Evaluating Action Programs

Consulting Editor: Amitai Etzioni

EVALUATING ACTION PROGRAMS
Readings in Social Action and Education

CAROL H. WEISS
Columbia University

Allyn and Bacon, Inc.
Boston • London • Sydney • Toronto

To My Mother

LIBRARY OF CONGRESS CATALOG CARD NUMBER: 70–165609
ISBN: 0-205-03247-8
Seventh printing . . . June, 1976

Contents

vi CONTENTS

PREFACE

Preface

While the primary audience for this book is the evaluator-in-training, it has much to offer the working evaluator, be he novice or old hand, in conducting competent and useful studies in an action-program setting. Present and future consumers of evaluation research—policy-makers, program administrators, program staff in the gamut of professional fields, and laymen—will also learn what evaluation is all about and how its results fit into the process of program decision-making.

The book aims to help the reader conceptualize and understand the purposes of evaluation and the methods by which it obtains information and generates conclusions. It assumes an elementary knowledge of social science research methods; even a passing acquaintance will get the reader through the book. Rather than giving a set of prefabricated rules and instructions, it points out the constraints within which evaluation operates and suggests alternative strategies of design, measurement, structure, relationship, and communication in order to accommodate to existing constraints and to serve the informational needs of programs.

There is a tremendous need today for skilled and astute evaluators, a need far in excess of supply. Most federal programs in the field of "human resources" are currently demanding evaluation of program outcomes, and unlike the situation of even a few years ago, they are providing large sums of money for large-scale studies. A recent review of only *federally* funded evaluations with budgets in excess of $25,000 turned up approximately a thousand such studies in one year (1970). In contrast, the number of people being trained to design and conduct evaluation research remains bizarrely low.

Nor is the need likely to diminish. Indications are bullish for further expansion of support for evaluation. For example, moves in the direction of decentralization of program initiative and management from the federal level to state and local levels—block grants, revenue sharing, and the like—will probably be accompanied by strong emphasis on evaluation as a means to determine whether program objectives are being met. If for no other reason than to maintain existing authority relationships among federal, state, and local governmental units, and to assure that federal funds are being spent to accomplish federally determined purposes, evaluation is likely to be a component of decentralization plans.

Regardless of the patterns of federal aid, the nation is in a period when planned social change efforts will necessarily continue and grow. Whether the pace be slack or quickened over short periods, all the omens portend that the nation will have to respond to rapidly moving events (heightened expectations, changing priorities, technological developments) through further social intervention. In such an environment, the need is clear for objective evidence on the consequences of the new policies and programs. This means not only more evaluation, but more imaginative and skillful evaluation, well conceived, multidimensional, relevant to the issues, and meshed into policy-making and planning processes.

Since formal teaching of evaluation methods is only now entering college curriculums on a significant scale, evaluation research has been a trial-and-error, learn-by-doing craft. Most investigators have been unaware of the wealth of experience and practical wisdom painfully accumulated by others. The growth and development of evaluation methodology has been further limited by the balkanization of the territory. Evaluators working in one professional field have had little communication across program boundaries with others in education, mental health, social work, health care, corrections, job training, international development, rehabilitation, law, personnel development, recreation, planning, and other fields.

By collecting the contributions of evaluators experienced in a range of substantive fields, the book identifies areas of consensus that have emerged across professional specialties. It also highlights issues that remain controversial. The author's introduction compares and contrasts the individual papers and places them in perspective.

I would like to thank a great many people who wittingly and unwittingly provided the opportunities, ideas, and encouragement out of which this volume grew. For tossing me into the water (often hot) of evaluation, my thanks go particularly to Eva H. Dirkes, Theresa Crowley, Jeanne Noble, Livingston Wingate, Jack Otis, Israel Gerver,

Virginia Burns, Bernard Russell, Leonard Stern, Richard Langendorf, and Alice Brophy. For insights, ideas, and encouragement, I owe much to David Kallen, Denise Kandel, Herbert Hyman, Amitai Etzioni, Allen Barton, David Caplovitz, Kathleen Archibald, and to Howard Davis and Irma Lann of the National Institute of Mental Health, whose support provided me a chance to survey the state of the art in evaluation. Finally, I thank the authors for permission to reprint a stimulating collection of papers.

1 / OVERVIEW

Evaluating Educational
& Social Action Programs:
A Treeful of Owls

Before a study is begun, researchers often call together an advisory committee to help develop the plans, specify the hypotheses or objectives to be studied, decide on design and measures, consider unexpected events and consequences that will affect the research, and, in applied research, prepare for later use of study results. This book represents an advisory committee of a high order. It provides the knowledge and insight of a score of the best informed people in the evaluation field, what a colleague calls "wise old owls." In this sense, the book is truly the product of "a treeful of owls."

Like most advisory committees, the members do not always agree. Their differences arise largely from differing assumptions about why evaluation is undertaken and what uses it serves. Once these are clarified, it is possible to consider each expert's advice in terms of its suitability for the conditions of a particular evaluation.

The book is designed to be used as a text in courses on evaluation research and as supplementary reading in courses on research methods. It has much help to offer the evaluator—be he evaluator-in-training, novice, or old hand—and much information for consumers of evaluation research—policymakers, program administrators, program staff, and laymen. It aims to explain what evaluation is all about, how its practice can be improved, and how its results can help make program decisions more rational. Rather than giving a set of instructions and rules, this book will help the reader conceptualize and understand the process of evaluation and alert him to potential pitfalls.

Basically, evaluation research is concerned with finding out how well action programs work. It represents the application of social science research methods to discover information of importance to program practice and public policy.

Over the last decade or two, the nation has become increasingly aware of the social problems that plague special groups of the population, and it has undertaken an array of programs to improve their lot. There are new programs—experimental, innovative, or extensions and improvements of ongoing programs—for such victims of social ills as pupils in inner-city schools, dropouts, delinquents, the unemployed, the ill, the mentally ill, and so on. Many established programs in education and welfare are experimenting with new methods and materials to accomplish their missions more effectively. Special training programs are being mounted for the professionals and subprofessionals who serve in the programs.

Such programs represent the extension of a tradition of social betterment efforts. As a nation, we have long supported programs of public education, health care, rehabilitation, youth work, corrections, public housing, veterans' benefits, urban planning, agricultural extension services, and the like. We believe in trying to improve the human condition and alleviate its attendant ills, and as new problems become visible, our response—both publicly through government action and privately through social agencies—has been to set up programs to cope with the problems.

How well do the host of programs, new and old, succeed in achieving the goals for which they were established? That seems a rational question, but not everyone is interested in the answers. Some people justify a program because it is "doing something" to deal with an obvious need. Others declare themselves content if a program saves one youth from crime, prepares one pupil for college. Agencies, staff, and constituencies form around a program, and they often develop an interest in perpetuating the program—and expanding it. As program advocates, they are interested in assessing the program only for the purpose of demonstrating its worth and justifying further funding. Long-established programs seldom see the need for rigorous proof of success since they "know" that they are doing good.

But there comes a time in the life of many programs when it is important to ask: How are we doing? Are we accomplishing what we set out to do?

A crisis can precipitate the inquiry—shortage of funds, competing needs, obvious failures, disorders. Those who fund the program may want to know if they are getting their money's worth. In the case of innovative programs, there is often a concern with learning whether the program represents a fruitful approach that should be adopted on a large-scale basis. Sometimes program staffs want to learn how to improve the effectiveness of what they are doing.

When there is a serious interest in finding out how well the program is working, the investigation can proceed by several routes. One way is through an impressionistic inquiry: an individual, a team, or a committee can go in and ask questions. Proceeding much as a good journalist does, the investigators talk to the program director, staff members, and recipients of service (students, clients, patients). They sit in on sessions, attend meetings, look at reports, and usually in a few weeks or months come up with a report. Much useful information can be ferreted out in this way, but the procedure has obvious limitations. It relies heavily on what people are willing to tell, and if the investigators are people from outside or "upstairs"—who can punish the program for inadequacies or departures from "the book"—the flow of information is likely to be far from candid. The journalistic inquiry depends, too, on the skill and insight of the investigators, and on their objectivity. If they are rushed, bland, or biased, their assessments can be wide of the mark. Perhaps the most significant disadvantage is the focus on the here and now. Whatever the merit of its findings, the investigation usually can tell little about *outcomes* of the program—what effect it has in helping participants achieve the goals for which the program was undertaken. If a program aims to teach students the principles of scientific method or equip them with the skills to get and hold a job, the impressionistic "look-see" can hardly gauge the extent of their knowledge and skills.

Another assessment technique is to administer questionnaires or interviews that ask people's opinions about the program. Superficially, this appears more scientific and objective than the first type of investigation, and it does prevent the more patent intrusion of observers' biases. On the plus side, it also yields clues about program strengths and weaknesses. But again, as a method of evaluation it is limited by what people divulge and by their immediate time perspective. Programs generally aim to change how people behave over time, and merely finding out that people like the program, find it interesting, or prefer it shortened or lengthened, tells little about its long-run effects on their behavior.

In some fields, there are well accepted standards of program operation that can form the basis for another type of assessment. For example, higher education accreditation groups look into such things as pupil-teacher ratio, number of books in the library, percentage of Ph.D.'s on the faculty. This procedure has obvious merits. But as an evaluation of how well a program is succeeding (in this case, educating students), it makes some leaping assumptions. It assumes a clear and direct relation between certain program "input" standards and desired program outcomes. Few programs indeed have a verified body of knowledge on the connections between inputs and outputs, and settling for an inquiry into the attainment of "program standards" finesses the question of whether the program achieves its purposes.

Whenever the real question is how well the program accomplishes its purposes, objective evidence on outcomes is needed. Securing such evidence is the function of evaluation research. We have now come to the subject, object, and hero of the book. Like most heroes, evaluation research has weaknesses and limitations, but it has an interesting and complex character, a high potential for improving the rationality of decisions.

Evaluation Problems

Evaluation research is designed for utility. Its purpose is to answer practical questions of decision-makers who want to know whether to continue a program, extend it to other sites, modify it, or close it down. If the program is found to be only partly effective in achieving its goals, as is often the case, evaluation research is often expected to say something about the *aspects* that are going awry and the kinds of changes that are needed. Since only a rare program staff is willing to consider complete abandonment of the program even in the face of bleak evaluation evidence, the response to evaluation is generally a search for improvement; so evaluators are called on to be diagnosticians as well as judges.

What does evaluation research look like? In traditional formulation, it consists of five basic stages:

1. Finding out the goals of the program;
2. Translating the goals into measurable indicators of goal achievement;
3. Collecting data on the indicators for those who have been exposed to the program;
4. Collecting similar data on an equivalent group that has not been exposed to the program (control group);
5. Comparing the data on program participants and controls in terms of goal criteria.

As a general procedure, this seems simple enough. It is very similar to the classical research experiment. In this case, the research hypothesis is that program goals are met. Data are collected about subjects who receive the program "treatment" and controls who do not. When data are analyzed, it becomes possible with a given level of confidence to accept or reject the hypothesis that the program is succeeding and to specify the extent of its success.

However, evaluation research is much easier to describe in the ideal than to do. A series of obstacles almost inevitably besets its path. Let us tour some of the most pervasive ones.

1. Evaluation research deals with people and programs in a real-life action environment. The research is not the primary activity; the program is. When there are conflicts between requirements of research and needs of the program, priority generally goes to the program. The evaluator, whose basic function is to provide information useful to decision-makers, can hardly justify interference with optimal operation of the program, and thus he may be called upon to adapt his strategies (or less benevolently, compromise his standards) to accord with realities of program life.

2. The goals of programs are rarely simple and clear cut. Sometimes a program has a straightforward goal, such as improving reading ability. But more often, program goals are many and diffuse, as to teach good citizenship, to inculcate respect for authority, to increase knowledge of safety rules, to improve group cooperation. In fact, it is frequently difficult to find out beyond the vaguest generalities what the goals of the program are. Program staff find it difficult to articulate or agree on a statement of goals in terms specific enough to measure. They find it even harder to recognize possible inconsistencies among goals or to rank varying goals in order of priority.

Yet the evaluator has to proceed on the basis of some accepted formulation of the specific changes in knowledge, attitudes, or behavior that the program aims to produce, or else his work is not likely to be relevant or usable. Unless there is consensus on goals beforehand, program decision-makers can later dismiss results of even the best evaluation study by saying, "But that's not what we were trying to do." If an evaluation of a preschool program shows that pupils did not learn verbal and numerical concepts, program advocates can claim that they were improving the children's medical and dental care or creating positive attitudes in parents toward the school.

3. Program staff may be reluctant to cooperate with evaluators. Particularly when the study relies on program staff for data, for access to records, for maintaining control groups, or other vital functions, their lack of interest or outright intransigence can have baleful effects on the evaluation.

Program staff have different interests and professional norms from evaluators. The staff's concern is service. To them, evaluation often means disruption and delay. They do not want to take time from their primary role—helping people—in order to fill out long, complicated forms or engage in other diversions that evaluators seem to think essential.

Moreover, many program staff are convinced of the program's worth and see little need for evaluation. If results of the study are positive, they knew it all along. If the results are negative, it is probably the fault of the evaluators and the grossness of their measures, which are too insensitive to capture the subtle and important changes that are going on. Furthermore, if people take negative findings seriously, the consequence of the study may be to imperil the program —and possibly the staff's own jobs. It is not remarkable that they are uncooperative when they view evaluation as a sitting-in-judgment on their work. Even when defensiveness is not a salient element in their view, they often see little potential payoff from evaluation.

4. Another obstacle to evaluation research is the difficulty of obtaining control groups. Why do we need controls? If we measure the relevant knowledge or behaviors of program participants before the program begins and after its end, doesn't the difference between the two measures indicate the program's effectiveness? Not necessarily. People do a lot of things besides attend program sessions. They talk to friends, watch television, read newspapers. Their ideas, aspirations, and responsibilities may change. For example, much delinquency research suggests that beyond the late teen years, youths become less likely to engage in delinquent acts—with or without program service. Historical events and economic conditions have an effect, too. Thus, in evaluation of a job training program, success in finding a job may be related less to program participation than to a general improvement in economic activity in the area. Another consideration is that people who voluntarily attend programs are likely to have higher motivation than those who do not; their post-program performance sometimes reflects the effect of motivation more than the effect of the program. With control groups, the evaluator is able to recognize the effects of such extraneous nonprogram factors, since they operate on the controls as well as the participants, and he can then identify the degree of change attributable to the program itself.

The essential condition for controls is that they be very much like the participants. The best way to assure similarity is to draw participants and controls from the same population pool and randomly assign individuals to one group or the other. Now there's the rub. In evaluation, the evaluator can rarely randomize assignments. Sometimes the program has to be offered to intact natural groups, such as classrooms or hospital wards; other classrooms or wards available for control purposes may have markedly different composition. Sometimes the program is offered on a voluntary basis and serves everyone who applies. How can you find controls for an after-school homework help program when everyone eligible and motivated is already participating in the program? On occasion, program directors and staff reject the whole concept of control groups as a denial of service to people in need.

A second-best procedure is to match participants and controls on characteristics assumed relevant to outcomes, such as age, sex, IQ, motivation. While often the best that can be done, matching procedures are frequently limited by ignorance of what variables are significant enough to require matching and by other potential biases as well.[1]

Probably the most important consideration is that even non-equivalent controls are better than no controls at all, and additional safeguards can be introduced through design, statistical treatment, and further research to compensate for inadequacies.

Even when the evaluator succeeds in setting up controls, problems arise in maintaining them. Program staff may undermine the control groups by accepting their members into the program when vacancies open up. They may become "contaminated" by informal exposure to program content, as when pupils in an experimental curriculum share the new materials with friends in neighboring control classes. Further, it is sometimes hard to maintain contact and cooperation with controls when the program periodically asks them for information but offers nothing in return.

5. *The program that the evaluator studies is rarely a simple entity.* Although there are programs that are well defined and relatively unchanging from one setting to another, such as a series of films or a course of programmed instruction, most programs depend heavily on the way that staff perceive and administer them. In large-scale programs, large variations can occur in types of staff, their skill, style of service, the amount of time they devote to the program, participants' attendance, even the content and basic direction of services provided. At the extreme, such diffuse programs as "community action" include a conglomeration of shifting activities that require enormous efforts to specify and describe.[2]

For the evaluator, complexity of the program means that even after he discovers the extent of change ensuing from the program, he is hard put to explain which components were responsible for observed effects (or lack of effects). Unless from the outset he builds in appropriate measures of program factors, his study will say little about which features of the program are productive, which should be

[1] See Donald T. Campbell and Julian C. Stanley, "Experimental and Quasi-Experimental Designs for Research on Teaching," in N. L. Gage (ed.), *Handbook of Research on Teaching* (Chicago: Rand McNally & Co., 1963), particularly pp. 217–220, 240–241, for an excellent discussion of research design.
[2] New programs may bumble around searching for a rationale, a strategy of action, and procedures of operation for quite a while before they settle on course. Because of initial confusion, evaluation from the outset is sometimes premature. In these cases, it may be better to wait until it is clear what the program is.

retained, which modified or abandoned.[3] If the program has positive results and other schools or agencies wish to adopt it, he can offer little guidance about which elements are essential and which are extraneous baggage.

Some programs are not only complex in content and method, they also shift course in midstream. A new director is hired; new regulations come through from Washington or the state agency; funds are cut or expanded; staff turns over; the original program seems to be making little headway; clients demand new types of service; the winds of ideological fashion change. For any of a dozen reasons, programs can drastically alter direction, either abruptly or by slow accretion. The evaluator, even one who had the foresight to take measurements of important program variables, is faced with a dilemma. He will be able to discover the extent of change that occurred in participants on the outcome indicators, but to what does he attribute the change: the original program, the subsequent program, the transition, or some admixture of everything going on?

6. *The traditional model of evaluation described on page 6 discovers how well the program has achieved its goals only after its completion.* A full cycle of the program has to operate before such data can be collected, or if longer term effects are to be assessed (as is often desirable), even more time must elapse. In order to ensure clarity about which program strategies are responsible for observed effects, the program should remain stable over its course. Staff should be discouraged from tinkering with ("improving") the program while it is under way, or the confusions noted in (5) above will hinder interpretation of results. Furthermore, the evaluation generally comes up with overall judgments: this number of participants achieved x level of success; or at best, this number of participants of types $A, B,$ and $C,$ under conditions $J, K,$ and $L,$ achieved certain levels of success.

But what of program directors and staff who want quicker feedback to help improve the program as it goes along? What of their need for guidance in dealing with issues of operation? Is evaluation irrelevant to their concerns? If evaluation to date has tended to scant these needs, such neglect is neither inevitable nor always justified.

7. *Evaluation research is meant for immediate and direct use in improving the quality of social programming. Yet a review of evaluation*

---

[3] For an excellent discussion of program conceptualization, see Herbert H. Hyman and Charles R. Wright, "Evaluating Social Action Programs," in P. F. Lazarsfeld, W. N. Sewell, and H. L. Wilensky (eds.), *The Uses of Sociology* (New York: Basic Books, Inc., 1967), particularly pp. 744–756.

experience suggests that evaluation results have generally not exerted significant influence on program decisions. Some reasons are obvious. Decision-makers respond to a host of factors besides evidence of program effectiveness. They are concerned with the political and organizational feasibility of the program; its acceptability to funders, staff, and constituents; the availability of money. They may have an ideological commitment to the program or an interest in maintaining the agency's position in the field. They may fear the unknown consequences of change and feel more comfortable in the status quo.

One complicating factor is that results of evaluation research, more often than not, show little positive change. "Using" such results implies serious overhaul of accepted theories, strategies, staff skills, and ways of work. Nor do these negative reports generally point the way to clearly defined alternatives of higher promise. Even when a study has analyzed the effects of different conditions on program outcomes, it is likely to find small differences in effects and yield only tantalizing clues about factors favorable to success. The decision-maker is rarely presented with clear and unambiguous direction, and his reluctance to leap into uncharted waters is understandable. Particularly when he has to dredge implications for action out of a long, murky report, he may fail to consider seriously even those findings that do offer guidance for change.

This is an awesome list of obstacles to the effective conduct of evaluation research. The aim in presenting it is not to discourage the aspiring evaluator, but rather to alert him to the difficulties of the terrain ahead. There are few sadder sights than a well intentioned researcher embarking on an evaluation study, armed only with his research methods textbook and his experience in laboratory or survey research, who comes a-cropper on the organizational, interpersonal, and political barriers in the program setting. I know, I've been there.

One of the first evaluation studies I conducted involved a program for training young people for service in an urban ghetto. After three months' formal training, the participants spent nine months on supervised jobs in schools, a hospital, settlement houses, a center for the aged, block organizations, and any other opportunity that presented itself. The program was a forerunner of VISTA. The goals of the program were global; the staff talked about improving community services, helping people, making agencies more responsive to needs of the poor, and similar generalizations. As a consequence of the open-endedness of program goals, which I never managed to pin down to specifics, I decided to study just about everything in sight. Basically, I tried to find out: How well did trainees learn what the training was teaching? How well did they apply their learning on community jobs? How much change was there in the clients they served? I blanketed the area with questionnaires and interviews—asking questions of trainees before the training, after the training, and after several months on the job; administering IQ tests and interest inventories; pestering trainers and other staff members for data and ratings; interviewing the agency supervisors; trying to collect record data on clients of the trainees. I was so afraid I might miss some item relevant to a possible goal, some vital piece of data in the chain of events, that questions and indices proliferated.

Control groups? We never even tried. The assembled group of trainees was a relatively unusual collection of people and included everyone who applied to the program. In fact, not until the day the program began did we know who, or how many, would actually show up. At the time, there seemed no possible way of finding an equivalent group to serve as a comparison. In our study of changes in the clients whom trainees served on their community jobs, we made some feeble attempts to compare them with clients of other workers in the same agencies. But extracting client information from most agencies (except the schools, who allowed us access to "before" and "after" reading scores) was difficult at best.

The program staff of our agency, in retrospect, put up very little fuss about the constant intrusions for data collection. The secret of our success on this score, I suspect, was that the federal agency funding the program *required* evaluation as a condition of the grant. Even staff members of the community agencies where the trainees worked were patient with our questions. They had an interest in helping advise us on how the program could be made more useful in terms of their own organization's interests. The trainees themselves went along, because evaluation was an integral part of the program and they seemed to take it for granted.

As for use of evaluation results to improve future programming, a critical problem was timing. Our reports were not completed until the second group of trainees was well into its training period. Our recommendations about training content, its relevance to job assignments, and the type and scope of job assignments with community agencies had limited impact because the report was out of phase with the program. Furthermore, the program staff was preoccupied with survival issues—seeing that the federal grant was continued, drumming up and maintaining support from community groups, recruiting new trainees, engaging a competent training staff. Our long and bulky report was not a matter of priority attention, even when supplemented with verbal presentations.

Looking back on it, I think, too, that because we were not sure that the program grant would be renewed, we pitched our report to the federal granting body, rather than the internal staff. That did not imply whitewash of the data, but it did involve casting the results in generalized, somewhat abstract terms. While the local staff was, with a few exceptions, content to pass along the evaluation unread, the Washington office did pay some heed. However, the VISTA program, then getting under way, probably never heard about our results. I later read of some VISTA projects that ran into exactly the same difficulties that our program did.

Although we did some interesting and ingenious things, this exercise in evaluation was less than a roaring success. Possibly its major use was to teach the evaluators the differences between "textbook" evaluation and evaluation in the setting of a developing action program and to educate us in methods and contrivances for overcoming difficulties. Unfortunately, our experience was not atypical of evaluations still being done. In fact, this book is dedicated to overcoming the kind of naivete that I began with.

The Readings

The readings are drawn from a variety of fields: education, job training, community action, crime and delinquency, antipoverty, psychotherapy, health. An interesting thing about evaluation research is that, regardless of the substantive field, the same issues constantly reappear. These selections make sense across a range of program areas.

The field of education has a tremendous interest and investment in evaluation—of curricula, instructional methods, programs, pupils, teachers, materials, practices. Educational evaluation has tended to consider its problems unique and its methods special and different from evaluation of other kinds of programs. As this book illustrates, the issues are very similar. Moreover, as educational evaluation follows innovative programming beyond the walls of the classroom to involve the social issues of the day, it becomes almost indistinguishable from evaluation of other planned social interventions.

Educational evaluators have much to learn from—and to teach—those in other fields, and they have much to lose by developing special perspectives and a special vocabulary that inhibits communication and interchange of experience. Thus, the program range of the readings in this book has extra benefits for evaluators in education as well as those in other fields. It pools a great deal of intelligence, of which no single field has either a monopoly or a superfluity, and it gives a sense of comfort, a huddling together in companionship, for those facing similar problems across the range of program areas.

In selecting the readings, the major criteria were the importance of what the author had to say and the good sense with which he said it. Therefore, each author's argument is left intact. The different perspectives highlight what remain as critical issues for evaluators.

Most of the papers deal with more than one issue. Robert E. Stake's paper provides general background on the logic of evaluation research. The papers by Henry W. Riecken and Edward A. Suchman are particularly broad-gauge discussions. One interesting feature of Riecken's paper is that, although never published before, it was written in 1953, long before the recent upsurge in evaluative activity. His advice remains as relevant and cogent today as much that is currently being written. (Would that I had read it, and had had the wit to appreciate it, before I began my trial-and-error evaluation career.)

While there is considerable overlap, the papers can fruitfully be considered under four headings. The following section introduces these topics and indicates the major contributions of each author. The topics, which are particularly problematic ones in evaluation research, are:

A. Purposes of evaluation,
B. Study designs appropriate for specified purposes,
C. Measurement of program outcomes and inputs,
D. Use of evaluation results in future program decisions.

Issues in Evaluation Research

A. PURPOSES OF EVALUATION

The purpose of evaluation research is to provide information for decision-making about programs. Almost all the authors agree on this, and some, like Marvin C. Alkin and Egon G. Guba, are emphatic on the subject.

But in practice, evaluation is sometimes undertaken for less noble motives. Program decision-makers may turn to evaluation to delay a decision; to justify and legitimate a decision already made; to extricate themselves from controversy about future directions by passing the buck; to vindicate the program in the eyes of its constituents, its funders, or the public; to satisfy conditions of a government or foundation grant through the ritual of evaluation. For a brief catalog of these "eyewash-whitewash" kinds of motivations, see Edward A. Suchman's article.

Such non-informational reasons for evaluation are not as rare as one might suppose. When the purpose underlying evaluation is of this ilk, the evaluator should be forewarned. He needs to spend enough time investigating who wants to know what, and why, to find out whether his study will serve a genuine purpose or whether it is likely to be ignored or used for political ends. If there is no commitment to using the study for decision-making, the evaluator may well decide to use his talents elsewhere. Or, if he decides to stay and conduct the study, he might profit from the advice given in the readings by Donald T. Campbell and Jack Elinson, each of whom provides a tongue-in-cheek method for making results come out "right."

Even when evaluation is honestly undertaken to serve as a basis for future decisions, questions arise: Whose decisions? At what level? What kinds of decisions? There are many actors on the program scene and each has a different order of concern. The cast of characters with an interest in the results of evaluation may include program developers, direct program staff, program directors, higher policy-makers (at the state or federal level), program directors in other similar agencies, social scientists.

Program developers seek all kinds of information on ways to make an emerging program more relevant, feasible, and effective. Program staff are likely to be interested in information about ways to improve specific practices of operation. The directors of the program are usually interested in knowing how effective the basic strategy of the program is, but they are more concerned with finding out what modifications in organization and procedure will improve it. Higher policy-makers are concerned with allocation issues: should the program be continued as is, given more resources, institutionalized as an ongoing activity, or abandoned? Other agencies want to know whether the program is effective enough to warrant adoption. Social scientists may seek to compare the effects of different program strategies and generalize about the factors responsible for success. Nowadays there may be a further player—the consumer of services who has a client's perspective on purposes, decisions, and uses. Some black communities, for example, are becoming concerned with the political legitimacy of the program, in terms such as "community control." Out of all these competing interests, whose decisional purposes shall an evaluation serve?

Michael Scriven introduces a useful distinction between "formative" and "summative" evaluation. Formative evaluation is designed to aid in the development of a program in its early phases. Its users are program developers and probably program staff as well. Summative evaluation, on the other hand, judges the worth of a program after it has been in operation. It is aimed at decision-makers in other systems who are considering adoption of the program and those who will decide on its continuation or termination at the initial site. As Scriven suggests, different evaluation designs are needed for the two purposes, as well as different types of measures and time schedules.

The program that Scriven discusses is a curriculum, and the

formative-summative distinction has special aptness to this situation. However, many programs are never "finished" in the way a curriculum is; they continue to grow and develop while in operation. Formative information needs may continue to be important.

In recent years there has been discussion of a "system model" of evaluation rather than a "goal model."[4] There is little agreement on what the elements of such a model should be, with almost as many interpretations offered as there are discussants. But there is a common underlying recognition that programs fulfill other functions and have other consequences besides achieving official goals, and that these are worthy of study. Further, if evaluation is viewed as part of the "system," it seems possible to develop an evaluation design that contributes information at each stage of the program. Program activities might be broken down into a logical series of consecutive phases, and the evaluator could analyze the consequences of each phase and report his findings in time to affect planning of later phases. In some cases, this might well be a productive approach, and further development of workable procedures deserves careful attention. But obviously, this kind of evaluation model forecloses opportunities for overall judgment about the utility of one basic program strategy over another. Evaluators need to be very clear about what the program's information needs are, then conduct the type of evaluation best adapted to filling the information requirements.

Edward A. Suchman discusses several phases in the life cycle of a program: a pilot phase when development proceeds on a trial-and-error basis, a model phase when a particular program strategy is run under controlled conditions to judge its effectiveness, a prototype phase when the model program is subjected to realistic operating conditions, the institutionalized phase when the program is an ongoing part of the organization. Ideally, these phases should occur in sequence. Often, of course, the program is (and remains) lodged at one of the stages. Each phase requires different kinds of information for decision-making. The next section will return to Suchman's suggestions for the types of evaluation design appropriate to each phase.

Marvin C. Alkin widens the range of informational needs that

4 For example, Amitai Etzioni, "Two Approaches to Organizational Analysis: A Critique and a Suggestion," *Administrative Science Quarterly*, vol. 4, no. 2 (1960), pp. 257–278; Herbert C. Schulberg and Frank Baker, "Program Evaluation Models and the Implementation of Research Findings," *American Journal of Public Health*, vol. 58, no. 7 (1968), pp. 1248–1255; Herbert C. Schulberg, Alan Sheldon, and Frank Baker, "Introduction," in *Program Evaluation in the Health Fields* (New York: Behavioral Publications, Inc., 1970); Alfred P. Parsell, "Dynamic Evaluation: The Systems Approach to Action Research," SP-2423 (Santa Monica: Systems Development Corporation, 1966); Perry Levinson, "Evaluation of Social Welfare Programs: Two Research Models," *Welfare in Review*, vol. 4, no. 10 (1966), pp. 5–12.

evaluation is called upon to serve. Building on the seminal work of Daniel Stufflebeam[5] and others, he considers not only the decisions to be made after the program is going, but also the decisions involved in program planning. Thus he includes in his definition of evaluation all the research efforts that go into assessing the needs of the system, planning the program, and installing and monitoring it. Important as these kinds of applied research are, there is some doubt that stretching the term "evaluation" to include them improves clarity. Evaluation has traditionally had a distinctive focus on outcomes—how well the program, either in the long or short run, is achieving certain goals. But the emphasis on feed-in to decision-making is all to the good. And as Riecken notes, some of these early applied research activities provide important information for traditional evaluation: system assessment helps to specify program goals and gives baseline information on the initial state of the system with which post-program data can be compared; monitoring of program implementation provides descriptors of the content and practice of the program in action, which enables the evaluator to analyze features of the program that are related to better or poorer outcomes.

The readings by Michael Scriven and Egon G. Guba emphasize the use of evaluation results to help improve the program. Donald T. Campbell and Peter H. Rossi are concerned primarily with judgments about the worth of the program. Thomas K. Glennan, Jr., writes from the viewpoint of the higher policy-maker who makes decisions about allocating resources among major programs. Robert S. Weiss and Martin Rein are also concerned about policy decisions, but they see the need for information less in terms of data on comparative *outcomes* of programs (because broad programs' outcomes are so complex and difficult to conceptualize and measure), and more in terms of understanding the forces that shape community programs. They recommend studying how communities resist and programs adapt, the dynamics of the intervention process. David K. Cohen discusses how evaluation purposes become entangled in political competition among levels of decision-makers—federal, state, and local, and notes that evaluation can become a political instrument to assert federal priorities. John Mann writes as a social scientist, reviewing evaluations in psychotherapy, counseling, human relations, and education, in a search for generalizations about their comparative effectiveness in changing human behavior. He seeks to add to the store of scientific knowledge. Differences in viewpoint among authors derive largely from their emphasis on different purposes and types of evaluative activity.

[5] Daniel L. Stufflebeam, *Evaluation as Enlightenment for Decision-making* (Columbus: Evaluation Center, Ohio State University, 1969).

Can one evaluation study serve all these purposes, or even several of them? Many of the contributors have grave doubts. Part of the trouble with many past evaluations is that they tried to serve too many masters. With careful design and adequate resources, perhaps two kinds of information needs can be met by a single study, but research requirements for different purposes are often incompatible. The evaluator should take pains to find out which decisions are pending, which pending decision has priority, and to which decision his study is expected to contribute. Then he can gear his study to serve the most important purposes.

In this connection, the structural location of the evaluation unit is important. Whether the evaluation is conducted by outsiders or by evaluators on the agency staff, it should be responsible to the organizational level where the decision is made. For example, an evaluation that makes "go or no-go" judgments on program merit should probably not be under the jurisdiction of the program director. He is rarely ready to countenance the total dismantling of his program and is unlikely to give results a fair hearing. The paper by Joseph S. Wholey, et al. recommends that an evaluation concerned with overall assessment of program success be responsible to the highest policy-maker; an evaluation that weighs effects of alternative methods or strategies within a program should be responsible to the program director.

B. DESIGN OF THE EVALUATION

Experimental design has long been considered the ideal for evaluation. The design requires that people be randomly assigned either to the program or to a control group. The controls may receive a placebo program (the social equivalent of a sugar pill), the standard service (e.g., the regular science curriculum rather than the innovative one), or no program at all. Relevant measurements are taken before and after the program.[6] If program recipients show greater positive change than the controls, the outcome can clearly be attributed to the program. The readings by Campbell, Glennan, Rossi, Aronson and Sherwood, Scriven, and Wholey discuss the elegance and power of experimental design.

The fly in the ointment is that experimental procedures are often impossible to introduce in the busy agency setting. There is resistance

---

[6] If assignments were randomly made from the pool of eligibles, "before" measures are not strictly necessary. It is assumed that the two groups were alike at the start. However, when dealing with small numbers, "before" measures are a check on initial similarity. If the two groups are not comparable, "before" measures provide the necessary data for statistical adjustment. Further, they make it easier to compute change scores.

from agency staff, from the very nature of the program (Aronson and Sherwood cite the case of a drop-in, multi-service center; how can you randomize service to people who come in?), from the nature of recipient groups, and from outside events that "contaminate" the controls. However, several of the authors caution against abandoning control group design too lightly.

Campbell suggests that the experiment as the method of choice is more feasible than many suspect. When there are too few openings to serve all eligible recipients, or when the program is introduced in stages so that some groups have to wait for entry, experimental design is possible. With careful planning and administrative backing, control groups can be used even in somewhat turbulent programs. Riecken suggests that systematic variations within the program can create alternatives that are the equivalent of, or a reasonable substitute for, control groups.

When circumstances preclude experimental design, quasi-experimental designs are often suitable. Campbell offers three types useful in evaluation research: interrupted time-series, control series, and regression discontinuity designs. While they do not have the power of the true experiment in ruling out all rival explanations of change (explanations that something besides the program was responsible for the change observed), they effectively guard against most of the important threats to valid interpretation.

Rossi, too, prefers experimental design wherever conditions allow. But in recognition of the common problems, he offers a two-step compromise: a "soft" correlational reconnaissance study to gauge whether the program is producing change, and a later experimental study to specify the extent and source of change more precisely.

Suchman gears his proposals for research design to the phase and needs of the program. In the developmental phase of the pilot program, he proposes flexible, quick-and-easy evaluation. The emphasis is on success or failure, but design need not be rigorous. In the model phase, a carefully controlled experiment is called for. The prototype and operating phases require continual feedback of information on the whole interacting system. Instead of before and after measures, he proposes repeated "during-during-during" measures of persons exposed and unexposed to the program. This procedure bears a passing resemblance to Campbell's control series design, but it does not control for important potential biases, such as selective exposure to the program. If program participation is voluntary, comparisons between participants and nonparticipants remain risky.

Guba, focusing on immediate improvement of programs, is impatient with experimental design. He finds it too restrictive, time-consuming, and unrealistic to be useful, and calls for more flexible ways to feed relevant information quickly into decision processes.

Weiss and Rein, while recognizing the utility of the experiment for well defined programs, cite its limitations when programs are broad-ranging, constantly developing, and have multiple objectives and multiple strategies. Under such circumstances, they find it artificial and misleading to examine a handful of outcome indicators. It is more important to understand the whole process of program development, adaptation, and effect. Here a historical, qualitative approach becomes productive.

Mann, on the basis of his review of evaluations, concludes that the best studies (even with control-group design) are inadequate for developing scientific generalizations. The evaluations and indeed the programs are, in Scriven's word, too "messy" to produce scientifically acceptable knowledge, and he proposes a return to the true experiment under laboratory conditions.

When the purpose of evaluation is to compare the effectiveness of different program strategies, several authors favor comparative evaluation of a number of programs on the same indicators. Such comparative study will not be rigorous enough to satisfy Mann's criteria, but it may be the most feasible way to provide information suitable for decision-making purposes. Looking at program content and outcomes on a cross-program basis makes possible broader generalizations about the effects of particular strategies and greater specificity about the conditions associated with better or poorer performance. Wholey, Glennan, and Cohen look toward more planned variations in federal programs, which will lend themselves to evaluative study.

While the potential of cross-program study is high, past experience cautions that the problems are legion. The difficulties that confront the evaluator of a single program are compounded manyfold. Comparative evaluation calls for large resources of skill, money, planning, patience, diplomacy, and administrative talent. The programs should be sufficiently strong and well defined and have a high enough likelihood of effecting change to warrant the investment.

Cohen surveys the experience of the Follow-Through cross-program evaluation, probably the most sophisticated attempt to compare the effectiveness of different program strategies. In his catalog of the problems it has encountered, a major issue is that Follow-Through projects, like many federally sponsored programs, are controlled at the local level. The federal agency has insufficient authority to impose necessary research conditions. For future evaluations of this type, program arrangements need to provide greater leverage to higher policy-makers, and to the evaluators whom they engage, to more closely approximate experimental conditions.

The readings, then, offer differing prescriptions for evaluation design because they are based on different assumptions about the purposes that evaluation should serve. It is apparent, too, that the authors have different images of programs in mind—simple/complex, stable/emergent, clear/ambiguous, apolitical/political—and are sensitive to different traps and entanglements. After review of their perspectives, the working evaluator has to develop a research design appropriate to the special conditions with which he is engaged.

Since evaluation often takes place in intransigent settings, and compromises in design are almost inevitable, two additional factors become particularly important. One is locating the study in a theoretical perspective. The "Utilization" article by Weiss has advice on this score. The other factor is replicating the evaluation. Few studies of the same type of program are repeated under comparable conditions. As Campbell urges, more should be done. It is only through repeated study that knowledge will accumulate.

C. MEASUREMENT

Evaluation is concerned with how well a program is meeting its goals, either at some intermediate stage (so that the information can be fed back into the program) or at the end. The first step in evaluation, then, is to discover what the program goals are and to formulate them in clear, specific, measurable terms.

This is often a formidable task. Many program directors and staff have very general goals expressed as vague abstractions. They find it difficult to translate them into concrete specifications of the changes in behavior, attitude, or knowledge that they hope to effect. Aronson and Sherwood recount the kinds of problems that arise when the evaluator presses staff to define goals. If the evaluator sits back and waits for the staff to come up with an operational statement, then "he should bring lots of novels to the office to read while he waits."[6] Moreover, as Scriven remarks, espoused goals are not always consistent with the program's content. It frequently is productive for the evaluator to participate in discussions with program staff to hammer out and clarify program goals. Scriven suggests that the evaluator undertake the task of evaluating proffered goals so that his study is not confined to trivial issues or to misleading or misguided ones.

Programs often have multiple goals. Some are more important than others; some are closer in time; some are more accessible to study; some may be incompatible with others. The evaluator has to have a sense of goal priorities in order to study the most significant issues. Again, he may have to work actively with program decision-makers and staff to sort out priorities.

The frequency of ambiguous and fuzzy goal statements has led

[6] Howard E. Freeman and Clarence C. Sherwood, "Research in Large-Scale Intervention Programs," *Journal of Social Issues,* vol. 21, no. 1 (1965), p. 17.

some observers to speculate about the origins of the state of affairs. Part of the reason is that it usually requires support from diverse groups and individuals to get a program accepted. Program goals have to be formulated in ways that satisfy the diversity of interests represented. Another reason, Aronson and Sherwood suggest, is programmers' lack of experience with analytical modes of thought and their concentration on the specifics of program operation. In one sense, ambiguity serves a useful function: it can mask differences in interpretation among supporting groups, between these groups and staff, or within the staff, that could rip the program apart if brought into the open. However, when there is little consensus on what the program is specifically attempting to achieve, progress is difficult. Each staff member may be pulling in a different direction. Not the least of the contributions that evaluation can make to practice is to insist on clear goal formulation, the setting of priorities among goals, and the reconciliation of divergent viewpoints.

Measuring outcomes is the core of the evaluator's job. He has to operationalize the program's goals in a set of indicators of desired outcomes. Scriven contrasts intrinsic measures—of internal characteristics of a program—and payoff measures—of outcomes, and finds advantages in both. The utility of intrinsic measures depends largely on program goals (to use his examples, is it an aim of the program to be elegant, modern, well structured?) and on the audience for whom the evaluation is intended. Most of the other contributors focus on payoffs as indicative of the extent to which goals are being realized.

One common difficulty is that the desired payoff lies far in the future. The program's real aims are to turn delinquents into law-abiding citizens or poor children into economically productive adults. It would take decades to find out whether the outcomes were in fact achieved. In the interim, evaluators have to rely on surrogate measures of attitudes, knowledge, skills, or behaviors that are presumably related to the ultimate payoff. School achievement scores, for example, are often used as criteria for the success of educational programs. But as Cohen notes, the relation between school achievement and social and economic advancement is by no means proved. Nor does existing theory or knowledge give leads to better proximate measures.

This is a problem that is not unique to evaluation but is basic to program design as well. A program is geared to producing certain intermediate changes on the assumption that they are necessary for the attainment of ultimate goals. In such cases, probably the best that evaluation can do, at least under the usual time constraints, is discover whether intermediate goals are being met. It is up to basic research to investigate the relation between these goals and desired final outcomes.

Whether goals are long- or short-term, the evaluator has to locate or develop suitable measures of outcomes. Usually, multiple measures are required. If a program has several goals, the use of a simple summary measure is likely to be obfuscating and misleading. If the evaluator can find available measures that are relevant to program intents, he is several steps ahead. He saves time, he may have the benefit of tested and validated instruments, and he has data on the responses of other groups to use as comparison. However, if existing measures are not directly relevant to the program goals, if they were developed for different age groups or different sets of conditions, or if experience has demonstrated important weaknesses, the evaluator is better advised to develop his own. In all events, efforts should continue to build up a repertoire of measures suitable for a broad array of programs. Glennan urges the use of similar outcome measures for programs with common aims. Use of the same measures facilitates comparison of relative effectiveness across many programs and adds significantly to the body of knowledge.

Riecken, among others, suggests that the evaluator pay attention, too, to unanticipated consequences that are byproducts of program operation. He should have the foresight to develop measures of important unintended outcomes that may negate (or enhance) the achievement of planned goals.

Data for evaluation are collected from a variety of sources using the whole arsenal of research techniques. Tests, interviews, and questionnaires are most commonly used, but consideration should also be given to observational data and agency records.[7] If they are accurate and complete, records can be particularly useful as an inexpensive and systematic source of information. But Aronson and Sherwood give examples of some problems that arise in their use.

Constant intrusions into the program in order to collect data can be a source of friction with program staff. The evaluator can reduce discord by limiting his demands. One thoughtfully constructed test or questionnaire is often better than three imperfectly conceived ones. When the evaluator is clear about what he needs to know and

---

[7] There are many catalogs and discussions of available tests, including Oscar Buros (ed.), *Sixth Mental Measurements Yearbook* (Highland Park, New Jersey: Gryphon Press, 1965). Attitude measures are listed and discussed in J. P. Robinson, R. Athanasiou, and Kendra B. Head, *Measures of Occupational Attitudes and Occupational Characteristics* (1967); J. P. Robinson, Jerrold G. Rusk, and Kendra B. Head, *Measures of Political Attitudes* (1968); J. P. Robinson and Phillip R. Shaver, *Measures of Social Psychological Attitudes* (1969); (all Ann Arbor: Survey Research Center, University of Michigan). Also Marvin E. Shaw and Jack M. Wright, *Scales for the Measurement of Attitudes* (New York: McGraw-Hill Book Company, 1967). A charming guide to the use of observational and archival data is Eugene J. Webb, Donald T. Campbell, R. D. Schwartz, and L. B. Sechrest, *Unobtrusive Measures: Nonreactive Research in the Social Sciences* (Chicago: Rand McNally & Co. 1966).

why, he can frame measures and schedule data collection with a minimum of disruption.

Programs may intend to bring about changes not only in people, but in agencies, larger social systems, or the public at large. Measures have to be relevant to such changes.[8]

Social indicators—collected government statistics on social conditions—are another possible source of outcome data, for example, unemployment rates, dropout rates. However, these data deal with conditions in a given geographical location and are probably appropriate only for programs large enough and intensive enough to expect to make a dent on an area-wide basis. Moreover, Sheldon and Freeman argue that they have limited utility for evaluative purposes because there is no way of telling whether changes in the indicator are the result of the program or of a host of other factors. Campbell is concerned that social indicators are subject to politically motivated biases in recordkeeping, and that the goal of the program may be to change the indicators rather than to change the social conditions that they imperfectly represent. Instances remain where their information can be important and complementary. Cohen, for example, proposes a system of indicators on schools and schooling to measure change in the distribution of educational resources and educational outcomes. Given the massive nature of the educational enterprise, such time-series data would help to answer some major questions in education, particularly if supplemented by special experimental studies.

Cost–benefit analysis is another measurement technique. As Glennan's paper indicates, cost–benefit analysis is not a substitute for usual methods of evaluation but a logical extension of it. Evaluation defines the program's benefits; cost–benefit analysis adds consideration of the value of benefits. Costs of the program are compared with benefits, as a way of judging whether the program is a worthwhile investment. Glennan discusses some of the methodological problems that arise, such as estimating the value of intangible benefits in dollar terms and appraising costs and benefits for different groups in society.

Knowing outcomes is only part of the job. Unless the evaluator can describe the program that brought about the outcome, he is telling only part of the story. He must learn enough about what is actually going on (rather than what was planned) to categorize the program's basic features. Sometimes the program is providing minimal service or non-treatment. Stake gives high priority to observation and de-

---

[8] One useful compendium of measures on organizations is Allen H. Barton, *Organizational Measurement* (Princeton: College Entrance Examination Board, 1961). For programs of national development, a series of measures on nations appears in Bruce M. Russett, *et al., World Handbook of Political and Social Indicators* (New Haven: Yale University Press, 1964).

scription of "instructional transactions," the program in action, and he proposes systematic comparison of plans and actuality. His diagram of the evaluation process specifies examination of congruence between intents and observations. Riecken stresses the value of direct observation of the program.

Further, the evaluator may need to know not only what the whole program is like, but something about its component parts and variations. If he is to understand the process of change, he will inquire into which parts of the program work, with which kinds of people, under which conditions. This requires systematic analysis and measurement of program variables, that is, variations in program conditions and events, that are likely to affect results. Mann presents a provocative list of program variables that may be germane to the types of programs that he examined. Data on outcomes can then be analyzed to see the extent to which success is contingent upon each particular prior condition.

How does an evaluator decide which program variables to measure? Cohen discusses the difficulties that arise when theory and knowledge are inadequate to define the factors that affect success. In most program areas, enough practical experience exists to suggest relevant dimensions. To aid in the identification of such important variables, several authors (Riecken, Aronson and Sherwood, and Weiss) suggest the construction of a model of how the program is expected to work. Such a model highlights the presumably significant aspects of the program that deserve classification and measurement. It also incorporates and makes explicit the assumptions about which program inputs lead *through which proximate stages* to achievement of final goals. To take a simple illustration, a program of nonprofessional teacher aides is expected to improve learning of arithmetic. It is assumed that effects will be accomplished because aides relieve teachers of clerical chores (measure: To what extent do they?), the teachers spend more time on arithmetic teaching (measure: To what extent do they?), and therefore student learning improves (measure: To what extent does it?). Tests of students' arithmetic achievement not only indicate outcomes for the program as a whole, but they can also be analyzed by the extent of aides' clerical work and teachers' increased teaching time in order to test the program's basic assumptions. Suchman similarly, if less formally, proposes investigation of the cause-and-effect linkages in the program.

D. USING THE RESULTS OF EVALUATION

Once the evaluation is completed, the logical expectation is that decision-makers will use the results to make rational decisions about future programming. All too often, however, the results are ignored.

With all the money, time, effort, skill, and irritation that went into the acquisition of information, why does it generally have so little impact?

One reason may be that the evaluation results do not match the informational needs of decision-makers. If they want to know how to improve the program, and evaluation reveals only that it led to X change in skill A, and Y change in attitude B, there is not much direction for improvement—except possibly, try harder! Guba insists that evaluators should have a better understanding of decision processes and of informational requirements relevant to decision-making. An allied issue is that of timing. As Weiss notes in "Utilization of Evaluation : Toward Comparative Study," evaluation results should be ready in time to be considered, not after the decision is reached.

Moreover, the results may not be relevant to the level of decision-maker who receives them. For example, overall assessments of program merit may be most useful to directors in other agencies who want to know whether or not a new program strategy works, and under what conditions. Weiss's first paper suggests that such people may never receive the report or may receive it in a nearly unreadable form. Most fields need better mechanisms for disseminating evaluative information. Even education, with its extensive Educational Resources Information Center (ERIC) system, may need a way to select the competent and important evaluation reports and make them more visible.

Another constraint on the use of results may be a lack of clear direction for future programming. Results may be ambiguous, implications unclear. They have to be translated into terms that make sense for pending decisions and that delineate alternatives that are indicated. There seems to be an uninhabited ground between the findings of evaluation research and the planning of future programs. In industrial reseach, units of research and development are a common phenomenon; they not only conduct research but continue to develop promising products up to the stage of commercial production. While analogies with the natural sciences are frequently misleading, there does seem to be recognition of a function that is largely unfilled in social programming. Somebody or some body should fill the gap of translating the evaluation research results into explicit recommendations for future programs.

Evaluators are often reluctant to draw conclusions from their data. Stake is representative of those who question whether evaluators *should* make judgments, although he believes that they can process the judgments of others. But judgments and recommendations for action have to be made somewhere. Unless the evaluator plays a leading role in the process, it may not get done. Riecken recommends that the evaluator interpret the findings and, more than that, help to implement them. Longood and Simmel also believe that the evaluator has a responsibility to the organization to work for the use of evaluative results, and they encourage the evaluator to emerge from his sheltered nook and engage in the rough and tumble of organizational decision-making.

Rossi, Ward and Kassebaum, Longood and Simmel, Campbell, and Weiss identify a further constraint on utilization of results. Organizations are comfortable in the status quo. When presented with negative results, their prestige, ideology, and even resources are threatened. They frequently react by rejecting the results.

Elinson documents the frequency with which evaluations produce negative findings. As Rossi notes, the easy things have been done; most current programs are trying to cope with the left-over hard-core social ills. If "no change" is a common evaluative product, it is small wonder that agencies find it hard to swallow.

Ward and Kassebaum recount an episode where a particularly able evaluation was ignored by administrators. They fear that the consequence of persistent unfavorable findings, with their potential for legislative budget cuts, will be *not* to close down ineffective programs but to close down outside evaluation.

Campbell suggests that one way out of this dilemma is for reformers to change their stance. Instead of committing themselves to new programs as though they were proven solutions, they would do better to commit themselves to seeking solution of the problem. Then they could run a phased series of experimental programs until genuine solutions were found.

Until the halcyon day arrives when administrators are experimenters, what can be done to counter program resistance? Riecken offers a series of proposals, for example, secure support from top levels, involve program staff in the evaluation, make results known in small doses, remain attached to the agency to work for implementation. In the "Utilization" paper, Weiss indicates further possibilities, with emphasis on improving the conduct of evaluation, and proposes that research be undertaken to analyze the effectiveness of a range of strategies for increasing utilization.

Even if evaluation results are not used immediately, over time they can have a cumulative impact on the climate of opinion and the legitimacy of programs. The final paper in the volume, Weiss's "The Politicization of Evaluation Research," suggests that the prevalence of negative findings in a wide range of program fields is not something to bemoan or cover up, even when it provokes political controversy or organizational resistance. Rather, the evidence that so many programs are having little constructive effect represents a fundamental critique of current approaches to social programming. This is a matter to which our society will, in time, have to respond.

2/READINGS

ROBERT E. STAKE

The Countenance of
Educational Evaluation

President Johnson, President Conant, Mrs. Hull (Sara's teacher)
and Mr. Tykociner (the man next door) are quite alike in the faith
they have in education. But they have quite different ideas of what
education is. The value they put on education does not reveal their
way of evaluating education.

Educators differ among themselves as to both the essence and
worth of an educational program. The wide range of evaluation purposes and methods allows each to keep his own perspective. Few
see their own programs "in the round," partly because of a parochial
approach to evaluation. To understand better his own teaching and to
contribute more to the science of teaching, each educator should examine the full countenance of evaluation.

Educational evaluation has its formal and informal sides. Informal evaluation is recognized by its dependence on casual observation, implicit goals, intuitive norms, and subjective judgment. Perhaps because these are also characteristic of day-to-day, personal
styles of living, informal evaluation results in perspectives which are
seldom questioned. Careful study reveals informal evaluation of education to be of variable quality—sometimes penetrating and insightful,
sometimes superficial and distorted.

Formal evaluation of education is recognized by its dependence

Robert E. Stake, "The Countenance of Educational Evaluation," *Teachers
College Record,* vol. 68, no. 7 (April 1967), pp. 523–540. Reprinted by permission.

on checklists, structured visitation by peers, controlled comparisons, and standardized testing of students. Some of these techniques have long histories of successful use. Unfortunately, when planning an evaluation, few educators consider even these four. The more common notion is to evaluate informally: to ask the opinion of the instructor, to ponder the logic of the program, or to consider the reputation of the advocates. Seldom do we find a search for relevant research reports or for behavioral data pertinent to the ultimate curricular decisions.

Dissatisfaction with the formal approach is not without cause. Few highly-relevant, readable research studies can be found. The professional journals are not disposed to publish evaluation studies. Behavioral data are costly, and often do not provide the answers. Too many accreditation-type visitation teams lack special training or even experience in evaluation. Many checklists are ambiguous; some focus too much attention on the physical attributes of a school. Psychometric tests have been developed primarily to differentiate among students at the same point in training rather than to assess the effect of instruction on acquisition of skill and understanding. Today's educator may rely little on formal evaluation because its answers have seldom been answers to questions *he* is asking.

Potential Contributions of Formal Evaluation

The educator's disdain of formal evaluation is due also to his sensitivity to criticism—and his *is* a critical clientele. It is not uncommon for him to draw before him such curtains as "national norm comparisons," "innovation phase," and "academic freedom" to avoid exposure through evaluation. The "politics" of evaluation is an interesting issue in itself, but it is not the issue here. The issue here is the *potential* contribution to education of formal evaluation. Today, educators fail to perceive what formal evaluation could do for them. They should be imploring measurement specialists to develop a methodology that reflects the fullness, the complexity, and the importance of their programs. They are not.

What one finds when he examines formal evaluation activities in education today is too little effort to spell out antecedent conditions and classroom transactions (a few of which visitation teams do record) and too little effort to couple them with the various outcomes (a few of which are portrayed by conventional test scores). Little attempt has been made to measure the match between what an educator intends to do and what he does do. The traditional concern of educational-measurement specialists for reliability of individual-student scores and predictive validity (thoroughly and competently stated in the American Council on Education's 1950 edition of *Educational Measurement*)[1] is a questionable resource. For evaluation of curricula, attention to individual differences among students should give way to attention to the contingencies among background conditions, classroom activities, and scholastic outcomes.

This paper is not about what should be measured or how to measure. It is background for developing an evaluation plan. What and how are decided later. My orientation here is around educational programs rather than educational products. I presume that the value of a product depends on its program of use. The evaluation of a program includes the evaluation of its materials.

The countenance of educational evaluation appears to be changing. On the pages that follow, I will indicate what the countenance can, and perhaps, should be. My attempt here is to introduce a conceptualization of evaluation oriented to the complex and dynamic nature of education, one which gives proper attention to the diverse purposes and judgments of the practitioner.

Much recent concern about curriculum evaluation is attributable to contemporary large-scale curriculum-innovation activities, but the statements in this paper pertain to traditional and new curricula alike. They pertain, for example, to Title I and Title III projects funded under the Elementary and Secondary Act of 1966. Statements here are relevant to any curriculum, whether oriented to subject-matter content or to student process, and without regard to whether curriculum is general-purpose, remedial, accelerated, compensatory, or special in any other way.

The purposes and procedures of educational evaluation will vary from instance to instance. What is quite appropriate for one school may be less appropriate for another. Standardized achievement tests here but not there. A great concern for expense there but not over there. How do evaluation purposes and procedures vary? What are the basic characteristics of evaluation activities? They are identified in these pages as the evaluation acts, the data sources, the congruence and contingencies, the standards, and the uses of evaluation. The first distinction to be made will be between description and judgment in evaluation.

The countenance of evaluation beheld by the educator is not the same one beheld by the specialist in evaluation. The specialist sees himself as a "describer," one who describes aptitudes and environments and accomplishments. The teacher and school administrator, on the other hand, expect an evaluator to grade something or someone as to merit. Moreover, they expect that he will judge things against external standards, on criteria perhaps little related to the local school's resources and goals.

Neither sees evaluation broadly enough. *Both* description and

judgment are essential—in fact, they are the two basic acts of evaluation. Any individual evaluator may attempt to refrain from judging or
from collecting the judgments of others. Any individual evaluator may
seek only to bring to light the worth of the program. But their evaluations are incomplete. To be fully understood, the educational program
must be fully described and fully judged.

Towards Full Description

The specialist in evaluation seems to be increasing his emphasis on
fullness of description. For many years he evaluated primarily by
measuring student progress toward academic objectives. These
objectives usually were identified with the traditional disciplines, e.g.
mathematics, English, and social studies. Achievement tests—standardized or "teacher-made"—were found to be useful in describing
the degree to which some curricular objectives are attained by individual students in a particular course. To the early evaluators, and to
many others, the countenance of evaluation has been nothing more
than the administration and normative interpretation of achievement
tests.

In recent years a few evaluators have attempted, in addition, to
assess progress of individuals toward certain "inter-disciplinary" and
"extracurricular" objectives. In their objectives, emphasis has been
given to the integration of behavior within an individual; or to the
perception of interrelationships among scholastic disciplines; or to the
development of habits, skills, and attitudes which permit the individual
to be a craftsman or scholar, in or out of school. For the descriptive
evaluation of such outcomes, the Eight-Year Study[2] has served as
one model. The proposed National Assessment Program may be
another—this statement appeared in one interim report:

> . . . all committees worked within the following broad definition of
> 'national assessment:'
> 1. In order to reflect fairly the aims of education in the U.S., the
> assessment should consider both traditional and modern curricula, and
> take into account ALL THE ASPIRATIONS schools have for de-
> veloping attitudes and motivations as well as knowledge and skills . . .
> [Caps added].[3]

In his paper, "Evaluation for Course Improvement,"[4] Lee Cronbach urged another step: a most generous inclusion of behavioral-
science variables in order to examine the possible causes and effects
of quality teaching. He proposed that the main objective for evaluation
is to uncover durable relationships—those appropriate for guiding

future educational programs. To the traditional description of pupil achievement, we add the description of instruction and the description of relationships between them. Like the instructional researcher, the evaluator—as so defined—seeks generalizations about educational practices. Many curriculum project evaluators are adopting this definition of evaluation.

The Role of Judgment

Description is one thing, judgment is another. Most evaluation specialists have chosen not to judge. But in his recent *Methodology of Evaluation*[5] Michael Scriven has charged evaluators with responsibility for passing upon the merit of an educational practice. (Note that he has urged the evaluator to do what the educator has expected the evaluator to be doing.) Scriven's position is that there is no evaluation until judgment has been passed, and by his reckoning the evaluator is best qualified to judge.

By being well experienced and by becoming well-informed in the case at hand in matters of research and educational practice the evaluator does become at least partially qualified to judge. But is it wise for him to accept this responsibility? Even now when few evaluators expect to judge, educators are reluctant to initiate a formal evaluation. If evaluators were *more* frequently identified with the passing of judgment, with the discrimination among poorer and better programs, and with the awarding of support and censure, their access to data would probably diminish. Evaluators collaborate with other social scientists and behavioral research workers. Those who do not want to judge deplore the acceptance of such responsibility by their associates. They believe that in the eyes of many practitioners, social science and behavioral research will become more suspect than it already is.

Many evaluators feel that they are not capable of perceiving, as they think a judge should, the unidimensional *value* of alternative programs. They anticipate a dilemma such as Curriculum I resulting in three skills and ten understandings and Curriculum II resulting in four skills and eight understandings. They are reluctant to judge that gaining one skill is worth losing two understandings. And, whether through timidity, disinterest, or as a rational choice, the evaluator usually supports "local option," a community's privilege to set its own standards and to be its own judge of the worth of its educational system. He expects that what is good for one community will not necessarily be good for another community, and he does not trust himself to discern what is best for a briefly-known community.

Scriven reminds them that there are precious few who can judge complex programs, and fewer still who will. Different decisions must be made—P.S.S.C. or Harvard Physics?—and they should not be made on trivial criteria, e.g. mere precedent, mention in the popular press, salesman personality, administrative convenience, or pedagogical myth. Who should judge? The answer comes easily to Scriven partly because he expects little interaction between treatment and learner, i.e., what works best for one learner will work best for others, at least within broad categories. He also expects that where the local good is at odds with the common good, the local good can be shown to be detrimental to the common good, to the end that the doctrine of local option is invalidated. According to Scriven the evaluator must judge.

Whether or not evaluation specialists will accept Scriven's challenge remains to be seen. In any case, it is likely that judgments will become an increasing part of the evaluation report. Evaluators will seek out and record the opinions of persons of special qualification. These opinions, though subjective, can be very useful and can be gathered objectively, independent of the solicitor's opinions. A responsibility for processing judgments is much more acceptable to the evaluation specialist than one for rendering judgments himself.

Taylor and Maguire[6] have pointed to five groups having important opinions on education: spokesmen for society at large, subject-matter experts, teachers, parents, and the students themselves. Members of these and other groups are judges who should be heard. Superficial polls, letters to the editor, and other incidental judgments are insufficient. An evaluation of a school program should portray the merit and fault perceived by well-identified groups, systematically gathered and processed. Thus, judgment data and description data are both essential to the evaluation of educational programs.

Data Matrices

In order to evaluate, an educator will gather together certain data. The data are likely to be from several quite different sources, gathered in several quite different ways. Whether the immediate purpose is description or judgment, three bodies of information should be tapped. In the evaluation report it can be helpful to distinguish between *antecedent, transaction,* and *outcome* data.

An antecedent is any condition existing prior to teaching and learning which may relate to outcomes. The status of a student prior to his lesson, e.g. his aptitude, previous experience, interest, and willingness, is a complex antecedent. The programmed-instruction specialist calls some antecedents "entry behaviors." The state accrediting agency emphasizes the investment of community resources. All of these are examples of the antecedents which an evaluator will describe.

Transactions are the countless encounters of students with teacher, student with student, author with reader, parent with counselor—the succession of engagements which comprise the process of education. Examples are the presentation of a film, a class discussion, the working of a homework problem, an explanation on the margin of a term paper, and the administration of a test. Smith and Meux studied such transactions in detail and have provided an 18-category classification system.[7] One very visible emphasis on a particular class of transactions was the National Defense Education Act support of audio-visual media.

Transactions are dynamic whereas antecedents and outcomes are relatively static. The boundaries between them are not clear, e.g. during a transaction we can identify certain outcomes which are feedback antecedents for subsequent learning. These boundaries do not need to be distinct. The categories should be used to stimulate rather than to subdivide our data collection.

Traditionally, most attention in formal evaluation has been given to outcomes—outcomes such as the abilities, achievements, attitudes, and aspirations of students resulting from an educational experience. Outcomes, as a body of information, would include measurements of the impact of instruction on teachers, administrators, counselors, and others. Here too would be data on wear and tear of equipment, effects of the learning environment, cost incurred. Outcomes to be considered in evaluation include not only those that are evident, or even existent, as learning sessions end, but include applications, transfer, and relearning effects which may not be available for measurement until long after. The description of the outcomes of driver training, for example, could well include reports of accident-avoidance over a lifetime. In short, outcomes are the consequences of educating—immediate and long-range, cognitive and conative, personal and community-wide.

Antecedents, transactions, and outcomes, the elements of evaluation statements, are shown in Figure 1 to have a place in both description and judgment. To fill in these matrices the evaluator will collect judgments (e.g. of community prejudice, of problem solving styles, and of teacher personality) as well as descriptions. In Figure 1 it is also indicated that judgmental statements are classified either as general standards of quality or as judgments specific to the given program. Descriptive data are classified as intents and observations. The evaluator can organize his data-gathering to conform to the format shown in Figure 1.

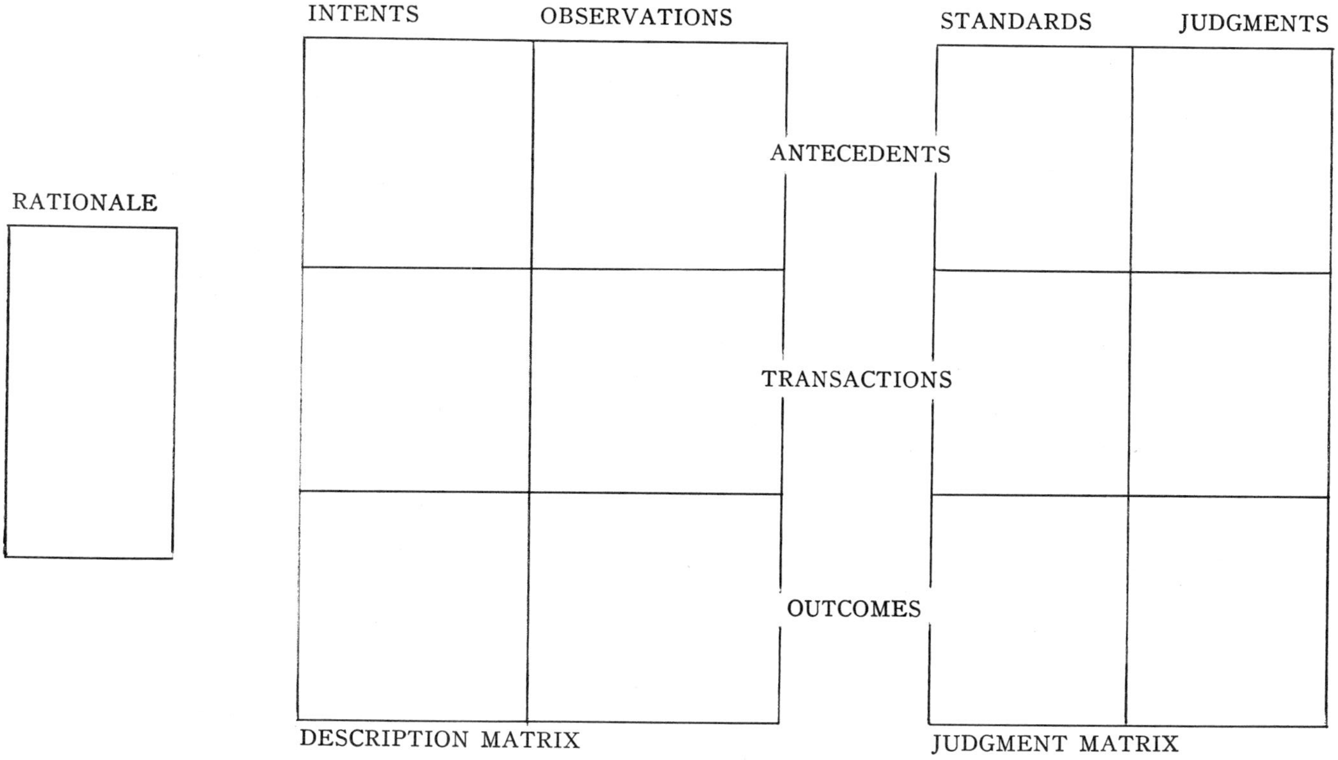

RATIONALE

	INTENTS	OBSERVATIONS		STANDARDS	JUDGMENTS
ANTECEDENTS					
TRANSACTIONS					
OUTCOMES					

DESCRIPTION MATRIX   JUDGMENT MATRIX

FIGURE 1. A LAYOUT OF STATEMENTS AND DATA TO BE COLLECTED BY THE EVALUATOR OF AN EDUCATIONAL PROGRAM

The evaluator can prepare a record of what educators intend, of what observers perceive, of what patrons generally expect, and of what judges value the immediate program to be. The record may treat antecedents, transactions, and outcomes separately within the four classes identified as *Intents, Observations, Standards,* and *Judgments,* as in Figure 1. The following is an illustration of 12 data, one of which could be recorded in each of the 12 cells, starting with an intended antecedent, and moving down each column until an outcome judgment has been indicated.

> *Knowing that (1) Chapter XI has been assigned and that he intends (2) to lecture on the topic Wednesday, a professor indicates (3) what the students should be able to do by Friday, partly by writing a quiz on the topic. He observes that (4) some students were absent on Wednesday, that (5) he did not quite complete the lecture because of a lengthy discussion and that (6) on the quiz only about 2/3 of the class seemed to understand a certain major concept. In general, he expects (7) some absences but that the work will be made up by quiz-time; he expects (8) his lectures to be clear enough for perhaps 90 percent of a class to follow him without difficulty; and he knows that (9) his colleagues expect only about one student in ten to understand thoroughly each major concept in such lessons as these. By his own judgment (10) the reading assignment was not a sufficient background for his lecture; the students commented that (11) the lecture was pro-vocative; and the graduate assistant who read the quiz papers said that (12) a discouragingly large number of students seemed to confuse one major concept for another.*

Evaluators and educators do not expect data to be recorded in such detail, even in the distant future. My purpose here was to give twelve examples of data that could be handled by separate cells in the matrices. Next I would like to consider the description data matrix in detail.

Goals and Intents

For many years instructional technologists, test specialists, and others have pleaded for more explicit statement of educational goals. I consider "goals," "objectives," and "intents" to be synonymous. I use the category title *Intents* because many educators now equate "goals" and "objectives" with "intended student outcomes." In this paper Intents includes the planned-for environmental conditions, the planned-for demonstrations, the planned-for coverage of certain subject matter, etc., as well as the planned-for student behavior. To be in-cluded in this three-cell column are effects which are desired, those which are hoped for, those which are anticipated, and even those which are feared. This class of data includes goals and plans that others have, especially the students. (It should be noted that it is not the educator's privilege to rule out the study of a variable by saying, "that is not one of our objectives." The evaluator should include both the variable and the negation.) The resulting collection of *Intents* is a priority listing of all that may happen.

The fact that many educators now equate "goals" with "intended student outcomes" is to the credit of the behaviorists, particularly the advocates of programmed instruction. They have brought about a small reform in teaching by emphasizing those specific classroom acts and work exercises which contribute to the refinement of student responses. The A.A.A.S. Science Project, for example, has been successful in developing its curriculum around behavioristic goals.[8] Some curriculum-innovation projects, however, have found the emphasis on behavioral outcomes an obstacle to creative teaching.[9] The educational evaluator should not list goals only in terms of anticipated student behavior. To *evaluate* an educational program, we must examine what teaching, as well as what learning, is intended. (Many antecedent conditions and teaching transactions can be worded behavioristically, if desired.) How intentions are worded is not a criterion for inclusion. Intents can be the global goals of the Educational Policies Commission or the detailed goals of the programmer.[10] Taxonomic, mechanistic, humanistic, even scriptural—any mixture of goal statements are acceptable as part of the evaluation picture.

Many a contemporary evaluator expects trouble when he sets out to record the educator's objectives. Early in the work he urged the educator to declare his objectives so that outcome-testing devices could be built. He finds the educator either reluctant or unable to verbalize objectives. With diligence, if not with pleasure, the evaluator assists with what he presumes to be the educator's job: writing behavioral goals. His presumption is wrong.

As Scriven has said, the responsibility for describing curricular objectives is the responsibility of the evaluator. He is the one who is experienced with the language of behaviors, traits, and habits. Just as it is his responsibility to transform the behaviors of a teacher and the responses of a student into data, it is his responsibility to transform the intentions and expectations of an educator into "data." It is necessary for him to continue to ask the educator for statements of intent. He should augment the replies by asking, "Is this another way of saying it?" or "Is this an instance?" Is is not wrong for an evaluator to teach a willing educator about behavioral objectives—they may facilitate the work. It is wrong for him to insist that every educator should use them.

Obtaining authentic statements of intent is a new challenge for the evaluator. The methodology remains to be developed. Let us now shift attention to the second column of the data cells.

Observational Choice

Most of the descriptive data cited early in the previous section are classified as *Observations*. In Figure 1 when he described surroundings and events and the subsequent consequences, the evaluator* is telling of his Observations. Sometimes the evaluator observes these characteristics in a direct and personal way. Sometimes he uses instruments. His instruments include inventory schedules, biographical data sheets, interview routines, check lists, opinionnaires, and all kinds of psychometric tests. The experienced evaluator gives special attention to the measurement of student outcomes, but he does not fail to observe the other outcomes, nor the antecedent conditions and instructional transactions.

Many educators fear that the outside evaluator will not be attentive to the characteristics that the school staff has deemed most important. This sometimes does happen, but evaluators often pay *too much* attention to what they have been urged to look at, and too little attention to other facets. In the matter of selection of variables for evaluation, the evaluator must make a subjective decision. Obviously, he must limit the elements to be studied. He cannot look at all of them. The ones he rules out will be those that he assumes would not contribute to an understanding of the educational activity. He should give primary attention to the variables specifically indicated by the educator's objectives, but he must designate additional variables to be observed. He must search for unwanted side effects and incidental gains. The selection of measuring techniques is an obvious responsibility, but the choice of characteristics to be observed is an equally important and unique contribution of the evaluator.

An evaluation is not complete without a statement of the rationale of the program. It needs to be considered separately, as indicated in Figure 1. Every program has its rationale, though often it is only implicit. The rationale indicates the philosophic background and basic purposes of the program. Its importance to evaluation has been indicated by Berlak.[11] The rationale should provide one basis for evaluating Intents. The evaluator asks himself or other judges whether the plan developed by the educator constitutes a logical step in the implementation of the basic purposes. The rationale also is of value in

---

* Here and elsewhere in this paper, for simplicity of presentation, the evaluator and the educator are referred to as two different persons. The educator will often be his own evaluator or a member of the evaluation team.

choosing the reference groups, e.g. merchants, mathematicians, and mathematics educators, which later are to pass judgment on various aspects of the program.

A statement of rationale may be difficult to obtain. Many an effective instructor is less than effective at presenting an educational rationale. If pressed, he may only succeed in saying something the listener wanted said. It is important that the rationale be in his language, a language he is the master of. Suggestions by the evaluator may be an obstacle, becoming accepted because they are attractive rather than because they designate the grounds for what the educator is trying to do.

The judgment matrix needs further explanation, but I am postponing that until after a consideration of the bases for processing descriptive data.

Contingency and Congruence

For any one educational program there are two principal ways of processing descriptive evaluation data: finding the contingencies among antecedents, transactions, and outcomes and finding the congruence between Intents and Observations. The processing of judgments follows a different model. The first two main columns of the data matrix in Figure 1 contain the descriptive data. The format for processing these data is represented in Figure 2.

The data for a curriculum are *congruent* if what was intended actually happens. To be fully congruent the intended antecedents, transactions, and outcomes would have to come to pass. (This seldom happens—and often should not.) Within one row of the data matrix the evaluator should be able to compare the cells containing Intents and Observations, to note the discrepancies, and to describe the amount of congruence for that row. (Congruence of outcomes has been emphasized in the evaluation model proposed by Taylor and Maguire.) Congruence does not indicate that outcomes are reliable or valid, but that what was intended did occur.

Just as the Gestaltist found more to the whole than the sum of its parts, the evaluator studying variables from any two of the three cells in a column of the data matrix finds more to describe than the variables themselves. The relationships or *contingencies* among the variables deserve additional attention. In the sense that evaluation is the search for relationships that permit the improvement of education, the evaluator's task is one of identifying outcomes that are contingent upon particular antecedent conditions and instructional transactions.

Lesson planning and curriculum revision through the years has been built upon faith in certain contingencies. Day to day, the master

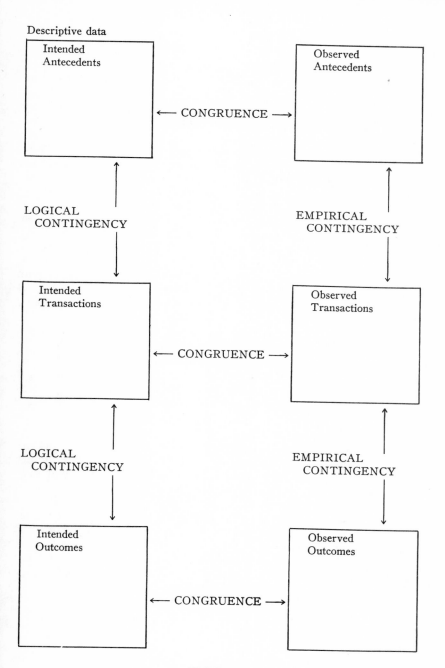

FIGURE 2
A REPRESENTATION OF THE PROCESSING
OF DESCRIPTIVE DATA

teacher arranges his presentation and selects his input materials to fit his instructional goals. For him the contingencies, in the main, are logical, intuitive, and supported by a history of satisfactions and endorsements. Even the master teacher and certainly less-experienced teachers need to bring their intuited contingencies under the scrutiny of appropriate juries.

As a first step in evaluation it is important just to record them. A film on floodwaters may be scheduled (intended transaction) to expose students to a background to conservation legislation (intended outcome). Of those who know both subject matter and pedagogy, we ask, "Is there a logical connection between this event and this purpose?" If so, a logical contingency exists between these two Intents. The record should show it.

Whenever Intents are evaluated the contingency criterion is one of logic. To test the logic of an educational contingency the evaluators rely on previous experience, perhaps on research experience, with similar observables. No immediate observation of these variables, however, is necessary to test the strength of the contingencies among Intents.

Evaluation of Observation contingencies depends on empirical evidence. To say, "this arithmetic class progressed rapidly because the teacher was somewhat but not too sophisticated in mathematics" demands empirical data, either from within the evaluation or from the research literature.[12] The usual evaluation of a single program will not alone provide the data necessary for contingency statements. Here too, then, previous experience with similar observables is a basic qualification of the evaluator.

The contingencies and congruences identified by evaluators are subject to judgment by experts and participants just as more unitary descriptive data are. The importance of non-congruence will vary with different viewpoints. The school superintendent and the school counselor may disagree as to the importance of a cancellation of the scheduled lessons on sex hygiene in the health class. As an example of judging contingencies, the degree to which teacher morale is contingent on the length of the school day may be deemed cause enough to abandon an early morning class by one judge and not another. Perceptions of importance of congruence and contingency deserve the evaluator's careful attention.

Standards and Judgments

There is a general agreement that the goal of education is excellence—but how schools and students should excell, and at what sacrifice, will always be debated. Whether goals are local or national, the measurement of excellence requires explicit rather than implicit standards.

Today's educational programs are not subjected to "standard-oriented" evaluation. This is not to say that schools lack in aspiration or accomplishment. It is to say that standards—benchmarks of performance having widespread reference value—are not in common use. Schools across the nation may use the same evaluation checklist** but the interpretations of the checklisted data are couched in inexplicit, personal terms. Even in an informal way, no school can evaluate the impact of its program without knowledge of what other schools are doing in pursuit of similar objectives. Unfortunately, many educators are loathe to accumulate that knowledge systematically.[13, 14]

There is little knowledge anywhere today of the quality of a student's education. School grades are based on the private criteria and standards of the individual teacher. Most "standardized" tests scores tell where an examinee performing "psychometrically useful" tasks stands with regard to a reference group, rather than the level of competence at which he performs essential scholastic tasks. Although most teachers are competent to teach their subject matter and to spot learning difficulties, few have the ability to *describe* a student's command over his intellectual environment. Neither school grades nor standardized test scores nor the candid opinions of teachers are very informative as to the excellence of students.

Even when measurements are effectively interpreted, evaluation is complicated by a multiplicity of standards. Standards vary from student to student, from instructor to instructor, and from reference group to reference group. This is not wrong. In a healthy society, different parties have different standards. Part of the responsibility of evaluation is to make known which standards are held by whom.

It was implied much earlier that it is reasonable to expect change in an educator's *Intents* over a period of time. This is to say that he will change both his criteria and his standards during instruction. While a curriculum is being developed and disseminated, even the major classes of criteria vary. In their analysis of nationwide assimilation of new educational programs, Clark and Guba[15] identified eight stages of change through which new programs go. For each stage they

** One contemporary checklist is *Evaluative Criteria*, a document published by the National Study of Secondary School Evaluation (1960). It is a commendably thorough list of antecedents and possible transactions, organized mostly by subject-matter offerings. Surely it is valuable as a checklist, identifying neglected areas. Its great value may be a catalyst, hastening the maturity of a developing curriculum. However, it can be of only limited value in *evaluating*, for it guides neither the measurement nor the interpretation of measurement. By intent, it deals with criteria (what variables to consider) and leaves the matter of standards (what ratings to consider as meritorious) to the conjecture of the individual observer.

identified special criteria (each with its own standards) on which the program should be evaluated before it advances to another stage. Each of their criteria deserves elaboration, but here it is merely noted that there are quite different criteria at each successive curriculum-development stage.

Informal evaluation tends to leave criteria unspecified. Formal evaluation is more specific. But it seems the more careful the evaluation, the fewer the criteria; and the more carefully the criteria are specified, the less the concern given to standards of acceptability. It is a great misfortune that the best trained evaluators have been looking at education with a microscope rather than with a panoramic view finder.

There is no clear picture of what any school or any curriculum project is accomplishing today partly because the methodology of processing judgments is inadequate. What little formal evaluation there is is attentive to too few criteria, overly tolerant of implicit standards, and ignores the advantage of relative comparisons. More needs to be said about relative and absolute standards.

Comparing and Judging

There are two bases of judging the characteristics of a program, (1) with respect to absolute standards as reflected by personal judgments and (2) with respect to relative standards as reflected by characteristics of alternate programs. One can evaluate SMSG mathematics with respect to opinions of what a mathematics curriculum should be or with regard to what other mathematics curricula are. The evaluator's comparisons and judgments are symbolized in Figure 3. The upper left matrix represents the data matrix from Figure 2. At the upper right are sets of standards by which a program can be judged in an absolute sense. There are multiple sets because there may be numerous reference groups or points of view. The several matrices at the lower left represent several alternate programs to which the one being evaluated can be compared.

Each set of absolute standards, if formalized, would indicate acceptable and meritorious levels for antecedents, transactions, and outcomes. So far I have been talking about setting standards, not about judging. Before making a judgment the evaluator determines whether or not each standard is met. Unavailable standards must be estimated. The judging act itself is deciding which set of standards to heed. More precisely, judging is assigning a weight, an importance, to each set of standards. Rational judgment in educational evaluation is a decision as to how much to pay attention to the standards of each reference

FIGURE 3

*A REPRESENTATION OF THE PROCESS OF JUDGING
THE MERIT OF AN EDUCATIONAL PROGRAM.*

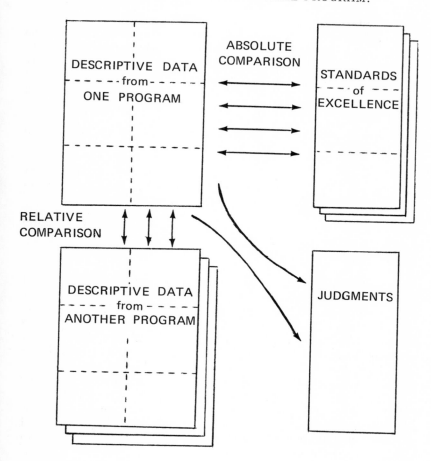

group (point of view) in deciding whether or not to take some administrative action.‡

Relative comparison is accomplished in similar fashion except that the standards are taken from descriptions of other programs. It is

‡ Deciding which variables to study and deciding which standards to employ are two essentially subjective commitments in evaluation. Other acts are capable of objective treatment; only these two are beyond the reach of social science methodology.

hardly a judgmental matter to determine whether one program betters another with regard to a single characteristic, but there are many characteristics and the characteristics are not equally important. The evaluator selects which characteristics to attend to and which reference programs to compare to.

From relative judgment of a program, as well as from absolute judgment we can obtain an overall or composite rating of merit (perhaps with certain qualifying statements), a rating to be used in making an educational decision. From this final act of judgment a recommendation can be composed.

Absolute and Relative Evaluation

As to which kind of evaluation—absolute or relative—to encourage, Scriven and Cronbach have disagreed. Cronbach[4] suggests that generalizations to the local-school situation from curriculum-comparing studies are sufficiently hazardous (even when the studies are massive, well-designed, and properly controlled) to make them poor research investments. Moreover, the difference in purpose of the programs being compared is likely to be sufficiently great to render uninterpretable any outcome other than across-the-board superiority of one of them. Expecting that rarely, Cronbach urges fewer comparisons, more intensive process studies, and more curriculum "case studies" with extensive measurement and thorough description.

Scriven, on the other hand, indicates that what the educator wants to know is whether or not one program is better than another, and that the best way to answer his question is by direct comparison. He points to the difficulty of describing the outcomes of complex learning in explicit terms and with respect to absolute standards, and to the ease of observing relative outcomes from two programs. Whether or not Scriven's prescription is satisfying will probably depend on the client. An educator faced with an adoption decision is more likely to be satisfied, the curriculum innovator and instructional technologist less likely.

One of the major distinctions in evaluation is that which Scriven identifies as *formative* versus *summative* evaluation. His use of the terms relates primarily to the stage of development of curricular material. If material is not yet ready for distribution to classroom teachers, then its evaluation is formative; otherwise it is summative. It is probably more useful to distinguish between evaluation oriented to developer-author-publisher criteria and standards and evaluation oriented to consumer-administrator-teacher criteria and standards. The formative-summative distinction could be so defined, and I will use the terms in that way. The faculty committee facing an adoption choice asks, "Which is best? Which will do the job best?" The course developer, following Cronbach's advice, asks, "How can we teach it better?" (Note that neither are now concerned about the individual student differences.) The evaluator looks at different data and invokes different standards to answer these questions.

The evaluator who assumes responsibility for summative evaluation—rather than formative evaluation—accepts the responsibility of informing consumers as to the merit of the program. The judgments of Figure 3 are his target. It is likely that he will attempt to describe the school situations in which the procedures or materials may be used. He may see his task as one of indicating the goodness-of-fit of an available curriculum to an existing school program. He must learn whether or not the intended antecedents, transactions, and outcomes for the curriculum are consistent with the resources, standards, and goals of the school. This may require as much attention to the school as to the new curriculum.

The formative evaluator, on the other hand, is more interested in the contingencies indicated in Figure 2. He will look for covariations within the evaluation study, and across studies, as a basis for guiding the development of present or future programs.

For major evaluation activities it is obvious that an individual evaluator will not have the many competencies required. A team of social scientists is needed for many assignments. It is reasonable to suppose that such teams will include specialists in instructional technology, specialists in psychometric testing and scaling, specialists in research design and analysis, and specialists in disseminaton of information. Curricular innovation is sure to have deep and widespread effect on our society, and we may include the social anthropologist on some evaluation teams. The economist and philosopher have something to offer. Experts will be needed for the study of values, population surveys, and content-oriented data-reduction techniques.

The educator who has looked disconsolate when scheduled for evaluation will look aghast at the prospect of a team of evaluators invading his school. How can these evaluators observe or describe the natural state of education when their very presence influences that state? His concern is justified. Measurement activity—just the presence of evaluators—does have a reactive effect on education, sometimes beneficial and sometimes not—but in either case contributing to the atypicality of the sessions. There are specialists, however, who anticipate that evaluation will one day be so skilled that it properly will be considered "unobtrusive measurement."[16]

In conclusion I would remind the reader that one of the largest investments being made in U.S. education today is in the development of new programs. School officials cannot yet revise a curriculum on rational grounds, and the needed evaluation is not under way. What is to be gained from the enormous effort of the innovators of the 1960's if in the 1970's there are no evaluation records? Both the new innovator and the new teacher need to know. Folklore is not a sufficient repository. In our data banks we should document the causes and effects, the congruence of intent and accomplishment, and the panorama of judgments of those concerned. Such records should be kept to promote educational action, not obstruct it. The countenance of evaluation should be one of data gathering that leads to decision-making, not to trouble-making.

Educators should be making their own evaluations more deliberate, more formal. Those who will—whether in their classrooms or on national panels—can hope to clarify their responsibility by answering each of the following questions: (1) Is this evaluation to be primarily descriptive, primarily judgmental, or both descriptive and judgmental? (2) Is this evaluation to emphasize the antecedent conditions, the transactions, or the outcomes alone, or a combination of these, or their functional contingencies? (3) Is this evaluation to indicate the congruence between what is intended and what occurs? (4) Is this evaluation to be undertaken within a single program or as a comparison between two or more curricular programs? (5) Is this evaluation intended more to further the development of curricula or to help choose among available curricula? With these questions answered, the restrictive effects of incomplete guidelines and inappropriate countenances are more easily avoided.

References

1. American Council on Education. *Educational Measurement*. E. F. Lindquist (Ed.). Washington, D.C., 1951.

2. Smith, E. R. and Tyler, Ralph W., *Appraising and Recording Student Progress*. New York: Harper and Row, 1942.

3. Educational Testing Service. "A Long, Hot Summer of Committee Work on National Assessment of Education," *ETS Developments,* Vol. XIII, November, 1965.

4. Cronbach, Lee. "Evaluation for Course Improvement," *Teachers College Record,* 64, 1963, pp. 672–683.

5. Scriven, Michael. "The Methodology of Evaluation," *AERA Monograph Series on Curriculum Evaluation,* No. 1. Chicago: Rand McNally, 1967, pp. 39–89.

6. Taylor, Peter A. and Maguire, Thomas O., "A Theoretical Evaluation Model," *The Manitoba Journal of Educational Research,* 1, 1966, pp. 12–17.

7. Smith, B. Othanel and Meux, M. O., *A Study of the Logic of Teaching.* Urbana: Bureau of Educational Research, University of Illinois. No date.

8. Gagné, Robert M., "Elementary Science: A New Scheme of Instruction," *Science,* Vol. 151, No. 3706, pp. 49–53.

9. Atkin, J. M., "Some Evaluation Problems in a Course Content Improvement Project," *Journal of Research in Science Teaching,* 1, 1963, 129–132.

10. Mager, R. F., *Preparing Objectives For Programmed Instruction.* San Francisco: Fearon Publishers, 1962.

11. Berlak, Harold. Comments recorded in *Concepts and Structure in the New Social Science Curricula.* Irving Morrissett (Ed.). Lafayette, Indiana: Social Science Education Consortium, Purdue University, 1966, pp. 88–89.

12. See Bassham, H., "Teacher Understanding and Pupil Efficiency in Mathematics: A Study of Relationship," *Arithmetic Teacher,* 9: 1962, pp. 383–387.

13. Hand, Harold C., "National Assessment Viewed as the Camel's Nose," *Phi Delta Kappan,* 47, September, 1965, 8–12.

14. Tyler, Ralph W., "Assessing the Progress of Education," *Phi Delta Kappan,* 47, September, 1965, 13–16.

15. Clark, David L. and Guba, Egon G., "An Examination of Potential Change Roles in Education." Columbus: The Ohio State University, 1965. (Multilith.)

16. Webb, Eugene J.; Campbell, Donald T., Schwartz, Richard D., and Sechrist, Lee. *Unobtrusive Measures: Nonreactive Research in the Social Sciences.* Chicago: Rand McNally, 1966.

EDWARD A. SUCHMAN

Action for What?
A Critique of Evaluative Research

One generation ago, Robert S. Lynd published his classical challenge to research scientists—*Knowledge for What?* (Lynd, 1939). In the midst of a period of breathtaking advances in all of the physical and social sciences, he proposed a time for stock-taking to evaluate the purposes and utility of such rapidly accumulating knowledge. Basic or "pure" research, he argued, had an objective beyond that of expanding disciplinary knowledge. The scientist, as a member of society whose research was supported by society, had an obligation to concern himself with the possible application of his discoveries to the needs of society.

While this proposition may have given rise to a great debate in the 1940's, it has become largely academic in The Great Society of the 1960's. The explosion of the first atomic bomb destroyed forever the detachment of the physical scientist. For better or worse, he found himself unavoidably in the center of the arena of national affairs. It wasn't long before he was joined there by the social scientist. If the physical sciences could produce such a shattering impact upon the world of nature, why shouldn't the behavioral sciences have an equally telling effect upon the world of man? Why couldn't man's knowledge of the forces governing himself and the societies he had created be applied to the remedying of the defects within those societies?

Edward A. Suchman, "Action for What? A Critique of Evaluative Research," in *The Organization, Management, and Tactics of Social Research,* edited by Richard O'Toole (Cambridge, Mass.: Schenkman Publishing Company, 1970). Reprinted by permission.

Lynd's challenge of "Knowledge for What?" has been answered one generation later by the resounding battle cry of, "Knowledge for action!" The emphasis today is clearly upon the application of knowledge to the amelioration of social problems. The same scientific methodology that had been so successful in discovering knowledge was now to be brought to bear upon the utilization of that knowledge. Social change could be planned and implemented by scientific research upon the causes of society's ills and by the development of intervention programs to meet these causes. Man, it seems, had now entered a period of widespread planned social change or innovation. Action programs in all areas of health, education, and welfare have become the watchword of the day (Bennis, 1960; Fairweather, 1967).

But action for what? Just as Lynd had challenged the purpose of knowledge in an era of new discoveries, we might today challenge the purpose of action in an era of frenzied and ever-increasing activity on an international, national, and local scale. What are we trying to accomplish with these action programs? Is knowledge for knowledge's sake to be replaced by action for action's sake?

Evaluation—the Study of Planned Social Change

To answer this question of action for what, social scientists are developing methods for studying planned social change in an attempt to evaluate the purposes and effectiveness of such change. These evaluative research studies attempt to apply the methods of science to service and action programs in order to obtain objective and valid measures of what such programs are accomplishing. Underlying these efforts are three implicit assumptions: (1) that man can change his social environment; (2) that change is good; and (3) that such change is measurable. Thus, social problems are viewed as amenable to deliberate intervention, while the success or failure of such intervention is subject to demonstration through scientific, evaluative research studies (Suchman, 1967).

From the point of view of this report, evaluation connotes some judgment concerning the effects of planned social change. The target or object of the evaluation is usually some program or activity which is deliberately intended to produce some desired result. The evaluation itself attempts to determine the degree of success or failure of the action in attaining this result. Thus, evaluation represents a measurement of effectiveness in reaching some predetermined goal.

The key elements in this definition of evaluation are: (1) an objective or goal which is considered desirable or has some positive value; (2) a planned program of deliberate intervention which one hypothesizes is capable of achieving the desired goal; and (3) a method for determining the degree to which the desired objective is attained *as a result of* the planned program. All three must be present before evaluation can take place.

These three elements can be recognized in Riecken's definition of evaluation as "the measurement of desirable and undesirable consequences of an action that has been taken in order to forward some goal that we value" (Riecken, 1952: 4). The emphasis upon the study of change is clearly seen in the four questions posed by Herzog for "a satisfactory evaluation of effort": (1) what kind of change is desired?; (2) by what means is change to be brought about?; (3) what is the evidence that the changes observed are due to the means employed?; and (4) what is the meaning of the changes found? (Herzog, 1959: 2). Unless one can visualize an *objective* involving change from some less desirable to some more desirable state, an *activity* or program designed to produce this change, and *criteria* by which one can judge that change has taken or is taking place, one cannot formulate the necessary evaluative hypothesis, viz., "Activities A, B, C will achieve objectives X, Y, Z."

The Need for Evaluation

To some extent, all programs of planned social change, whether educational, economic, medical, political, or religious, are required to provide "proof" of their legitimacy and effectiveness in order to justify public support. The demand for "proofs of work" will vary depending upon such factors as degree of faith in authority and competition between opposing programs or objectives. The current proliferation of new types of social intervention which challenge traditional approaches to health, education, and welfare and which compete for both public and financial support are under constant pressure to show that they are better than established programs and deserve a larger proportion of available resources. There probably comes a time in the development of any new approach to a social problem when, after an initial outburst of enthusiastic activity, a breathing period of evaluation sets in.

The need for evaluation rarely occurs in an atmosphere of complacency. Dissatisfaction and puzzlement lie behind most demands for evaluation. The natural tendency of an entrenched program is to resist change. Only when the public voices its displeasure at the way a social problem is being met or a public service is being rendered, or when professional conscience becomes too uneasy about its efforts at correcting social conditions or providing public services does talk of evaluation begin. The same factors that create public concern about the social problem to begin with also underlie the demand for evaluation: (1) a "perceived discrepancy" between what exists and what is desired, (2) a feeling of a "need for adjustive activity" to resolve this discrepancy, and (3) an "awareness of ignorance or doubt" about what should be done (Merton and Devereaux, 1964). As stated by Borgatta: "When conditions are bad enough and social conscience is brought into play, both the need and the potential for improvement may lead to the development of a program designed to be corrective. Most programs that receive systematic attention for evaluation occur in the context of correcting an existing situation" (Borgatta, 1966).

Before an evaluation is undertaken, it is important that the sources of "dissatisfaction and puzzlement" be identified as clearly as possible. Unless this is done, it becomes difficult to formulate the study in such a way as to provide the answers that will be needed to remedy the dissatisfaction or dispell the puzzlement. Thus, an evaluation study should be a problem-solving enterprise with a clear-cut relationship to some decision-making function. Perhaps the most crucial question to be asked before an evaluation is undertaken is, "What decisions about the program or its objectives will be affected by the results of the evaluation?" Further development of this question would force consideration of why the evaluation was being done, what alternative courses of action were being considered, who was in favor of or opposed to the evaluation, how much weight would the results of the evaluation carry, and what resources existed or could be marshalled to support the recommendations of the evaluation. A good exercise is to "suppose" positive or negative results and then to predict what would be done as a result of either outcome.

The answers to questions such as the above will increase the likelihood that the results of an evaluation will be utilized and help to forestall unnecessary and unproductive studies. Unless a reasonable assumption can be made that the results of the evaluation will be utilized, there is probably little need for the evaluation. Much too often evaluation studies are undertaken when there is very little likelihood that anything will change regardless of how the evaluation comes out. The attitude seems to be "let's do the evaluation and then decide what to do with the results." In such a case, the evaluation is probably unnecessary and certainly inadequately conceived.

One further consideration has to do with the appropriate and desirable time for evaluation. An evaluation study should not be undertaken until an activity or program has had enough time to prove its possible effectiveness. Obviously, the program has to have become operational before it can be evaluated. To some extent an evaluation can be limited to determining whether or not a program has succeeded in establishing itself; but, as we shall see later, this is a limited evaluation that has little to do with the actual effectiveness of the program.

However, while a program should not be evaluated too soon, neither should it be evaluated too late. The evaluation should occur while there is still time to apply the results to the operation of the program. This means before the activity has become so entrenched that change is no longer possible or can only be made with great difficulty and disruption. It is well known that evaluation has its greatest success with new, experimental activities and its least success with established, traditional programs. In the case of newly developed programs, it may be possible to "build-in" evaluative research in such a way as to feed-back information to the program. Such built-in evaluation can also serve the purpose of "quality control" and redirection for an on-going program.

Evaluation is most productive when it can become a continuous process of program assessment and improvement. Too often the need for evaluation is narrowly defined in terms of a one-shot, "pass-fail" decision. Not only is this unrealistic, since very seldom are the results of an evaluation study so definitive as to "prove" a program a complete failure, nor are the administrative considerations usually such as to permit the total termination of a program, but also an important function of the evaluation should be to improve shortcomings of the program in order to increase its effectiveness. Evaluative research is best viewed as a learning process with the focus of interest being an analysis of *why* a program is failing or succeeding.

The answer to this question "why" might encompass an analysis of: (1) the attributes of the program itself that make it more or less successful; (2) the population exposed to the program in terms of which sub-groups are reached and which affected; (3) the situational context within which the program takes place, such as auspices, locale, competing programs, and community support; and (4) the different kinds of effects produced by the program, such as cognitive, attitudinal, or behavioral, long or short-term, unitary or multiple, including special attention to any negative side-effects. Information on the above aspects of program operation represents the research contribution which evaluation can make to any programmatic activity (Suchman, in press). In this sense evaluation involves more than judging; it also includes an understanding of process and a constant feed-back of information for program revision.

Functions and Types of Evaluation

Evaluation is an important component of administration, whether such evaluation be formal or informal. If we view the administrative process as a "cycle" which includes the following special activities: (a) decision-making, (b) programming, (c) communicating, (d) controlling, (e) reappraising (Litchfield, 1956: 12), it becomes apparent that evaluation is an essential tool of management. Since the major focus of administration is the organization of resources and activities so as to achieve some desired objective, and since we have defined evaluative research as the study of the relationship of planned activities to desired objectives, we place evaluative research at the heart of the administrative process. In fact, we would argue that evaluative research constitutes the methodological and empirical backbone of any attempt to build a field of administrative science or practice theory.

From this point of view, evaluation becomes programmatic research whose major function is to aid administrators or program operators to plan and adjust their activities in an attempt to increase the probability of achieving the desired action or service goals. Evaluation is, thus, an integral part of any operating system. It is present at all stages of the system and not confined, as is commonly thought, to the terminal effects of a program. This conception of evaluation as a self-contained, one-shot study of the effectiveness of a disembodied, clearly defined program or activity stems, in part, from the model of experimental research which calls for before and after comparisons of the results of some single "stimulus." Overwhelmingly, action and service programs are continuous, on-going events, however, which cannot be meaningfully segmented and disengaged from the entire operational process. As we shall see, the design of evaluative research becomes strongly influenced by this important consideration.

We may identify a sequence of development which relates four major aspects of programmatic activity. While these stand in a logical progression as diagrammed below, it is important to visualize a constant interaction among them with success at one stage moving the process forward to the next stage, but with failure at any stage leading to a "recycling" to some earlier stage. This sequence is as follows:

Research → Planning → Demonstration → Operation

This process model has been applied by Guba and Clark to educational programs in terms of the following series of steps: *research* leads to two stages of *development* (invention and design) which is followed by two stages of *diffusion* (dissemination and demonstration) which, in turn, leads to three steps of *adoption* (trial, installation, and institutionalization) (Guba and Clark, 1111:8). Each step has its own objectives and its own appropriate criteria of success or failure and, thus, is subject to separate evaluation. In turn, the evaluation is also subject to an evaluation of its effectiveness.

In discussing this model, Gideonse points out that innovation or change does not necessarily begin with research, but that the initiative for different actions can occur at any point in the continuum and may originate from sources not directly involved in the program process itself. He proposes an output model based on a separation of research, development, and operation each with its own rather distinct objectives and unique orientation. Research has a *knowledge* orientation with the objective being the testing of a "non-action" hypothesis. Development has a *process* orientation aimed at formulating organizational formats, materials, and techniques of operations. Operations has a *production* orientation whose objective is to install and administer programs designed to achieve the desired change or output (Gideonse, 1968). However, Gideonse also points out that, while they are distinct, there is a constant flow backwards and forwards between the various steps of the model.

Evaluation may occur at each stage of the above sequence, since each of these processes may be viewed as a series of purposive activities designed to achieve its own specified goal. Thus, we may evaluate research in terms of its ability to provide the necessary knowledge-base for planning; in turn, planning may be evaluated according to its success or failure in developing a program which can be tried out on a demonstration basis. Similarly, the demonstration program can be evaluated in terms of its utility for the establishment of an operating program, while the operating program becomes evaluated according to its effectiveness in achieving the desired objective.

From the point of view of this progression, we may view the objective of any earlier stage as being one of providing the *means* towards the achievement of some objective at a later stage. Thus, the objective of research is to provide knowledge as the means for planning, whose objective, in turn, is to provide a plan which becomes the means for setting up a demonstration project, whose objective now becomes the development and testing of procedures which becomes a means toward establishing the desired operational program—whose objective, to push the process further, becomes the means of achieving the desired goal. At each point in the above flow from research to operation, evaluation provides the necessary information to determine whether one should move ahead to the next stage or perhaps back to a previous stage. For example, a demonstration program which fails to produce the desired effects may require the planning of a new approach, which, in turn, may call for more research. This is why we have stressed evaluation as a continuous process.

In general, the major emphasis of most evaluation studies will be upon the demonstration and operation stages, although there is no reason, as we have formulated the process above, why research and planning cannot also be evaluated. This becomes obvious when the major function of the organization is research or planning *per se* and where the administration of such an organization is evaluated in terms of its own specific research or planning objectives. In a similar sense, evaluation itself is subject to evaluation as a form of administrative enterprise. In other words, any program of activities designed for some specified purpose may be evaluated in terms of its degree of success or failure in achieving those purposes. This rather all-encompassing statement underscores the emphasis of the previous section on the importance of determining as clearly as possible *why* any particular evaluation is needed.

Demonstration Programs

The demonstration program occupies a strategic and central place in the scheme of evaluative research. Its major purpose is the development of an "experimental" program which will permit an evaluation of probable success or failure on a "laboratory" or trial basis. The administrator has greater flexibility in designing and carrying out the program, while the evaluator has an opportunity to apply more methodological controls than he could in an operating situation. As described in the above systems model, the demonstration project is the product of research and planning and the precursor of program operations.

It is important to distinguish clearly between the objectives and research designs for the evaluation of demonstration as opposed to operational programs. The objective of a demonstration program is to develop a model or prototype for future operational programs or to test on a small scale the effectiveness of some large-scale program. First and foremost, it has an evaluative research objective; demonstration without evaluation is meaningless. The goal of an operational program, on the other hand, is to attempt to meet some existing need by means of whatever programs can be realistically established. Its primary orientation is that of immediate service. Confusion of the two may find the administrator attempting to meet a service need with a demonstration project or a research need by means of an operating program—usually with little success. To be sure, there may be an element of service in a demonstration program and of research in an operating program, but the differing *primary* foci must be kept clear.

This confusion may carry over into the types of evaluation designs used. A demonstration project is usually set up as a one-shot trial while an operating program is an on-going affair. The purpose of developing a demonstration program is to permit one to have greater control over both the "stimulus" and its administration, to

offer the possibility of matching experimental with control populations, and to make before and after measurements. Obviously, an
evaluation of this type of program calls for an experimental research
design. And yet many demonstration projects are carried out as
miniature operating programs with little or no attempt at methodological rigor. On the other hand, a service program is a continuous,
on-going operation in which there is usually little possibility of withholding services from a matched control group or of making before
and after measures. This type of program requires a systems research
model which accentuates the feed-back of information and constant
revision of the program. And yet many program evaluators attempt
to apply a rigorous experimental design to such operating programs,
and wonder why they have failed, or blame the program administrator
for not cooperating with them. As we shall see, this distinction between demonstration and operational programs has many highly
significant implications for both the methodology and the administrative aspects of evaluative research.

There are several types of demonstration projects which have
different purposes and require somewhat different evaluation designs.
These variations are related to the state of existing knowledge about
the objectives and the means for achieving these objectives, as well as
to the resources and opportunities available for carrying out the evaluation. In a general way, we may classify demonstration projects as:
(1) pilot programs, (2) model programs, and (3) prototype programs. To some extent, these variations are related in time, with the
pilot program coming first, followed by the development of a model
program, and then the prototype program. We look at each briefly.

The *pilot program* represents a trial-and-error period during
which new approaches and new organizational structures or procedures can be tried out on a rather flexible and easily revisable basis.
James stresses the importance of this type of program as an opportunity for doing program research and for learning from experience.
He recommends that in this type of project, "Great stress should be
laid upon selection of objectives, exploration of the strategic factors
involved, building evaluation into the project, and retaining enough
flexibility to keep the demonstration useful during its entire development. Instead of stressing only the services to be achieved, careful
attention must be given in program development to the elements
of failure and what can be done about them. Rather than be annoyed
at the problems which arise, their appearance should be welcomed as
learning opportunities" (James, 1961 : 133).

The emphasis of pilot programs should be upon variation—
variation in the way the program is organized, in how and by whom
it is carried out, where it is located, whom it reaches, etc. Flexibility,
innovation, redirection, reorganization are all desirable, and attempts

to structure or "freeze" a program at this stage are premature. Obviously, the pilot project requires "quick-and-easy" evaluation with primary emphasis upon the "feedback" of results for program changes. This does not mean that success or failure are not to be judged, but that the basis for such judgments need not depend upon rigorous experimental designs. This pilot stage is one of exploratory research and the main objective is to learn enough to be able to move ahead to the development of a program which can then be evaluated in a more systematic manner.

The *model program* represents the end result of a series of productive pilot projects. Based on what has been learned in the pilot projects, a program can be designed which stands the greatest chance of success. In one sense, the administrator who sets up a model project is still feeling his way. He believes that he can achieve the desired objectives given the proper circumstances, but he is not certain enough to want to try out the program under regular operating conditions. He is seeking to demonstrate that success is possible, not that it is practicably achievable. In a way he is now ready to design a definitive experiment as a test of his hypothesis that activities A, B, C can achieve objectives X, Y, Z, but wishes to assure himself that activities A, B, C have really been put into effect under the most desirable circumstances.

The evaluative design for a model program is almost the exact opposite of that of a pilot project. Now, more than anywhere else, a carefully controlled experiment is in order. The program input must be highly structured and well-defined. Any variations of input must be controlled and keyed to expected variations in output. Extraneous "stimuli" must be eliminated insofar as possible. Experimental and control groups need to be closely matched. Criteria of effectiveness have to be defined, and valid, reliable instruments of sufficient precision constructed. Before and after measurements with these instruments need to be made. This is when the experimental design for evaluative research is most appropriate.

Caution must be exercised in the evaluation of model programs not to generalize the conclusions to standard programs. The temptation is to feel that if the model program has been proven to be effective, it may now be put into effect on a broad scale. This is justified only if the same exemplary program can be translated into a routine operating program—which is rarely, if ever, the case. Perhaps one of the most common disappointments in evaluative research is to prove that, given the right circumstances, a program can be successful and then find that programs set up without control of these circumstances turn out to be failures.

To develop and test programs as operationally feasible, it is necessary to utilize the third type of demonstration program—the *prototype.* This is probably what most people have in mind when they think of demonstration projects. As defined by the Office of Vocational Rehabilitation, these demonstration projects have as their objective, "the application in a practical setting of results, derived from either fundamental research or from experience in life situations, for the purpose of determining whether these knowledges or experiences are actually appliable in the practical setting chosen" (Criswell, 1962 : 1).

Most important for prototype programs is that the program be practical and realistic in terms of what can be done on a large scale with available resources. The evaluation design can attempt to approximate the experimental approach and should compare the new prototype program with traditional programs as controls. But, since the prototype and traditional programs must be carried out under normal operating conditions if one is to be able to generalize the findings, rigorous controls over matched experimental and control groups may not be readily obtainable. It is absolutely essential for the prototype program to be evaluated under conditions as similar as possible to the proposed operational program for the results to be applicable to these programs. A research dimension can profitably be added, however, in order to determine how and why the prototype program was a success or failure and to specify what aspects of the program were relatively more successful than others, and among which population sub-groups.

If we view the evaluative process as a double test of: (1) the validity of a particular approach as a means toward the achievement of some desired change or objective, and (2) the ability to institute a workable program based on that approach, then we see that the model demonstration program evaluates the first condition, while the prototype demonstration program is aimed at the second condition. The failure of an operational program may, thus, be due to either the use of a wrong or invalid approach (which could be tested by a model program) or to the unfeasibilty of the approach, even though valid, as a viable means of operationalizing the approach (which could be tested by a prototype program).

Operational Programs

Once a program is already in operation—as is the case in the vast majority of instances—a different form of evaluation is required than that which we have been discussing for demonstration programs. The continuous nature of an on-going service, by and large, neither requires nor permits the use of an experimental design. The focus of interest is more upon the improvement of services than upon evaluating whether or not a service is worth keeping. Health, education, and welfare programs will continue to operate regardless of the results of any evaluation study and the key question is not so much "Are they any good?" as "How can they be made better?"

This latter question requires the development of an evaluation model which stresses the feed-back of a continuous stream of information into the on-going program. Such models have been called process models and have had their major development in the field of operations research. While it is beyond the scope of this paper to discuss operations research as a whole, we can look at some of its more evaluative aspects.

Underlying the operations approach to program or organizational analysis is the belief that modern complex organizations are characterized by "the study of relations rather than 'entities' with an emphasis on process and transition probabilities as the basis of a flexible structure with many degrees of freedom" (Buckley, 1967: 39). An intricate net of information and communication furnishes the basis for constant feed-back and readjustment of activities. The emphasis of this model is upon an adaptive system, as opposed to equilibrium or homeostatic models, consisting of, "a complex of elements or components directly or indirectly related in a causal network, such that each component is related to at least some others in a more or less stable way within any particular period of time" (Buckley, 1967). The process is continually in operation and constantly changing in response to external as well as internal pressures.

It is clear that evaluative research within such a system cannot meaningfully carve out a single segment of the process for evaluation as a self-contained unit. The separate component *per se* is not as important as its relationship to other components and can best be evaluated as an inherent part of the on-going system. The parts of a total system, i.e., health, education, welfare, are not independent, stable, permanent structures, but rather interrelated, alterable, and temporary, subject to the workings of the system as a whole with changes in any part of the system influencing other parts of the system.

"Operations research" constitutes an attempt to formalize on-going program or organizational evaluation. More generally, it represents the entire process of program development and management with the focus of evaluation being upon the day-to-day operation of the system as a whole (Rivett, 1968). The results of this type of evaluative research become applicable to decision-making at all stages of program planning, development, and operation. One of the best developed of these systems approaches to evaluation is that of PERT —Program Evaluation and Review Technique (Cook, 1966). This plan requires the development of a network of interrelated work paths showing the intermediate steps or events and time estimates for their achievement. The various events are linked together by the activities that constrain the completion of these events. Critical paths are evaluated in terms of time and cost estimates related to the attainment of desired goals. A crucial element is the use of continuous evaluation for correcting and revising program plans.

The experimental design for the evaluation of demonstration projects becomes rather contrived and inapplicable to the evaluation of operational systems. Both its logic and practicality are questionable. Instead of the "before-after" design, we have what might be called, a "during–during–during" design. The major objective is no longer the proof or disproof of the single S-R hypothesis of experimental research, but the feed-back of information about progress along a never-ending continuum of action. The model of the "definitive" experiment is an anachronism for this type of programmatic research. The evaluation must accordingly be developed in terms of its value for direction and redirection, under determinable probabilities of relative success or failure for various stages of the process, with a key emphasis upon decisions to recycle, terminate or progress from one stage to another. The evaluative problem, accordingly, must be formulated not as one of success or failure, but rather of stop, go back, revise, or continue. The objective of such an evaluation is one of constant program assessment and improvement where there is no question that programs must and will continue, i.e., education, health, welfare, and where the emphasis of the evaluation is upon increasing program effectiveness.

The Design of Evaluative Research

The in-put → process → output model of planned social change described above has highly significant implications for evaluative research methodology. Basically it implies some hypothesis about the ability of a program activity (the input) to influence the "causal" factors (the process) which promote or inhibit the desired objective (the output). The evaluative hypothesis reads, "Activities A, B, C will achieve objectives X, Y, Z because they are able to influence the process producing X, Y, Z" (Suchman, 1967). This statement of the problem underscores three major methodological requirements in evaluative research: (1) a description and analysis of input which identifies as clearly as possible the "active" components or change stimuli in the program or service and how these may vary; (2) an understanding of the "cause/effect" process which underlies the occurrence of the desired objective and which is capable of being influenced by the program input; and (3) a definition of the objective or desired goal in terms of criteria which permit valid and reliable measurements of attainment.

Various research designs have been proposed for testing the evaluative hypothesis as stated above (Campbell, 1967; Campbell, 1957; and Chapin, 1957). Basically these designs represent some adaptation of either the experimental or systems model. We have already discussed these models and some of their methodological implications elsewhere. Further elaboration of research designs would require more detail than would be appropriate in this paper. We would only like to emphasize, once again, the need to relate the type of design to the type of program or service being evaluated.

In this connection, it is worthwhile to note that evaluation can occur on several levels and use different research designs which vary in their approximation to the ideal scientific experiment. A necessary requirement, therefore, of any evaluation project is recognition of the level of its evaluation and a clear statement of what adaptations of the ideal design, and the consequent limitations of "proof," have taken place. A common error in evaluation is to claim more than the research design permits one to show.

The logical requirements of an evaluation study can be represented by the familiar model of the laboratory experiment (Stouffer, 1950).

	Before	After	
Experimental	X_1	X_2	$d = X_2 - X_1$
Control	X_1^1	X_2^1	$d^1 = X_2^1 - X_1^1$

Before a program begins, two equivalent groups are selected at random or by matching from the target population. A "before" measurement is made to determine the base line from which change is to be evaluated. One of the groups (the experimental group) is exposed to the program or activity being evaluated while the other (the control group) is either not exposed at all, given a placebo, or exposed to some alternative program. Where possible, neither the experimenter nor the subject should know which is the experimental or control program (to control suggestibility and unconscious bias). At the conclusion of the evaluation (or at appropriate time intervals), an "after" measure is made which is compared for change from the "before" measure (d vs d^1) for both the experimental and control groups.

The logic of this design is largely infallible. As we have pointed out, however, only rarely can it be put into practice outside the laboratory. Instead, in field research, we use various adaptations of this design. The most important of these for evaluative research are:

1. *The case study.* Individuals or groups are observed or measured for the desired change only after exposure to the program being evaluated (cell X_2 in above table). There is no base-line measurement and no unexposed control group. This is obviously the weakest, if most common, of evaluation designs. The program administrator, clinician, or therapist may be reassured if his subject shows improvement, and he may solicit testimonials to this effect, but he has no way of really knowing whether such improvement was due to his intervention, or for that matter, whether greater improvement might not have occurred without his intervention.

2. *The survey design.* After a program has been put into operation, a survey is made to determine who in the population was exposed to the program and what changes, if any, have taken place in them as compared to those who were not exposed (cells X_2 and X_2^1 in above table). This represents an improvement over the previous design in that a control group is present. However, its major weakness is the absence of any "before" measure to compare the equivalence of the experimental and control group and to provide a check on the self-selection bias of the exposed group (e.g., those individuals who expose themselves may be more favorable or susceptible to the program to begin with). To some extent, this bias can be treated statistically by *ex-post-facto* matching of exposed and non-exposed groups on relevant characteristics (e.g., those which might produce an exposure bias). However, the "proof" is still based on correlational analysis, rather than controlled exposure.

3. *The panel or prospective study design.* "Before" measures are made of an unexposed target population. The program is initiated and "after" measures of the desired effect are made to compare changes that have taken place in those who became exposed with those who did not. If the program is an on-going one, these measures can be repeated periodically in a "during–during–during" design. Information can be fed back to the program which can then undergo a series of revisions with the effects of various changes being measured at different points in time.

This field study design comes closest to satisfying the methodological requirements of the experimental model and offers perhaps the most acceptable compromise for evaluative research. It still lacks the requirement of a random assignment of experimental and control groups before exposure, but as in the case of the survey design, such matching can be done to some extent by equating exposed and non-exposed groups on various relevant characteristics. A great deal has been written about this prospective or panel design and it is well worth the careful attention of the evaluator (Glock, 1967).

There can be little question from a methodological point of view that, insofar as possible, the evaluator should strive for as close an approximation to the experimental model as possible. It will probably be more productive to use some realistic alternative program for the control rather than a placebo or no treatment at all. A comparison with alternative programs provides more powerful evidence than showing that one's program is better than nothing at all. If the program to be evaluated is being conducted on a wide scale, it is also necessary to take into account the problem of sampling programs for evaluation. For example, the findings of an evaluation of a single rehabilitation workshop cannot automatically be generalized to all such workshops. Selecting a sample of workshops also permits an analysis of the effect of variations in the operation of the workshop.

In line with our previous discussion of demonstration programs, the rigorousness of an evaluation study design needs to be related to the type of program being evaluated, as well as to reality. Model programs are most demanding of the best experimental design that can be developed. Pilot projects, on the other hand, may make-do with case study or survey evaluation designs. Prototype and operational projects can probably have their needs best satisfied by a panel design which permits continuous evaluation and feed-back for program assessment and improvement. In any case, the decision about what design to use should stem as much as possible from the requirements of the type of program being evaluated and while reality factors may necessitate compromises, these should not be made too easily or quickly and always with an awareness of the limitations they inevitably impose upon the validity of one's findings.

Evaluative Objectives and Criteria

The crucial element in any evaluation study is the presence of some valued goal or objective. Evaluation cannot exist in a vacuum—one must always ask "evaluation of what?" Unless a program can specify what value its activities are seeking to further, whether this be the amelioration of some specific social problem or the advancement of some broad humanistic goal, evaluation becomes meaningless (Gruenberg (ed.), 1966). To evaluate means to assess value, and before the assessment can take place, the desired value must be understood.

This problem of defining the values underlying a program or activity is perhaps the most subjective and difficult aspect of evaluative research. For one thing, values differ for different people. The values of program personnel may differ from those of their clients or the public. Furthermore, different program personnel and different segments of the public may have conflicting values among themselves, as witness the current controversy over "middle-class" professional values as opposed to the "lower-class" values of the poverty class. The desirability of planned social change or intervention is itself a value judgment. Social values in general define what will be called a social problem, what the acceptable and appropriate means will be to meet this problem, and who shall be given the power and resources to do so.

The statement of specific program objectives combines the value judgments discussed above with the theoretical assumptions of the "cause/effect" process. These assumptions concern the validity of the means being used for achieving the desired objective. Such assumptions underlie all forms of purposive action. We may refer to the assumptions underlying the desirability of objectives as "value" assumptions, while the assumptions as to means or process of attaining the objectives constitute "validity" assumptions. The former are largely a matter of subjective belief, while the latter are subject to empirical verification.

Objectives are commonly classified according to three different levels of generality ranging from immediate to intermediate to ultimate. In principle, one may visualize an unlimited universe of possible objectives and sub-objectives corresponding to the various levels that make up a total program and arranged according to some organizational hierarchy. On the bottom of this hierarchy, we usually find the field personnel whose objectives are largely those of delivery of services and whose success or failure is measured against the *immediate* criteria of effort expended and quantity and quality of services delivered. On the next higher level, we may find the supervisory or administrative personnel whose objectives are those of program direction where effectiveness is evaluated on an *intermediate* level according to the accomplishments or results of the efforts of the service personnel. At the top of the hierarchy is the central staff whose major function is that of program planning and development and whose policy decisions guide the performance goals of the field personnel and are evaluated on the *ultimate* level of success in meeting the social problem under attack.

A similar division of labor is implied by the distinction between "objectives," "activities," and "practices" arranged in a descending order. Policy *objectives* are formulated and evaluated at the highest level of administration, while program *activities* are designed and evaluated at the intermediate level as the means toward achieving the higher level policy objectives. In turn, personnel *practices* are developed as the means of operationalizing the program activities and are evaluated at the immediate level of worker performance. Each of the lower level steps denotes an action taken to implement an upper level objective. Thus, evaluation objectives can be conceived as making up an ordered series of means-ends relationships.

This interdependence is reflected in organizational structure and function, with the organization and techniques of work at an upper level becoming the objectives of the immediately lower level, with the objectives at any level being derived from the methods of the immediately higher level. Thus, any program can be subdivided into a continuous chain of actions in which each action is the result of the one that comes before it and a necessary condition to the one that comes after it. Evaluation then proceeds to validate the means-ends relationships between each adjacent pair comprising the program.

In terms of our previous discussion of the relationship of input to process to output, immediate goals are evaluated according to the degree to which services can be delivered (effort) while intermediate goals are evaluated according to the degree of intervention in the "causal" process that takes place as a result of these services (accomplishment). Whether such intervention results in the subsequent attainment of the ultimate goal will depend largely upon the validity of the underlying theory relating process to objective. Perhaps this formulation of the problem will help to explain why most evaluations are limited to immediate and intermediate objectives, and to dispel some of the heated controversy over whether such limited goals constitute legitimate objectives for evaluation in and of themselves (MacMahon, Pugh, and Hutchison, 1961). They do so to the extent that the "causal" process linking performance to ultimate objectives is valid.

Evaluation, in the above sense, may be divided into two parts. An evaluation of *"technique"* which tests the ability of a particular program to change the "causal" process and an evaluation of *"theory"* which tests the ability of the change in "causal" process to produce the desired objective. This latter function is more properly the province of basic or "non-evaluative" research, but it does indicate how evaluative research may also contribute to basic knowledge, and how dependent any intervention program is upon a valid theory of change. For example, an educational program designed to get people to stop smoking may be evaluated on the immediate level in terms of its success in organizing a program in such a way that people are reached with the educational materials (effort), and on the intermediate level in terms of how many people actually stop smoking (accomplishment), but whether or not the ultimate goal of a decrease in the incidence of lung cancer occurs (outcome) will depend upon the validity of the "cause/effect" theory that links smoking to lung cancer.

As one moves from immediate to intermediate to ultimate objectives, one encounters greater complexity in the number and type of factors influencing each. On the immediate level, the factors affecting the performance of personnel are relatively limited and can be more or less directly controlled. Specific effort criteria are relatively easy to develop, i.e., many-days of teaching, cases treated, literature distributed. On the intermediate level, the number of factors affecting program operation and accomplishment becomes increasingly complex, including external influences over which one can have little control. Measures of achievement reflect this complexity and often cannot be directly related to effort expended. On the ultimate level, the particular program becomes only one part of a vast array of factors which influence high-level policy goals and, not only is the magnitude of its effects diminished, but the causal links become greatly attenuated. Rossi cautions against expecting any great effects at the ultimate level. He warns, "We cannot ordinarily expect that the new treatments we can devise will produce massive results. . . . The problem of evaluation in this historical period is that new treatments can be expected to yield marginal improvements over present treatments and the cost-to-benefit ratio can be expected to rise dramatically" (Rossi, 1966).

Institutional objectives: Evaluations on the ultimate level deal almost entirely with societal indicators, such as incidence of illness, rather than measures of individual change (Sheldon and Moore, 1968). As such, these evaluations very rarely study the effects of specific programs. More appropriately they may be viewed as institutional evaluations and reflect the impact of a broad spectrum of events. Objectives are defined for the society in general and reflect social goals such as "an informed citizenry." In education, for example, such institutional evaluations have become increasingly important as the American educational system as a whole has come under critical review (Perkins, 1966). We may refer to evaluations on this level as "policy" evaluations which are system oriented.

Organizational objectives: The evaluation of complex organizations, such as a school system, hospital, or large industrial concern, requires the formulation of objectives and criteria of accomplishment on a much broader scale than program evaluation. The need for assessment on this level, however, is perhaps even greater than on the program level. Planned social change will, in the long run, be much more affected by organizational or system changes than by specific program innovations. The latter have often been referred to as "tinkering" as opposed to any meaningful intervention on a policy level involving the restructuring of an entire organizational approach.

In a general way, we may contrast two broad organizational objectives: (1) *maximizing,* or seeking the maximum attainment of objectives for any given amount of resources, and (2) *sufficing,* or seeking the attainment of acceptable or desirable states (Simon, 1957).

These notions of maximizing and sufficing reflect two rather different approaches to complex organizations. The first views such organizations as rational systems which can be evaluated according to criteria of maximum output and is usually associated with the private sector, i.e., profit, efficiency. The second treats organizations as natural systems and evaluates them according to social criteria, i.e., service, amelioration, and is most applicable to the public sector. Obviously, these two differing objectives play a major role in determining the type of criteria for the assessment of success or failure in organizations.

Maximizing criteria probably attain their greatest utility in evaluations of cost-effectiveness. Few programs can be justified at any cost and effort—cost ratios are required to measure comparative efficiency. Cost-effectiveness is, thus, becoming an increasingly important tool in management. Briefly described, cost refers to the value of the resources expended to achieve a certain goal, while effectiveness refers to the quality or level of achievement. A cost-effectiveness analysis attempts to strike a balance between these two factors or a ratio of input to output. The goal is to maximize results for a given cost—to obtain the most optimal use of available resources for achieving the desired objective. This evaluation design requires a comparison of alternative courses of action in terms of their costs and their effectiveness. For example, a comparison of individualized instruction with closed circuit television would have to balance the two in terms of their cost-effectiveness ratio. The specific techniques for a cost-effectiveness analysis are rather specialized, requiring the development of special models and criteria for weighing cost against effectiveness (Morse, 1967). Such evaluations are largely limited to highly standardized and well-established programs. They rarely make sense until prior evaluations have shown program effectiveness and therefore represent the most advanced stage of evaluation.

Thompson has developed an interesting set of propositions about the evaluation of organizations based upon the completeness of knowledge about "cause/effect" relationships and the degree of crystallization of the standards of desirability (Thompson, 1967: 83–100). Where "cause/effect" understanding is fairly complete and the standards of desirability have become crystallized, an organization would tend to employ a maximizing approach to evaluation. with a major emphasis upon *efficiency*. Lacking knowledge of cause and effect, but possessing well-formulated standards, the criteria of success are apt to be instrumental in terms of the desired state of affairs, with the emphasis being on sufficing rather than maximizing. Where knowledge is incomplete and standards ambiguous, *social* criteria involving the approval or disapproval of appropriate reference groups will become substituted for efficiency or instrumental tests of achievement. We recognize this to be the case in many, if not most, social action programs.

Evaluative Criteria

The problem of criteria in evaluative research has traditionally been discussed in the literature as one of finding reliable and valid operational indices for measuring the attainment of some objective. The emphasis has been technical, rather than conceptual. The result has been a long history of methodological disputation to the neglect of conceptual definition and clarification.

Conceptually, evaluative criteria represent the basis upon which decisions are made about means towards ends. We may divide this decision-making process into the following three components each of which requires different criteria of effectiveness :[1]

1. *An information component*—A reference system, model, process, or standard according to which information may be selected, collected, and evaluated. This represents a criterion of relevance—but relevance to action, and not simply construct revelance.
2. *An interpretation component*—A value position or preference system representing the desirable, the appropriate, the acceptable means and ends for making decisions. This represents a *weighting* process or decision rule by which alternatives may be assigned priorities.
3. *An action component*—A risk-taking approach to problem-solving in which criteria function to set the limits of acceptable error. This represents an *operational* process or an administrative rule by which error costs are matched against potential outcomes.

Each of the above components involves a different type of analysis; the first concerns information retrieval and utilization systems, the second, decision-making systems, and the third, risk-taking choice situations. Each of these is a key element in "operations research" and reflects the intimate relationship between evaluative research and these program management processes as discussed previously. The central role of criteria in all three underscores our concern with a more adequate conceptualization of this measure.

Given the above classification, criteria become linked to an action process. The model is that of an on-going system which at any moment is in a state of equilibrium, but which contains within it conflictual elements pushing toward resolution by means of a new equilibrium. These conflictual elements represent "discrepancies" between desired objectives and current attainments—"what is" vs. "what should be." The discovery and description of such discrepancies depends upon feed-back informational criteria, while the resolution, either in terms of changed objectives or changed operations, depends upon interpretative criteria of decision-making, followed by action criteria of risk-taking. Evaluation and the use of criteria within this model is obviously not a one-shot affair, but becomes a continuous chain of discrepancy determinations and resolutions for the on-going system. Criteria, in this sense, are ever-lasting and ever-changing, and not static measures that become standardized and routinized.

In terms of the above model, evaluative hypotheses may be derived by relating a series of activities at some point in the action process to a series of objectives for this same stage. Since deliberate intervention in the on-going process is being contemplated, a theory of "causation" is usually implied. The criteria are derived from the evaluative hypothesis and reflect this "cause/effect" process. Information criteria must be relevant to the independent variable (Activities A, B, C) and interpretive of the dependent variable (Effects X, Y, Z). Action criteria must be linked to the process which underlies the relationship of the information to the interpretive criteria, or else we may attempt to change a "spurious cause" (i.e., the Hawthorne effect).

Tied in as they are to decision-making and risk-taking, the criteria of evaluative research strongly reflect the professional value-system of the program personnel in relation to the value system of significant-others, i.e., the public, the clients, the "official" governmental body, and other professionals in and out of the program. Criteria will therefore tend to be selected from the virtually unlimited universe of possible criteria on the basis of their relevance to value-laden objectives and results and then defined in terms which permit relative weighting for determining a balance among the inevitable value conflicts in any action program. Competing values constitute one of the most important elements of criteria selection and definition. Such values underlie all criteria.

A more technical aspect of criteria selection and definition concerns its "operationalism"—both in terms of its measurability and its manipulatability. Ease and refinement of measurement become important technical aspects in addition to the usual scientific standard of reliability. (Validity, we have already seen, is determined by answering the all-important question, "Validity for what?" in terms of validity for information, interpretation, and action.) Criteria, to have utility in evaluative research, must be practical enough to provide measures which do not interfere too greatly with program routines and which produce answers in time enough for them to permit program changes. Refinement is determined by that level of precision which permits meaningful distinctions of success or failure to be made in terms of decisions to revise or proceed, rather than some absolute judgment of instrument precision. The old adage of not using a scalpel in a butcher shop is highly appliable to evaluative research.

Similarly, degree of manipulatability becomes extremely important for the selection of evaluative variables for which criteria are to be developed. Criteria which refer to variables which permit little deliberate intervention are not too useful for program change. While such variables may have high explanatory power, they offer little leeway for administrative action; i.e., heredity or sex. In effect, the evaluator needs to look for criteria of those variables which permit interference with the "causal process" or change in the social system.

Thus, it can be seen that evaluative criteria may be used:

1. To monitor a steady state so as to determine when a correction is necessary (as in an automated system involving servomechanisms).
2. To identify alternatives in a problem (non-steady) situation and provide relevant information (as in a changing curriculum).
3. To weigh alternative courses of decision-making in terms of relative gains and losses.
4. To determine corrective action and the error-risks involved in various approaches to change.

These four uses may be viewed as "validity" indices for evaluative criteria. Technically they function as predictive criteria and are judged in terms of their ability to achieve certain desirable ends and/or to forestall undesirable consequences. They represent validity for action rather than validity for measurement or description. They are prospective predictions rather than *ex-post-facto* explanations and involve making predictions about the outcomes of induced change and matching those predictions against actual outcomes.

The above approach to the criterion problem requires further conceptual development and, even more important, empirical testing. It does seem to re-open a classical problem of scientific measurement to new formulations that make more sense for evaluative as compared to non-evaluative research. A challenging approach to this problem is offered by Etzioni and Lehman in terms of the possible dysfunctional aspects of utilizing invalid criteria in evaluative research. In general, they point out two broad classes of dysfunctions: (1) arriving at invalid conclusions which become the bases for erroneous policy decisions, and (2) ignoring those dimensions and indicators of a concept that are most susceptible to social manipulation (Etzioni and Lehman, 1967). This paper offers a convincing argument for increased attention to "social validity" as opposed to "methodological validity."

Administrative Considerations in Evaluative Research

Evaluative research is applied research and, as such, it encounters all of the problems of research management in general and of applied research in particular. Other papers in this conference are specifically aimed at these problems and there would be little point in discussing them in detail in the present paper. Instead we will focus upon some of those aspects of research administration which we feel are of special importance for evaluative research.

Evaluative research is judgmental—its major function is to determine whether certain activities are attaining their objectives. As such, it inevitably constitutes a threat to those individuals whose responsibility it is to see that the activities do achieve their objectives. No matter what is done to lessen this feeling of threat, few administrators or program personnel can be expected to view an evaluation of their efforts with detached objectivity. Since the evaluation usually is undertaken only when some dissatisfaction or puzzlement is present, the evaluation is in itself a challenge of their effectiveness. Program administrators and especially program personnel have to operate under assumptions of success and an evaluation constitutes a questioning of these assumptions. Furthermore, the conduct of the evaluation itself produces demands upon the operation of the program which may interfere with the routine administration of the program. As described by Wright and Hyman, "The staff . . . have invested considerable time, effort, and sentiment in their programs. They may be ego-involved in their activities. They may be sensitive to the cold-blooded objective probing of the scientific researcher. Even under favorable circumstances, it is common to find that action-oriented and dedicated persons are unreceptive to social science . . . how much more likely a hostile reaction may be if such measurements threaten to reveal unfavorable information" (Wright and Hyman, 1964: 23). It is a rare practitioner who welcomes an evaluation study.

There can be no denying that the basic relationship between evaluator and practitioner is one of the former evaluating the work of the latter. As Wilensky and Lebeaux have stated, "What the social scientist thinks of as 'objective investigation' the practitioner often takes as 'hostile attack' " (Wilensky and Lebeaux, 1958: 20). Evaluative research seeks change while most of the natural tendencies of program operation are to resist change. This difference in focus gives rise to a host of administrative problems and conflicts between the evaluator and the practitioner. These interpersonnel problems, perhaps more than anything else, make evaluative research unattractive to research workers and account for the reluctance of many social scientists to become involved in program evaluation.

In general, the administrative problems of evaluative research will vary according to the type of evaluation being attempted. In terms of their implications for the conduct of evaluative research, we may classify evaluation studies as follows, ranging from general to specific objectives and from large-scale to small-scale activities:

A. *System-oriented evaluations*
  1. Institutional or social sub-systems (i.e., health, education, or welfare systems).
  2. Complex organizations (i.e., hospitals, public schools, welfare agencies).
B. *Program-oriented evaluations*
  1. Simple organizations (i.e., clinics, classrooms, employment offices).
  2. Simple programs (i.e., immunization program, reading improvement, enrollment campaign).

The conduct of evaluation in the above four types of settings will create somewhat different problems in the formulation of the evaluation study, in the structure of the evaluation unit and its relationship to other units, in the personal interrelationships of evaluation and program staff, and in the utilization of evaluative research findings.

System or institution oriented evaluations are more likely to be concerned with broad objectives and policy questions. Strangely enough this type of evaluation, basic as it is, may not constitute a serious threat to the administrator. While the institution as a whole may be under attack, and the administrator may be called upon to defend the "establishment," the threat is likely to be impersonal and his own position in the institutional system is not too much at stake.

Similarly, systems-oriented evaluations of complex organizations will tend to stress adjustive recommendations rather than judgments of success or failure. Since the major function of the evaluator is to help the administrator run his organization in a more effective manner, much of the personal threat is removed. In such cases of system-oriented evaluation, the integration of the evaluation unit into the system itself becomes quite natural. In fact, it is on this level of evaluation that one is most likely to encounter the organization of an evaluation unit within the institution or complex organization itself. Since policy decisions are usually involved, such evaluation units tend to be located in the upper echelons and to have high-prestige and status. Whatever conflicts occur between evaluator and program staff tend to be quite similar to those that occur between the administrative staff and the operating staff in general. One possible shortcoming of this type of arrangement would be the tendency to work within the system and to take for granted its general legitimacy.

Thus the evaluation would be corrective rather than challenging to the existing structure or operation. While the system may become more efficient as a result of such evaluation efforts, it is not likely to undergo any basic changes.

On the other hand, program oriented evaluations directly challenge the worthwhileness of specific activities or the performance of specific individuals. Since they attempt directly to relate activities to outcomes, the conclusions are apt to focus around the success or failure of some specific organization or program to the extent that such judgments may well determine the future existence of the organization or program. Under such circumstances, the program staff may be expected to be highly anxious about the evaluation.

Sources of conflict between the evaluator and staff on the program evaluation level may begin as early as the statement of program objectives. The program staff has a strong, vested interest in the program as it is now operating. In many cases, professional identity as well as employment is at stake. Behind any program lies a host of untested assumptions, not only in regard to basic theory but also in relation to techniques of operation. The first task of the evaluator often is to compile a list of program objectives and to examine their underlying assumptions. While being asked to specify one's objectives may be difficult for the program staff, being forced to justify these objectives and to defend one's beliefs in why one's program can be expected to attain them may actually be painful.

There are no easy answers to the administrative problems in evaluation. The major positive force lies in the promise of help that evaluation can give to policy-making and program effectiveness. Given a supportive climate and a program staff dedicated to program improvement, evaluative research can make a significant contribution and need not prove traumatic. Lacking such conditions, evaluative research may have to make its way against the resistances of program directors and staff, largely through the force of governmental and public demand for "proof of works."

Perhaps the most hopeful note in the above somewhat discouraging analysis of administrative problems is the increasing dissatisfaction that many of the practicing professions are experiencing with their traditional approaches to social problems. The stubborn resistance to solution of many of these problems has led to a growing willingness to challenge the basis of established programs—both theoretical and technical. The chance to experiment with new approaches has excited many practitioners to try to develop innovative programs. Government and public support and increased professional prestige are now being given to the evaluative research. As proclaimed by Hilleboe, "The age of accountability is upon us. If we strain against it, we will plunge ourselves into the obscure backwash of ceremonial duties. . . . But if we accept accountability as a way of thinking and a way of life, we can propel public health to a grand new era of achievement and acclaim" (Hilleboe, 1964 : 48).

It is this atmosphere of a "brave new world" based upon carefully planned and evaluated social change that has given rise to the current interest in evaluative research. Such research makes little sense in a self-satisfied world content to do things the way they always were done. It becomes essential in a troubled world, anxious and willing to seek change. Social experimentation in health, education, and welfare has not only become acceptable, it is strongly encouraged in a host of new attempts to solve old problems. Within the evaluation of such experimentation, perhaps, lies the answer to the question "Action for What?"

And yet to the evaluative researcher, such questioning is not only essential to the design of the study but also constitutes the challenge and reward of the research process. From this questioning of established procedures comes the research hypothesis and the possibility of new discoveries. His aim is not to justify an existing program but to diagnose its ills and to prescribe a course of treatment. If the program is "sick," such help may be welcome, but if it feels "well," such evaluation can only be viewed as unjustified interference.

To such differing values, goals, and perceptions of the problem is added the need for close working relationships between evaluator and operating staff in the conduct of the program evaluation study itself. These daily role relationships are apt to be quite conflictual. The evaluation study must make demands upon the operation of the program—it is foolish to think otherwise. It must ask for as much control as possible over the assignment of subjects or clients; it may require some form of change in how the program is run; it must insist upon the collection of data beyond that of routine record-keeping. And it must ask these things at the same time that it threatens the existence of the program. Little wonder that smooth working relationships are difficult!

Add to the above, the usual dearth of resources in time, money, personnel, and facilities offered the evaluator, and one can begin to understand why evaluative research today is almost universally deficient. Many of these problems exist in regard to working relationships between researcher and administrator in any applied setting, but they become magnified when the applied research is also an evaluation.

In many cases, furthermore, the evaluator is apt to be an "outsider." In fact, one of the major administrative questions concerning evaluation is whether the evaluator should be a staff member of the organization or program being evaluated or whether he should be brought in as an independent researcher or consultant. There are advantages and disadvantages to either arrangement and the decision must depend upon the particular circumstances. The advantages of an outside evaluator are increased objectivity and the ability to see and challenge what someone close to the program may have come to take for granted. The outside evaluator will have less personal involvement in the outcome of the evaluation and is, therefore, under fewer pressures to produce a favorable report. He is also more likely to be trained in evaluative research and to have had experience in evaluating other programs.

On the other hand, the outsider is less likely to understand the objectives and procedures of the program, especially if these require technical or professional competence. He is more likely to miss subtle aspects of program operation or objectives, especially possible "negative" effects. In addition, as an outsider, he is less likely to be acceptable to the operating staff, and more likely to encounter obstacles in carrying out the evaluation. As described by Metzner and Gurin, "Any attempt at evaluation, particularly from the outside, may well be conceived as a threat. It is an examination and report concerning how well people are doing. Very few people are so secure, or unaware of their own deficiencies, that an unknown with a notebook will arouse no anxieties. This is particularly true if the evaluations are not responding to local desire, but are brought in from above, and the purposes and relations are unclear" (Metzner and Gurin, 1960: 8). However, the closer personal relationships of an inside evaluator can interfere seriously with objectivity. There will be a natural tendency to stress the successes and to overlook the failures.

Regardless of whether an outsider or insider does the evaluation, it is important to recognize that complete detachment is almost impossible. Inevitably, the evaluator tends to be co-opted to a greater or lesser degree by the system. He begins to identify with the program and its goals; he forms interpersonal relationships with the program staff; he gets caught up in the daily operations of the program—in short, he becomes involved and can rarely just hit-and-run.

Probably the best solution is to recognize the inevitability of the conflict and to attempt to structure the situation so that the program staff plays an important part in developing the evaluation and in carrying out any recommendations. Early in the evaluation, the program staff should help to formulate the objectives of the program to be evaluated. This self-examination of program goals and procedures will also increase the likelihood of developing criteria of effectiveness which are meaningful and acceptable to the staff. In fact, it is probably unwise to proceed with an evaluation until some degree of consensus has been reached by program and evaluation staff.

The evaluation itself should be conducted with an obvious concern for the program staff's routine. Disruption should be kept to a minimum and where unavoidable should be carefully explained and justified. Finally, findings should be discussed thoroughly with the program staff and possible remedies of deficiencies explored. The follow-up component of the evaluation should be left as much as possible in the hands of the program staff, with the evaluator presenting his findings and making recommendations, but not being in a position to enforce change. Certainly, the findings of an evaluation are much more likely to be utilized if the program staff has played a part in the evaluation and is given direct responsibility for implementing its findings (Sadofsky, 1966).

In short, rather than attempting to find ways to keep the administrator and staff out of the evaluation, the better strategy may be to increase their commitment to the evaluation by stressing program improvement rather than a pass-fail judgment. Since a primary criterion for evaluating the evaluation will be its ability to produce program change, the cooperation of program staff is extremely important. While the evaluation may be a tremendous success from a methodological point of view, unless its findings are utilized it may well be judged a failure in terms of accomplishment.

Weiss lists the following conditions as important for increasing the potential of utilization for evaluative research findings:

1. The explication of the theoretical premises underlying the program, and direction of the evaluation to analysis of these premises.
2. Specification of the "process model" of the program—the presumed sequence of linkages that lead from program input to outcome, and the tracking of the processes through which results are supposed to be obtained.
3. Analysis of the effectiveness of components of the program, or alternative approaches, rather than all-or-nothing, go or no-go assessment of the total program.

In addition to these general factors, utilization is likely to reflect: (1) early identification of potential users of evaluation results and selection of the issues of concern to them as the major focus of study; (2) involvement of administrators and program practitioners, from both inside and outside the project, in the evaluation process; (3) prompt completion of evaluation and early release of results; (4) effective methods for presentation of findings and dissemination of information (Weiss, 1966).

A brief word should be added about some of the indirect uses of evaluation. Some of these are "legitimate" by-products of an evaluation while others represent abuses of evaluative research. Among the desirable secondary benefits of an evaluation, we may list the following:

1. A clarification and re-examination on the part of program administrators of the objectives and underlying assumptions of their programs.
2. A more careful analysis of the content and operation of the program in order to specify what the essential aspects of the program are.
3. The identification and definition of the target population and the situational context of the programs.
4. A re-evaluation of the theoretical or knowledge base of the program especially in terms of how principles are translated into practices.
5. The formulation of hypotheses for further research to fill in gaps in knowledge especially as these would affect program planning.
6. The development of a more critical attitude among personnel including an opportunity to suggest ways of improving services.
7. An increase in staff morale and commitment as a consequence of a sincere attempt to improve the program—especially if the staff itself is disappointed in their accomplishments.

The following list of possible misuses of evaluation may serve as a deterrent to such "pseudo-evaluations."

1. *Eye-wash*—an attempt to justify a weak or bad program by deliberately selecting for evaluation only those aspects that "look good" on the surface. Appearance replaces reality.
2. *White-wash*—an attempt to cover up program failure or errors by avoiding any objective appraisal. Vindication replaces verification.
3. *Submarine*—an attempt to "torpedo" or destroy a program regardless of its effectiveness. Politics replaces science.
4. *Posture*—an attempt to use evaluation as a "gesture" of objectivity or professionalism. Ritual replaces research.
5. *Postponement*—an attempt to delay needed action by pretending to seek the "facts." Research replaces service.

Notes to the Chapter

1. We are indebted to Malcolm Provus for one development of this classification.

References

BENNIS, WARREN G., KENNETH D. BENNE, and ROBERT CHIN. 1960. *The Planning of Change*. New York: Holt, Rinehart and Winston.

BORGATTA, EDGAR F. 1966. "Research problems in evaluation of health service demonstration." *Milbank Memorial Fund Quarterly,* 44 (October) : 183–184.

BUCKLEY, WALTER. 1967. *Sociology and Modern Systems Theory.* Englewood Cliffs, New Jersey : Prentice-Hall, Inc.

CAMPBELL, DONALD T. 1957. "Factors relevant to the validity of experiments in social settings." *Psychological Bulletin,* 54: 297–312.

CAMPBELL, DONALD T. 1963. "From description to experimentation interpreting trends in quasi-experiment." In Chester W. Harris (ed.), *Problems in Measuring Change.* Madison : University of Wisconsin Press.

CHAPIN, F. STUART. 1957. *Experimental Designs in Sociological Research.* New York : Harper and Brothers (revised 1955).

COOK, DESMOND L. 1966. *Program Evaluation and Review Technique: Applications in Education.* Washington : U.S. Department of Health, Education, and Welfare, Office of Education.

CRISWELL, JOAN H. 1962. *The Place of Demonstration Projects in the Program of the Office of Vocational Rehabilitation.* Washington : Office of Vocational Rehabilitation (August). (Mimeo.)

ETIZIONI, AMITAI, and EDWARD W. LEHMAN. 1967. "Some dangers in 'valid' social measurement." *The Annals of the American Academy of Political and Social Science,* (September) : 1–15.

FAIRWEATHER, GEORGE W. 1967. *Methods for Experimental Social Innovation.* New York : John Wiley and Sons.

GIDEONSE, HENDRICK D. 1968. "Research development, and the improvement of education." *Science,* 164 (November 1) : 541 :45.

GLOCK, CHARLES (ed.) 1967. *Survey Research in the Social Sciences.* New York : Russell Sage Foundation.

GRUENBERG, ERNEST M. (ed.) 1966. "Evaluating the effectiveness of mental health services." *Milbank Memorial Fund Quarterly,* 44 : Part 2 (January).

GUBA, E. A., and D. C. CLARK. Undated. "An examination of potential change roles in education." Virginia : Airlie House. (Mimeo.)

HERZOG, ELIZABETH. 1959. *Some Guide Lines for Evaluative Research.* Washington : U.S. Department of Health, Education, and Welfare, Social Security Administration, Children's Bureau.

HILLEBOE, HERMAN E. 1964. "Improving performance in public health." *Public Health Reports* (January).

JAMES, GEORGE. 1961. "Planning and evaluation of health programs." *Administration of Community Health Services.* Chicago : International City Managers' Association.

LITCHFIELD, EDWARD H. 1956. "Notes on a general theory of administration." *Administrative Science Quarterly* (June).

LYND, ROBERT S. 1939. *Knowledge for What?* Princeton, New Jersey: Princeton University Press.

MACMAHON, BRIAN, THOMAS F. PUGH, and GEORGE B. HUTCHISON. 1961. "Principals in the evaluation of community mental health programs." *American Journal of Public Health,* (July): 963–968.

MERTON, ROBERT K., and EDWARD C. DEVEREAUX, JR. 1964. "Practical problems and the uses of social science." *Transaction,* Vol. I (July): 18–21.

METZNER, CHARLES A., and CHARLES GURIN. 1960. *Personal Response and Social Organization in a Health Campaign.* Ann Arbor: University of Michigan. Bureau of Public Health Economics. Research Series No. 9.

MORSE, PHILIP M. (ed.) 1967. *Operations Research for Public Systems.* Cambridge: M.I.T. Press.

PERKINS, JAMES A. 1966. *The University in Transition.* Princeton: Princeton University Press.

RIECKEN, HENRY W. 1952. *The Volunteer Work Camp: A Psychological Evaluation.* Cambridge, Massachusetts: Addison-Wesley Press.

RIVETT, PATRICK. 1968. *An Introduction to Operations Research.* New York: Basic Books.

ROSSI, PETER H. 1966. "Boobytraps and pitfalls in the evaluation of social action programs." *Proceedings of the American Statistical Association.* Social Statistics Section.

SADOFSKY, STANLEY. 1966. "Utilization of evaluation results: Feedback into the action program." In June L. Shmelzer, *Learning in Action.* Washington: Government Printing Office.

SHELDON, ELEANOR, and WILBERT E. MOORE (eds.) 1968. *Indicators of Social Change.* New York: Russell Sage Foundation.

SIMON, HERBERT A. 1957. *Models of Man, Social and Rational.* New York: John Wiley and Sons, Inc.

STOUFFER, SAMUEL A. 1950. "Some observations on study design." *American Journal of Sociology,* 56 (January): 355–361.

SUCHMAN, EDWARD A. "Evaluation as Research." *Urban Review.* In press.

SUCHMAN, EDWARD A. 1967. *Evaluative Research: Principles and Practice in Public Service and Social Action Programs.* New York: Russell Sage Foundation.

SUCHMAN, EDWARD A. 1967. "Principles and practice of evaluative research." In John T. Doby (ed.), *An Introduction to Social Research,* pp. 327–351. New York: Appleton-Century-Crofts.

THOMPSON, JAMES D. 1967. *Organizations in Action.* New York: McGraw-Hill.

WEISS, CAROL H. 1966. "Utilization of evaluation: Toward comparative study." Paper presented at the American Sociological Association Meeting. Miami Beach: September 1.

WILENSKY, HAROLD L., and CHARLES N. LEBEAUX. 1958. *Industrial Society and Social Welfare.* New York: Russell Sage Foundation.

WRIGHT, CHARLES R., and HERBERT H. HYMAN. 1964. "The evaluators." In Philip E. Hammond (ed.), *Sociologists at Work.* New York: Basic Books.

HENRY W. RIECKEN

Memorandum on
Program Evaluation

I. Introduction

This memorandum is based on a preliminary reconnaissance of recent evaluative studies of programs of social action in a number of different substantive areas. The reconnaissance is necessarily incomplete, and one aim in distributing this memorandum is to stimulate suggestions for gathering more information about evaluative studies.

The main purpose of the memorandum, however, is to provide a common basis for discussion by social scientists and social practitioners of the problems that evaluation studies face and the formulation of a strategy for improving such studies. In the following pages, I shall attempt to state what I mean by "program evaluation"; to indicate some of the range of techniques and their application; some of the purposes for which evaluative studies are carried out; and, finally, some of the suggestions that have been made by researchers and practitioners for developing and expanding evaluation studies.

One point has become quite apparent in the investigation so far: namely, that there are a large number and variety of studies being carried on for the purpose of examining and suggesting changes in programs of intentional social action, and that the demand for such studies from social practitioners is increasing. It seems reasonable

Henry W. Riecken, Memorandum on Program Evaluation, internal memorandum to the Ford Foundation, October 1953. Reprinted by permission.

to ask whether social scientists should coordinate their efforts to meet this demand, and, if so, what means they should choose in order to make the best use of available resources. In short, it is proposed that we should evaluate the field of evaluation studies and make suggestions for its future development.

II. Definitions

It is assumed that evaluation is always undertaken with reference to some intentional action designed to influence persons or to change a material situation. *Evaluation* is the measurement of desirable and undesirable consequences of an action intended to forward some goal that the actor values. *Action* means a conscious attempt to change something about another individual or group and/or his situation. (The limiting case occurs when the intent of the action is to maintain the status quo against (negatively valued) changes—e.g., the prevention of delinquency.) A *program* or *treatment* is the set of operations or actions intended to produce the desired effects, and such effects can be called the *objectives* of the program. A program is ordinarily carried out through an organization called the *agency*. The *action personnel* or *staff* are those individuals who plan and execute the operations of the program, while those who are to be changed or affected by the action can be called the *subjects* of the program. For the sake of convenience, anyone who undertakes investigation of program operations or effects will be called an *evaluator*.

III. Types of Evaluation

Although the foregoing definitions focus attention on one kind of evaluation (the study of *effects*), it is apparent that the term "evaluation'" is currently used in several different senses. A rough typology, in which purpose and method are combined, suggests that evaluation studies take the following principal forms:

(1) *Effect studies*—The most important form of evaluation study, for present purposes, is that in which the focus of attention is on *ends,* or the degree to which program objectives are achieved (and unintended consequences occur). Studies of effects represent the maximum contribution that social science can make to social practice, since they are usually intended to feed back results into program planning or policy making. Because of their importance, and because full-scale effect studies subsume several other types of evaluation, a detailed treatment of the procedures

and major problems of effect studies is reserved for Part V.
(2) *Operations Analysis*—In studies of this type the emphasis is on *means* or operations of the program without specific attention to ends. The efficacy of the means is usually assumed. Operations analysis has two special forms:

    (a) *Compliance with standards.* A program or institution may be examined in terms of a list of standard criteria—e.g., number of pupils per teacher, number of clients per case-worker, presence or absence of specified services, and adequacy of buildings or equipment.

    (b) *Report of activities.* A kind of administrative evaluation technique is the periodic report of activities made without reference to predetermined standards. Thus a division head may be required to report to an agency head on the amount of work performed, number of personnel on duty, etc. Reports of activities are sometimes used in connection with "program justification"—e.g., the Bureau of the Budget bases its evaluation of government agency requests for funds partly on activity reports which may include number of letters written, phone calls made, clients interviewed or publications distributed.

(3) *Surveys of Need*—Prior to the formulation of an action program a survey may be conducted to assess the need for or desirability of a contemplated action. Such surveys also implicitly try to assess the probable worth of the action in terms of what could be done if available resources were used in a particular way. Or the surveyors may be asked to help develop a plan to achieve the intended aims.

(4) *Investigations*—A form of evaluation that is often punitive or hostile to an action program is the investigation or "independent audit." It is distinguished not so much by method as by intent and by the policing role played by the evaluators who may be a congressional committee, a presidential commission, or a board of independent experts. Most often the investigation is an instrument of a supervisory administrative unit and is used to abolish a program, change its directors or curtail certain activities. Sometimes the investigation is simply an attempt to assess the current status of operations and achievements of a program, in which case it takes a type (1) or (2) form.

IV. Types of Programs Evaluated

The list of programs that have been or are being evaluated by social scientists is extremely long and quite diverse. The following list briefly samples major substantive areas:

Social case work
Foreman training
Parole systems
Vocational guidance
International broadcasting
School lunches
Air-raid protection information
Volunteer work camps
Product advertising
Training in leadership
Participation of youth in politics

Adult education courses
Education in cancer control
War Bond sales drives
Infant and maternal care
  centers
Agricultural technology
Rural rehabilitation
Student exchanges
General education (under-
  graduates)
Reduction of prejudice

The list could be endlessly multiplied, but the systematization of knowledge about evaluation can better be served by attempting to classify the types of programs to which evaluation can be or has been applied. The following typology is crude and multi-dimensional, grouping action programs according to the greatest communalities in : subject-matter, "size" and flexibility of the program, degree of control over the situation that an investigator can achieve, and techniques used in gathering data. Fundamentally, the typology is based on an intuitive belief that individual social scientists will feel more comfortable and be able to communicate better within one type than across two or more types:

(1) *Information and education programs:* Programs to reduce prejudice, spread health information, foster citizens' interest in the United Nations, change attitudes toward dental hygiene, alter opinions of students about foreign nations, and the like have certain communalities of discipline and method. Almost all of these programs employ as evaluators psychologists, sociologists, public opinion pollers and educators. Techniques usually stress questionnaires, attitude scales, interviews and content analysis. Most of the programs are fairly confined and finite in space and time. Almost all of them lend themselves (with greater or lesser readiness) to evaluation employing the model of the scientific experiment. It is *relatively* easy to define program objectives, specify targets of change, standardize the "treatment" or operations, and introduce variations into the attempted action. Control groups can usually be found and held untreated.

(2) *Skill or performance training programs:* Besides in-school courses, there are programs for training foremen in "human relations skills," soldiers in the use of medical aid kits, farmers in soil conservation practices, non-literate peasants and workers in infant hygiene, nurses in handling psychological aspects of somatic illness. Such programs as these usually involve the

efforts of subject matter specialists and materials technicians (e.g., engineers, chemists, agronomists, medical doctors, etc.) as well as those of behavioral scientists. Evaluation procedures usually include performance tests, observations of behavior, and, very often, the study of rates or incidence data in addition to interviewing and questionnaires. The possibilities for experimental variation in program may be more limited, and the cost of failure in terms of wasted man hours and palpable injury or damage to subjects is generally much greater than in the case of type (1) programs.

(3) *Microcosmic social welfare programs:* This category includes programs designed to improve the economic well-being, standard of living, morality, self-reliance; to reduce the criminality, delinquency, or morbidity of individuals, families, sub-community or locality groups; to "rehabilitate" ex-convicts, unwed mothers, displaced persons, alcoholics, and former psychotic patients of mental hospitals; to increase the participation of "young adults" in political action, foster character development in adolescents, and improve the "adjustment" of the aged. Such programs as these have broader aims (and greater ambiguity of criteria for success) than do type (1) and (2) schemes, use a multiplicity of means, and usually attempt to adjust the "treatment" to the needs of the particular subject rather than trying to standardize operations. Furthermore, such programs tend to have less control over the variables that affect the outcome of action since the program is ordinarily carried out in the context of normal social life over a considerable period of time and "extraneous" influences are likely to be very important in determining the achievement of objectives. Type (3) programs also present new problems in design, since they deal with a wider variety of characteristics and problems in the subjects, thus making it difficult to obtain adequate control groups or baseline measurements without very large samples. Similarly, it is harder to introduce experimental variations into the program and, again, the cost of negative or zero outcomes of particular treatments is high in terms of injury to the participants and prestige of the agency, as well as in sheer dollar volume, since type (3) programs usually require large staffs and long periods of work. Lastly, social scientists attempting to evaluate such programs usually need considerably more advice and counsel from social practitioners and will benefit more from the latters' store of practical wisdom than is the case in type (1) and (2) programs.

(4) *Macrocosmic social welfare programs:* These are the massive social change and economic welfare programs such as AAA, SCS, FOA, technical assistance programs, the Full Employment

Act of 1946, rural rehabilitation schemes in Central and South America, nationalization of industry in Britain, and like programs. Programs of this type border upon continuous or "normal" social action such as taxation policy, immigration legislation, price and wage control policies, Federal Reserve Board action, and so forth, where it is hard to delineate a finite "program." The primary differentiating characteristic of macrocosmic programs is their extreme complexity, both in operations and effects, which makes for great difficulty in determining baselines and in segregating "treatment" from "extraneous influences." Furthermore, the possibility of experimental variations in treatment undertaken for the sake of evaluating alternative means is almost ruled out. A very wide range of disciplinary specialists and practitioners must be represented on the evaluation team.

COMMENT:

Two further considerations affecting evaluation studies must be mentioned in delineating types of programs:

(a) *Degree of institutionalization.* When a program is identified or coordinate with an established agency (e.g., social case work, public school education, agricultural extension work, etc.) an evaluator faces considerably greater problems of entree, rapport, resistance to research procedures and, later, to changes in program that may be suggested by findings, than he does in *ad hoc,* frankly experimental, or non-institutionalized programs. The opportunity to introduce program innovations for the purpose of testing their effects is also limited. It may also be more difficult to determine objectives and to describe the operations of institutionalized programs since their routinization usually leads to a lack of self-consciousness about them among the action staff. Type (3) and (4) programs are ordinarily more institutionalized than types (1) and (2).
(b) *Manifest and latent objectives.* Besides the possibility that an institutionalized program may incorporate the latent objective of self-perpetuation, it is clear that some action programs (notably type (4)) have other important latent objectives. Thus, certain technical assistance programs may have foreign policy objectives that exceed the manifest objective of raising the standard of living in the "subject" country; a domestic agricultural program may have political importance that, in the minds of representatives, outweighs the technical or economic effects of the program;

an action agency may continue to carry on a program that some sponsor believes in, even though the staff may feel or know that the manifest objective of the program is not being achieved. Aspects of operations (or entire programs) that have latent objectives of this sort are highly resistant to change in the face of evidence that the manifest aims are not being accomplished. Finally, there may exist in staff and sponsors alike a kind of "absolute value" orientation toward an activity. Thus, Margaret Blenkner quotes P. R. Lee as saying: "Much of what we do in social work we do because, on the whole, we prefer a civilization in which such things are done to one in which they are not. Some values are beyond measurement."

V. Technical Problems

The following pages discuss in detail some of the major technical and procedural problems of evaluation research. The first section consists of a "model" for evaluation studies presented as a vehicle for organizing some of the technical difficulties that social scientists and practitioners have experienced in evaluating action programs; next, larger procedural problems are discussed in connection with program planning and utilization of results; finally, two sections are given over to consideration of some long-term strategy problems.

A. A MODEL FOR EVALUATION STUDIES

Both because of their importance and because of the methodological difficulties they present, Effect Studies (type (1) in section III above) seem to be the most appropriate place for social scientists to direct their attention and efforts. Furthermore, it can be shown that type (2) studies (Operations Analysis) are a necessary step in an Effect Study, and that Surveys of Need (type (3) above) are a special case of one step in Effect Studies, namely, the definition of objectives.

With these points in mind, the following model for evaluation studies is proposed. The model has obviously been inspired by the design commonly employed in scientific experiments. It is equally obvious that because of practical constraints (time, money, power to manipulate variables) and because of ignorance (lack of substantive knowledge and of adequate theory about social and behavioral systems), few evaluation studies will be able to satisfy the rigorous demands the model makes. Nevertheless, the model may direct attention to means for improving current procedures and point to problems appropriate for systematic study.

1. *Determining program objectives.* It is essential not only that the major objectives of an action program be clearly defined, but also that they be stated in operational terms—i.e., in terms of concrete behavior, specific accomplishments or states of affairs—in order that an evaluator can devise appropriate measuring instruments (in the broadest sense of the term, including tests, interviews, ratings, objective indices of rate, frequency or quantity). Operational statement of objectives is usually the most difficult task in conducting an evaluation study.

Comment: It is obvious that objectives must be stated in advance of taking action in order to prevent the trivial occurrence that the stated objectives are merely the observed results of action.

In spite of the foregoing warning, it is sometimes possible to derive objectives by closely scrutinizing a series of successful outcomes of action (in the ongoing programs or in pre-tests of alternative actions) and enlisting the aid of practitioners in determining the specific criteria that lead them to rate an outcome as "successful." Thus, Hunt, Blenkner and Kogan asked social caseworkers to rate a series of casework records, then carefully went over the successfully treated ones with workers and therefrom derived the criteria used in building their "Movement Scale."

It is known that, in any but the simplest programs, action staff may differ among themselves as to what the objectives of the program are. In order to minimize resistance to results and to maximize the usefulness of research, it is essential to have advance agreement on objectives and on the procedures to be used in appraising their attainment.

Objectives should be differentiated from expectations or level of aspirations. For example, an objective of social case work may be economic rehabilitation of the client, defined operationally as his holding a job steadily for a period of one year. A level of aspiration for the economic rehabilitation program is the percentage of cases in which the objective had been achieved. A major question that is not often faced is: what is a reasonable (realistic) expectation of success—5, 50, or 95 percent of the cases treated?

Definition of the objectives in operational terms is a step frequently omitted in evaluation studies, sometimes because the objectives are, in fact, too vague and general to be specified, because neither the action staff nor the evaluator are sufficiently aware of the importance of such a step, or because the evaluator was not called into consultation until after the program had been launched.

Concomitant with the defining of objectives is choosing the means for their achievement. Action personnel often do not distinguish these steps but it will be to the evaluator's advantage to do so, at least analytically. If the evaluator conceives his role as more than that of a passive observer, and if he arrives on the scene before the program has become fixed, he may want to suggest alternative operations. (See section B below for further comments on "program planning.")

As promised above, it can be shown that Surveys of Need are a part of determining objectives. Sometimes an action staff does not know how to direct its efforts and ask social scientists for assistance in planning. A Survey of Need can ordinarily be predicated on hypotheses proferred by the action staff, sponsors and consultant practitioners. By helping the staff decide on criteria for the existence of a Need (or problem) and by conducting a survey to determine whether or not the criteria are met, an evaluator can help to determine realistic objectives for action. Such a survey will serve a double purpose in that it also establishes a baseline, or measure of the state of affairs existing before action has been taken.

Often no Survey of Need is made before beginning an action program but, instead, the program is based on "self-evident" or "obvious" propositions that, when examined empirically, may well turn out to be incorrect. Many such assumptions revolve around motivation of subjects, with programs being designed to exploit nonexistent motives (e.g., "voluntary rationing" programs during World War II, certain kinds of appeals used to sell war bonds).

2. *Describing operations.* Besides defining objectives operationally, an evaluator must find out what concrete actions are being employed to achieve the ends. An accurate, factual, first-hand account of what is actually being done under the program is important, especially where complex and diffuse programs are being administered from a central agency. Very often, actual operations differ from the plan or blueprint for them. An evaluator cannot safely assume that the operations planned (or even alleged to exist) by a headquarters staff are in fact being carried out in the field. There may be a number of reasons for the discrepancy, including misperceptions or wishful thinking on the part of the staff, unrecognized conflict between agency conceptions and local law or customs, availability of resources and personnel, and the like. Finally, it is clear that adequate information about operations can almost never be obtained retrospectively. Observation, especially participant observation where feasible, should be carried on while operations are proceeding.

Comment: An evaluator can get a strategic advantage from the comparison of different means for achieving the same objectives. In short, if it is feasible to introduce systematic variations into the treatment, the evaluator can conduct a comparative study of means and perhaps isolate important variables in this way, thus adding greatly to his knowledge.

A factor over which the evaluator may have little control but which should engage his attention is the adequacy of the operations— that is, the impact of the program upon the subjects. The impact of a program should be differentiated from its effects. Impact is a question of the intensity, duration, and appropriateness of treatment rather than its consequences. To illustrate: an information or propaganda campaign may succeed in influencing virtually all the people it reaches but may reach only a small proportion of the available audience; a counseling program for preventing juvenile delinquency may be well designed but the case load of counsellors may be so large that they do not have a strong impact on any cases.

3. *Measuring effects.* Finding or devising techniques for detecting changes in subjects and estimating the degree to which observed phenomena approach the objectives of the program is perhaps the second most difficult task in evaluation studies. It is made easier by clear, operational definitions of objectives, but it is never a simple problem. The usual requirements of reliability and validity must be met of course. The application of measurement techniques is usually costly and time consuming, with data collection and analysis taking the largest share of the total time budget.

Comment: Measuring devices, especially questionnaires and tests, too often are invested with magic qualities, especially by action staff, but, regrettably, also by social scientists. Although the choice of appropriate techniques is important, it must depend upon, not substitute for, thinking through the problem of objectives and means for achieving them.

The development of measuring devices is a technical problem of social science rather than one peculiar to evaluation studies. There seems to be no reason to believe that anything more or less is involved in developing measures for evaluative purposes than for any other social science endeavor.

A practical difficulty of measurement in many studies is that of obtaining adequate information about the subjects' experiences outside of the program. For example, in studies of the effects of a school lunch program on pupils' health, the evaluators had trouble securing precise information on quantity and type of food eaten at home. This kind of difficulty arises principally in connection with programs that have only intermittent influence on subjects or control only a narrow sphere of relevant forces. In one sense, it is a problem of the degree of control or manipulation that can be achieved; but, since the usual substitute for manipulation of forces is their measurement, the difficulty deserves to be mentioned here.

Especially when objectives have not been operationally defined, it happens that reliable and valid objective measurement techniques are omitted and one of the following procedures substituted:

(a) *Expert judgment:* reputable and skillful practitioners or subject-matter specialists may be asked to render a judgment about the effectiveness of the program. Such judgments usually fail to make explicit the assumptions, procedures for collecting information and criteria for appraising data that the experts have used. This remark is not intended to condemn expert judgment but merely to point out that it is difficult to know exactly what was done, to repeat it and to get consistent agreement among judges.

(b) *Illustrative incidents or case reports:* the experience of some or most of the subjects of the program are collected as evidence of program impact. Besides the possibility of sampling bias such a technique usually suffers from lack of comparability between subjects' reports and, hence, severe limitation on both generalizability and quantification, or statements of the extent to which particular effects were produced.

(c) *Testimonial* letters or reports, whether volunteered or solicited not only involve multiple frames of reference for viewing the program effects, but are even more likely to be unrepresentative since they are rarely written by individuals who were unaffected by or moderately dissatisfied with the program. Lastly, reliance on testimonials tends to equate satisfaction with effectiveness.

4. *Establishing a baseline.* If an action program intends to produce changes in individuals or their situations, it is necessary to measure the state of affairs prior to action in order to have a basis for estimating effects. This requirement is almost always recognized as important but practical obstacles may arise to its fulfillment: (1) the action agency may feel that immediate action is needed and it cannot wait for an evaluator to complete a thorough survey; (2) establishing the baseline means at least doubling the expense of the study since, in the simplest case, the same measurement operations must be undertaken both before and after the program. There are counterbalancing advantages, however, if time and cost are not ruling factors, for an investigator can learn much about the situation, his instruments and about hitherto unforeseen problems while he is attempting to establish the baseline.

Comment: A technical problem about which relatively little is known is the effect of pre-treatment measurement upon the impact of the program. One research by R. L. Solomon suggests that the effect of pre-testing in an attitude change study is to reduce the effectiveness of the subsequent communication. It is conceivable that pre-testing could function in the opposite direction under other conditions—i.e., to heighten the effectiveness of the action by "sensitizing" subjects to what was being done to them.

It has been suggested that baseline measurement can serve the same function as a Survey of Need (see section III above), revealing the extent to which the conditions assumed by program planners actually exist. Furthermore, the baseline survey can provide information about factors not encompassed in program plans and perhaps to be fed back into planning in a helpful way. Thus Simmons has suggested, in connection with the evaluation of district health centers in Santiago, that an adequate baseline survey should not stop with collecting data on morbidity and mortality incidence, dietary and sanitation practices, etc., but should also attempt to determine the nature and extent of "native" beliefs and practices in the area of health and medicine. He points out that no health program is launched into a complete vacuum of ideas and that a knowledge of likely sources of resistance to the "modern medicine" program could be gotten from surveying the existing situation. This recommendation has wide applicability.

Baseline measurement is most often omitted when the evaluator has not been called upon for consultation until the program is under way. In this case, the evaluator must depend either on retrospective report (with attendant risks of memory distortions) or on whatever documentary evidence there happened to be at the time the program was instituted; such evidence is ordinarily inadequate. Sometimes baseline measurements are incomplete simply because of lack of experience and foresight about what data might be needed later.

5. *Controlling extraneous factors.* Ideally the evaluator attempts to determine the effectiveness of the program by comparing the changes observed in a treated group with those in a matched control group, in order to eliminate the possibility that the observed effects are the consequences of random or irrelevant forces that happen to occur simultaneously with the program. This requirement is more often observed in theory than in practice because of the great practical difficulty in obtaining and studying a control group. Not only is it difficult to know what are the relevant variables on which to match controls with experimentals, but it is also difficult to measure or restrict the forces acting on the control group. Measuring costs are doubled. It is usually harder to per-

suade control subjects to submit to tests or interviews. Sometimes humanitarian, political or other policy considerations prevent using a control group. Finally, in massive programs designed to affect an entire society or community there may literally be no possibility of obtaining an exactly comparable control group.

Comment: Instead of the traditional design of a treated experimental group and an untreated control group, it may be more feasible to divide the experimental group into two or more parts and carry out different operations on each part, thus making, in effect, a comparison study (cf. "Describing Operations" above).

It can be argued that, where the program is extensive enough and the direction of its influence clearly enough differentiated from other concurrent forces, no control group is needed to demonstrate effectiveness. Such an argument does not negate the possible advantage of studying alternative programs directed toward the same objectives.

6. *Detecting unanticipated consequences.* A common experience of social planners and practitioners is that their actions produce effects that are unintended, whether "beneficial" or "harmful." The two most common reasons for the occurrence of unanticipated consequences are (1) correlation (simultaneous variation) between phenomena, and (2) back effects in an interrelated system whose equilibrium is upset by the intentional action. It is desirable to make provision in the evaluation design for detecting unanticipated consequences, but, by definition, it is hard to anticipate the unanticipated, and ways of dealing with this problem are not well known.

Comment: Intuitive familiarity with the subject matter of the program and a close acquaintance with subjects may help to detect unexpected effects. Deliberate attentiveness to disturbances and complaints among the subjects may be rewarding. Pre-testing operations would often help. Where feasible (e.g. in small scale programs of attitude change and skill training) the evaluator may gain some insight into program effects by means of role-playing the intended program. Lastly, it would, in principle, help greatly to avoid unanticipated outcomes if there were a clear, explicit and adequate model of the action process and how it is supposed to work. For example, if one is evaluating a program to prevent delinquency, it would be useful to make explicit the assumptions and the mechanisms believed to be operative in the process of influence (e.g., identification with father figures, repression through fear of punishment, catharsis through athletics, etc.) and the manner in which these are believed to change the subjects.

B. RELATIONSHIP OF EVALUATION TO ACTION

I. *Planning.* It is generally agreed that successful evaluation studies cannot be performed retrospectively—i.e., after the program has been completed, but, rather, that evaluation must be "built into" programs at their inception. A number of considerations are advanced for such a position:

(1) By being present at the beginning, the idea of evaluation is less threatening to the action personnel, both because it is less likely to be seen as a hostile or threatening act, and because personnel come to feel that they have had a hand in planning the evaluation. Therefore, the activities of evaluators will encounter less resistance both to providing data and to accepting the results of the study. Further, it is argued, the presence of evaluators conveys to action staff an "experimental" attitude and minimizes their personal commitment to any particular phase of the program.

(2) If evaluators are an integral part of the planning phase of programs they can often help to clarify objectives, since their attention is focused on measuring program achievements.

(3) Evaluators may be able to contribute substantively to planning by drawing on established findings of social science or their own experience with similar programs. Thus they may be able to suggest methods of known effectiveness and point out known difficulties in operations that action staff may conceive.

(4) Above all, if he is present at the start of things the evaluator can follow the entire program through planning, pre-testing and full-scale operations, thereby enabling him to secure information and keep records of actual happenings which are rarely recalled in full detail by action staff at a later time.

The scheme outlined above is sometimes called "program planning." It raises the interesting question of how deeply an evaluator should become involved in actual planning of a program, for objectivity, resistance to research findings and degree of "stake" in a program must concern the evaluator not only in relation to the action staff but also to himself.

A second point on which there is considerable agreement among social scientists who have conducted evaluation studies is that no such study can be successfully executed or its findings utilized in further planning unless the evaluator has been requested by the agency to conduct the study, and, further, unless he has the approval and support of the highest echelon of power in the agency. Such support is essential for gaining entree into units where observations must be made, in securing records, permission to test, to question or interview staff or subjects, and is vital for implementing program changes, especially experimental variations. The importance of powerful backing is especially well illustrated by the accounts of two evaluation studies (of the Investigation type) where the requesting agencies (FCC and Food and Drug Administration) had police power over the program.

A third question concerning the relationship between evaluator and action staff revolves around formal role or organizational connection: should the evaluation be conducted by investigators who are formally independent of the agency or by a "research department" within the agency itself? The arguments for the *latter* view are:

(1) resistance to research is minimized because the evaluators are "insiders" not potentially hostile strangers;
(2) little or no time is lost acquainting evaluators with the substantive details of the operating program;
(3) the evaluation personnel remain attached to the organization and can help interpret findings and oversee their implementation.

For the point of view that advocates the "independent investigator," the arguments are:

(1) an "insider" cannot maintain independence and objectivity of judgment both because of his identification with the existing program and because of organizational (social) pressures from his colleagues in the action sections of the agency to endorse their activities;
(2) little of the time spent in getting acquainted with the program is wasted, since this period often produces profitable research ideas and may reveal aspects of the operation to which the action personnel are so accustomed that they are unaware of alternatives;
(3) an outsider often has greater freedom of movement in an agency because he has the ambiguity of status associated with the stranger, can often achieve the intimacy of the stranger, and is not identified with any faction or interest group within the agency.

These conflicting points of view probably cannot be resolved without extensive experience with different kinds of programs.

II. *Utilization of Results.* In addition to the relationship of evaluation to planning, it is important to consider how research results are fed back into the program. A number of evaluators have reported instances in which the results of a study were directly and importantly influential in making changes in action programs, and some things are known about instances in which research findings have not been used. The question, however, needs further study. A serious complication arises from the fact that it is usually difficult to tell how weighty the results of a study, as such, have been in changing the plans of an action staff. An administrator must often take into account considerations (such as overall policy, non-utilitarian values, latent objectives) that go beyond or sometimes counter recommendations arising from research. Occasionally too, research results merely reaffirm a decision that the administrator had already reached.

There have been some attempts to collate the experiences of applied social research and to systematize knowledge about the conditions under which research is likely to be influential. It is generally agreed that favorable conditions include some of the matters that have already been mentioned in connection with program planning: i.e., incorporating evaluation plans into program planning; involving action staff in research; securing support from the power figures in the agency; and remaining in close touch with program operations at every step of the way. If these precautions are taken, it seems likely that the research will be germane to the interests of the action staff and also that their expectations of it will be realistic. In addition, it has been claimed that research which focuses on operations rather than on personnel (especially personal qualities) will minimize defensive anxiety and increase acceptance of findings. Again, if research results are made known in small doses and program or agency changes are introduced gradually rather than abruptly, there is less likelihood of resistance. Finally, if an evaluator remains attached to the agency to help interpret and implement findings, they are more likely to be adopted than if a report is simply dropped in the lap of the action staff and no provision made for explaining findings or helping to follow them through into action.

C. CHOICE OF PROBLEMS

In trying to formulate an optimum strategy for evaluation studies, one is inevitably confronted with the question of whether social scientists should attempt to evaluate any sort of program whose sponsors request help, shall accept whatever role relationship is offered, and make whatever compromises with ideal conditions that circumstances may demand; or whether evaluators should confine their attention and efforts to cases where there is maximum likelihood of success.

The question is an extremely important one, involving not only professional prestige, financial support for research, the advancement of technique and accumulation of knowledge, but, quite as important, responsibility to society, assistance to practitioners, the cost of failure in terms of wasted effort and unfulfilled expectations, and, not least, the probability that research results can have some effect on action. Furthermore, both long- and short-run considerations must be balanced in making the decision, since immediate rewards in the form of prestige, popularity, power and temporary or partial help for action agencies may interfere with longer run gains such as the gradual growth of skill and knowledge.

The remarks made so far in this memorandum suggest some of the conditions under which it is possible to carry out successful evaluation studies—i.e., studies which meet minimum standards of scientific acceptability in their data collection and interpretation, and which lead to promising recommendations for action that are in turn accepted and put to use by the action staff. These conditions can be summarized as follows:

(1) The evaluator must be requested by the action agency to conduct the study.

(2) The request, or at least the subsequent support, must come from the highest echelon of power in the agency.

(3) The evaluator must begin work before the program is under way and preferably before it is well formulated; and he must be allowed to take at least a passive part in discussions of program objectives. He must further be allowed to propose his research plan (including techniques, criteria for determining program effects and like matters) to the action staff and be given an opportunity to gain their acceptance of the plan as well as to get their suggestions concerning it.

(4) The evaluator must be able to conduct his research in such a way that he can minimize resistance to and anxiety about data collection and future use of information. Correspondingly, he must be able to avoid being forced into the role of policeman or spy, except when engaged by an agency legitimately charged with such functions.

(5) There must be sufficient time, money, and patience to allow for familiarization with the agency, scouting the situation, building the necessary research staff, devising and pre-testing instruments and techniques to achieve ordinary standards of acceptability.

(6) The evaluator must have access to any portion of the program, personnel, records and procedures of the agency that fall within the legitimate scope of his problem interest and be able to observe and examine these unhampered by constraints other than scientific canons and ordinary standards of decent conduct.

(7) The evaluator should have maximum opportunity to suggest and to help implement variations in and/or systematic controls upon the program operations as long as these are both potentially helpful in attributing causal significance to events and are not harmful to subjects, staff, or the reputation of the agency and are consistent with its values and aims.

(8) The evaluator must be able to play a neutral, non-partisan role within the agency, not becoming identified with any faction or section, or any particular operation.

In addition to these procedural "musts," there are some conditions that will probably increase the chances of a successful outcome for evaluation studies:

(9) Since it usually requires a long time to determine the effects of social action, it seems wise to avoid programs where there is likely to be instability of conditions—e.g., changes in program objectives required by changing environmental conditions; doubt about the continuation of the program or the agency; doubt about the availability of subjects for follow-up study; uncertainty about the continued existence of the forces responsible for creating the action program, etc.

(10) Since the effectiveness of evaluation studies is related in part to the possibility that effective action can be taken, research efforts might best be invested in programs that can exercise influence over the subjects or their environment—i.e., where an agency can have an important impact on the problem conditions it wants to deal with and where intentional action can exert maximum control over natural forces.

(11) The store of accumulated knowledge about human behavior is greater for some problems than for others. Evaluation studies that can draw on a considerable body of existing data and theory, or, at least, on prior investigation, are more likely to be fruitful than studies that tackle completely novel problems.

It is not at all clear that the best strategy for evaluation research is to hew close to the conditions and cautions listed above. All that has been said is that these are the conditions under which evaluation is most easily and successfully performed. It will certainly be necessary to accept research invitations whose terms fall short of the ideal, but perhaps it is unwise to attempt studies where only a minority of the conditions can be met. Perhaps also, the list will provide a basis for planning a systematic attack on the manifold problems that presently confront evaluation reearch.

D. PROGRAMS VERSUS VARIABLES

A further serious question in the strategy of evaluation research is whether effort should be directed toward the study of programs or the study of variables. The distinction here is, broadly, between assessing the effects of a program as it stands, as a totality, or, alternatively, retreating from the full complexity of everyday life and simplifying inquiry by selecting the aspects, cases, or phenomena within the program that appear most amenable to inquiry.

It is clear that the categories of subjects and of action that an agency employs are often not the preferred categories of social science. Thus, the cases accepted by a social work agency are likely to include a wide variety of human problems with (often enough) several problems presented simultaneously by the same subject. The case worker's simultaneous attack on the several problems of the subject, while fully justified of course, does tend to spoil any attempt at neat design and close control over such variables as diagnosed difficulty and technique of treatment. Again, the criteria of admission or inclusion in a program may overlap or cross-cut the established categories of a social science discipline. For example, the category "parolees" may include some but not all of the existing individuals whose mothers died before they were five years old and who have been convicted of robbery. There may be a perfectly reasonable hypothesis about the psychodynamics of such robbers, taken as a class, and even a feasible suggestion as to how to supervise their period of parole in order to maximize success in rehabilitation. Testing such an hypothesis is usually not feasible under existing parole programs, however, for they must be somewhat more standardized than specialized for the benefit of the hypothesis.

It is not sufficient to dismiss the present question by replying that the practitioner must take life as it occurs and that he needs help with his immediate problems; nor is it appropriate to reply that "the institution does not exist for the purpose of being experimented upon," as one practitioner has remarked. Such comments are correct, of course, and social scientists do not have the right of irresponsibility. But, what is being argued here is not that the world should be made into a gigantic laboratory for the convenience of social scientists, but rather, that *in the long run,* advances in knowledge will come more surely from working with variables well grounded in systematic theory and related to previous research than they will from *catch-as-catch-can* engagements of social science with social practice. If this point is admitted, the only question remaining is whether social science and social practice can afford to wait out the long run.

A reasonable compromise between the "program" and the "variable" approach would seem to be that, with proper foresight in design and data collection, proper choice of programs, and with good fortune in attendance, both programs and variables can be studied. There may arise, however, choice points where a social scientist will have to make a strategic decision. There are few guideposts to help him make it at the present time, and some deliberation and discussion over strategy may repay us well.

MARVIN C. ALKIN

Evaluation Theory
Development

. . . A theory of evaluation should: (1) offer a conceptual scheme by
which evaluation areas or problems are classified; (2) define the
strategies including kinds of data, and means of analysis and reporting
appropriate to each of the areas of the conceptual scheme; (3) provide systems of generalizations about the use of various evaluation
procedures and techniques and their appropriateness to evaluation
areas or problems.

At their best the propositions presented in a theory of evaluation
should enable one to predict, fully, the appropriateness of utilizing
various evaluation strategies within a system. Development of an
evaluation theory is thus an "end" rather than a means, guiding the
research activities of the Center for the Study of Evaluation.* Development of a theory is a difficult enterprise. The process of working
toward the achievement of this end requires a conceptual framework
to guide and coordinate our efforts. What is presented in this paper
represents months of conceptual efforts and may be thought of as a
first approximation of an attempt to develop an evaluation theory.
In other words, we have constructed a rationale for cónducting evaluations in a certain way that is based on a specified set of assumptions
which in turn underlie a precise definition of what an evaluation is
supposed to do or be.

Marvin C. Alkin, "Evaluation Theory Development," *Evaluation Comment,*
vol. 2, no. 1 (October 1969), pp. 2–7. Reprinted by permission.
* At the University of California at Los Angeles.

To start with, in the development of a theory, it is necessary to reach agreement on a definition of evaluation. Most would agree that a major failing of evaluation today stems from the lack of an adequate definition. Past definitions of evaluation have either equated it with: (1) measurement and testing, (2) statements of congruence between performance and objectives, or (3) professional judgments. None of these definitions by itself is sufficient to provide all the necessary information or to include the multiplicity of activities now regarded as evaluation.

In the past year, there has been increasing evidence of a developing consensus on a broader, more comprehensive definition of evaluation. This expanded view has necessarily taken into consideration that the judgments from evaluators are intended to be of use to decision-makers in selecting among various courses of action. This view of evaluation also acknowledges the uniqueness of specific situations or programs and the necessity of recognizing this uniqueness in the evaluation as well as in the manner in which the evaluation information is ultimately reported.

Our definition of evaluation, therefore, is based on the following assumptions:

1. Evaluation is a process of gathering information. Most past definitions of evaluation are inadequate since they do not cover the full range of activities requiring information.
2. The information collection in an evaluation will be used mainly to make decisions about alternative courses of action, rather than being employed in some other fashion. Thus, the manner in which the information is collected, as well as the analysis procedures, must be appropriate to the needs of the decision-maker or of potential decision-involved publics. This requirement might necessitate quite different analyses than those which might be employed if the purpose were understanding the education process per se.
3. Evaluation information should be presented to the decision-maker in a form that he can use effectively and which is designed to help rather than confuse or mislead him.
4. Different kinds of decisions may require different kinds of evaluation procedures.

While there are any number of variations of a specific wording that might serve equally well for a definition of evaluation, we have devised one which fits our conceptions of evaluation and meets our biases. We would maintain that evaluation must take into consideration the ultimate decision-making functions to be served, as well as the nature of the specific problem or situation under analysis. We prefer the following definition:

Evaluation is the process of ascertaining the decision areas of concern, selecting appropriate information, and collecting and analyzing information in order to report summary data useful to decision-makers in selecting among alternatives.

The first part of the definition of evaluation presented here deals with *ascertaining the decision areas of concern.* The decision-maker, and not the evaluator, determines the nature of the domain to be examined. The evaluator can and should, however, point out inconsistencies, potential difficulties, or additional data that might modify the decision-maker's views on the relevance of certain concerns.

For example, if the evaluator is called upon by a specific decision-maker to provide an evaluation, first, he will want to know what should be evaluated. Decision areas of concern may be stated relative to explicit statements of goals or objectives of the system or relative to various implicit goals. In his interactions with the decision-maker, the evaluator may wish to point out the necessity for broadening the area of concern because of interrelated aspects of the school program, or to consider, as well, various areas of potential unanticipated outcomes.

On the other hand, if the evaluator is conducting an evaluative study of an educational institution without having been commissioned by a specific decision-maker, he has available greater flexibility. A professor, for example, might conduct an evaluative study of his university. There is a preconception on the part of the evaluator as to which decision-maker or potential decision groups he is directing his work towards. Thus, the decision area of concern in such an endeavor is framed by the unique nature of the potential decision-maker or decision groups along with either actual data or judgments on the part of the evaluator as to the concerns of this group (individual).

We consider this "preconception of decision-maker" notion a fundamental and useful distinction between evaluation and some kinds of research. If one realizes that the purpose of what he does is to provide the best possible basis for informed judgments or decisions, his thinking about his task will surely be influenced; and this will be a different influence than that which operates on the researcher whose purpose is to discover or explain some phenomenon.

Another part of the definition and, therefore, another task of evaluation deals with *selecting appropriate information* in light of the decision areas to be considered. If the decision area relates to the assessment of the needs of a total system, the information requirements will be quite different than when the decision area is related to the relative success of two specific alternative programs conducted under experimental conditions. The task of the evaluator in specifying information requirements includes the development of the evaluation design of the project, and the selection and/or development of instruments designed to provide the information appropriate to the decision areas.

Collecting and analyzing the information are tasks of prime concern to the evaluator. He will encounter different problems associated with these tasks, depending upon the unit being evaluated, the nature of the decision-maker, and other considerations.

One of the most vital parts of the evaluation process is *reporting summary data* to the decision-maker. Most evaluators often overlook this function as being merely a pro forma exercise. The evaluator's role requires that he make judgments about the relative worth of various courses of action. These judgments may be in the form of statements or recommendations to the decision-maker(s), or may be general descriptive material. But in all instances the evaluator should attempt to be explicit in the specification of the value system that led to the judgments made. Indeed, if the purpose of evaluation is to provide information that will enable decision-makers to reach decisions about alternatives, then the nature and form of the reporting should be appropriate to the problem and the audience.

The summary data is provided to be of use to the *decision-maker*. It has already been alluded to in this paper that we are using the term "decision-maker" to apply both to an explicit contractor of evaluation services as well as a potential but only implicit decision-maker or group. Moreover, we are using the term "decision-maker" to apply both to an individual with organizational "line" authority (e.g., a school principal) as well as to other publics that participate in the decision process or in the development of educational policy decisions. Throughout this paper, whenever we refer to "decision-maker" it is in the generic sense discussed above.

Information is provided to "decision-makers," in order to enable sounder decisions in *selecting among alternatives*. By definition, a "decision" involves making a choice among alternatives. However, the form of alternatives has a wide range. Alternatives may range from a "go/no-go" category regarding a given textbook for a particular classroom to a complex aggregation of a number of budget categories related to an optimum expenditure level. In general, the number of categories of alternatives increases as the size of the program or system increases; e.g., pupil achievement, teacher morale, teacher practices, etc.

The summary evaluation data should ordinarily be presented in the form of statements and/or recommendations about alternatives. An exception would be when such information is designed to describe the status (past, present, or future) of the system. For example, "the students at your school are weak in mathematics." In this instance, there are no alternatives and the decisions are implied (e.g., something should be done to correct this situation.)

Evaluation Need Areas

The foregoing definition and assumptions are closely tied to the decision-making process, which in turn leads to a consideration of what kinds of educational decisions require evaluative information. Inquiry along these lines has led to the development of a decision-oriented classification of the various types of evaluation. Five areas of evaluation may be identified.

These five areas represent attempts to provide evaluative information to satisfy unique decision categories. In other words, there are evaluations necessary in providing information for decisions about the state of the system. (We call such evaluations *systems assessment.*) There are evaluations necessary in providing information to assist in the selection of particular programs likely to be effective in meeting specific educational needs. (We call this kind of evaluation, which takes place prior to the implementation of the program, *program planning.*) There are evaluations necessary in providing information relative to the extent to which a program has been introduced in the manner in which it was intended and to the group for which it was intended (*program implementation*). There are evaluations necessary in providing information during the course of a program about the manner in which the program is functioning, enroute objectives are being achieved, and what unanticipated outcomes are being produced. Such information can be of value in modifying the program (*program improvement*). Evaluations are necessary in providing information that might be used by decision-makers in making judgments about the worth of the program and its potential generalizability to other related situations (*program certification*).

The evaluation areas outlined above seem to represent a growing consensus among a number of people engaged in the study of evaluation. The first two and the last need areas discussed are somewhat similar, respectively, to "context," "input," and "product" presented by Stufflebeam (1968). What he refers to as "process" we have chosen to think of as two separate stages, program implementation and improvement. Major differences of emphasis are found between the descriptions of our need areas and his stages. However, Stufflebeam's work contributed substantially to our thinking. The discrepancy model presented by Provus (1969) outlines five stages: "definition," "installation," "process," "product," and "cost benefit analysis." The first four of these are somewhat similar to our stages two through five. Provus does not include systems assessment as a part of his model. With respect to cost benefit analysis, we would maintain that cost benefit considerations are a part of each need area of the evaluation and cannot be thought of as simply an additional task to be attacked when all of the other evaluations have been completed. The general notion that cost benefit considerations are a part of each stage of the evaluation process also would seem to be sub-scribed to by John Hemphill in his recent NSSE Yearbook chapter (1969). The evaluation types outlined by Rodney Skager (1969) are also quite similar to the framework presented here. A better under-standing of the need areas will be gained by a more complete descrip-tion of each.

SYSTEMS ASSESSMENT

Systems assessment is a means of determining the range and specifi-city of educational objectives appropriate for a particular situation. The needs may be represented as a gap between the goal and the present state of affairs. The evaluative problem, then, becomes one of assessing the needs of students, of the community, and of society in relation to the existing situation. Assessment, therefore, is a state-ment of the status of the system as it presently exists in comparison to desired outputs or stated needs of the system.

A systems assessment might be related to evaluation of a specific instructional program and thus the charge would be to determine the present status relative only to a specific objective and related ob-jectives. We would refer to this as a "sub-system assessment."

Systems assessment does not refer to specification of process characteristics appropriate for a district, school, or classroom. A statement such as "this district needs a lower pupil-teacher ratio" or "a need of this district is to install team teaching" is not a systems assessment. The systems assessment must be related to the ultimate behavior of clients of one type or another (pupils, parents, community, etc.—all clients of the school). To put it simply, systems assessment must result in a statement of objectives in terms of outputs of the school.

The process in the systems assessment area of ascertaining the decision area, specifying and collecting information and reporting summary data, requires methodology and techniques different from that which might be employed, for example, in a typical experimental design. The data are concerned with the status of the system. The summary data might be comparative, historical, or other descriptive information.

PROGRAM PLANNING

Program planning, the second need area, is concerned with providing information which will enable the decision-maker to make planning decisions—to select among alternative processes in order to make a judgment as to which of them should be introduced into the system to fill most efficiently the critical needs previously determined. In an instance where we are proceeding through severe need areas in sequential fashion, the following might occur. After the decision-maker receives the systems assessment evaluation, he might make a decision as to the appropriate means of fulfilling that need. Alternatively, he might designate several possibilities and ask the evaluator to provide information on the possible impact of each. Hence, in program planning, the evaluator provides the data for an evaluation of a program prior to its inception. The task of the evaluator is to anticipate the attainment of goals and to assess the potential relative effectiveness of different courses of action.

It is quite obvious that the collection and analysis of data of the type required for this evaluation need area will be quite different from collection and analysis problems for other areas. The techniques may require both internal and external evaluation procedures. (See Lumsdaine, 1965.)

By way of internal evaluation, programs may be examined to determine the extent to which their reproducible segments purport to achieve the objectives of the program being evaluated. Technical features of style or construction, practicality and cost are other means of providing internal evaluation. To date, the evaluations of products by EPIE . . . have been primarily based upon internal evaluations.

External evaluations of programs yet to be implemented might take the form of examining research data on the results of implementation in similar or near-similar situations. Or external evaluations might attempt to utilize some of the various educational planning techniques to obtain data. Computer simulations might be developed; Delphi analysis might provide insights into the potential outcomes of a program; gaming and various other systems analytic approaches might also provide external evaluation data.

PROGRAM IMPLEMENTATION

After the decision-maker has selected the program to be implemented, an evaluation of program implementation determines the extent to which the implemented program meets the description formulated in the program planning decision. In the case of an existing program where no known changes have been implemented, the evaluation task at this stage is to determine the degree to which planning descriptions of the program coincide with the implemented program and the extent to which assumed descriptions of inputs to the system (students) correspond with observed inputs.

There have been numerous examples in the educational literature of conflicting results relative to the impact of a specific instructional treatment. We would maintain that in large part this is attributable to the lack of specificity of the precise nature of the instructional treatment that was employed. Team teaching is *not* always team teaching. More precisely, team teaching in Santa Rosa might be quite different from team teaching in Boston or from team teaching in Palo Alto, California. The precise definition of the parameters defined as team teaching in a given situation would help to insure an understanding of what is being evaluated and whether what is being evaluated is what the investigator thought the program was.

PROGRAM IMPROVEMENT

The evaluator can play an important role in program improvement, the fourth need area, by providing as much information as possible about the relative success of the parts of the program. In order to perform program improvement evaluation, it is necessary to recognize the basically interventionist role that the evaluator has been asked to take.

The key point in the understanding of the role of the evaluator in performing evaluations in this need area is that he is first and foremost an interventionist attempting to provide data which will lead to the immediate modification and, hopefully, improvement of the program. As the evaluator identifies problems and collects and analyzes related information, data are presented immediately to the decision-maker so that changes may be executed within the system to improve the operation of the program. Information might include data on the extent to which the program appears to be achieving the prescribed objectives, as measured by regular tests; information also might be presented which relates to the impact of the program on other processes or programs.

This need area has often been overlooked or ignored by the traditional evaluator who has attempted to impose the antiseptic sterility of the laboratory on the real world. Such an approach may make for a fine experiment, but it does little to improve a program which is often not in its final form.

PROGRAM CERTIFICATION

In the fifth evaluation need area, program certification, the role of the evaluator is to provide the decision-maker with information that will enable him to make decisions about the program as a whole and its potential generalizability to other situations. The evaluator might attempt to provide information which will enable the decision-maker to determine whether the program should be eliminated, modified, retained, or introduced more widely.

The kind of information collected for program certification decisions is in large part dependent upon who is the intended decision-maker. It is obvious that different information will be required if the potential decision-maker is the teacher, the principal, or a funding agency. Evaluations in this area will be concerned with examining the extent to which the objectives have been achieved, as well as with the impact on the outcomes of other programs.

In program certification evaluations, there is a requirement for valid and reliable data which would generally require that the evaluator attempt to apply as rigid a set of controls as possible. The evaluator might use pre- and post-test designs and employ sophisticated methods for analyzing the data. Intervention should be avoided in evaluations in this need area. Here the traditional evaluator is "at home."

In considering the situations in which evaluation might take place in various need areas, we have found it helpful to differentiate between the evaluation of educational systems and the evaluation of instructional programs. In terms of the conceptual framework that has been presented, one can view the evaluation of educational systems as involving the first two need areas and the evaluation of instructional programs as largely involving the last three.

In evaluating any educational system it is necessary to determine the educational needs in terms of the most appropriate objectives for the given system and to devise a procedure for providing regular information on the progress of the system relative to these dimensions. This procedure is the evaluative device for decision-making about the assessment of system needs (Systems Assessment). When decisions have been made about the objectives of the system which are inadequately met, the decision-maker might then be concerned with the selection of programs to meet these objectives. Evaluation information might be sought relative to the possible impact of various courses of action or programs (Program Planning).

Thus, if one followed through on the full cycle of evaluation in an educational system, including the allowance of feedback and recycling, the process might be depicted as in Figure 1.

The evaluation of an instructional program assumes the prior assessment of the program or of a larger system, a decision about objectives to be attended to, and the selection of programs considered to be appropriate for meeting these objectives. That is, the evaluation of an instructional program ordinarily begins after the decisions related to need areas 1 and 2 of the evaluation have been made. In evaluating an instructional program, the objectives to be achieved and the program which it is assumed will be most successful in achieving these objectives are generally considered as "given." Thus, the evaluation of an instructional program focuses primarily on the last three need areas of evaluation.

Where the evaluation task commences with the evaluation of the instructional program, we envisage the necessity for a sub-system

FIGURE 1

EVALUATING EDUCATIONAL SYSTEMS

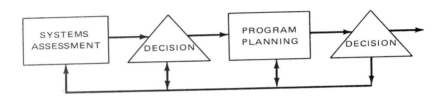

assessment dealing with the area of concern of the selected instructional program. Thus, it is seen that the evaluation need areas are not necessarily sequential with the steps easily defined. In some instances, moreover, the data collection, analysis, and reporting appropriate to a decision might be so easy to obtain or so inextricably tied to the making of the decision that the decision-maker and his staff would perform the evaluation themselves. In some instances, the project begins for the evaluator after a number of decisions have already been made. Thus, the evaluator might have to attend to only selected evaluation need areas.

For the sake of convenience, in Figure 2 we have depicted a way in which the evaluation need areas might be interrelated in the evaluation of instructional programs.

A final explanatory note is in order concerning the role of the evaluator in this evaluation model. It might be possible to draw the conclusion that the evaluator does all things—that he is curriculum designer, administrator, program implementor, test officer, budget manager, etc. This is a misconception. We have partially dispelled this notion by commenting earlier that what has been described in this section is the full range of the evaluation cycle. We are describing functions to be performed rather than a role in each evaluation need area for a specific individual.

Evaluation Theory Development
Through Programmatic Research

The conception of evaluation which has just been formulated has influenced the Center's organizational structure and current research

FIGURE 2

EVALUATING INSTRUCTIONAL PROGRAMS

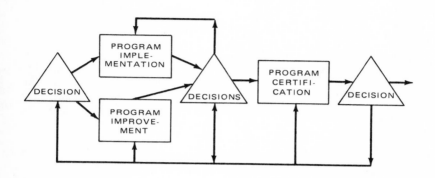

activities. The Center's theory building activities are contained within two programs: a program on Evaluation of Instructional Programs and a program on Evaluation of Educational Systems. The Center is supporting one major project in the first program and two in the second.

Examination of the two major programs of the Center shows that they do not represent discrete entities separate and distinct from each other. Rather, they represent ends of a continuum. On one end of the continuum, where the object being evaluated is relatively discrete and definable in terms of the objectives of the system, and where the instructional treatment is rather easily described, the nature of the evaluation is quite different from that which would be appropriate for a large educational system. In the first case, the most important requirement for evaluation is a clear, precise specification of the objectives of the system and the means of measuring these objectives.

.   .   .

On the other end of the continuum are broad-scale educational systems in which outcomes are not clearly definable and in which the process of specifying objectives is an iterative one. The complexities of this kind of system are often so great that to speak of objectives in any concrete sense is to mask the real outputs of the system. The outcomes and consequences of all of the many interactions within the system are great and are often at variance with the objectives of the system.

While the most important element in evaluation at the micro-level is the specification of objectives, at the macro-level of large educational systems the social and organizational context is of prime significance, having tremendous impact on the outcomes of the system. Therefore, it is necessary in an evaluation to consider the input, contextual and criterion variables and their interactions.

Other difficulties in the evaluation of complex systems involve the accurate specification of the instructional treatment. That is, the instructional treatment is often neither clear and easily identifiable nor easily reproducible. It is instead a vast array of complex, interactive elements loosely called instruction.

It is apparent that this kind of evaluation requires not simply a specification of the objectives but rather a total examination of a system, with all of the implications that derive from systems theory. The implications of the data requirements for the evaluation of complex educational systems are readily apparent. In addition to specifying the objectives of the system and the degree to which the system has met these objectives, evaluation must provide data on other outcomes of the system (unanticipated outcomes or consequences), on the inputs of the system, on accurate descriptions of the alternative processes used within the system, and on the input-output relationships—especially as they relate to the factors which can be considered malleable by the decision-maker. . . .

References

HEMPHILL, J. K. The relationships between research and evaluation studies. In R. W. Tyler (Ed.), *Educational evaluation: New roles, new means; the sixty-eighth yearbook of the National Society for the Study of Education, part II*. Chicago: NSSE, 1969. Pp. 189–220.

LUMSDAINE, A. A. Assessing the effectiveness of instructional programs. In R. Glaser (Ed.), *Teaching machines and programmed learning, vol. II: Data and directions*. Washington, D.C.: National Education Association, 1965. Pp. 267–320.

PROVUS, M. Evaluation of ongoing programs in the public school system. In R. W. Tyler (Ed.), *Educational evaluation: New roles, new means; the sixty-eighth yearbook of the National Society for the Study of Education, part II*. Chicago: NSSE, 1969. Pp. 242–283.

SKAGER, R. W. *Evaluation and the improvement of compensatory educational programs.* CSE Report No. 54. Los Angeles: Center for the Study of Evaluation, 1969.

STUFFLEBEAM, D. L. *Evaluation as enlightenment for decision-making.* Columbus: Evaluation Center, Ohio State University, 1969.

J. S. WHOLEY, H. G. DUFFY
J. S. FUKUMOTO, J. W. SCANLON
M. A. BERLIN, W. C. COPELAND
J. G. ZELINSKY

Proper Organizational Relationships

Assignment of Responsibility

Differences in the responsibilities of policy makers and program managers imply a natural division of evaluation responsibilities. This division of responsibility, though the division will be blurred in practice, is useful both for removing bureaucratic obstacles to evaluation and for improving the objectivity of evaluation studies.

Program managers may view evaluation as a threat to their own positions, or at least as a process from which they have more to lose than gain. One possible finding of an evaluation study, for example, is that they are not performing their jobs competently, or that the principles underlying a program have proven faulty. In either case, administrators may prefer to take their chances on

Joseph S. Wholey, *et al.,* "Federal Evaluation Policy: An Overview," A Summary of the Urban Institute Study of Social Program Evaluation by Federal Agencies, September 1969, pp. 22–27. Reprinted by permission.
The authors distinguished four types of evaluation: (1) *program impact evaluation* is assessment of the overall effectiveness of a national program in meeting its objectives, or assessment of the relative effectiveness of two or more programs in meeting common objectives; (2) *program strategy evaluation* is assessment of the relative effectiveness of different techniques used in a national program; (3) *project evaluation* is assessment of the effectiveness of an individual project in achieving its stated objectives; (4) *project rating* is assessment of the relative effectiveness of different local projects in achieving program objectives. *Monitoring,* unlike evaluation, focuses on program inputs and assesses the managerial and operational efficiency of programs.

ignorance about the worth of their programs—rather than risking the judgment of an objective evaluation, which might show the program to be ineffective in whole or in part. (There also may be legitimate fears that evaluation might give misinformation or unbalanced views of the worth of programs.)

RECOMMENDATIONS

- It makes obvious sense to place the responsibility for evaluation *at a level appropriate to the decisions which the evaluation is to assist.* No program manager should be expected to evaluate the worth of his program, for example, nor should a member of the manager's staff be put in the position of having to criticize his boss.

Specifically, we offer these recommendations for various levels of government:

a. *White House/Bureau of the Budget.* The Urban Affairs Council and the Bureau of the Budget should be responsible for identifying major questions to be answered through evaluation studies. (For example: What are the financial and non-financial costs and benefits of the various federally funded education programs? What strategies and techniques are most useful for bringing various disadvantaged groups into productive employment? What is the value of the Model Cities program as a device for organizing the planning for, and delivery of, services for an urban area?)

The Bureau of the Budget should be responsible for requiring development of evaluation plans and for using the results of evaluation studies in the budget-making process.

The Bureau of the Budget should be responsible for initiating evaluations that cross agency lines to compare the effectiveness of similar or related programs (e.g., the OEO–DOL evaluation of five manpower programs, or the BOB-VA-DOL-HEW-DOD evaluation of programs for disadvantaged returning veterans).

b. *Agencies.* Responsibility for national program impact evaluation should rest with the agency head (Office of the Secretary or equivalent), rather than with the program manager.[1] Responsibility for eval-

[1] Congress is giving limited but increasing evaluation responsibilities to the General Accounting Office. GAO has in the past two years moved from major emphasis on program/project monitoring to accomplishment of a limited number of national program impact evaluations. GAO intends to perform program strategy evaluation as well.

uating projects and alternative strategies *within* a program should rest with the operating bureau chiefs and program managers.

Agency heads should establish a central evaluation office *responsible to the agency head,* with the following functions: (1) conduct national program impact evaluations; (2) help program managers define program objectives in measurable terms; (3) help program managers (or their evaluators) develop project rating systems and design high-priority program strategy evaluations; (4) approve the design of all evaluation studies financed by the agency; and (5) disseminate the results of significant evaluation studies to program managers and policy makers (including legislative and budget analysts).

c. *Operating Bureaus/Program Managers.* Operating bureau chiefs and program managers should assess the effectiveness of projects within their programs through project rating and project monitoring and, when feasible, should undertake comparative evaluations of the relative effectiveness of different strategies and techniques within their programs.

In addition, managers of operating programs should be given responsibility for introducing planned variations and possibly even controlled experiments within a portion of their operating program or in a related experimental demonstration program. They should be given the authority and responsibility to function as experimenters, when experimentation is feasible, altering components of projects (e.g., eligibility, duration of services, intensity of services, per capita investment) as a physical scientist alters temperature, chemical concentrations, etc., to assess the effects. For those Federal operating programs in which decisions on project operation are very decentralized (e.g., Title I of the Elementary and Secondary Education Act), the relative value of alternative strategies and techniques can often be best assessed through systematic introduction of major variations into a small portion of the program or into a related demonstration program, with comparable evaluation of the relative effectiveness of these strategies and techniques. It will often be reasonable to allocate 5 to 10% of program funds to such experimental demonstration projects and to field experiments. (The New Jersey negative income tax experiment and the major variations introduced into the Follow Through program are examples of the approach suggested.)

State and Local Relationships

The evaluation of Federal social programs is complicated by the fact that most are administered by State and local governments. A long-standing tradition of local autonomy and the lack of precedents for Federal monitoring of local efforts (e.g., in State grant-in-aid programs and in education programs) often leads to reluctance on the part of some Federal managers to insist on evaluation.

Administrators in the Office of Education's Division of Vocational Education, for example, argue that since their programs are implemented at the local level, they should be evaluated there—even though, they admit, local resources for evaluation are minimal. Owing partly to this ambivalence, the division has no formal system for evaluating vocational education programs.

RECOMMENDATION

- Federal agencies should examine each of their programs to determine what types of evaluation (program impact evaluation, program strategy evaluation, project rating, and monitoring) are appropriate at the Federal level. Whenever Federal funds are being expended, the Federal government should retain some evaluation role to discharge its duty to administer public funds efficiently.

For programs like education, in which State and local governments contribute the major share of support and Federal programs tend to be grant-in-aid programs to States, Federal agencies should place most emphasis on program strategy evaluation (perhaps in conjunction with field experiments or experimental demonstration programs) and on development and demonstration of project rating systems for use at State and local levels. For such programs, Federal agencies should consider the following approaches:

Programs administered by States: cooperative arrangements among the States should be encouraged to test common approaches to evaluation of similar programs, so that an evaluation conducted in California will supplement the results of a study conducted in New York, and vice versa. To foster such cooperation, the Federal government should consider making grants for evaluation to *groups* of States.

Programs administered by local governments: local communities should be encouraged to discharge Federal project evaluation requirements by cooperative evaluations based on the collection and analysis of comparable data. (As we indicate [earlier] allowing communities complete freedom in designing and conducting their own evaluations will result in large numbers of small, unrelated studies that offer policy makers cloudy insights at great cost.)

Groups of large and medium-size cities with similar problems should further be encouraged to develop evaluation systems that assess the effectiveness of local programs, such as their school programs, through collection and analysis of comparable data. (The school systems or the welfare programs of many cities, for example, offer a population representative, for many purposes, of the entire nation's urban students and welfare recipients. Each provides a kind of universe-in-miniature; several cities working together could make the kinds of comparisons that are the essence of evaluation.) To demonstrate *local evaluation* of local programs, the Federal government should supply funds and technical assistance.

finished curriculum, refined by use of the evaluation process in its first role, represents a sufficiently significant advance on the available alternatives to justify the expense of adoption by a school system.

One of the reasons for the tolerance or indeed encouragement of the confusion between roles and goals is the well-meaning attempt to allay the anxiety on the part of teachers that the word "evaluation" precipitates. By stressing the constructive part evaluation may play in nonthreatening activities (roles) we slur over the fact that its goals always include the estimation of merit, worth, value, etc., which all too clearly contribute in another role to decisions about promotion and rejection of personnel and courses. But we cannot afford to tackle anxiety about evaluation by ignoring its importance and confusing its presentation; the loss in efficiency is too great. Business firms can't keep executives or factories when they know they are not doing good work and a society shouldn't have to retain textbooks, courses, teachers, and superintendents that do a poor job when a good performance is possible. The appropriate way to handle anxiety of this kind is by finding tasks for which a better prognosis is possible for the individuals whose positions or prestige are threatened. Failure to evaluate pupils' performance leads to the gross inefficiencies of the age-graded classroom or the "ungraded" reports on pupils, and failure to evaluate teachers' performances leads to the correlative inefficiency of incompetent instruction and the substitution of personality for performance. A little toughening of the moral fiber may be required if we are not to shirk the social responsibilities of the educational branch of our culture. Thus, it may even be true that "the greatest service evaluation can perform is to identify aspects of the course where revision is desirable" (Cronbach,[1] p. 236), though it is not clear how one would establish this, but it is certainly also true that there are other extremely important evaluation services which must be done for almost any given curriculum project or other educational innovation. And there are many contexts in which calling in an evaluator to perform a final evaluation of the project or person is an act of proper recognition of responsibility to the person, product, or taxpayers. It therefore seems a little excessive to refer to this as simply "a menial role," as Cronbach does. It is obviously a great service if this kind of terminal, overall, or "outcome" evaluation can demonstrate that a very expensive textbook (etc.) is not significantly better than the competition, or that it is enormously better than any competitor. In more general terms it may be possible to demonstrate that a certain type of approach to (for example) mathematics is not yielding significantly better pupil performance on any dimension that mathematicians or vocational users are prepared to regard as important. This would certainly save a great deal of expenditure of time and money and constitute a valuable contribution to educational development, as would the converse, favorable, result. Thus there seems to be a number of qualifications that would have to be made before one could accept a statement asserting the greater importance of formative evaluation by comparison with summative. ("Evaluation, used to improve the course while it is still fluid, contributes more to improvement of education than evaluation used to appraise a product already placed on the market."—Cronbach,[1] p. 236) Fortunately we do not have to make this choice. Educational projects, particularly curricular ones, clearly must attempt to make best use of evaluation in both these roles. As a matter of terminology, I think that novel terms are worthwhile here, to avoid inappropriate connotations, and I propose to use the terms "formative" and "summative" to qualify evaluation in these roles.

Now any curriculum builder is almost automatically engaged in formative evaluation, except on a very strict interpretation of "evaluation." He is presumably doing what he is doing because he judges that the material being presented in the existing curriculum is unsatisfactory. So, as he proceeds to construct the new material, he is constantly evaluating his own material as better than that which is already current. Unless entirely ignorant of one's shortcomings as a judge of one's own work, he is also presumably engaged in field-testing the work while it is being developed, and in so doing he gets feedback on the basis of which he again produces revisions; this is of course formative evaluation. If the field-testing is elaborate, it may amount to summative evaluation of *the early forms* of the new curriculum. He is usually involved with colleagues, e.g. the classroom teacher or peers, who comment on the material as they see it—again, this is evaluation, and it produces changes which are allegedly for the better.

If a recommendation for formative evaluation has any content at all, it presumably amounts to the suggestion that a *professional* evaluator should be added to the curriculum construction project. There certainly can be advantages in this, though it is equally clear from practical experience that there can be disadvantages. But this question is clearly not the same as the question whether to have summative evaluation. . . .

Evaluation Versus Estimation of Goal Achievement

One of the reactions to the threat of evaluation, or perhaps to the use of over-crude evaluative procedures, was the extreme relativization of evaluation research. The slogan became: How well does the course achieve its goals? instead of How good is the course? but it is correlate with pay-off evaluations. Since these correlations are largely a priori in our present state of knowledge, they argue, the intrinsic approach is too much an armchair affair. The intrinsic evaluator is likely to counter by talking about important values that do not show up in the outcome study to which the pay-off man restricts himself, due to the deficiencies of present test instruments and scoring procedures: he is likely to exemplify this claim by reference to qualities of a curriculum such as elegance, modernity, structure, integrity, readiness considerations, etc., which can best be judged by looking at the materials directly.

The possibility obviously emerges that an evaluation involving some weighting of intrinsic criteria and some of pay-off criteria might be a worthwhile compromise. There are certain kinds of evaluation situations where this will be so, but before any assessment of the correct relative weighting is possible it is necessary to look a little further into the nature of the two pure alternatives.

It was maintained in the preceding section that evaluation in terms of goal achievement is typically a very poor substitute for good summative evaluation, since it merely relativizes the problem. If we are going to evaluate in a way that brings in goals at all, then we shall typically have some obligation to evaluate the goals. The trouble with "intrinsic" evaluation is that it brings in what might be called intermediate goals or criteria, and hence automatically raises the question of the value of these criteria, presumably by reference to the pay-off criteria. One of the charms of the pay-off type of evaluation is the lack of charm, indeed the messiness, of a thorough intrinsic evaluation.

A major difficulty with evaluation involving intermediate goals, which is the key feature of an "intrinsic" approach, lies in the *formulation* of the goals. In the first place the verbally espoused goals of a curriculum-maker are often not the implicit goals of his curriculum. Moreover, it is not always the case that this kind of error should be corrected in favor of the espoused goals by revising the curriculum or in favor of the implicit goals by revising the espoused goals. How do we decide which should receive precedence? Even if we were able to decide this, there is the perennial headache of translating the description of the goals that we get from the curriculum-maker or the curriculum-analyst into testable terms. Many a slip occurs between that lip and the cup.

In addition to this, there is the problem already mentioned, that putting pressure on a writer to formulate his goals, to keep to them, and to express them in testable terms may enormously alter his product in ways that are certainly not always desirable. Perhaps the best way of handling this third problem is to give prospective curriculum-builders an intensive short course in evaluation techniques and problems prior to their commencing work. Such a course would

be topic-neutral, and would thereby avoid the problems of criticism
of one's own "baby." Interaction with a professional evaluator can
then be postponed substantially and should also be less anxiety-
provoking. Short courses of the kind mentioned should surely be
available for subsidized attendance every summer at one or two
centers in the country. Ignoring any further consideration of the
problem of in-group harmony, and this proposal for improving
formative evaluation, we can turn to the practical problem of
evaluation. . . .

The Possibility
of Pure Pay-Off Evaluation

The operationalist in this area, the "pay-off" evaluator, watches the
developing intricacies of the above kind of experimental design with
scorn, for he believes that the whole idea of bringing in goal- or con-
tent-assessment is not only an irrelevant but also an extremely unreliable procedure for doing the job of course evaluation. In his view
it isn't very important to examine what a teacher says he is doing,
or what the students say he is doing (or they are learning), or even
what the teacher says in class and the students read in the texts; the
only important datum is what the student says (does, believes, etc.)
at the end of the course that he wouldn't have said at the beginning
(or, to be more precise, would not have said at the end if he had
not taken this course). In short, says the hard-headed one, let's just
see what the course does, and let's not bother with the question of
whether it had good intentions.

But the operationalist has difficulties of his own. He cannot
avoid the construct validity issue entirely, that is, he cannot avoid
the enormous difficulties involved in correctly describing *at a useful
level of generality* what the student has learned. It is easy enough
to give the exact results of the testing in terms of the percentage
of the students who gave certain answers to each specific question;
but what we need to know is whether we can say, in the light of
their answers, that they have a *better* understanding of the elements
of astronomy, or the chemical-bond approach to chemistry, or the
ecological approach to biology. And it is a long way from data about
answers to specific questions, to that kind of conclusion. It is not
necessary for the route to lie through a discussion of abstract, intermediate goals—the operationalist is quite right about this. But *if* it
does not lie through a discussion of goals, then we shall not have
available the data that we need (a) to distinguish between importantly
different explanations of success or failure, (b) to give reasons for

striking improvements on the same criteria (with some exceptions, of which the most notable is the performance of students in studies of good programmed texts). Initially, one's tendency is to feel that the mountain has labored and brought forth a mouse—and that it is a positive mouse and not a negative one entirely depends upon the evaluation of the criteria, i.e., (mainly) tests used. A legitimate reaction is to look very seriously into the question of whether one should not weight the judged merit of content and goals by subject-matter experts a great deal more heavily than small differences in level of performance on unassessed criteria. If we do this, then relatively minor improvements in performance, on the right goals, become very valuable, and in these terms the new curriculum looks considerably better. Whether this alteration of weights can really be justified is a matter that needs very serious investigation; it requires a rather careful analysis of the real importance to the understanding and use of contemporary physics, as it is seen by, e.g., physicists, of the missing elements in the old curriculum. It is all too tempting to feel that the reweighting must be correct because one is so thoroughly convinced that the new course is better.

Another legitimate reaction is to wonder whether the examinations are really doing a good job testing the depth of understanding of the people trained on the new curriculum. Here the use of the oversize question pool becomes extremely important. Cronbach speaks of a 700-item pool (without flinching!) and this is surely the order of magnitude that makes sense in terms of a serious evaluation of a one- or two-year curriculum. Again, it is going to be tempting to put items into the pool that reflect mere differences of terminology in the new course, for example. Of course if the pool consists mainly of questions of that kind, the new-curriculum students will do much better. But their superiority will be almost entirely illusory. Cronbach warns us against this risk of course-dependent terminology, although he goes too far in segregating understanding from terminology (this point is taken up below). So here, too, we must be certain to use external evaluators in the construction or assessment of the question pool.

Illegitimate reactions run from the charming suggestion that such results simply demonstrate the weaknesses of evaluation techniques, to a more interesting suggestion implicit in Cronbach's paper. He says:

> Since group comparisons give equivocal results, I believe that a formal study should be designed primarily to determine the post-course performance of a well-described group, with respect to many important objectives and side-effects.*

* This and the succeeding quotation are from p. 238.

Cronbach is apparently about to suggest a way in which we can avoid comparison, not with goals or objectives, but with another group, supposedly matched on relevant variables. What is this non-comparative alternative procedure for evaluation? He continues:

> Ours is a problem like that of the engineer examining a new automobile. He can set himself the task of defining its performance characteristics and its dependability. It would be merely distracting to put his question in the form: 'Is this car better or worse than the competing brand?'

It is perfectly true that the automobile engineer *might* only just be interested in the question of the performance and dependability of the new automobile. But no automobile engineer ever has had this pure interest, and no automobile engineer ever will have it. Objectives do not become "important" except in a context of practical choice. Unrealistic objectives, for example, are not important. The very measures of the performance and dependability of an automobile and our interest in them spring *entirely* from knowledge of what has and has not so far proved possible, or possible within a certain price-class, or possible with certain interior space, or with a certain overall weight, etc. The use of calibrated instruments is not an alternative to, but only a mediated way of, doing comparative studies. The same applies in the field of curriculum development. We already have curricula aimed at almost every subject known to man, and there isn't any real interest in producing curricula for curricula's sake; to the extent that there is, there isn't any interest in evaluating them. We are interested in curricula because they may prove to be better than what we now have, in some important way. We may assign someone the task of rating a curriculum on certain variables, without asking them simultaneously to look up the performance of other curricula on these variables. But when we come to *evaluate* the curriculum, as opposed to merely describing its performance, then we inevitably confront the question of its superiority or inferiority to the competition. To say it's a "valuable contribution," a "desirable" or "useful" course, even to say—in the usual context—that it's very good, is to imply relative merit. Indeed the very scales we use to measure its performance are often percentile scales or others with a built-in comparison.

There are even important reasons for putting the question in its comparative form immediately. Comparative evaluations are often very much easier than noncomparative evaluations, because we can often use tests which yield differences instead of having to find an absolute scale and then eventually compare the absolute scores. If we are discussing chess-teaching courses, for example, we might match two groups for background variables, and then let them play each other off in a round-robin tournament. Attempting to devise a measure of skill of an absolute kind would be a nightmare, but we might easily get consistent and significant differences from this kind of comparative evaluation. Cronbach is not making the "pure pay-off" mistake of thinking that one can avoid all reference to general goals; but he is proposing an approach which underestimates the implicit comparative element in any field of social engineering including automobile assessment and curriculum evaluation, just as the pay-off approach underestimates the implicit appeal to abstract intermediate qualities.

Cronbach continues in this paragraph with a line of thought about which there can be no disagreement at all; he points out that in any cases of comparisons between importantly different teaching instruments, no real understanding of the reason for a difference in performance is gained from the discovery that one of them *is* notably superior to the other: "No one knows which of the ingredients is responsible for the advantages." But understanding is not our *only* goal in evaluation. We are also interested in questions of support, encouragement, adoption, reward, refinement, etc. And these extremely important questions can be given a useful though in some cases not a complete answer by the mere discovery of superiority. It will be recalled that in an earlier section we argued that the pure pay-off position suffers by comparison wih the supporter of mediated evaluation in that his results will not include the data we need in order to locate sources of difficulty, etc. Here Cronbach is arguing that his noncomparative approach will be more likely to give us the data we need for future improvement. But this is not in any way an advantage of the noncomparative method as such. It is simply an advantage of methods in which more variables are examined in more detail. If we want to pin down the exact reasons for differences between programs, it is quite true that "small-scale, well-controlled studies can profitably be used to compare alternative versions of the same course" whereas the large-scale overall comparison will not be so valuable. But that in no way eliminates the need for comparative studies at some point in our evaluation procedures. In short, his argument is simply that in order to get *explanations,* one needs more control groups, and possibly more short-run studies, than one needs for summative *evaluation*. This is incontestible; but it does not show that for the purposes of overall evaluation we can or should avoid overall comparison.

One might put the point in terms of the following analogy: in the history of automobile engine design there have been a number of occasions when a designer has turned out an engine that was quite inexplicably superior to the competition—the Kettering GM V8, the

Coventry Climax and the Weslake Ford conversions are well-known examples. Perhaps thirty variables are significantly changed in the design of any new engine and for a long time after these had been in production nobody, including the designer, knew which of them had been mainly responsible for the improvement. But the decision to go into production, the decision to put the further research into the engine that led to finding out what made it great, indeed the beginning of a new era in engine design, required *only the comparative evaluation.* You set a great team to work and you hope they are going to strike gold; but then you assay the ore before you start the big capital expenditure involved in finding out the configuration of the lode and mining. This is the way we have to work in any field where there are too many variables and too little time.

Note

1. Lee Cronbach, "Evaluation for Course Improvement," *Teachers College Record,* vol. 64, no. 8, May 1963, reprinted in *New Curricula* (R. Heath, Ed., New York: Harper & Row, 1964, pp. 231–248). References in this paper are to the latter version.

DAVID K. COHEN

Politics and Research:
Evaluation of Social Action
Programs in Education

Although program evaluation is no novelty in education, its objects have changed radically. The national thrust against poverty and discrimination introduced a new phenomenon with which evaluators must deal: large-scale programs of social action in education. In addition to generating much activity in city schools, these programs produced considerable confusion whenever efforts were made to find out whether they were "working." The sources of the confusion are not hard to identify. Prior to 1964, the objects of evaluation in education consisted almost exclusively of small programs concerned with such things as curriculum development or teacher training: they generally occurred in a single school or school district, they sought to produce educational change on a limited scale, and they typically involved modest budgets and small research staffs.

This all began to change in the mid-1960's, when the federal government and some states established broad educational improvement programs. The programs—such as Project Headstart, Title I of the 1965 ESEA, and Project Follow-Through—differ from the traditional objects of educational evaluation in several important

David K. Cohen, "Politics and Research: Evaluation of Social Action Programs in Education," *Review of Educational Research,* vol. 40, no. 2 (1970), 213–238. Copyright by American Educational Research Association, Washington, D.C.

Research for this paper was supported by a grant from the Carnegie Corporation of New York to the Center for Educational Policy Research, Harvard University. Henry Dyer, Frederick Mosteller, and Martin Rein served as consultants to Dr. Cohen on the preparation of this chapter.

respects: (1) they are social action programs, and as such are not focused narrowly on teachers' in-service training or on a science curriculum, but aim broadly at improving education for the disadvantaged; (2) the new programs are directed not at a school or a school district, but at millions of children, in thousands of schools in hundreds of school jurisdictions in all the states; (3) they are not conceived and executed by a teacher, principal, a superintendent, or a researcher—they were created by the Congress and are administered by federal agencies far from the school districts which actually design and conduct the individual projects.

Simply to recite these differences is to suggest major new evaluation problems. How does one know when a program which reaches more than eight million children "works"? How does one even decide what "working" means in the context of such large-scale social action ventures? Difficulties also arise from efforts to apply the inherited stock-in-trade evaluation techniques to the new phenomena. If the programs seek broad social change, is it sensible to evaluate them mainly in terms of achievement? If they are national action programs, should evaluation be decentralized?

This chapter is an effort to explore these and other questions about evaluating large-scale social action programs. It has three major parts. First, I delineate the political character of the new programs, in order to distinguish them from the traditional objects of educational evaluation. Second, to illustrate this point and define the major obstacles to evaluation, I review some evaluations of the new programs. Finally, I suggest some elements of a strategy which might improve the evaluation of social action programs.

Politics and Evaluation

There is one sense in which any educational evaluation ought to be regarded as political. Evaluation is a mechanism with which the character of an educational enterprise can be explored and expressed. These enterprises are managed by people, and they take place in institutions; therefore, any judgment on their nature or results has at least a potential political impact—it can contribute to changing power relationships. This is true whether the evaluation concerns a small curriculum reform program in a rural school (if the program is judged ineffective the director might lose influence or be demoted), or a teacher training program in a university (if it is judged a success its sponsors might get greater authority). Evaluation, as some recent commentators have pointed out, produces information which is at least potentially relevant to decision-making (Stufflebeam, 1967;

Guba, 1968). Decision-making, of course, is a euphemism for the allocation of resources—money, position, authority, etc. Thus, to the extent that information is an instrument, basis, or excuse for changing power relationships within or among institutions, evaluation is a political activity.

These political aspects of evaluation are not peculiar to social action programs. They do, however, assume more obvious importance as an educational program grows in size and number of jurisdictions covered: the bigger it is, the greater the likelihood for the overt appearance of political competition.

There is another sense in which evaluation is political, for some programs explicitly aim to redistribute resources or power; although this includes such things as school consolidation, social action programs are the best recent example. They were established by a political institution (the Congress) as part of an effort to change the operating priorities of state and local governments and thus to change not only the balance of power within American education but also the relative status of economic and racial groups within the society. One important feature of the new social action programs, then, is their political origin; another is their embodiment of social and political priorities which reach beyond the schools; a third is that their success would have many far-reaching political consequences.

One political dimension of evaluation is universal, for it involves the uses of information in changing power relationships; the other is peculiar only to those programs in which education is used to rearrange the body politic. Although one can never ignore the former dimension, *its salience in any given situation is directly proportional to the overt political stakes involved;* they are small in curriculum reform in a suburban high school, somewhat larger in a state-wide effort to consolidate schools, and very great in the case of national efforts to eliminate poverty. The power at stake in the first effort is small, and its importance slight. In the social action programs, however, the political importance of information is raised to a high level by the broader political character of the programs themselves.

This should be no surprise. Information assumes political importance within local school jurisdictions, but political competition *among* school jurisdictions usually involves higher stakes—and the social action programs promote competition among levels of government. These programs are almost always sponsored by state or federal government, with at least the implicit or partial intent of setting new priorities for state and local governments. In this situation evaluation becomes a political instrument, a means to determine whether the new priorities are being met and to assess the differential effectiveness of jurisdictions or schools in meeting them. As a result, evaluation is affected by the prior character of intergovernmental relations. State resistance to federal involvement, for example, pre-dates recent efforts to evaluate and assess federal social action pro-grams. The history colors the evaluation issue and the state response reflects the prior pattern of relations, for evaluation is correctly seen as an effort to assert federal priorities. Evaluation also can affect patterns of intergovernmental relations for it can help consolidate new authority for the superordinate government. In general, how-ever, evaluation seems to reflect the established pattern of inter-governmental relations.

Of course, not all the novelties in evaluating large-scale social action programs are political. There are serious logistical difficulties —the programs are bigger than anything ever evaluated in education, which poses unique problems—and there is no dearth of methodo-logical issues. These mostly center around making satisfactory com-parisons between "treated" subjects and some criterion presumed to measure an otherwise comparable condition of non-treatment. These are difficult in any program with multiple criterion variables, and when the program is spread over the entire country the problems multiply enormously. But difficult though these issues may be, they are in all formal respects the same, irrespective of the size, age, aim, or outcome of the program in question. The large-scale programs do not differ in some formal property of the control-comparison problem, but only in its size. The bigger and more complicated the programs, the bigger the associated methodological headaches. What distinguishes the new programs are not the formal problems of knowing their effects, but the character of their aims and their or-ganization. These are essentially political.

The politics of social action programs produce two sorts of evaluation problem. Some are conceptual—the programs' nature and aims have not been well understood or adequately expressed in eval-uation design. Others are practical—the interested parties do not agree on the ordering of priorities which the programs embody. As a result of the first, evaluation is misconceived; as a result of the second, evaluation becomes a focus for expressing conflicting political interests.

Conceptual Problems

The central conceptual difficulty can be simply summarized: while the new programs seek to bring about political and social change, evaluators generally approach them as though they were standard efforts to produce educational change. This results in no small part from ambiguity of the programs—since they are political endeavors in education, the program content and much of the surrounding rhetoric is educational. It also occurs because evaluation researchers identify professionally and intellectually with their disciplines of origin (mostly education and psychology), and thus would rather not study politics. They prefer education and psychology; since that is what they know, what their colleagues understand, and—if done well—what will bring them distinction and prestige (Dentler, 1969).

But whatever the sources of the incongruence, it produces inappropriate evaluation. The aims and character of the programs are misconceived, and as a result evaluation design and execution are of limited value. Title I of ESEA (U.S. Congress, 1965a) is a good example with which to begin.

In the four years ESEA has been in existence, the federal government completed several special evaluation studies, undertaken either by the Office of the Secretary of HEW or the Office of Education.[1] They concentrated mainly on one question—has the program improved achievement over what otherwise might have been expected? The answer in each case was almost entirely negative, and not surprisingly, this led many to conclude that the Title I program was not "working." This, in turn, raised or supported doubts about the efficacy of the legislation or the utility of compensatory education. Yet such inferences are sensible only if two crucial assumptions are accepted:

(a) children's achievement test scores are a sufficient criterion of the program's aims—the consequences intended by the government—to stand as an adequate summary measure of its success; and

(b) the Title I program is sufficiently coherent and unified to warrant the application of *any* summary criterion of success, be it achievement or something else.

Both assumptions merit inspection.

It does not seem unreasonable to assume that improving the achievement of disadvantaged children is a crucial aim of the Title I program. Much of the program's rhetoric suggests that it seeks to reduce the high probability of school failure associated with poverty. Many educators and laymen regard achievement test scores as a suitable measure of school success, on the theory that children with higher

---

[1] The National evaluations of Title I are little more than annual reports based on the state evaluation reports, which are little more than compilations of LEA reports. This is not to say that the reports are useless—but simply that they are not evaluations. The Office of the HEW Secretary was responsible for a study by Tempo, 1968. Also, see Piccariello, undated.

achievement will have higher grades, happier teachers, more positive attitudes toward school, and therefore a better chance of remaining and succeeding.

There are, however, two difficulties with this view. One is that achievement scores are not an adequate summary of the legislation's diverse aims. The other is that hardly anyone cares about the test scores themselves—they are regarded as a suitable measure of program success only because they are believed to stand for other things.

The second point can easily be illustrated. Aside from a few intellectuals who think that schooling is a good thing in itself, people think test scores are important because they are thought to signify more knowledge, which will lead to more years in school, better job opportunities, more money, and more of the ensuing social and economic status Americans seem to enjoy. Poor people, they reason, have little money, undesirable jobs (if any) and, by definition, the lowest social and economic status presently available. The poor also have less education than most of their countrymen. On the popular assumptions just described, it is easy to argue that "poverty can be eliminated" by increasing the efficiency of education for the poor.

Although much abbreviated, this chain of reasoning is not a bad statement of the reasons why improved achievement is an aim of Title I. Improved schooling was a major anti-poverty strategy, and higher school achievement simply a proxy for one of the program's main aims—improving adults' social and economic status. The principal problem this raises for evaluation is that the criterion of program effectiveness is actually only a surrogate for the true criterion. This would pose no difficulty if reliable estimates of the causal relationship between schoolchildren's achievement and their later social and economic status existed. Unfortunately, no information of this sort seems to be available. There is one major study relating years of school completed and occupational status; it shows that once inherited status is controlled, years of school completed are moderately related to adult occupational status (Blau and Duncan, 1968). Other studies reveal no direct relationship between intelligence and occupational status, but they do show that the education-occupation relationship is much weaker for Negroes than whites (Duncan, 1968). The first of these findings should not encourage advocates of improved achievement, and the second is hardly encouraging to those who perceive blacks as a major target group for anti-poverty programs.

There are studies which show that more intelligent people stay in school longer (Duncan, 1968), but it is hardly clear a priori that raising achievement for disadvantaged children will keep them in school, nor is it self-evident that keeping poor children in school longer will get them better jobs.[2] It is, for example, not difficult to imagine that the more intelligent children who stay in school longer do so because they also have learned different behavior patterns, which include greater tolerance for delayed gratification, more docility, less overt aggression, and greater persistence. Several compensatory programs are premised on these notions, rather than the achievement-production idea. Without any direct evidence on the consequence of either approach, however, it is difficult to find a rational basis for choice.

This does not mean that compensatory education programs founded on either view are a mistake—absent any data, one could hardly take that position. It does suggest, however, that using achievement—or any other form of school behavior—as a proxy for the actual long-range purpose of compensatory education is probably ill-founded. The chief difficulty with this variety of agnosticism, of course, is that the only alternative is evaluation studies whose duration would make them of interest only to the next generation. What is more, they would be extremely expensive. The current proportion of program budgets devoted to evaluation indicates that the probability of undertaking such studies is nil.

Even if this scientific embarrassment were put aside, there is the other major difficulty with using achievement as an evaluation criterion. Schoolmen must be expected to assume that the greater application of their efforts will improve students' later lives, but there is no evidence that the Congress subscribed to that view by passing Title I of the 1965 ESEA. Although the title did contain an unprecedented mandate for program evaluation—and even specified success in school as a criterion—this is scant evidence that the sole program aim was school achievement. The mandate for evaluation—like many Congressional authorizations—lacked any enabling mechanism: responsibility for carrying out the evaluation was specifically delegated to the state and local education authorities who operated the programs. It was not hard to see, in 1965, that this was equivalent to abandoning much hope of useful program evaluation.

The main point, however, is that the purposes of the legislation were much more complex: most of them could be satisfied without any evidence about children's achievement. Certainly this was true for aid to parochial school students, and it most likely was also true for many of the poorer school districts: for them (as for many of the

---

[2] By "achievement," I mean measures of reading or general verbal ability; I do not include therein more specialized measures of achievement such as math, social studies, science, or driver education.

congressmen who voted for the act) more money was good in itself. Moreover, the Congress is typically of two minds on the matter of program evaluation in education—it subscribes to efficiency, but it does not believe in Federal control of the schools. National evaluations are regarded as a major step toward Federal control by many people, including some members of Congress.

Although the purposes of the Congress may be too complicated to be summarized in studies of test scores, they are not by that token mysterious. The relevant Committee hearings and debates suggest that the legislative intent included several elements other than those already mentioned.[3] One involved the rising political conflict over city schools in the early 1960's; many legislators felt that spreading money on troubled waters might bring peace. Another concerned an older effort to provide federal financial assistance for public education: the motives for this were mainly political and ideological, and were not intimately tied to achievement. A third involved the larger cities; although not poor when compared to the national average expenditure, they were increasingly hard-pressed to maintain educational services which were competitive with other districts in their areas as property values declined, population changed, and costs and taxes rose. Educators and other municipal officials were among the warmest friends of the new aid scheme, because it promised to relieve some of the pressure on their revenues.

Indeed, many purposes of the legislation—and the Congress's implicit attitude toward evaluation—can be summarized in the form which it gave to fund apportionment. Title I is a formula grant, in which the amount of money flowing to any educational agency is a function of how many poor children it has, not of how well it educates them. In a sense, Title I is the educational equivalent of a rivers and harbors bill. There is no provision for withdrawing funds for non-performance, nor is there much suggestion of such intent in the original committee hearings or floor debates. Given the formula grant system, neither the Federal funding agency or the states have much political room to maneuver, even if they have the results of superb evaluation in hand. Without the authority to manipulate funds, achievement evaluation results could only be used to coax and cajole localities: the one major implicit purpose of program evaluation—more rational resource allocation—is seriously weakened by the Title I formula grant system.

[3] A good general treatment is Bailey and Mosher, 1968. See also: U.S. Congress, 1965b; U.S. House Education and Labor Committee, 1965a and b; U.S. Senate Appropriations Committee, 1965; and U.S. Senate Labor and Public Welfare Committee, 1965.

It is, therefore, difficult to conclude that improving schools' production of poor children's achievement was the legislation's major purpose. The legislative intent embraced many other elements: improving educational services in school districts with many poor children, providing fiscal relief for the central cities and parochial schools, reducing discontent and conflict about race and poverty, and establishing the principal of federal responsibility for local school problems. The fact that these were embodied in a single piece of legislation contributed heavily to its passage,. but it also meant that the resulting program was not single-purpose or homogeneous. If any supposition is in order, it is precisely the opposite. Title I is typical of reform legislation in a large and diverse society with a federal political system: it reflected various interests, decentralized power, and for these reasons a variety of programatic and political priorities.

Additional References: Bateman, 1969; Campbell, 1969; Campbell and Stanley, 1966; Dyer, in press; Evans, 1969; Hyman and Wright, 1966; Marris and Rein, 1967; McDill, McDill and Spreche, 1969; Rivlin, 1969; Rivlin and Wholey, 1967; Rothenberg, 1969; Swartz, 1961; Weiss and Rein, 1969; Wholey, 1969 a and b; Williams and Evans, 1969.

Consequences for Evaluation

Misconceptions about program aims result in omissions in evaluations and in distortions of the relationship among various aspects of evaluation. The first problem is mainly confined to program delivery. For Title I, for example, there are several criteria of program success which appear never to have been scrutinized. One involves impact of Title I on the fiscal position of the parochial schools: as nearly as I can tell, this purpose of the Act has never been explored.[4] Another involves the impact of Title I upon the fiscal situation of the central cities and their position vis-à-vis adjacent districts. Although the redistributive intent of the title was clear, there is little evidence of much effort to find out whether it has had this effect. With the exception of one internal Office of Education paper— which showed that Title I had reduced the per pupil expenditure disparity between eleven central cities and their suburbs by about half—

---

[4] The most recent report of the National Advisory Council on the Education of Disadvantaged Children (1969) contains a brief section on this issue. It does not deal with program impact, but with private-parochial school relations.

this subject appears to have received no attention.[5] A third involves the quality of education in target as compared with non-target schools. Thus far no data have been collected which would permit an assessment of Title I's effectiveness in reducing intra-district school resource disparities, although this was one of the most patent purposes of the Act. There has been an extended effort, covering 465 school districts (Project 465) to gather information on resource delivery to Title I target schools. This might turn up interesting data on differences in Title I services among schools, districts, or regions, but comparison with schools which do not receive Title I aid is not provided. Since Title I seeks to provide better-than-equal education for the disadvantaged, measuring its impact upon resource disparities between Title I and non-Title I schools within districts would be crucial. This is recognized in the Office of Education regulations governing the Title, which provide that Title I funds must add to existing fiscal and resource equality between Title I and non-Title I schools.[6] Important as this purpose of the legislation is, only a few federal audits have been conducted; for the most part, states satisfy the federal requirements simply by passing on data provided by the local education agencies, most of which are so general they are useless.

Such things do not result simply from administrative lapses. Evidence on whether Title I provides better-than-equal schooling would permit a clear judgment on the extent to which Federal priorities were being met. But the legislation allocates money to jurisdictions on a strict formula, and it delegates the responsibility for monitoring performance to those same jurisdictions: this reflects both the decentralization of power in the national school system and the sense of the Congress that it should remain just so. An important source of inadequate program delivery studies is inadequate Federal power or will to impose its priorities on states and localities; the priorities are enunciated in the statute, but the responsibility for determining whether they are being met is left with the states and localities.

The distribution of power is not the sole source of such problems in evaluating program delivery; the sheer size and heterogeneity of the society, and the unfamiliarity of the problems are also important. Project Headstart is illustrative. This program was not initially established within the existing framework of education. It existed

---

[5] Jackson, P. B. (1969). Hartman (undated) concluded that the aims of Title I are so vague as to make the act little more than a general (i.e., non-categorical) vehicle for redistributing educational revenues.

[6] The requirement is found in U.S. Dept. of Health, Education, and Welfare (1968). There also is a special memorandum (Howe, 1968) covering this issue.

mostly outside the system of public schools; its clients were below the age of compulsory education, and its local operating agencies often were independent of the official school agencies. Since the program came into existence, several million dollars have been spent on evaluation, and not a little of it on studies of program delivery. Yet it is still impossible to obtain systematic information on this subject. Several annual national evaluations and U.S. Census studies of program delivery are unpublished. But even if these studies had all been long since committed to print, they would only allow comparisons within the Headstart program. They would provide no basis for comparing how the services delivered to children under this program compare with those available to more advantaged children. That is no easy question to answer, but it is hardly trivial: without an estimate of this program's efficacy in delivering services to children, its efficacy as an anti-poverty program could hardly be evaluated.

There have been some recent efforts to remedy the relative absence of information on Title I program delivery, through an extensive management information program under development in 21 states. Data are to be collected from a sample of schools which receive Federal aid under several programs; it is estimated that the universe of schools and districts from which the sample will be drawn includes roughly 90% of all public school students in those states. Extensive information on teachers, on district and school attributes, and funding will be collected from self-administered questionnaires. Principals and teachers will provide information on school and classroom characteristics and programs, including compensatory efforts. In elementary schools the teachers will provide information on student background, but in secondary schools these data may be taken from the students themselves. Some effort also will be made to measure the extent of individual student's exposure to programs. In addition, common testing (using the same instruments in all schools) is planned, beginning with grades four and eleven. If this ambitious effort becomes operational in anything approaching the time planned, in a few years extensive data will be available with which to assess program delivery for Title I.

In summary, then, an underlying purpose of social action programs is to deliver more resources to the poor, whether they are districts, schools, children, or states. It is therefore essential to know how much more and for whom. It is important both because citizens should know the extent to which official intentions have been realized, and because without much knowledge on that score, it is hard to decide what more should be done. Satisfying these evaluative needs implies measurement that is both historical (keyed to the target population before the program began) and comparative (keyed to the non-target population).[7]

Studies of program delivery also serve a building-block function with respect to evaluating program outcomes. Whatever criterion of program effect one might imagine, it could not intelligibly be evaluated in the absence of data which describe the character of the program. Improved health, for example, is a possible outcome of the health care components of Title I and Headstart: one could not usefully collect evidence on changes in students' health without evidence on the character and intensity of the care they received from the program. And if one were interested in the impact of health care on school performance, it would be necessary to add some measure of students' achievement, classroom behavior, or attitudes. In the case of achievement outcomes, of course, evaluators commonly try to associate information about the type and intensity of academic programs with students' scores on some later test.

Despite the logical simplicity of these relationships, it is not easy to find large-scale social action programs in which outcome evaluation is linked to appropriate program delivery data. Without any direct evidence on program delivery, the only "input" which can be evaluated is inclusion in a program. But an acquaintance with national social action ventures leads quickly to the conclusion that an important aspect of such endeavors is the "non-treatment project." There is no reason to believe that mere inclusion necessarily leads to change either in the substance of education or in the level of resources. This phenomenon takes many forms: it may consist of teachers or

---

[7] Not all the purposes of social action programs are so neat or abstract, nor can they all be evaluated by counting dollars, teachers, or special programs. One of the aims of large-scale social action programs is to produce peace, or at least to reduce conflict. Whether or not they serve these ends is well worth investigating.

Similarly, little is known about the ways in which educational institutions change. This has been highlighted by the ability of many big-city school systems to absorb large amounts of activity and money designed to change them, and emerge apparently unchanged. If any question about the efficacy of social action programs is crucial, it is how such efforts at change succeed or fail. The requirement here may not be quantitative research, but political and social analysis, which follows the political and administrative history of social change programs. It may be possible to learn as much about the sources of programs' success from studying the politics of their intent and execution as from analyzing the quantitative relationships between program components and some summary measure of target group performance. Although such studies would be inapplicable in traditional educational evaluation, they are crucial in the evaluation of social action programs. These programs represent an effort to rearrange political relationships, and the sources of variation in their success are therefore bound to have as much to do with political and administrative matters as with how efficiently program inputs are translated into outcomes.

specialists who never see the target children; it may involve supplies and materials never unpacked, or educational goods and services which reach students other than those for whom they were intended; in still other cases it may consist of using program monies to pay for goods and services already in use. Whatever the specific form the non-treatment project takes, however, recognizing it requires extensive program delivery data. In a decentralized educational system the probability of such occurrences must be fairly high, and the obstacles to discovering them are considerable.

Even if the non-treatment project problem could be ignored, inadequate evidence on program delivery has other consequences for the evaluation of program outcomes. One of them is illustrated by the following excerpt from one Office of Education study of pre- and post-test scores in 33 big-city Title I programs (Piccariello, undated, p. 4):

> For the total 189 observations [each observation was one classroom in a Title I program], there were 108 significant changes (exceed 2 s.e.). Of these 58 were gains and 50 were losses. In 81 cases the change did not appear to be significant.

> As the data in Appendix D show, success and failure seem to be random outcomes, determined neither clearly nor consistently by the factors of program design, city or state, area or grade level.

When one reads Appendix D, however, he finds that the categorization by program design rests exclusively on one-paragraph program descriptions of the sort often furnished by the local project directors in grant applications. This makes it difficult to grasp the meaning of the study's conclusions. Perhaps success and failure were random with respect to program content, but given the evidence at hand it is just as sensible to argue that program content is unrelated to project descriptions, and that some underlying pattern of causation exists.[8] Without evidence on program delivery, it is not easy to see what can be learned from evaluations of this sort.

There is, however, an important counter-argument on this point. The recent Westinghouse evaluation of Project Headstart, for example, took as its chief independent variable *inclusion in Headstart projects*. The premise for this was that the government has a legitimate interest in determining whether a program produces the ex-

---

[8] Actually, the evaluation found that gains were more common among classrooms which had low scores on the pre-tests and that losses were more common among those classrooms which had higher pre-tests. The most economical hypothesis, then, is a regression effect (Piccariello, undated).

pected results. On this view, arguments about program delivery are irrelevant, since from the sponsoring agency's perspective, inclusion in the program is of overriding interest. (See Evans, 1969.)

There certainly is no question that in principle over-all program evaluation is justified. But the principle need not lead to a single summary evaluation in practice. Judgments about a program's over-all impact can just as well be derived from an evaluation which distinguishes program types or differentiates program delivery as from one which ignores them. From this perspective, rather than reporting whether the "average" Headstart project raised achievement, it would be more meaningful to identify the several program types and determine whether each improved achievement.

This may seem sensible, but it is not easy to put into practice. How does one collect data on program types or distinguish program characteristics? Assume a hypothetical program in which the outcome variable is school achievement. The first step would be to drop all projects whose purpose is not to improve achievement. But if one reads any compilation of project aims in Title I, he finds that only a minority aim only to improve achievement. Another minority aims to improve something else, and a majority aim to do both, or more. Given this heterogeneity of aims and the non-treatment project problem, one could not proceed on the basis of project descriptions— the stated purpose of improving achievement would have to be validated by looking at programs. The second step would be to distinguish the main approaches (the program types), from all those which actually sought to raise achievement. The main purpose of the evaluation is to distinguish the relative effectiveness of several approaches to this goal.

But if the logic seems clear, the procedure does not. To empirically distinguish the class of projects aimed at raising achievement one must first know what it is about schooling that affects achievement. Only on the basis of such information would it be possible to sort out those projects whose execution was consistent with their aims from those which were not. But when the new programs were established very little was known on this point: prior compensatory education efforts were few, far between, and mostly failures. The legislation was not the fruit of systematic experimentation and program development, but the expression of a paroxysm of concern. Although a good deal has been learned in the last four or five years, researchers are still a good way from an inventory of techniques known to improve school achievement. The only way one can tell if a project is of the sort which improves achievement, then, is not to inspect the treatment but to inspect the results.

This creates an awkward situation. If there is no empirical

typology of compensatory or remedial programs, what basis is there for distinguishing among programs? What basis is there for deciding which program characteristics to measure—if one does not know what improves achievement, how does one select the program attributes to measure? Some choice is essential, for evaluations cannot measure everything.

These questions focus attention on one important attribute of the new programs. To the extent that they seek to affect some outcome of schooling, such as attitudes or achievement, they represent a sort of muddling-through—an attempt at research and development on a national scale. This is not a comment on the legislative intent, but simply a description of existing knowledge. If program managers and evaluators do not know what strategies will affect school outcomes, it is not sensible to carry out over-all, one-shot evaluations of entire national programs: the results of strategies which improved achievement might be canceled out by the effects of those which did not. If the point is to find what "works," the emphasis should be on defining distinct strategies, trying them out, and evaluating the results. The highest priority should be maximum definition and differentiation among particular approaches. Program managers and evaluators must therefore devise educational treatments based on relatively little prior research and experience, carry them out under natural conditions, evaluate the results, and compare them with those from other similarly developed programs. Insofar as school outcomes are the object of evaluation, the work must take place in the context of program development and comparative evaluation. This requirement raises a host of new problems related to the intentional manipulation of school programs and organization within the American polity.

Experimental Approaches

The problem, then, is not only to identify what the programs deliver, but also to systematically experiment with strategies for affecting school outcomes. This idea has been growing in the Federal bureaucracy as experience with the social action programs reveals that the system of natural experiments (every local project does what it likes on the theory that good results would arise, be identified, and disseminated) has not worked. The movement toward experimentation presumes that the most efficient way to proceed is systematic trial and discard, discovering and replicating effective strategies.

Under what conditions might social action programs assume a partly experimental character? For Title I this would not be easy, because the legislation did not envisage it. It is a major operating program, and several of its purposes have nothing to do with achievement. Activities in Washington designed to carry out systematic research and development would generate considerable opposition among recipient state and local educational agencies, and in the Congress. Experimentation requires a good deal of bureaucratic and political control, and there is little evidence of that. The Office of Education, for example, does not require that the same tests be used in all Title I projects—indeed, it does not require that *any* tests be used. The Title I program's managers have neither the power nor the inclination to assign educational strategies to local educational agencies. Even if they did, the legislation would be at cross-purposes with such efforts. It aims to improve resource delivery—to ease the fiscal hardships of city and parochial schools, and to equalize educational resource disparities. Although the formula grant system is quite consistent with these aims, it is not consistent with experimentation. The two aims imply different administrative arrangements, reporting systems, and patterns of Federal-state-local relations. The experimental approach requires a degree of control over school program which seems incompatible with the other purposes of Title I.

The question is whether other programs offer a better prospect for experimentation in compensatory education. In mid-1968, the White House Task Force on Child Development recommended that Federal education programs adopt a policy of "planned variation"; the Task Force report argued that no learning from efforts to improve education was occurring with existing programs, and that it would result only from systematic efforts to try out different strategies under a variety of school and community conditions (White House Task Force, 1968).

The Task Force report focused its attention on Project Follow-Through. Follow-Through was originally intended to extend Headstart services from preschool to the primary grades, but severe first year budgetary constraints had greatly reduced its scope. Largely for this reason, the program seemed a natural candidate for experimentation. The Task Force (1968) recommended that Federal officials select a variety of educational strategies and develop evaluation plans using common measures of school outcomes in all cases.

> The administration should explicitly provide budget and personnel allowances for a Follow-Through staff to stimulate and develop projects consistent with these plans . . .

> The Office of Education should select all new Follow-Through projects in accordance with these plans for major variation and evaluation.

After three years, can the effort be termed a success? Since the program is still under development it would be unwise to deal with the strategies or their impact upon achievement. My concern is only with the quality of the evaluation scheme and the discussion is meant to be illustrative; the evaluation design may change, but the underlying problems are not likely to evaporate.

The Follow-Through program of experimentation is designed to determine which educational strategies improve achievement over what might otherwise be expected, and what the relative efficiency of the strategies is. The program began with little knowledge about the determinants of academic achievement, and as a consequence, equating schools and programs becomes much more difficult. Assume, for example, that all the Follow-Through projects sought to change student achievement by changing teachers' classroom behavior, but no two projects used the same treatment or attacked the same dimension of behavior. Suppose further that in half the projects achievement gains for students resulted. How could one be sure that the gains derived from the Follow-Through strategies, and not from selection or other teacher attributes than those manipulated by the program? The obvious answer is to measure teacher attributes and use the data to "control" the differences. But, since the program begins with little knowledge of what it is about teachers and teaching that affects achievement, evaluators must either measure *all* the teacher attributes which might affect achievement or closely approximate an experimental design. The first alternative is logically impossible, for the phenomena are literally unknown. The second alternative poses no logical problems; it requires only that the Federal experimenter have extensive control over the assignment of subjects (schools, school systems, and teachers) to treatment. The problems it raises are administrative and political.

The Follow-Through program has not been able to surmount them. Neither the districts nor the schools appear to have been selected in a manner consistent with experimental design. The districts were nominated by state officials; those nominated could accept or decline, and those who accepted could pretty much choose the strategy they desired from several alternatives. There was, then, room for self-selection. In addition, the purveyors of the strategies—the consultants who conceived, designed, and implemented or trained others to implement the strategies—seem also to have been recruited exclusively by self-selection. The usual ways of dealing with selection problems (never entirely satisfactory) seem even less helpful here. Although experimental and non-experimental schools could be compared to see if they differed in any important respects, the relevance of this procedure is unclear when little is known about what those "important respects" (vis-à-vis improving education for disadvantaged children) happen to be.

The weight of the evaluation strategy seems to fall on comparison or control groups. The present plan calls for selecting a sample of treatment and control classrooms, carrying out classroom observation, measuring teachers' background and attitudes, and using variables derived from these measurements in multivariate analyses of student achievement. Most of the instruments are still under development. But since there is neither a compulsion nor an incentive for principals in non-Follow-Through schools to participate as controls, how representative will the control classrooms be? What is more, these control or comparison groups cannot serve as much of a check on selectivity among the participants. Many of the comparison schools are in the same districts which selected themselves into the program and chose particular treatments; even those that are not are bound to be somewhat selected, because of the voluntary character of participation. Even if no "significant differences" are found between experimental and control schools, this would only prove that selected experimental schools are not very different from selected control schools.

There also may be some confounding of Follow-Through with related programs. Follow-Through operates in schools which are likely to receive other federal (and perhaps state and local) aid to improve education for disadvantaged children. Students will have the benefit of more than one compensatory program, either directly or through generally improved services and program in their school. There is little evidence at the moment of any effort to deal with this potential source of confounding.

In addition to selection, there are problems related to sample size. The design assumes that classrooms are the unit of analysis; this is appropriate, since they are the unit of treatment. Almost all measurements of program impact are classroom aggregates—i.e., they measure a classroom's teacher, its climate, its teaching strategy, etc. But it seems that relatively few classrooms will be selected from each project for evaluation (the 1969–70 plans call for an average of almost five per project, distributed over grades K–2). Since there are only a few classrooms per grade per project, it appears that in the larger projects there might be a dozen experimental units (classrooms) per grade. That is a very small number, especially when it is reasonable to expect some variation among classrooms on such things as teacher and student attributes, classroom styles, etc. In fact, since only six or eight of the strategies that are being tried involve large numbers of projects, the remaining strategies (more than half the total) probably will not have sufficient cases for much of an evaluation.

There has been some effort to deal with this problem by expanding the student achievement testing to cover almost all classrooms in Follow-Through. This has not, however, been paralleled by .expanded measurement of what actually is done in classrooms, a procedure which is helpful only on the assumption that there is no significant variation among classrooms within projects or strategies on variables related to the treatment or the effect. If this is true, of course, then measuring *anything* about the content, staff, or style of the classroom is superfluous—one need only designate whether or not it is an experimental or control unit. Despite the evaluators' view that this approach is warranted, the inclusion of some classrooms for which the only independent variable is a dummy (treatment–nontreatment) variable seems dubious. This will inflate the case base and therefore produce more statistical "confidence" in the results, but it may so sharply reduce the non-statistical confidence that the exercise will be useless. The evaluators argue that given the fixed sum for evaluation, they cannot extend measurement of classroom content.

Sample size problems are compounded because the evaluation is longitudinal. Since there is inter-classroom mobility in promotion (all classes are not passed on from teacher to teacher *en bloc*), following children for more than one year will sharply reduce the number of subjects for which two- or three-year treatment and effect measures can be computed. Add to this the rather high inter-school pupil mobility which seems to be characteristic of slum schools, and nightmarish anxieties about sample attrition result. Although nothing is certain at this point, there will be considerable obstacles to tracing program effects over time.

A fourth problem relates to student background measures. Apparently these data are being collected only for a relatively small sample of families. The evaluators are not sure that it will be large enough to allow consideration of both project impact and family background variables at once, but budget constraints preclude expanding the sample.

There are a few additional difficulties that merit mention, though they do not arise from the evaluation strategy, but from the nature of social action programs. There are reports of "leakage" of treatments from Follow-Through to comparison schools in some communities; there also seem to have been shifts in program goals in some projects; and apparently there has been conflict in definition of aims between the Follow-Through administration and some projects. In fact, there appears to be an element of non-comparability emerging among the strategies. Some involve very broad approaches, whose aims center around such things as parent involvement in or control of schools; others are more narrowly-defined and research-based strategies for improving cognitive growth. As long as traditional evaluation questions are asked (did treatment produce different results than an otherwise comparable non-treatment?), this poses no problem, but comparing treatments is close to the heart of Follow-Through. It is difficult to see how such comparative questions can be answered when the programs are so diverse. The general change programs, for example, appear to be hostile to the idea of evaluations based on achievement. They seem to be moving toward establishing other outcomes—"structural change" in schools, for example—as the program aim of primary concern. This heterogeneity of aims may well restrict the scope of comparative analysis for Follow-Through.

The common element in all these difficulties is that the Office of Education is largely powerless to remedy them. Random assignment of schools to treatments and securing proper control groups are the most obvious cases; lack of funds to generate adequate samples of experimental classrooms or parents are other manifestations of the same phenomenon. Although there is no doubt that some problems could have been eased by improved management, no amount of forethought or efficiency can produce money or power where there is none. Nor is it easy to see how the Office of Education could effectively compel project sponsors not to change some aspects of their strategies or not to alter their motion of program aims.

The experience thus far with Follow-Through suggests, then, that the serious obstacles to experimentation are political: first, power in the educational system is almost completely decentralized (at least from a national perspective), and federal experimentation must conform to this pattern; second, the resources allocated to eliminating educational disadvantage are small when compared to other federal priorities, which indicates the government's relatively low political investment in such efforts. Consequently, federal efforts to experiment begin with a grave deficit in the political and fiscal resources required to mount them, and there is little likelihood of much new money or more power with which to redress this imbalance. These difficulties are not peculiar to evaluation: they result from the same conditions which make it difficult to mount and operate effective reform programs. The barriers to evaluation are simply another manifestation of the obstacles to federally-initiated reform when most power is local and when reform is a relatively low national priority.

Several dimensions of social action program evaluation emerge from this analysis. My purpose here is not to provide a final typology of evaluation activities, but simply to suggest the salient elements. First among these is the identification of program aims; this ordinarily will involve the recognition of diversity, obscurity, and conflict within programs, and greater attention to program delivery. Evaluators of social action programs often complain that the programs lack any clear and concise statement of aims, a condition which they deplore because it muddies up evaluations. Their response generally has been to bemoan the imprecision and fuzzy-mindedness of the politicians and administrators who establish the programs, and then to choose a summary measure of program accomplishment which satisfies their more precise approach. I propose to stand this on its head and question the intellectually fuzzy single-mindedness of much educational evaluation. It generally has not grasped the diverse and conflicting nature of social action programs, and therefore produces unrealistically constrained views of program aims.

The second element is clarity about the social and political framework of measurement. In traditional evaluation the ideal standard of comparison (the control group or pre-measure) is one that is just like the treatment group in all respects except the treatment. But in social action programs the really important standard of comparison is the non-treatment group—what one is really interested in is how much improvement the program produces *relative to those who do not need it*. As a result the evaluation of social action programs is essentially comparative and historical, despite its often quantitative character: it seeks to determine whether a target population has changed, relative both to the same population before the program began and to the non-target population.

Finally, the evaluation of social action programs in education is political. Evaluation is a technique for measuring the satisfaction of public priorities; to evaluate a social action program is to establish an information system in which the main questions involve the allocation of power, status, and other public goods. There is conflict within the educational system concerning which priorities should be satisfied, and it is transmitted, willy-nilly, to evaluation. This puzzles and irritates many researchers; they regard it as extrinsic and an unnecessary bother. While this attitude is understandable; it is mistaken. The evaluation of social action programs is nothing if not an effort to measure social and political change. That is a difficult task under any circumstances, but it is impossible when the activity is not seen for what it is.

Suggestions for an Evaluation Strategy

What might be the elements of a more suitable evaluation strategy? The answer depends not only on what one thinks should be done, but on certain external political constraints. There is, for example, good reason to believe that federal education aid will be shifted into the framework of revenue sharing or block grants in the near future, and this is unlikely to strengthen the government's position as a social or educational experimenter. The only apparent alternative is continuing with roughly the present balance of power in education as categorical aid slowly increases the federal share of local expenditures. This seems unlikely to improve the government's position in the evaluation of large-scale social action programs. In addition, there seems to be a growing division over the criteria of program success.

Researchers are increasingly aware that little evidence connects the typical criteria of program success (high achievement and good deportment), with their presumed adult consequences (better job, higher income, etc.). More important, in the cities—particularly in the Negro community—there is rising opposition to the view that achievement and good behavior are legitimate criteria of success. Instead, political legitimacy—in the form of parent involvement or community control—is advanced as a proper aim for school change programs. It is ironic that the recent interest in assessing schools' efficiency—which gained much of its impetus from black discontent with white-dominated ghetto schools—now meets with rising opposition in the Negro community as blacks seek control over ghetto education. Nonetheless, this opposition is likely to increase, and the evaluation of social action programs in city schools is sure to be affected.

There is, then, little reason to expect much relaxation of the political constraints on social action program evaluation. This suggests two principles which might guide future evaluation: experiment only when the substantive issues of policy are considerable and reasonably well-defined; reorient evaluation of the non-experimental operating programs to a broad system of measuring status and change in schools and schooling.

The first principle requires distinctions among potential experiments in terms of the political constraints they imply. One would like to know, for example, which pre-school and primary programs increase cognitive growth for disadvantaged children; whether giving parents money to educate their children (as opposed to giving it to schools) would improve the children's education; whether students' college entrance would suffer if high school curriculum and attendance requirements were sharply reduced or eliminated; whether school decentralization would improve achievement; or whether it would raise it as much as doubling expenditures.

These are among the most important issues in American education, but they are not equally difficult when it comes to arranging experiments to determine the answers. In most cases, large scale experimentation would be impossible. Experiments with decentralization, tuition vouchers, doubling per-pupil expenditures, and radical changes in secondary education have two salient attributes in common: to have meaning they would have to be carried out in the existing schools, and few schools would be likely to oblige. If experimentation occurs on such issues it would be limited—a tentative exploration of new ideas involving small numbers of students and schools. While this is highly desirable, it is not the same thing as mounting an experimental social action program in education.

This may not be the case with one issue, however—increasing

cognitive growth for disadvantaged children. It already is the object of several social action programs and would not be a radical political departure. As a result of prior efforts, enough may be known to permit comparative experimental studies of different strategies for changing early intelligence. Several alternative approaches can be identified: rigid classroom drill, parent training, individual tutoring at early ages, and language training. Relatively little is known about the processes underlying these approaches, but there may be enough practical experience to support systematic comparative study. Since all the strategies have a common object, researchers probably could agree on common criterion measures. Since cognitive growth is widely believed to be crucial, investment in comparative studies seems worthwhile. But if such studies were undertaken, they should determine whether the treatment effect itself (higher IQ) is only a proxy for other things learned during the experiment, such as academic persistence, good behavior, and whether cognitive change produces any change on other measures of educational success, such as grades or years of school completed.

In effect, the chances for success of experimental approaches to social action will be directly related to a program's political independence, its specificity of aim, and its fiscal strength. The less it resembles the sort of broad-aim social action programs discussed in this paper, the more appropriate is an experimental approach and the more the "evaluation" looks like pure research. Of course, the further one moves down this continuum the less the program's impact is, and the less relevant the appellation "social action." Early childhood programs may be the only contemporary case in which the possibility of large-scale experimentation does not imply political triviality.

The second principle suggested above implies that the central purpose of evaluating most social action programs is the broad measurement of change. Evaluation is a comparative and historical enterprise, which can best be carried out as part of a general effort to measure educational status and change. The aims of social action programs are diverse, and their purpose is to shift the position of specified target populations relative to the rest of the society; their evaluation cannot be accomplished by isolated studies of particular aims with inappropriate standards of comparison. Evaluating broad social action programs requires comparably broad systems of social measurement.

A measurement system of this sort would be a census or system of social indicators of schools and schooling (not education). It would cover three realms: student, personnel, program, and fiscal inputs to schools; several outcomes of schooling, including achievement; temporal, geographic, political and demographic variation in both categories. If data of this sort were collected on a regular and recurring basis, they would serve the main evaluation needs for such operating programs as Title I. They would, for example, allow measurement of fiscal and resource delivery and of their variations over time, region, community, and school type. They would permit measurement of differences in school outcomes, as well as their changes over time. If the measurement of school outcomes were common over all schools, their variations could be associated with variations in other school attributes, including those of students, school resources, and the content and character of federal programs. Finally, if the measurement of outcomes and resources were particular to individual students, many of these comparisons could be extended from schools to individuals.

One advantage of such a measurement system would be its greater congruence with the structure and aims of large-scale multi-purpose programs. Another is that it would be more likely to provide data which could be useful in governmental decision-making—which, after all, is what evaluation is for. Most evaluation research in programs such as Title I is decentralized, non-recurring, and unrelated to either program planning or budgeting; as a result of the first attribute it is not comparable from community to community; as a result of the second it is not comparable from year to year; and as a result of the third it is politically and administratively irrelevant. Since the main governmental decisions about education involve allocating money and setting standards for goods, services, and performance, evaluation should provide comparable, continuing, and cumulative information in these areas. That would only be possible under a regular census of schools and schooling.

This is not to say there would be no deficiencies; there would be several, all of which are pretty well given in the nature of a census. By definition a census measures stasis, it quantifies how things stand. If done well, it can reveal a good deal about the interconnection of social structure; if it recurs, it can throw much light on how things change. But no census can reveal much about change other than its patterns—probing its causes and dynamics requires rather a different research orientation. And no census can produce qualitative data, especially on such complicated organizations as schools. There is, however, no reason why qualitative evaluation could not be systematically related to a census. Such evidence is much more useful when it recurs, and is connected with the results of quantitative studies. The same is true of research on the political dynamics and consequences of social action programs. Although valuable in itself, its worth would be substantially increased by relating it to other evidence on the same program.

The central problem, however, is experimentation. Using a census as the central evaluation device for large-scale multi-purpose programs assumes that systematic experimentation is very nearly impossible within the large operating programs and can best be carried on by clearly distinguishing census from experimental functions. It would be foolish to ignore experimentation—it should be increased—but it would be illusory to try to carry it out within programs which have other purposes. A clear view of the importance of both activities is unlikely to emerge until they have been distinguished conceptually and pulled apart administratively.

These suggestions are sketchy, and they leave some important issues open. Chief among them are the institutional and political arrangements required to mount both an effective census of schools and schooling and a long-term effort in experimentation.[9] Nonetheless, my suggestions do express a *strategy* of evaluation, something absent in most large-scale educational evaluation efforts. The strategy assumes that government has two distinct needs, which thus far have been confounded in the evaluation of large-scale action programs. One is to measure status and change in the distribution of educational resources and outcomes; the other is to explore the impact and effectiveness of novel approaches to schooling. If the first were undertaken on a regular basis the resulting time-series data would provide much greater insight into the actual distribution of education in America. It would thus build an information base for more informed decisions about allocation of resources, at both the state and Federal level. If the second effort were undertaken on a serious basis, it should be possible to learn more systematically from research and development. Perhaps the best way to distinguish this strategy from existing efforts is this: were the present approach to evaluating social action programs brought to perfection, it would not be adequate—it would not tell us what we need to know about the programs.

---

[9] Creating the capacity for experimentation would involve a few major decisions. One probably would be to separate the activity from the Office of Education, retaining its connection with HEW at the Assistant Secretary level. Another would be to create greater institutional capacity for support and evaluation in the private (or quasipublic) sector; at the moment, this important resource is not well enough developed to bear the load. A third would be to so arrange its management that the decisions about what experiments to fund resulted from systematic and sustained interaction between the political governors of such an institution, its scientific staffers and constituents, and the educational practitioners. Without this, it would probably do interesting but politically unimportant work.

Creating the capacity for a census or system of schooling indicators involves different issues. Here there is good reason for it to be part of USOE. The question is where, and what capacity would be required; though these require more detailed work than is possible here, a bit of speculation is possible. There is some reason to think, for example, that the new 21 state management information system might be a good base from which to begin. There already is an ongoing program, it seems to have promise conceptually, and there seems to be a good state–Federal relationship.

Second, my suggestions assume that the evaluation of social action programs is a political enterprise. This underlies the idea of separating experimentation from large-scale operating programs. It also underlies the notion of a census of schools and schooling, which would almost compel attention to the proper standards of comparison and would emphasize the importance of change. In addition, only a broad system of measurement can capture the political variety which social action programs embody. Perhaps most important, measuring the impact of social change programs in this way is not tied to a particular program or pattern of Federal aid.

Finally, such a strategy could be implemented within the existing political constraints. That is not a scientific argument, but that is the real point: evaluating social action programs is only secondarily a scientific enterprise. First and foremost it is an effort to gain politically significant information on the consequences of political acts. To confuse the technology of measurement with the real nature and broad purposes of evaluation will be fatal. It can only produce increasing quantities of information in answer to unimportant questions.

Bibliography

BAILEY, S. and MOSHER, E. ESEA: *The Office of Education Administers a Law.* Syracuse, N.Y.: Syracuse Univ. Press, 1968.

BLAU, P. and DUNCAN, O. *The American Occupational Structure.* New York: Wiley, 1968.

DENTLER, R. *The Phenomenology of the Evaluation Researcher.* Paper presented to the Conference on Evaluating Social Action Programs, American Academy of Arts and Sciences, May 1969. New York: Center for Urban Education, 105 Madison Avenue. (Typewritten.)

DUNCAN, O. *Socioeconomic Background and Occupational Achievement.* Ann Arbor: Univ. of Mich. Press, 1968.

GUBA, E. Development, Diffusion, and Evaluation. *Knowledge Production and Utilization in Educational Administration.* (Edited by Terry Eidell and Joanne Kitchel.) Eugene, Ore.: Univ. Council for Educational Administration and Center for the Study of Educational Administration, 1968. Chapter 3, pp. 37–63.

HARTMAN, R. *Evaluation in Multi-Purpose Grant-in-Aid Programs.* Washington, D.C.: The Brookings Institution, undated. (Typewritten.)

HOWE, HAROLD (Commissioner). *Special memorandum.* Washington, D.C.: U.S. Dept. of Health, Education, and Welfare, Office of Education, June 14, 1968.

JACKSON, P. B. *Trends in Elementary and Secondary Education Expenditures: Central City and Suburban Comparisons, 1965–1968.* Washington, D.C.: U.S. Dept. of Health, Education, and Welfare, Office of Education, Office of Program Planning and Evaluation, 1969. (Mimeo.)

National Advisory Council on the Education of Disadvantaged Children. *Title I ESEA: A Review and a Forward Look.* Washington, D.C.: the Council, 1969.

PICCARIELLO, H. *Evaluation of Title I.* Paper presented to the Dept. of Health, Education, and Welfare, Office of Education, Washington, D.C., undated. (Typewritten.)

STUFFLEBEAM, D. The Use and Abuse of Evaluation in Title III. *Theory into Practice* 6: 126–33; 1967.

TEMPO, G. *Survey and Analysis of Title I Funding for Compensatory Education.* Washington, D.C.: U.S. Dept. of Health, Education, and Welfare, Office of the Secretary, 1968.

U.S. Congress, Eighty-nine, First Session. Title I. *Elementary and Secondary Education Act of 1965* Public Law 89-10. U.S. Statutes at Large, 89th Congress, First Session. 1965a.

U.S. Congress, Eighty-nine, First Session. House Report No. 143. *Report of the Committee on Education and Labor, on the Elementary and Secondary Education Act of 1965.* 1965b.

U.S. Department of Health, Education, and Welfare. *Criteria for Applications Grants to Local Educational Agencies Under Title I, ESEA.* Washington, D.C.: the Department, 1968.

U.S. Department of Health, Education, and Welfare. *Summary Report of 1968 White House Task Force on Child Development.* Washington, D.C., USGPO, 1968.

U.S. House Education and Labor Committee. *Hearings before General Subcommittee on Education, Eighty-Ninth Congress, First Session, on Aid to Elementary and Secondary Education.* 1965a.

U.S. House Education and Labor Committee. *Hearings before General Subcommittee on Education, Eighty-Ninth Congress, First Session, on the Elementary and Secondary School Act Formulas.* 1965b.

U.S. Senate Appropriations Committee. *Hearings before Subcommittee on Departments of Labor and HEW Appropriations for 1966, Departments of Labor and HEW Supplemental Appropriations for 1966, Eighty-Ninth Congress, First Session.* 1965.

U.S. Senate Labor and Public Welfare Committee. *Hearings before Subcommittee on Education, Eighty-Ninth Congress, First Session, on the Elementary and Secondary Education Act of 1965.* 1965.

Additional References

ALDRICH, NELSON (Issues Editor). *The Urban Review* 2, No. 6 and No. 7; 1968.

BATEMAN, W. *An Experimental Approach to Program Analysis: Stepchild in the Social Sciences.* Paper presented to the Operations Research Society of America, Denver, Colo., June 1969. Washington, D.C.: The Urban Institute, 1969.

CAMPBELL, D. Reforms as Experiments. *American Psychologist* 24: 409–29; 1969.

CAMPBELL, D. and STANLEY, J. *Experimental and Quasi-Experimental Designs for Research.* Chicago: Rand McNally, 1966.

DYER, H. Some Thoughts About Future Studies. Draft manuscript for *Equal Educational Opportunity.* (Edited by D. Moynihan and F. Mosteller.) New York: Random House, in press.

EVANS, J. *Evaluating Social Action Programs.* Washington, D.C.: Office of Economic Opportunity, 1969. (Typewritten.)

HYMAN, H. and WRIGHT, C. Evaluating Social Action Programs. *The Uses of Sociology.* (Edited by Paul Lazarsfeld, William Sewall, and Harold Wilensky.) New York: Basic Books, 1966. Chapter 27, pp. 741–82.

MARRIS, P. and REIN, M. *Dilemmas of Social Reform.* Atherton, N.Y.: Atherton Press, 1967.

McDill, E.; McDill, M.; and Sprehe, T. *An Analysis of Evaluation of Selected Compensatory Education Programs.* Presented to the American Academy of Arts and Sciences Conference, May 1969. Baltimore, Md.: Johns Hopkins Univ., 1969. (Typewritten.)

RIVLIN, A. *PPBS in HEW: Some Lessons from Experience.* Paper prepared for the Joint Economic Committee, Mar. 1969. Washington, D.C.: The Brookings Institution, 1969. (Typewritten.)

RIVLIN, A. and WHOLEY, J. *Education of Disadvantaged Children.* Paper presented to the Symposium on Operations Analysis of Education, Nov. 1967. Washington, D.C.: The Brookings Institution, 1967. (Typewritten.)

ROTHENBERG, J. *Cost Benefit Analysis: A Methodological Exposition.* Paper presented to the American Academy of Arts and Sciences Conference, May 1969. Cambridge: Mass. Institute of Technology, 1969. (Typewritten.)

SWARTZ, R. Experimentation in Social Research. *Journal of Legal Education* 13: 401–10; 1961.

WEISS, R. and REIN, M. *Evaluation of Broad-Aim Social Programs.* Paper presented to the American Academy of Arts and Sciences

Conference, May 1969. Roxbury, Mass.: Harvard Medical School, 1969. (Typewritten.)

WHOLEY, J. *Federal Evaluation Practices.* Washington, D.C.: The Urban Institute, 1969a. (Typewritten.)

WHOLEY, J. Program Evaluation in the Department of Health, Education, and Welfare. *Federal Program Evaluation Practices.* Appendix I. Washington, D.C.: The Urban Institute, 1969b.

WILLIAMS, W. and EVANS, J. The Politics of Evaluation: The Case of Headstart. *Annals* 385: 118–32; 1969.

ELEANOR BERNERT SHELDON
HOWARD E. FREEMAN

Notes on Social Indicators:
Promises and Potential

There is a new social movement afoot today, one advanced by a peculiar consortium of social scientists, social commentators, political activists, and legislators. It most commonly goes by the name of "social indicators," although occasionally it is referred to as "social accounts" or "social bookkeeping" or "monitoring social change." The central referent, however, is the concept of social indicators.

Usually one thinks of quantitative measures when referring to social indicators, although there is no reason why qualitative ones cannot also be included under the rubric (Gross, 1966; Gross and Springer, 1967a, 1967b). Even if the term is reserved for quantitative measures, however, it should be pointed out that not all statistics are social indicators. There probably is general agreement among those who banter the term about that only measures which are employed repeatedly and at regular intervals are to be properly considered indicators; in other words, social indicators are time-series that allow comparisons over an extended period and which permit one to grasp long-term trends as well as unusually sharp fluctuations in rates.

There also may be considerable agreement that social indicators are statistics that can be disaggregated by relevant attributes of either the persons or the conditions measured (such as skin color or year of construction) and by the contextual characteristics that surround the measure (such as region or city size). Even if one agrees to

Eleanor Bernert Sheldon and Howard E. Freeman, "Notes on Social Indicators: Promises and Potential," *Policy Sciences,* vol. 1, no. 1, April 1970, pp. 97–101, 110–111. Excerpts reprinted by permission.

consider only statistics that can be disaggregated as social indicators, the meaning of the term "relevant" is most blurred. There is no agreement on the set of characteristics most relevant for purposes of disaggregation.

But beyond the notions of time-series and disaggregation, the multitude of additional restrictions placed upon the concept by some, but not by others, is staggering. Some maintain indicators must be of direct normative interest (U.S. Department of Health, Education, and Welfare, 1969). The inclusion of the term *direct* raises an interesting question. Probably an acceptable synonym for "indicator" is "reflector." Persons who use the dictionary as an authority might challenge whether or not an indicator can be a direct measure; they probably could properly hold if you have a direct measure of a phenomenon it is no longer aptly described by the term indicator.

Perhaps more restrictive and confusing is the position that indicators must be "normative." Obviously what is salient today may not be so next year and vice versa; if only statistics of a direct normative interest are maintained, currently invisible but subsequently critical social problems will not be encompassed by extant time-series. It also is held that indicators need to be measures of welfare: the number of doctors or policemen in these terms are not regarded as indicators, only figures on health status, acts of crime, and so on. Yet, if one is going to make assessments of present and future welfare services, do not we need to know how rapidly or slowly resources pools are being developed?

Moreover, it is claimed that indicators need to have "direction," one pole being regarded as "good" and the other as "bad." But what is good in the minds of some may be bad in the views of others, let alone that the direction may be evaluated in opposite ways by some persons at different times—like days lost from work for illness and disability. It could be argued, for example, that an increase in this indicator may reflect either a decline in the health status of the employed population or liberalization of employment policies on sick leave.

The term social indicator must be regarded as an elusive concept. Moreover, the boundaries of the indicator movement are amoebic, and partisans to the cause come and go, often deserters to it quietly returning only to slip away again. But the existence of the movement is real: social indicators have been the subject of editorials in our most prestigious newspapers; the deliberations of a citizen–government group have been transmitted by the Secretary of Health, Education, and Welfare to the President (U.S. Department of Health, Education, and Welfare, 1969); Senator Mondale and his associates introduced Bill S-5 in 1969 to establish a council of social advisors and to promote indicator development and use; and the outpouring of papers and monographs on indicators will undoubtedly soon occasion the continual publication of review articles and bibliographies.

The elusiveness of the concept of social indicators stems from the multitude of views on the relevance and purpose of developing and organizing statistics about the state of affairs in the country and its constituent parts. At the same time, however, the vagueness of the concept encourages persons to advocate their own particular perspectives, further increasing the confusion about the utility of social statistics for planning, program development, and scholarly endeavors. Perhaps the time has come to provide a reasonably extended scrutiny of some impossible uses of social indicators and to specify in a programmatic sense the possible, if only potentially so, uses of indicators.

Some Impossible Uses of Indicators

At least three claims of social indicators need to be regarded with extreme skepticism, for we are not only technically deficient at present, but the conceptual development required to fulfill the espoused promises has not taken place—and if the effort is not redirected may never take place. Each of the claims of indicator use, while overlapping, merits separate scrutiny:

1. The setting of goals and priorities
2. The evaluation of programs
3. The development of a balance sheet.

THE SETTING OF GOALS AND PRIORITIES

Among the partisans of social indicators are a relatively vocal group who regard the benefits of the movement to be primarily political, i.e., as to a key to social policy development. It may be of value to point out that government and business, as well as influential community groups, use statistics in order to support their ideas for action programs, and their own priority systems regarding what needs to be done. Further, it may be obvious that the more respectable the figures and the more prestigeful their source, the more potent a tool of political influence is available.

A robust social indicator movement permits well-intentioned politicians and program advocates access to statistics that can be presented with unusual persuasiveness. Dignifying a statistic by referring to it as an indicator may help, even though it may be no better conceptualized or measured before it is given status as an indicator. In the abstract it could be argued that, if one had a comprehensive and exhaustive set of social indicators available, it would be possible to identify those that show the most marked changes and to scrutinize the social problem phenomenon they reflect in order to locate areas that press for attention. As Henriot (1970) observes, however, the very process of developing indicators is value-laden; their very definition reflects sociopolitical values. Consequently, those indicators that may show startling changes if lodged in one system of measures might be regarded as of modest interest if placed in a different system.

It would be foolish to argue against the use of indicators in program planning and development, or to expect their employment to disappear as a means of influencing politicians and their electorates. But it is naive to hold that social indicators in themselves permit decisions on which programs to implement, especially that they allow the setting of priorities. The use of data to make a case either already decided on other grounds or one that inevitably is going to be determined by political rather than "objective" considerations—whether or not it is in a good cause—is a weak basis for the indicator effort. Priorities do not depend on assembled data. Rather, they stem from national objectives and values and their hierarchical ordering.

In short, when used for purposes of setting goals and priorities, indicators must be regarded as inputs into a complex political mosaic. That they are potentially powerful tools in the development of social policy is not to be denied. But they do not make social policy development any more objective. Advocates of policy can strengthen their position by citing hard data and so can critics of those policies. In a situation where all sides have equity of resources to gather, interpret, and communicate indicator information, it could be argued that social indicators can serve to develop a more rational decisionmaking process in social policy development. But this is unlikely to be the case very often and in instances of unfair competition indicators are essentially a lobbying device (Henriot, 1970).

THE EVALUATION OF PROGRAMS

Concurrent with the movement to promote social indicators, there has developed a strenuous effort on the part of key individuals in and outside of government to estimate the gains that are derived from the initiation and expansion of different types of preventive and rehabilitative action programs. The terms "evaluation research" and "cost benefits analysis" now are common jargon among a vast number of such practitioners, planners, and politicians. The rationality of being able to estimate the benefits of expenditures of money, time, and manpower is virtually incontestable, and the utility of knowing whether existing and innovative programs work clearly is desirable.

The empirical situation however is that there have been but a handful of respectable evaluation studies of social action programs: There simply are not very many craftsmanlike evaluations of national programs, and there is increasing dissatisfaction with the failure to document by careful research the current massive programs now underway to improve the occupational, educational, mental and physical health status of community members. As a consequence, there is the temptation to argue for social indicators as a substitute for experimental evaluations. The fact of the matter is, however, that social indicator analyses cannot approximate the necessary requirements of sound design in order to provide for program evaluation.

Investigators who have thought about the problems of evaluation generally agree that there is no substitute for experimental research that differentiates between the effects of treatments and programs on the one hand and of extraneous contaminating factors on the other. Experimentally designed evaluations often are not possible because of resistance to the requisite random assignment of persons to different treatment groups. Thus, there is a turning to efforts of evaluation through statistical controls or "systems analyses."

The use of indicators to evaluate programs would require one to be able to demonstrate, via statistical manipulations, that programs determine the outcomes measured by the indicators rather than other factors "causing" the results. The old example of a relationship between the number of storks in a community and its birth rate should suffice to make the point. There is no possibility at the present time of meeting the requirements of controlling for contaminating variables with available statistics that may be regarded as indicators, at least ones that cover large groups of individuals. In order to locate and identify factors that may be contaminating, knowledge of the determinants and interrelationships between determinants is required. Information is not available in many fields of social concern to do such analyses well, either on an empirical basis or a theoretical one.

Admittedly there are persons who are much more optimistic about the potential use of a feedback system for determining the full range of consequences of the society's actions and which thus would provide guidelines for future courses (Bauer, 1966). But the strongest proponents of the feedback system approach, who tell us that our knowledge can permit the development of a social system model and the derivation of measures from it to assess programmatic efforts, find it hard or impossible to supply guidance on how this is to be done. Even if it were possible in the abstract (and certainly most people in the evaluation research game would argue against the idea of evaluating programs by means of social indicators), realistically there is no basis or advice available on what to do and how to do it.

Modifications of trends and shifts in the behavioral conditions of populations either over time or for different groups do not provide enough opportunities for controlled analyses to muster any persuasive argument about the efficacy or efficiency of programmatic efforts. The development and refinement of social indicators and the activities of persons within the movement simply neither will satisfy the need nor serve as a substitute for evaluation studies of an experimental character. Arguing that the development of social indicators provides a means to decide on the cost-benefits and the efficiency of programs is a way of inhibiting the development of adequate means of evaluations and exaggerated claim of the potential of social indicators.

THE DEVELOPMENT OF A BALANCE SHEET

The most publicly appealing notion of social indicators is their use in a system of social accounts. The claim is that it is possible to develop a system of national social accounting that brings together in an integrated fashion the relative concepts developed by economists, political scientists, sociologists, anthropologists, psychologists, and social psychologists (Gross, 1966). It is maintained that "The great advances in the social sciences during recent decades make it possible to establish such a system. The needs of administrators, government leaders, and international agencies make it imperative" (Gross, 1966, p. 155). Though such proponents do describe the major outlines of "a social system at a national level," such notions scarcely provide a social system model or conceptual framework amenable to a national accounting system. . . .

Evoking the economic analogy and proposing the development of social indicators that parallel economic indicators is confusing and in part fallacious. Despite its weaknesses and limited rigor, economic theory provides a definition and the specifications of an economic system, and the linkages are at least hypothesized, if not empirically demonstrated, between many variables in the system. From such a point of departure, an administrator or a set of administrators can design policies that make possible the manipulation of one or more of the variables in the system, thereby causing the prior hypothesized changes of other variables in that system. Because the changes are of a relatively short-term nature, feedback is rather prompt, say six months to a year, and policies and programs are vulnerable to further modification, alteration, and manipulation. At least to some extent, this model has worked and economic indicators and accounts are useful policy tools.

Although some social scientists have promised similar usefulness for social indicators and social accounts, this is not even a reasonable anticipation. There is no social theory, even of a tentative nature, which defines the variables of a social system and the relationships between them. It is even difficult to locate partial theories or so-called middle-range ones covering any single aspect of society which have convincing explanatory potential. Yet, without the guidance of theoretical formulations concerning significant variables and their linkages, one can hardly suggest that there exists, even potentially, a set of measures that parallel the economic variables.

There is also a problem of scale construction that is not often faced in the call for social indicators. A balance sheet not only requires a set of categories—ones conceptually based and integrated—but some common interval measure, such as money, for adding and subtracting apples and oranges or cancers and rapes simply is not possible. Money has meaning and allows one to sum values across a large number of different domains. Neither the state of conceptualization nor technique in the social sciences other than economics has produced necessary measures.

The Potential of the Indicator Movement

The oversell of social indicators, which we have tried to confront in the preceding section, may suggest to some that the appropriate strategy of responsible persons should be an intensive and direct effort to render the movement ineffective. This need not be so; a viable alternative is to redirect and rechannel existing efforts, to reformulate the goals of the indicator movement, to modulate the promises on the utility of indicators in ways that make them realistic, and to exploit the momentum gained from the movement to improve the quantity and quality of data on the structural outlines and social processes of society. There are extensive needs and attractive possibilities of three types that can be promoted. The social indicator movement can contribute (1) to improved descriptive reporting; (2) to the analysis of social change; and (3) to the prediction of future social events and social life. The three tasks of course are interdependent. Adequate descriptive reporting is essential for the development of improved investigations of social change and correspondingly increased understanding of past social changes is required for the better prediction of future events. . . .

References

BAUER, RAYMOND A., ed. (1966), *Social Indicators*, Cambridge: M.I.T. Press.

Gross, Bertram M. (1966), "The State of the Nation: Social Systems Accounting," in Raymond A. Bauer, ed., *Social Indicators,* pp. 154–271. Cambridge: M.I.T. Press.

Gross, Bertram M., and Michael Springer (1967a), "A New Orientation in American Government," *The Annals* of the American Academy of Political and Social Science, May 1967, pp. 1–19.

Gross, Bertram M., and Michael Springer (1967b), "New Goals for Social Information," *The Annals* of the American Academy of Political and Social Science, September 1967, pp. 208–218.

Henriot, Peter J., "Political Questions about Social Indicators," *Western Political Quarterly,* 23 (June 1970).

U.S. Department of Health, Education, and Welfare (1969), *Toward a Social Report.* Washington, D.C.: U.S. Government Printing Office, January 1969.

THOMAS K. GLENNAN, JR.

Evaluating
Federal Manpower Programs:
Notes and Observations

. . . Benefit-Cost Evaluation
of Manpower Programs

In this section, a number of issues concerning the measurement and interpretation of benefits and costs are considered. For the moment, it is assumed that the major purpose for carrying out benefit–cost evaluations is to support the allocation of resources among a group of national manpower programs. A subsidiary purpose may be the justification of requests for additional funds to be utilized by manpower programs. . . .

DISTRIBUTION OF COSTS AND BENEFITS
AMONG ECONOMIC AND SOCIAL CLASSES

Statements about the economic efficiency of a social program do not take into account who pays for the program and who receives its benefits.* Clearly, in the Poverty Program the issue of who receives

Thomas K. Glennan, Jr., "Evaluating Federal Manpower Programs: Notes and Observations," Memorandum RM-5743-OEO, prepared for the Office of Economic Opportunity. RAND Corporation, Santa Monica, California, September 1969. Abridged by permission of the author.

* In many respects, my comments on treatment of distributional objectives parallels that of Rothenberg. See Jerome Rothenberg, *Economic Evaluation of Urban Renewal,* The Brookings Institution, Washington, D.C., 1967, particularly Chapter II.

benefits is a crucial one. The introduction of these issues complicates benefit-cost analysis ,because of the necessity of weighing gains and losses of one group (the poor) against the gains and losses of another group (the non-poor).

When programs have objectives that go beyond simply maximizing the return on public investments irrespective of who receives the benefits, a simple benefit-cost ratio is an insufficient indicator of program outcome. Several alternative approaches to this problem have been suggested. Perhaps the most frequently advanced idea is the use of a system of weights reflecting the relative value society places on increases in the well-being of specific groups in society. For example, a given increase in income to very poor families might be considered more significant or valuable than a similar increase in income to a "barely" poor family. An increase in the income of the barely poor is in turn more valuable than a similar increase in income of the non-poor. Or increases in the income of Negroes may be valued more highly by society than increases in the income of whites. If such a set of weights could be specified, a new figure of merit for the program's impact could be formed that consisted of the weighted sum of the benefits to differing segments of society. A similar weighted sum of the costs would also be needed.

It is difficult to conceive of a feasible way to arrive at an explicit set of weights. Clearly, however, a set of weights is implicit in the actions of Congress and various executive departments.* Because of the difficulty in arriving at a set of weights, the best the evaluator can do may be to simply portray the costs and benefits of a program for different subgroups in society. Thus, for example, analysis of poverty program outcomes might consider two groups, the poor and the non-poor (roughly speaking, these latter are the taxpayers). The benefits to the poor would include increased earnings resulting from program participation plus other increases in income from sources such as welfare or training allowances. Costs to the poor would include earnings foregone while in training plus out-of-pocket expenses for transportation or baby sitting services. . . .

When the outcomes of programs are portrayed in terms of their consequences for various segments of society many of the questions concerning the treatment of elements of costs and benefits are simplified. Transfer payments such as welfare payments, for example, are usually not considered either a cost or a benefit in benefit-cost analyses because such a transfer simply represents a shift of consump-

---

* For a discussion of the need to integrate distributional effects and efficiency in assessing the cost and benefits of a program, see Burton A. Weisbrod, "Income Redistribution Effects and Benefit-Cost Analysis" in Samuel B. Chase, Jr., Ed., *Problems in Public Expenditure Analysis,* The Brookings Institution, Washington, D.C., 1968.

tion from one group to another. No consumption is foregone by society as a whole. However, it is clear that such transfers have significant consequences for different groups in society and form an important effect of most social action programs.

Although a tabulation of costs and benefits to various segments of society are important, it is clear that the policymaker is likely to want a figure of merit for the program that summarizes its performance. This desire is part of the reason for the popularity of the benefit-cost ratio. The construction of such a figure of merit should depend upon the objectives of the program. For manpower programs targeted on poverty populations, the following formulation might be used. Basically the objective of the program is the increase in the economic welfare of the target population. The costs are the foregone consumption of the rest of society. With such a formulation the benefits are:

(1) the increased earnings (net of taxes) of the target population resulting from participation in the program
(2) plus the net increase in transfer payments to the target population during participation in the program
(3) less decreases in transfer payments to the target population because of higher earnings subsequent to program participation
(4) less losses of earnings from work that would have been performed if enrollee had not been in program
(5) less losses of earnings of poor individuals displaced by trainees.

The sum of these changes is simply the stream of increments (or decrements) of real income both during and after the program which are attributable to the program.

The costs should include:

(1) The direct costs of the program including subsistence payments
(2) less any decreases in other transfer payments occasioned by the existence of the program
(3) plus losses of income of the non-poor if they are displaced by the program enrollees
(4) plus any decreases in income to the non-poor that occur because trainees are temporarily withdrawn from the work force
(5) less long term decreases in transfer payments because of the higher earnings of target population resulting from program
(6) less net external benefits which accrue to the non-poor and are not reflected in earnings of target population
(7) less the increases in taxes paid by the target population on earnings increments resulting from the program.

Numerous assumptions must be made in order to obtain estimates of many of the cost components. This is particularly true for items 3, 4, 6, and 7. For example, increased taxes paid by program participants have value to the non-poor only if they result in lower taxes for the non-poor or the support of other government programs that benefit the non-poor. Calculation of such quantities depends upon assumptions concerning level of economic activity, the reaction of the government to increases (or potential increases) in tax revenues, and the distribution of the benefits of government programs among the poor and non-poor.

Costs and benefits occur over a considerable period of time. In order to compare costs with benefits, both streams are discounted back to the present time using some value of discount rate. The proper value of discount rate to use has been the subject of considerable debate, a debate I do not choose to enter.* It is worth noting, however, that the relative ranking of programs will not be affected by the choice of a discount rate unless the temporal patterns of costs and benefits differ between the programs. The absolute ratio of benefits to costs will be significantly affected by the choice of discount rates.

Because of the many assumptions that must be made, the probability that an evaluation by one investigator will be comparable to that of another is not high. Comparison of two programs using figures generated by two different analysts is usually unwise. Two practical suggestions to improve this situation can be advanced. First, whenever practical, programs having similar or overlapping objectives should be simultaneously evaluated using identical assumptions (and if possible identical data collection efforts). Second, efforts should be made to develop an agreed upon set of conventions for the evaluation of social action programs similar in concept to those contained in "Green Book" for water resource projects.

NON-MONETARY BENEFITS

The discussion has proceeded as if all program benefits could be reflected in monetary terms. This is clearly not the case. There are benefits to the poor that are not measurable in dollar terms. Improvements in self-image, improved access to public services because of better knowledge, less alienation from the world of work or from other segments of society, better health or improved reading and

* The choice of a proper rate of discount is extensively discussed in *Economic Analysis of Public Investment Decisions: Interest Rate Policy and Discounting Analysis*. Hearings Before a Subcommittee on Economy in Government of the Joint Economic Committee of the Congress of the United States, 90th Congress, 2nd Session, 1968, Washington, D.C.

computational skill are but a few of the non-monetary benefits that are thought to accrue to participants in various manpower programs. To some extent some of these may be positively associated with income increases. Hence, comparison of programs in terms of their impact on increasing incomes will implicitly consider these factors. There is no simple way to include those factors that are more directly associated with program experience in the calculation of benefits.

If two programs have the same monetary benefits relative to costs, it might be possible to choose between them on the basis of the probable relative impact on other non-monetary benefits. For situations where the benefit-cost ratios differ, the judgment is much more difficult. Consider, for example, a comparison of the Job Corps and the Neighborhood Youth Corps (NYC). Suppose the youths from both programs gain the same benefits in terms of increased income. The youths from Job Corps receive extensive medical and dental care, considerable counseling, remedial education and some vocational skills, all in a residential environment. The youths in NYC, on the other hand, receive only work experience with generally limited amounts of remedial education and counseling. The Job Corps costs about four times as much per trainee as the NYC. Hence, with the assumption of equal monetary benefits, the benefit-cost ratio of Job Corps would be one quarter of NYC's. How much of this difference can be attributed to the failure to adequately account for the improved individual welfare associated with good health or reading capability? This is a matter of judgment that is now made, in the case of manpower programs, by an ill-defined set of decisionmakers in OEO, the Department of Labor, the Budget Bureau, the White House, and Congress.

This problem must be carefully separated from the one in which these non-monetary program outcomes are thought to lead to subsequent increases in income. The benefits described in the previous paragraph are what the economist calls "consumption" benefits to program participants leading to improvements in his current well-being. However, many of these benefits, such as health status, reading skills, or degree of alienation from various groups in society may be related to long term work experience. Improvements along these lines may improve the capacity of the individual to find and keep a job, but this improvement may not be clearly discernible in the proximate work experience of the individual. In this case if the Job Corps provides the individual with capabilities that become useful only after some work experience or when the youth is older, then comparing the monetary benefits of the two programs only on the basis of proximate work experience is inappropriate. Unfortunately, there is little basis for determining the impact of many factors, such as health, upon the lifetime earnings of an individual. The analyst has to retreat to the rather unsatisfying activity of specifying the size of the improvement in employment or wage rates that would be required to equate the benefit-cost ratios so that the policymaker can more easily make a judgment about the probability that such a future difference can be expected to occur.

CONCLUSIONS

This section has touched on a few conceptual problems associated with benefit-cost analysis. A glance at any group of evaluations of manpower programs will be sufficient to indicate the great variety of ways analysts have approached the problems noted here. This variability has rendered the studies incomparable and to some extent has discredited benefit-cost analysis.* Steps should be taken to reduce this variability, perhaps by establishing conventions under which benefit-cost or cost effectiveness studies of human resource programs would be conducted.

*The Measurement
of Benefits and Costs*

In the previous section elements of a conceptual framework were established for comparing the costs and benefits of undertaking a manpower program. It was implicitly assumed that data on both the costs and benefits were available and that the major task of the evaluator was specifying what data to aggregate to obtain meaningful measures of costs and benefits.

Although it is true that many evaluations utilize questionable assumptions in calculating costs or benefits, the major difficulties seem to lie in empirically estimating these figures. Data produced routinely as a by-product of program operations suffer from two major flaws. They tend to be unreliable. Data for many projects are missing or contain numerous errors. More serious is the fact that few projects follow enrollees after the training period and hence are in a position to report earnings or employment histories.** Hence, the fundamental

* For example, three evaluations of the Job Corps using essentially the same data yielded estimates of benefit-cost ratios ranging from .3 to 5. See Lillian Regelson, "Applications of Cost-Benefit Analysis to Federal Manpower Programs," a paper presented at a meeting of the Operations Research Society of America, Denver, June 1969.
** The reporting system for the Manpower Development and Training Act includes data on work histories of enrollees subsequent to enrollment. These data are supposed to be collected by the Employment Service but the return rates are quite low.

data required to assess benefits of a training program, the earnings of the trainee, must be obtained by other means. In most cases, the other means is some form of survey.

In general, the increase in national output is measured by the increase in income of the trainee. The use of this measure can be justified by the assumption that wages are equal to the marginal product of the worker. Two further assumptions are required. First, wages should represent total compensation. If extensive fringe benefits are also "paid," the use of only wages understates the program benefits. Second, it must be assumed that the enhanced employment and income status of the trainee has not been at the expense of someone else—that there is no displacement of workers by the trainees. This is a hard assumption to validate, for displacement is difficult or impossible to measure. Displacement should be less during periods of high employment (labor shortages) than during periods of economic slack.*

If the objective of the program being evaluated is to enhance the economic welfare of a target population, increases in income experienced by the trainee as a result of his training must be measured. However, the change in income is made up of many more factors than simply changes in employment rate and wages. Changes in welfare payments, unemployment compensation, and other forms of transfer payments that result from program participation must be measured. Taxes must be netted out. Decreases in economic welfare of other members of the target population who are displaced by the trainee should be accounted for if such displacement takes place.

Measurement of all these effects poses significant problems. How much of the change in the wage income of a trainee should properly be attributed to his training? In many instances, individuals can expect normal increases in their income. During periods of increasing economic activity, labor markets tighten and unemployment rates decrease; wages frequently rise. In such circumstances, the income of most of the work force may be expected to increase. Young workers just entering the labor force typically experience considerable unemployment and only low wages, partly as a result of laws that prohibit them from taking certain jobs. More important, perhaps, is the fact that a youth is trying out jobs in search for work that appeals to him, a process that often leads to unemployment. As he ages, his wages and employment increase. If a training program has a large

---

* The displacement effect has an anologue on the cost side. Opportunity costs to society due to the withdrawal of labor from the work force depend upon the employment level. In conditions of high unemployment, opportunity costs should be much less than the earnings that would have been received by the trainee if he had not been working, since other labor stands ready to fill the demand the trainee does not meet.

number of youths, much of the observed increase of income of the trainees can be attributed to this maturation process.

The ideal measure of the increase in trainee income is a comparison of his actual income subsequent to training with what his income would have been without training—clearly an impossible comparison. In the absence of this measure, the best substitute is the work experience and earnings of a control group of individuals who are similar to the trainees in all respects except for the receipt of training. The most satisfactory control group is that formed when potential trainees are randomly assigned to either training or the control group. Such assignments are generally held to be socially unacceptable and I know of no case where such a procedure has been used to construct a control group for a large social action program evaluation.

Many other types of controls have been tried—none of which is very satisfactory. These include:

(1) The program enrollees themselves (before and after comparisons).
(2) Groups of individuals who signed up but failed to enter the program.
(3) Groups of individuals who stayed in the program only a short time.
(4) Groups of individuals having similar backgrounds who for one reason or another did not sign up for training.

The first type of control, the experiences of the enrollees prior to enrollment, has already been discussed. It has very limited credibility at times when labor market conditions change rapidly or in the evaluation of programs serving a large number of youths. The second, third, and fourth types of groups have grave problems of their own; the most pervasive and yet unanalyzable problem is the so-called self-selection problem. Because the trainee group chose to enter the program and the control group chose not to, the two groups may differ in systematic yet unmeasurable ways. In general, the dimensions of these unmeasurable differences are considered to be attitude and motivation.

RAND's experience in examining a comprehensive youth program illustrates this problem.* A retrospective survey of program enrollees was made. Short term enrollees, those staying less than a week, were used as a control group. Their average stay was less than two days. By various criteria, those in the control group did better than the longer term enrollees. In seeking an explanation for

* L. P. Holliday, *Appraising Selected Manpower Training Programs in the Los Angeles Area*, RM-5746-OEO, The RAND Corporation, May 1967, pp. 8–9.

this, the analysts reached the tentative conclusion that the "controls" were typically more motivated than the long term program participants. They left the program quickly because they felt they could do better elsewhere—in this case, by seeking a job by themselves. Indeed, there was some suggestion that the program facilitated this by providing placement counseling.

In contemplating this finding, however, we decided that had the result turned out otherwise, we would have had little confidence in the result. There appears to be an equally plausible set of arguments that would hold that short term stayers or no-shows (the second and third types of control groups listed on the previous page) are less motivated and able. Perhaps the distribution of motivation and attitude for this group is really bi-modal. It includes both the least and most motivated individuals in the population served by the program. One or the other type may predominate in any particular case.

Of the four types of control groups listed, the most satisfactory appears to be the last, a group of individuals who have similar work histories but have never come in contact with the program being evaluated. The choice of such a group has been accomplished in several ways. The Somers study in West Virginia utilized a random sampling of individuals in the files of the employment service.* Earl D. Main used a control group of friends, neighbors, or relatives of the trainee whose names were obtained from the trainee. Page and Gooding used persons who filed regular claims for unemployment compensation who reportedly had similar demographic characteristics.**

Although the last type of control seems most satisfactory, it is by no means obvious that it eliminates the self-selection bias. For this reason, lingering and reasonable doubts about the validity of the estimates of program effects will remain.

LONGITUDINAL VERSUS RETROSPECTIVE STUDIES

Further steps can be taken to satisfy doubts about the adequacy of a control group if the study is longitudinal and the control group is actually chosen *before* the trainees whose experiences are to be examined enter the program. Such a prospective and longitudinal study

*Gerald Somers, ed., *Retraining the Unemployed,* The University of Wisconsin Press, Madison, Wisconsin, 1968, p. 26.
** Main's, Page's and Gooding's results are reported in Einar Hardin, *Benefit Cost Analysis of Occupational Training Programs: A Comparison of Recent Studies,* paper presented at the North American Conference on Cost-Benefit Analysis of Manpower Policies, May 1969, University of Wisconsin, Madison, Wisconsin.

of a major manpower program has not to my knowledge been made, although OEO is now in the process of implementing one.

All of the studies reviewed in the course of preparing this Memorandum were retrospective and most obtained their data at only one point in time. The major limitation of a retrospective non-longitudinal sample is the inability to measure attitudes at different points in time. As a consequence, a control group can be compared with an enrollee group only on objective factors such as age, race, sex, or work experience. Questions about current attitudes or expectations are difficult to phrase and interpret but there is even less reason to place credence in such questions when they refer to a much earlier point in time. Thus, in none of the benefit-cost studies examined were attitudinal questions used to control for differences between a control group and the enrollee group.

In a prospective and longitudinal study, of course, attempts can be made to ascertain the attitudes and expectations of the two groups and differences in these dimensions can conceivably be controlled in comparing the work experiences of the two groups. Such control, however, is hampered by the absence of any well-developed and accepted theory concerning the relationship of attitudes and expectations to job search and retention behavior.*

Longitudinal studies can have other advantages of course. If repeated interviews are made, they may result in more reliable estimates of the sample's work experience because the respondent is not asked to recall information over long periods of time. Program experiences can be monitored in greater detail than that provided by program records. But such studies have disadvantages also. Most important perhaps is their expense. They take place over a longer period of time which means the evaluation staff has to be kept intact for a longer period. Longitudinal studies are susceptible to sample degradation as members of the original sample are lost because of moves, death, or simply because they cannot be found. This may result either in small ultimate sample sizes or a larger initial sample.** Since a prospective, longitudinal evaluation of a large social action program has yet to take place, the importance of both the potential benefits and problems cannot be realistically assessed.

* A preliminary example of such a study is contained in two publications by Ralph Underhill: *Youth in Poor Neighborhoods* and *Methods in the Evaluation of Programs for Poor Youth,* The National Opinion Research Center, Chicago, Illinois, 1967 and 1968.
** Such loss also results in biases because the lost group may be different from those that are found. But these biases are also present in retrospective surveys with low response rates. At least in the longitudinal survey, earlier data can be used to compare the characteristics of the group that is lost with those that are found.

One frequently voiced complaint about prospective and longitudinal studies is that they require longer to complete, increasing the probability that the evaluated programs will have changed; the chance that the evaluation will be irrelevant is higher than would be the case in a retrospective study. This complaint must be examined carefully. If a program is to be evaluated on the basis of the experiences of individuals entering in or terminating from a program during a specified period of time, either type of study will provide data at approximately the same time. But, the decision to undertake the longitudinal study must be made much earlier—sometime prior to when the enrollees whose experiences are to be examined enter the program.

Up to now, evaluation has been a fairly ad hoc activity. Once it was decided that an evaluation was to take place, there were substantial pressures to obtain information as soon as possible. If, however, evaluation becomes more routine, longitudinal study designs become more feasible with a continuing succession of such efforts in being at any given time. With such a commitment, longitudinal studies could provide data to decisionmakers at least as quickly as retrospective studies.

Clearly the desirability of instituting such a continuing program depends upon a variety of factors. Since such studies have not been carried out, we have little evidence on these factors. What is the cost per subject in the sample? Does the probable increase in confidence in the validity of control group/trainee comparisons seem worth the increase in cost? What is the probability that a major program reorganization will render the evaluation results irrelevant? The current OEO evaluation of manpower programs should clarify many of these questions.*. . .

THE EXAMINATION OF ALTERNATIVE DESIGNS

There are relatively few national manpower programs. Moreover, these have been established with only vague hypotheses concerning the combinations of services that are likely to be successful. It is tempting therefore to structure an evaluation in such a way as to provide insight on alternative designs. Suppose the projects examined differ in the mix of services provided or the type of personnel utilized. Would it be useful to view these projects as a form of natural experiment that could be used to cast light on superior project demands and hence suggest changes that should be made in program guidelines?

---

* OEO is currently carrying out a longitudinal evaluation of five manpower programs. Program enrollees in ten cities will be interviewed several times during a period of 18 to 20 months. The evaluators also hope to examine the impact of local labor market characteristics on program outcomes.

Two major problems limit the value of the natural experiment. The first problem has to do with multiple causality. In RAND's examination of a comprehensive youth program there was some indication that successful labor market performance was inversely related to length of stay in the program. There are a number of plausible explanations for such a phenomenon. Perhaps the most reasonable is that youths with more severe problems tend to stay in the program longer and also to have worse labor market performance after they leave the program. Ascribing all of the poor labor market performances to the length of stay rather than to some unmeasured personal characteristics of the enrollee results in the conclusion that the program may be detrimental.

The same may be true for attempts to relate the success of a project to the mix of services it provides. To the extent that the mix of services reflects the peculiar and unique (but unmeasured) needs of the enrollees of the project, attempts to relate success of the project to the mix of services will be frustrated. It will be impossible to separate the impact of the service mix of the project on the labor market performance from the impact of the quality of the enrollees.

Multiple causality frequently plagues the social sciences. Basically, this problem arises because of the lack of a theory of human behavior that relates measurable psychological variables to various forms of human performance. In the absence of such theory, it will be impossible to separate the effects of the multiple causes in natural experiments. This has led to suggestions that more formal experiments be carried out. In such experiments a more systematic attempt would be made to vary project inputs independently of the enrollee characteristics and so lessen the problems of multiple causality.**

The use of experimental projects as a means of systematic program development is likely to be more common in the future. Certainly OEO's experience with rapidly initiating large national programs on the basis of "theory" rather than proven experience would not support the contention that this approach to program development should be continued. Yet the value of experimental projects or social experiments as a means of program development and as a source of planning information remains to be demonstrated. Such experimentation will be expensive and may not lead to replicable de-

---

* See for example Glen G. Cain and Robinson G. Hollister, "Evaluating Manpower Programs for the Disadvantaged," a paper presented at the North American Conference on Cost-Benefit Analysis of Manpower Policies, May 14–15, 1969, University of Wisconsin, Madison, Wisconsin.

** The major current example of such an experiment is Project Follow Through which is seeking to try out a substantial variety of programatic approaches to helping disadvantaged youngsters succeed in the early years in school.

signs. It will take considerable periods of time and require an uncommon cooperation between project operators and evaluators. While the use of social experiments for program development and planning remains an exciting possibility, it should not be viewed as a panacea for the planner seeking to improve program design. . . .

DONALD T. CAMPBELL

Reforms as Experiments[1,2]

The United States and other modern nations should be ready for an
experimental approach to social reform, an approach in which we try
out new programs designed to cure specific social problems, in which
we learn whether or not these programs are effective, and in which
we retain, imitate, modify, or discard them on the basis of apparent
effectiveness on the multiple imperfect criteria available. Our readiness for this stage is indicated by the inclusion of specific provisions
for program evaluation in the first wave of the "Great Society"
legislation, and by the current congressional proposals for establishing "social indicators" and socially relevant "data banks." So long
have we had good intentions in this regard that many may feel we are
already at this stage, that we already are continuing or discontinu-
ing programs on the basis of assessed effectiveness. It is a theme of
this article that this is not at all so, that most ameliorative programs
end up with *no* interpretable evaluation (Etzioni, 1968; Hyman &
Wright, 1967; Schwartz, 1961). We must look hard at the sources of

Donald Campbell, "Reforms as Experiments," *American Psychologist,* vol.
24, no. 4 (April 1969), pp. 409–429. Revised by the author.

[1] The preparation of this paper has been supported by National Science
Foundation Grant GS1309X. Versions of this paper have been presented as the
Northwestern University Alumni Fund Lecture, January 24, 1968; to the Social
Psychology Section of the British Psychological Society at Oxford, September
20, 1968; to the International Conference on Social Psychology at Prague, Oc-
tober 7, 1968 (under a different title); and to several other groups.

[2] Requests for reprints should be sent to Donald T. Campbell, Department
of Psychology, Northwestern University, Evanston, Illinois 60201.

this condition, and design ways of overcoming the difficulties. This article is a preliminary effort in this regard.

Many of the difficulties lie in the intransigencies of the research setting and in the presence of recurrent seductive pitfalls of interpretation. The bulk of this article will be devoted to these problems. But the few available solutions turn out to depend upon correct administrative decisions in the initiation and execution of the program. These decisions are made in a political arena, and involve political jeopardies that are often sufficient to explain the lack of hard-headed evaluation of effects. Removing reform administrators from the political spotlight seems both highly unlikely, and undesirable even if it were possible. What is instead essential is that the social scientist research advisor understand the political realities of the situation, and that he aid by helping create a public demand for hard-headed evaluation, by contributing to those political inventions that reduce the liability of honest evaluation, and by educating future administrators to the problems and possibilities.

For this reason, there is also an attempt in this article to consider the political setting of program evaluation, and to offer suggestions as to political postures that might further a truly experimental approach to social reform. Although such considerations will be distributed as a minor theme throughout this article, it seems convenient to begin with some general points of this political nature.

Political Vulnerability
from Knowing Outcomes

It is one of the most characteristic aspects of the present situation that *specific reforms are advocated as though they were certain to be successful.* For this reason, knowing outcomes has immediate political implications. Given the inherent difficulty of making significant improvements by the means usually provided and given the discrepancy between promise and possibility, most administrators wisely prefer to limit the evaluations to those the outcomes of which they can control, particularly insofar as published outcomes or press releases are concerned. Ambiguity, lack of truly comparable comparison bases, and lack of concrete evidence all work to increase the administrator's control over what gets said, or at least to reduce the bite of criticism in the case of actual failure. There is safety under the cloak of ignorance. Over and above this tie-in advocacy and administration, there is another source of vulnerability in that the facts relevant to experimental program evaluation are also available to argue the general efficiency and honesty of administrators. The public availability of such facts reduces the privacy and security of at least some administrators.

Even where there are ideological commitments to a hard-headed evaluation of organizational efficiency, or to a scientific organization of society, these two jeopardies lead to the failure to evaluate organizational experiments realistically. If the political and administrative system has committed itself in advance to the correctness and efficacy of its reforms, it cannot tolerate learning of failure. To be truly scientific we must be able to experiment. We must be able to advocate without that excess of commitment that blinds us to reality testing.

This predicament, abetted by public apathy and by deliberate corruption, may prove in the long run to permanently preclude a truly experimental approach to social amelioration. But our needs and our hopes for a better society demand we make the effort. There are a few signs of hope. In the United States we have been able to achieve cost-of-living and unemployment indices that, however imperfect, have embarrassed the administrations that published them. We are able to conduct censuses that reduce the number of representatives a state has in Congress. These are grounds for optimism, although the corrupt tardiness of state governments in following their own constitutions in revising legislative districts illustrates the problem.

One simple shift in political posture which would reduce the problem is the shift from the advocacy of a specific reform to the advocacy of the seriousness of the problem, and hence to the advocacy of persistence in alternative reform efforts should the first one fail. The political stance would become: "This is a serious problem. We propose to initiate Policy A on an experimental basis. If after five years there has been no significant improvement, we will shift to Policy B." By making explicit that a given problem solution was only one of several that the administrator or party could in good conscience advocate, and by having ready a plausible alternative, the administrator could afford honest evaluation of outcomes. Negative results, a failure of the first program, would not jeopardize his job, for his job would be to keep after the problem until something was found that worked.

Coupled with this should be a general moratorium on ad hominum evaluative research, that is, on research designed to evaluate specific administrators rather than alternative policies. If we worry about the invasion-of-privacy problem in the data banks and social indicators of the future (e.g., Sawyer & Schechter, 1968), the touchiest point is the privacy of administrators. If we threaten this, the measurement system will surely be sabotaged in the innumerable ways possible. While this may sound unduly pessimistic, the recurrent anecdotes of administrators attempting to squelch unwanted research findings convince me of its accuracy. But we should be able to evaluate those alternative policies that a given administrator has the option of implementing.

Field Experiments and Quasi-Experimental Designs

In efforts to extend the logic of laboratory experimentation into the "field," and into settings not fully experimental, an inventory of threats to experimental validity has been assembled, in terms of which some 15 or 20 experimental and quasi-experimental designs have been evaluated (Campbell, 1957, 1963; Campbell & Stanley, 1963). In the present article only three or four designs will be examined, and therefore not all of the validity threats will be relevant, but it will provide useful background to look briefly at them all. Following are nine threats to internal validity.[3]

1. *History:* events, other than the experimental treatment, occurring between pretest and posttest and thus providing alternate explanations of effects.
2. *Maturation:* processes within the respondents or observed social units producing changes as a function of the passage of time per se, such as growth, fatigue, secular trends, etc.
3. *Instability:* unreliability of measures, fluctuations in sampling persons or components, autonomous instability of repeated or "equivalent" measures. (This is the only threat to which statistical tests of significance are revelant.)
4. *Testing:* the effect of taking a test upon the scores of a second testing. The effect of publication of a social indicator upon subsequent readings of that indicator.
5. *Instrumentation:* in which changes in the calibration of a measuring instrument or changes in the observers or scores used may produce changes in the obtained measurements.

---

3 This list has been expanded from the major previous presentations by the addition of *Instability* (but see Campbell, 1968; Campbell & Ross, 1968). This has been done in reaction to the sociological discussion of the use of tests of significance in nonexperimental or quasi-experimental research (e.g., Selvin, 1957; and as reviewed by Galtung, 1967, pp. 358–389). On the one hand, I join with the critics in criticizing the exaggerated status of "statistically significant differences" in establishing convictions of validity. Statistical tests are relevant to at best 1 out of 15 or so threats to validity. On the other hand, I join with those who defend their use in situations where randomization has not been employed. Even in those situations, it is relevant to say or to deny, "This is a trivial difference. It is of the order that would have occurred frequently *had* these measures been assigned to these classes solely by chance." Tests of significance, making use of random reassignments of the actual scores, are particularly useful in communicating this point.

6. *Regression artifacts:* pseudo-shifts occurring when persons or treatment units have been selected upon the basis of their extreme scores.

7. *Selection:* biases resulting from differential recruitment of comparison groups, producing different mean levels on the measure of effects.

8. *Experimental mortality:* the differential loss of respondents from comparison groups.

9. *Selection-maturation interaction:* selection biases resulting in differential rates of "maturation" or autonomous change.

If a change or difference occurs, these are rival explanations that could be used to explain away an effect and thus to deny that in this specific experiment any genuine effect of the experimental treatment had been demonstrated. These are faults that true experiments avoid, primarily through the use of randomization and control groups. In the approach here advocated, this checklist is used to evaluate specific quasi-experimental designs. This is evaluation, not rejection, for it often turns out that for a specific design in a specific setting the threat is implausible, or that there are supplementary data that can help rule it out even where randomization is impossible. The general ethic, here advocated for public administrators as well as social scientists, is to use the very best method possible, aiming at "true experiments" with random control groups. But where randomized treatments are not possible, a self-critical use of quasi-experimental designs is advocated. We must do the best we can with what is available to us.

Our posture vis-à-vis perfectionist critics from laboratory experimentation is more militant than this: the only threats to validity that we will allow to invalidate an experiment are those that admit of the status of empirical laws more dependable and more plausible than the law involving the treatment. The mere possibility of some alternative explanation is not enough—it is only the *plausible* rival hypotheses that are invalidating. Vis-à-vis correlational studies and common-sense descriptive studies, on the other hand, our stance is one of greater conservatism. For example, because of the specific methodological trap of regression artifacts, the sociological tradition of "ex post facto" designs (Chapin, 1947; Greenwood, 1945) is totally rejected (Campbell & Stanley, 1963, pp. 240–241; 1966, pp. 70–71).

Threats to external validity, which follow, cover the validity problems involved in interpreting experimental results, the threats to valid generalization of the results to other settings, to other versions of the treatment, or to other measures of the effect:[4]

---

[4] This list has been lengthened from previous presentations to make more salient Threats 5 and 6 which are particularly relevant to social experimentation.

1. *Interaction effects of testing:* the effect of a pretest in increasing or decreasing the respondent's sensitivity or responsiveness to the experimental variable, thus making the results obtained for a pretested population unrepresentative of the effects of the experimental variable for the unpretested universe from which the experimental respondents were selected.

2. *Interaction of selection and experimental treatment:* unrepresentative responsiveness of the treated population.

3. *Reactive effects of experimental arrangements:* "artificiality"; conditions making the experimental setting atypical· of conditions of regular application of the treatment: "Hawthorne effects."

4. *Multiple-treatment interference:* where multiple treatments are jointly applied, effects atypical of the separate application of the treatments.

5. *Irrelevant responsiveness of measures:* all measures are complex, and all include irrelevant components that may produce apparent effects.

6. *Irrelevant replicability of treatments:* treatments are complex, and replications of them may fail to include those components actually responsible for the effects.

These threats apply equally to true experiments and quasi-experiments. They are particularly relevant to applied experimentation. In the cumulative history of our methodology, this class of threats was first noted as a critique of true experiments involving pretests (Schanck & Goodman, 1939; Solomon, 1949). Such experiments provided a sound basis for generalizing to other *pretested* populations, but the reactions of unpretested populations to the treatment might well be quite different. As a result, there has been an advocacy of true experimental designs obviating the pretest (Campbell, 1957; Schanck & Goodman, 1939; Solomon, 1949) and a search for nonreactive measures (Webb, Campbell, Schwartz, & Sechrest, 1966).

These threats to validity will serve as a background against which we will discuss several research designs particularly appropriate for evaluating specific programs of social amelioration. These are the "interrupted time-series design," the "control series design," "regression discontinuity design," and various "true experiments." The order is from a weak but generally available design to stronger ones that require more administrative foresight and determination.

Discussion in previous presentations (Campbell, 1957, pp. 309–310; Campbell & Stanley, 1963, pp. 203–204) had covered these points, but they had not been included in the checklist.

Interrupted Times-Series Design

By and large, when a political unit initiates a reform it is put into effect across the board, with the total unit being affected. In this setting the only comparison base is the record of previous years. The usual mode of utilization is a casual version of a very weak quasi-experimental design, the one-group pretest-posttest design.

A convenient illustration comes from the 1955 Connecticut crackdown on speeding, which Sociologist H. Laurence Ross and I have been analyzing as a methodological illustration (Campbell & Ross, 1968; Glass, 1968; Ross & Campbell, 1968). After a record high of traffic fatalities in 1955, Governor Abraham Ribicoff instituted an unprecedentedly severe crackdown on speeding. At the end of a year of such enforcement there had been but 284 traffic deaths as compared with 324 the year before. In announcing this the Governor stated, "With the saving of 40 lives in 1956, a reduction of 12.3% from the 1955 motor vehicle death toll, we can say that the program is definitely worthwhile." These results are graphed in Figure 1, with a deliberate effort to make them look impressive.

In what follows, while we in the end decide that the crackdown had some beneficial effects, we criticize Ribicoff's interpretation of his results, from the point of view of the social scientist's proper standards of evidence. Were the now Senator Ribicoff not the man of stature that he is, this would be most unpolitic, because we could be alienating one of the strongest proponents of social experimentation in our nation. Given his character, however, we may feel sure that he shares our interests both in a progressive program of experimental social amelioration, and in making the most hard-headed evaluation possible of these experiments. Indeed, it was his integrity in using every available means at his disposal as Governor to make sure that the unpopular speeding crackdown was indeed enforced that make these data worth examining at all. But the potentials of this one illustration and our political temptation to substitute for it a less touchy one, point to the political problems that must be faced in experimenting with social reform.

Keeping Figure 1 and Ribicoff's statement in mind, let us look at the same data presented as a part of an extended time series in Figure 2 and go over the relevant threats to internal validity. First, *History.* Both presentations fail to control for the effects of other potential change agents. For instance, 1956 might have been a particularly dry year, with fewer accidents due to rain or snow. Or there might have been a dramatic increase in use of seat belts, or other safety features. The advocated strategy in quasi-experimentation is not to throw up one's hands and refuse to use the evidence because of this

FIGURE 1

CONNECTICUT TRAFFIC FATALITIES.

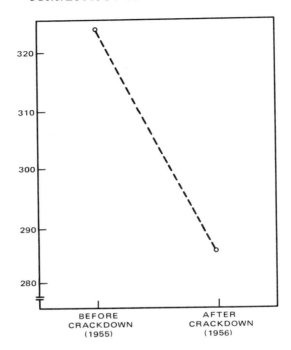

lack of control, but rather to generate by informed criticism appropriate to this specific setting as many *plausible* rival hypotheses as possible, and then to do the supplementary research, as into weather records and safety-belt sales, for example, which would reflect on these rival hypotheses.

Maturation. This is a term coming from criticisms of training studies of children. Applied here to the simple pretest-posttest data of Figure 1, it could be the plausible rival hypothesis that death rates were steadily going down year after year (as indeed they are, relative to miles driven or population of automobiles). Here the extended time series has a strong methodological advantage, and rules out this threat to validity. The general trend is inconsistently up prior to the crackdown, and steadily down thereafter.

Instability. Seemingly implicit in the public pronouncement was the assumption that all of the change from 1955 to 1956 was due to the crackdown. There was no recognition of the fact that all time series

FIGURE 2

CONNECTICUT TRAFFIC FATALITIES.

(*Same data as in Figure 1 presented as part of an extended time series.*)

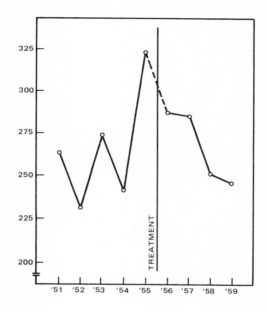

are unstable even when no treatments are being applied. The degree of this normal instability is the crucial issue, and one of the main advantages of the extended time series is that it samples this instability. The great pretreatment instability now makes the treatment effect look relatively trivial. The 1955–56 shift is less than the gains of both 1954–55 and 1952–53. It is the largest drop in the series, but it exceeds the drops of 1951–52, 1953–54, and 1957–58 by trivial amounts. Thus the unexplained instabilities of the series are such as to make the 1955–56 drop understandable as more of the same. On the other hand, it is noteworthy that after the crackdown there are no year-to-year gains, and in this respect the character of the time series seems definitely to have changed.

The threat of instability is the only threat to which tests of significance are relevant. Box and Tiao (1965) have an elegant Bayesian model for the interrupted time series. Applied by Glass (1968) to our monthly data, with seasonal trends removed, it shows a statistically significant downward shift in the series after the crackdown. But as we shall see, an alternative explanation of at least part of this significant effect exists.

Regression. In true experiments the treatment is applied independently of the prior state of the units. In natural experiments exposure to treatment is often a cosymptom of the treated groups' condition. The treatment is apt to be an *effect* rather than, or in addition to being, a cause. Psychotherapy is such a cosymptom treatment, as is any other in which the treated group is self-selected or assigned on the basis of need. These all present special problems of interpretation, of which the present illustration provides one type.

The selection-regression plausible rival hypothesis works this way: Given that the fatality rate has some degree of unreliability, then a subsample selected for its extremity in 1955 would on the average, merely as a reflection of that unreliability, be less extreme in 1956. Has there been selection for extremity in applying this treatment? Probably yes. Of all Connecticut fatality years, the most likely time for a crackdown would be after an exceptionally high year. If the time series showed instability, the subsequent year would on the average be less, *purely as a function of that instability.* Regression artifacts are probably the most recurrent form of self-deception in the experimental social reform literature. It is hard to make them intuitively obvious. Let us try again. Take any time series with variability, including one generated of pure error. Move along it as in a time dimension. Pick a point that is the "highest so far." Look then at the next point. On the average this next point will be lower, or nearer the general trend.

In our present setting the most striking shift in the whole series is the upward shift just prior to the crackdown. It is highly probable that this caused the crackdown, rather than, or in addition to, the crackdown causing the 1956 drop. At least part of the 1956 drop is an artifact of the 1955 extremity. While in principle the degree of expected regression can be computed from the autocorrelation of the series, we lack here an extended-enough body of data to do this with any confidence.

Advice to administrators who want to do genuine reality-testing must include attention to this problem, and it will be a very hard problem to surmount. The most general advice would be to work on chronic problems of a persistent urgency or extremity, rather than reacting to momentary extremes. The administrator should look at the pretreatment time series to judge whether or not instability plus momentary extremity will explain away his program gains. If it will, he should schedule the treatment for a year or two later, so that his decision is more independent of the one year's extremity. (The selection biases remaining under such a procedure need further examination.)

In giving advice to the *experimental* administrator, one is also inevitably giving advice to those *trapped* administrators whose political predicament requires a favorable outcome whether valid or not. To such trapped administrators the advice is pick the very worst year, and the very worst social unit. If there is inherent instability, there is nowhere to go but up, for the average case at least.

Two other threats to internal validity need discussion in regard to this design. By *testing* we typically have in mind the condition under which a test of attitude, ability, or personality is itself a change agent, persuading, informing, practicing, or otherwise setting processes of change in action. No artificially introduced testing procedures are involved here. However, for the simple before-and-after design of Figure 1, if the pretest were the first data collection of its kind ever publicized, this publicity in itself might produce a reduction in traffic deaths which would have taken place even without a speeding crackdown. Many traffic safety programs assume this. The longer time-series evidence reassures us on this only to the extent that we can assume that the figures had been published each year with equivalent emphasis.[5]

Instrumentation changes are not a likely flaw in this instance, but would be if recording practices and institutional responsibility had shifted simultaneously with the crackdown. Probably in a case like this it is better to use raw frequencies rather than indices whose correction parameters are subject to periodic revision. Thus per capita rates are subject to periodic jumps as new census figures become available correcting old extrapolations. Analogously, a change in the miles per gallon assumed in estimating traffic mileage for mileage-based mortality rates might explain a shift. Such biases can of course work to disguise a true effect. Almost certainly, Ribicoff's crackdown reduced traffic speed (Campbell & Ross, 1968). Such a decrease in speed increases the miles per gallon actually obtained, producing a concomitant drop in the estimate of miles driven, which would appear as an inflation of the estimate of mileage-based traffic fatalities if the

---

[5] No doubt the public and press shared the Governor's special alarm over the 1955 death toll. This differential reaction could be seen as a negative feedback servosystem in which the dampening effect was proportional to the degree of upward deviation from the prior trend. Insofar as such alarm reduces the traffic fatalities, it adds a negative component to the autocorrelation, increasing the regression effect. This component should probably be regarded as a rival cause or treatment rather than as artifact. (The regression effect is less as the positive autocorrelation is higher, and will be present to some degree insofar as this correlation is less than positive unity. Negative correlation in a time series would represent regression beyond the mean, in a way not quite analogous to negative correlation across persons. For an autocorrelation of Lag 1, high negative correlation would be represented by a series that oscillated maximally from one extreme to the other.)

FIGURE 3

NUMBER OF REPORTED LARCENIES UNDER $50 IN
CHICAGO, ILLINOIS, FROM 1942 TO 1962

(data from Uniform Crime Reports for the United States, 1942–62).

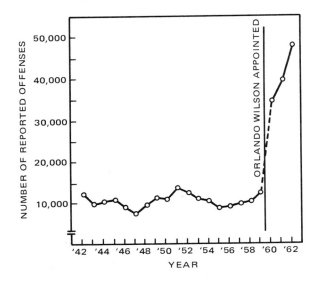

same fixed approximation to actual miles per gallon were used, as it undoubtedly would be.

The "new broom" that introduces abrupt changes of policy is apt to reform the record keeping too, and thus confound reform treatments with instrumentation change. The ideal experimental administrator will, if possible, avoid doing this. He will prefer to keep comparable a partially imperfect measuring system rather than lose comparability altogether. The politics of the situation do not always make this possible, however. Consider, as an experimental reform, Orlando Wilson's reorganization of the police system in Chicago. Figure 3 shows his impact on petty larceny in Chicago—a striking *increase!* Wilson, of course, called this shot in advance, one aspect of his reform being a reform in the bookkeeping. (Note in the pre-Wilson records the suspicious absence of the expected upward secular trend.) In this situation Wilson had no choice. Had he left the record keeping as it was, for the purposes of better experimental

FIGURE 4

NUMBER OF REPORTED MURDERS AND NONNEGLIGENT MANSLAUGHTERS IN CHICAGO, ILLINOIS, FROM 1942 TO 1962

(*data from* Uniform Crime Reports for the United States, *1942–62*).

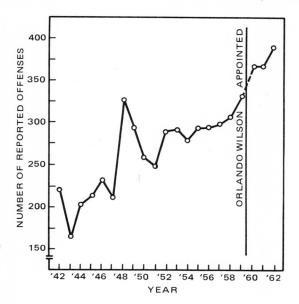

design, his resentful patrolmen would have clobbered him with a crime wave by deliberately starting to record the many complaints that had not been getting into the books.[6]

Those who advocate the use of archival measures as social indicators (Bauer, 1966; Gross, 1966, 1967; Kaysen, 1967; Webb et al., 1966) must face up not only to their high degree of chaotic error and systematic bias, but also to the politically motivated changes in record keeping that will follow upon their public use as social indicators (Etzioni & Lehman, 1967). Not all measures are equally susceptible. In Figure 4, Orlando Wilson's effect on homicides seems negligible one way or the other.

---

[6] Wilson's inconsistency in utilization of records and the political problem of relevant records are ably documented in Kamisar (1964). Etzioni (1968) reports that in New York City in 1965 a crime wave was proclaimed that turned out to be due to an unpublicized improvement in record keeping.

Of the threats to external validity, the one most relevant to social experimentation is *Irrelevant Responsiveness of Measures*. This seems best discussed in terms of the problem of generalizing from indicator to indicator or in terms of the imperfect validity of all measures that is only to be overcome by the use of multiple measures of independent imperfection (Campbell & Fiske, 1959; Webb et al., 1966).

For treatments on any given problem within any given governmental or business subunit, there will usually be something of a governmental monopoly on reform. Even though different divisions may optimally be trying different reforms, within each division there will usually be only one reform on a given problem going on at a time. But for measures of effect this need not and should not be the case. The administrative machinery should itself make mutiple measures of potential benefits and of unwanted side effects. In addition, the loyal opposition should be allowed to add still other indicators, with the political process and adversary argument challenging both validity and relative importance, with social science methodologists testifying for both parties, and with the basic records kept public and under bipartisan audit (as are voting records under optimal conditions). This competitive scrutiny is indeed the main source of objectivity in sciences (Polanyi, 1966, 1967; Popper, 1963) and epitomizes an ideal of democratic practice in both judicial and legislative procedures.

The next few figures return again to the Connecticut crackdown on speeding and look to some other measures of effect. They are relevant to the confirming that there was indeed a crackdown, and to the issue of side effects. They also provide the methodological comfort of assuring us that in some cases the interrupted time-series design can provide clear-cut evidence of effect. Figure 5 shows the jump in suspensions of licenses for speeding—evidence that severe punishment was abruptly instituted. Again a note to experimental administrators: with this weak design, *it is only abrupt and decisive changes that we have any chance of evaluating.* A gradually introduced reform will be indistinguishable from the background of secular change, from the net effect of the innumerable change agents continually impinging.

We would want intermediate evidence that traffic speed was modified. A sampling each year of a few hundred five-minute highway movies (random as to location and time) could have provided this at a moderate cost, but they were not collected. Of the public records available, perhaps the data of Figure 6, showing a reduction in speeding violations, indicate a reduction in traffic speed. But the effects on the legal system were complex, and in part undesirable. Driving with a suspended license markedly increased (Figure 7), at least in the biased sample of those arrested. Presumably because

FIGURE 5

SUSPENSIONS OF LICENSES FOR SPEEDING, AS A
PERCENTAGE OF ALL SUSPENSIONS.

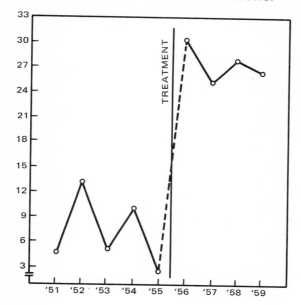

of the harshness of the punishment if guilty, judges may have become
more lenient (Figure 8) although this effect is of marginal significance.

The relevance of indicators for the social problems we wish
to cure must be kept continually in focus. The social indicators approach will tend to make the indicators themselves the goal of social
action, rather than the social problems they but imperfectly indicate.
There are apt to be tendencies to legislate changes in the indicators
per se rather than changes in the social problems.

To illustrate the problem of the irrelevant responsiveness of
measures, Figure 9 shows a result of the 1900 change in divorce
law in Germany. In a recent reanalysis of the data with the Box and
Tiao (1965) statistic, Glass (Glass, Tiao, & Maguire, 1969) has
found the change highly significant, in contrast to earlier statistical
analyses (Rheinstein, 1959; Wolf, Lüke, & Hax, 1959). But Rheinstein's emphasis would still be relevant: The indicator change indicates no likely improvement in marital harmony, or even in marital
stability. Rather than reducing them, the legal change has made the

FIGURE 6

SPEEDING VIOLATIONS, AS A PERCENTAGE
OF ALL TRAFFIC VIOLATIONS.

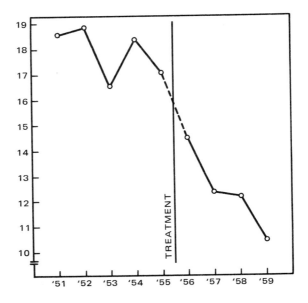

divorce rate a less valid indicator of marital discord and separation
than it had been earlier (see also Etzioni & Lehman, 1967).

Control Series Design

The interrupted time-series design as discussed so far is available
for those settings in which no control group is possible, in which
the total governmental unit has received the experimental treatment,
the social reform measure. In the general program of quasi-
experimental design, we argue the great advantage of untreated comparison groups even where these cannot be assigned at random. The
most common of such designs is the non-equivalent control-group
pretest-posttest design, in which for each of two natural groups, one of
which receives the treatment, a pretest and posttest measure is taken.
If the traditional mistaken practice is avoided of matching on pretest
scores (with resultant regression artifacts), this design provides a
useful control over those aspects of history, maturation, and test-retest

effects shared by both groups. But it does not control for the plausible rival hypothesis of *selection-maturation interaction*—that is, the hypothesis that the selection differences in the natural aggregations involve not only differences in mean level, but differences in maturation rate.

This point can be illustrated in terms of the traditional quasi-experimental design problem of the effects of Latin on English vocabulary (Campbell, 1963). In the hypothetical data of Figure 10B, two alternative interpretations remain open. Latin may have had effect, for those taking Latin gained more than those not. But, on the other hand, those students taking Latin may have a greater annual rate of vocabulary growth that would manifest itself whether or not they took Latin. Extending this common design into two time series provides relevant evidence, as comparison of the two alternative outcomes of Figure 10C and 10D shows. Thus approaching quasi-experimental design from either improving the nonequivalent control-group design or from improving the interrupted time-series design,

FIGURE 7

ARRESTED WHILE DRIVING WITH A SUSPENDED LICENSE, AS A PERCENTAGE OF SUSPENSIONS.

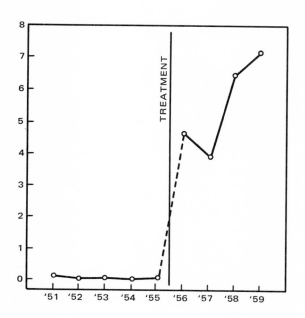

FIGURE 8

PERCENTAGE OF SPEEDING VIOLATIONS JUDGED
NOT GUILTY.

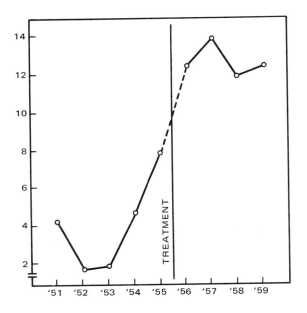

we arrive at the control series design. Figure 11 shows this for the Connecticut speeding crackdown, adding evidence from the fatality rates of neighboring states. Here the data are presented as population-based fatality rates so as to make the two series of comparable magnitude.

The control series design of Figure 11 shows that downward trends were available in the other states for 1955–56 as due to history and maturation, that is, due to shared secular trends, weather, automotive safety features, etc. But the data also show a general trend for Connecticut to rise relatively closer to the other states prior to 1955, and to steadily drop more rapidly than other states from 1956 on. Glass (1968) has used our monthly data for Connecticut and the control states to generate a monthly difference score, and this too shows a significant shift in trend in the Box and Tiao (1965) statistic. Impressed particularly by the 1957, 1958, and 1959 trend, we are willing to conclude that the crackdown had some effect, over and above the undeniable pseudo-effects of regression (Campbell & Ross, 1968).

The advantages of the control series design point to the advantages for social experimentation of a social system allowing subunit diversity. Our ability to estimate the effects of the speeding crackdown, Rose's (1952) and Stieber (1949) ability to estimate the effects on strikes of compulsory arbitration laws, and Simon's (1966) ability to estimate the price elasticity of liquor were made possible because the changes were not being put into effect in all states simultaneously, because they were matters of state legislation rather than national. I do not want to appear to justify on these grounds the wasteful and unjust diversity of laws and enforcement practices from state to state. But I would strongly advocate that social engineers make use of this diversity while it remains available, and plan cooperatively their changes in administrative policy and in record keeping so as to provide optimal experimental inference. More important is the recommendation that, for those aspects of social reform handled by the central government, a purposeful diversity of implementation be envisaged so that experimental and control groups be available for analysis. Properly planned, these can approach true experiments, better than the casual and ad hoc comparison groups now available.

FIGURE 9

DIVORCE RATE FOR GERMAN EMPIRE, 1881–1914.

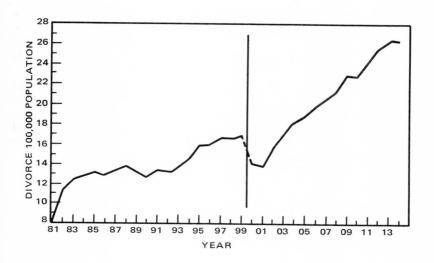

FIGURE 10

FORMS OF QUASI-EXPERIMENTAL ANALYSIS FOR THE EFFECT
OF SPECIFIC COURSE WORK, INCLUDING CONTROL
SERIES DESIGN.

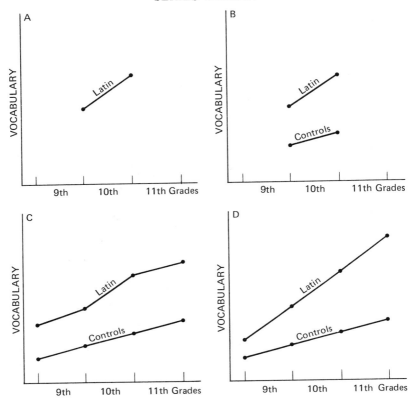

But without such fundamental planning, uniform central control can reduce the present possibilities of reality testing, that is, of true social experimentation. In the same spirit, decentralization of decision making, both within large government and within private monopolies, can provide a useful competition for both efficiency and innovation, reflected in a multiplicity of indicators.

The British Breathalyser Crackdown

One further illustration of the interrupted time series and the control series will be provided. The variety of illustrations so far provided have each illustrated some methodological point, and have thus ended

up as "bad examples." To provide a "good example," an instance
which survives methodological critique as a valid illustration of a
successful reform, data from The British Road Safety Act of 1967
are provided in Figure 11a (from H. R. Ross, D. T. Campbell, and
G. V. Glass. "Determining the social effects of a legal reform: The
British 'Breathalyser' Crackdown of 1967," *American Behavioral
Scientist,* 1970, vol. 13, no. 4, March–April, pp. 493–509).

The data on a weekly-hours basis are only available for a composite category of fatalities plus serious injuries, and Figure 11a
therefore uses this composite for all three bodies of data. The "Week-
End-Nights" comprises Friday and Saturday nights from 10:00 p.m.
to 4:00 a.m. Here, as expected, the crackdown is most dramatically
effective, producing initially more than a 40 percent drop, leveling
off at perhaps 30 percent, although this involves dubious extrapolations in the absence of some control comparison to indicate what the
trend over the years might have been without the crackdown. In this
British case, no comparison state with comparable traffic conditions
or drinking laws was available. But controls need not always be
separate groups of persons, they may also be separate samples of times

FIGURE 11

*CONTROL SERIES DESIGN
COMPARING CONNECTICUT FATALITIES
WITH THOSE OF FOUR COMPARABLE STATES*

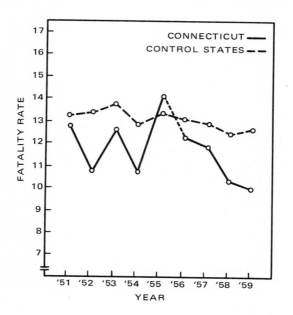

FIGURE 11a

BRITISH TRAFFIC FATALITIES PLUS SERIOUS INJURIES,
BEFORE AND AFTER THE BREATHALYSER CRACKDOWN OF
OCTOBER 1967 (SEASONALLY ADJUSTED)

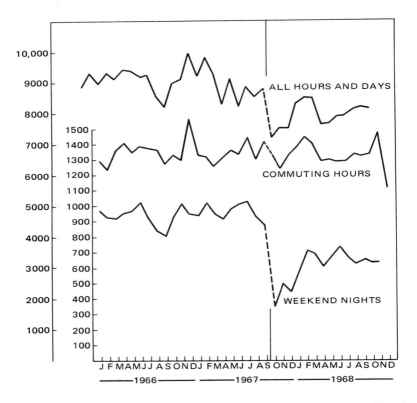

or stimulus materials (Campbell and Stanley, 1966, pp. 43–47). A
cigarette company may use the sales of its main competitor as a
control comparison to evaluate a new advertising campaign. One
should search around for the most nearly appropriate control comparison. For the Breathalyser crackdown, commuting hours when
pubs had been long closed seemed ideal. (The Commuting Hours
figures come from 7:00 a.m. to 10:00 p.m. and 4:00 p.m. to 5:00 p.m.
Monday through Friday. Pubs are open for lunch from 12:00 to 2:00
or 2:30, and open again at 5:00 p.m.)

These commuting hours data convincingly show no effect, but
are too unstable to help much with estimating the long term effects.
They show a different annual cycle than do the week-end nights or the

overall figures, and do not go back far enough to provide an adequate base for estimating this annual cycle with precision.

The use of a highly judgmental category such as "serious injuries" provides an opportunity for pseudo-effects due to a shift in the classifiers' standards. The overall figures are available separately for fatalities, and these show a highly significant effect as strong as that found for the serious injury category or the composite shown in Figure 11a.

More details and the methodological problems are considered in our fuller presentation (H. R. Ross, D. T. Campbell, and G. V. Glass, 1970). One further rule for the use of this design needs emphasizing. The interrupted time series can only provide clear evidence of effect where the reform is introduced with a vigorous abruptness. A gradually introduced reform has little chance of being distinguished from shifts in secular trends or from the cumulative effect of the many other influences impinging during a prolonged period of introduction. In the Breathalyser crackdown, an intense publicity campaign naming the specific starting date preceded the actual crackdown. Although the impact seems primarily due to publicity and fear rather than actual increase of arrests, an abrupt initiation date was achieved. Had the enforcement effort changed at the moment the act was passed, with public awareness being built up by subsequent publicity, the resulting data series would have been essentially uninterpretable.

Regression Discontinuity Design

We shift now to social ameliorations that are in short supply, and that therefore cannot be given to all individuals. Such scarcity is inevitable under many circumstances, and can make possible an evaluation of effects that would otherwise be impossible. Consider the heroic Salk poliomyelitis vaccine trials in which some children were given the vaccine while others were given an inert saline placebo injection —and in which many more of these placebo controls would die than would have if they had been given the vaccine. Creation of these placebo controls would have been morally, psychologically, and socially impossible had there been enough vaccine for all. As it was, due to the scarcity, most children that year had to go without the vaccine anyway. The creation of experimental and control groups was the highly moral allocation of that scarcity so as to enable us to learn the true efficacy of the supposed good. The usual medical practice of introducing new cures on a so-called trial basis in general medical practice makes evaluation impossible by confounding prior status with treatment, that is, giving the drug to the most needy or most hopeless. It has the further social bias of giving the supposed benefit to those

most assiduous in keeping their medical needs in the attention of the
medical profession, that is, the upper and upper-middle classes. The
political stance furthering social experimentation here is the recognition of randomization as the most democratic and moral means of
allocating scarce resources (and scarce hazardous duties), plus the
moral imperative to further utilize the randomization so that society
may indeed learn true value of the supposed boon. This is the ideology
that makes possible "true experiments" in a large class of social
reforms.

But if randomization is not politically feasible or morally justifiable in a given setting, there is a powerful quasi-experimental design
available that allows the scarce good to be given to the most needy or
the most deserving. This is the regression discontinuity design. All it
requires is strict and orderly attention to the priority dimension. The
design originated through an advocacy of a tie-breaking experiment
to measure the effects of receiving a fellowship (Thistlethwaite &
Campbell, 1960), and it seems easiest to explain it in that light.
Consider as in Figure 12, pre-award ability-and-merit dimension,
which would have some relation to later success in life (finishing col-

FIGURE 12

TIE-BREAKING EXPERIMENT AND REGRESSION
DISCONTINUITY ANALYSIS

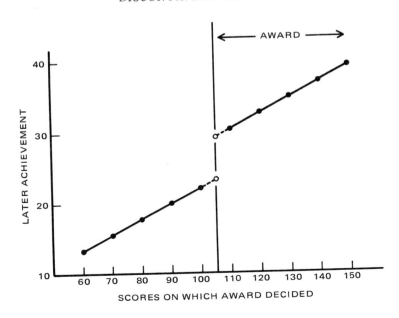

lege, earnings 10 years later, etc.). Those higher on the premeasure are most deserving and receive the award. They do better in later life, but does the award have an effect? It is normally impossible to say because they would have done better in later life anyway. Full randomization of the award was impossible given the stated intention to reward merit and ability. But it might be possible to take a narrow band of ability at the cutting point, to regard all of these persons as tied, and to assign half of them to awards, half to no awards, by means of a tie-breaking randomization.

The tie-breaking rationale is still worth doing, but in considering that design it became obvious that, if the regression of premeasure on later effects were reasonably orderly, one should be able to extrapolate to the results of the tie-breaking experiment by plotting the regression of posttest on pretest separately for those in the award and non-award regions. If there is no significant difference for these at the decision-point intercept, then the tie-breaking experiment should show no difference. In cases where the tie breakers would show an effect, there should be an abrupt discontinuity in the regression line. Such a discontinuity cannot be explained away by the normal regression of the posttest on pretest, for this normal regression, as extensively sampled within the nonaward area and within the award area, provides no such expectation.

Figure 12 presents, in terms of column means, an instance in which higher pretest scores would have led to higher posttest scores even without the treatment, and in which there is in addition a substantial treatment effect. Figure 13 shows a series of paired outcomes, those on the left to be interpreted as no effect, those in the center and on the right as effect. Note some particular cases. In instances of granting opportunity on the basis of merit, like 13a and b (and Figure 12), neglect of the background regression of pretest on posttest leads to optimistic pseudo-effects: in Figure 13a, those receiving the award do do better in later life, though not really because of the award. But in social ameliorative efforts, the setting is more apt to be like Figure 13d and e, where neglect of the background regression is apt to make the program look deleterious if no effect, or ineffective if there is a real effect.

The design will of course work just as well or better if the award dimension and the decision base, the pretest measure, are unrelated to the posttest dimension, if it is irrelevant or unfair, as instanced in Figure 13g, h, and i. In such cases the decision base is the functional equivalent of randomization. Negative background relationships are obviously possible, as in Figure 13j, k, and l. In Figure 13, m, n, and o are included to emphasize that it is a jump in intercept at the cutting point that shows effect, and that differences in

FIGURE 13

ILLUSTRATIVE OUTCOMES OF REGRESSION DISCONTINUITY ANALYSES

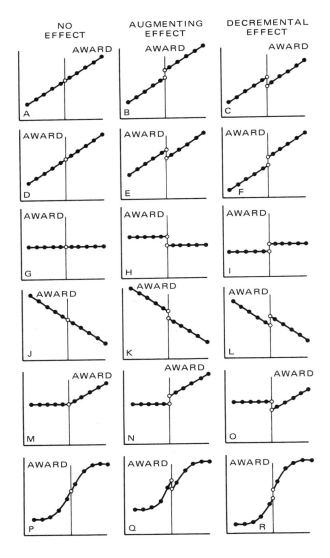

slope without differences at the cutting point are not acceptable as evidences of effect. This becomes more obvious if we remember that in cases like m, a tie-breaking randomization experiment would have shown no difference. Curvilinear background relationships, as in Figure 13p, q, and r, will provide added obstacles to clear inference in many instances, where sampling error could make Figure 13p look like 13b.

This design could be used in a number of settings. Consider Job Training Corps applicants, in larger number than the program can accommodate, with eligibility determined by need. The setting would be as in Figure 13d and e. The base-line decision dimension could be per capita family income, with those at below the cutoff getting training. The outcome dimension could be the amount of withholding tax withheld two years later, or the percentage drawing unemployment insurance, these follow-up figures being provided from the National Data Bank in response to categorized social security numbers fed in, without individual anonymity being breached, without any real invasion of privacy—by the technique of Mutually Insulated Data Banks. While the plotted points could be named, there is no need that they be named. In a classic field experiment on tax compliance, Richard Schwartz and the Bureau of Internal Revenue have managed to put together sets of personally identified interviews and tax-return data so that statistical analyses such as these can be done, without the separate custodians of either interview or tax returns learning the corresponding data for specific persons (Schwartz and Orleans, 1967; see also Schwartz and Skolnick, 1963).

Applied to the Job Corps illustration, it would work as follows: Separate lists of job-corps applicants (with social security numbers) would be prepared for every class interval on per capita family income. To each of these lists an alphabetical designation would be assigned at random. (Thus the $10.00 per week list might be labeled *M;* $11.00, *C,* $12.00, *Z,* $13.00, *Q,* $14.00, *N,* etc.) These lists would be sent to Internal Revenue, without the Internal Revenue personnel being able to learn anything interpretable about their traineeship status or family income. The Internal Revenue statisticians would locate the withholding tax collected for each person on each list, but would not return the data in that form. Instead, for each list, only the withholding tax amounts would be listed, and these in a newly randomized order. These would be returned to Job Corps research, who could use them to plot a graph like Figures 10 or 11, and do the appropriate statistical analyses by retranslating the alphabetical symbols into meaningful base-line values. But within any list, they would be unable to learn which value belonged to which person. (To ensure this effective anonymity, it could be specified that no lists shorter than 100 persons be used, the base-line intervals being expanded if necessary to achieve this.) Manniche and Hayes (1957) have spelled out how a broker can be used in a two-staged matching of doubly coded data. Kaysen (1967) and Sawyer and Schechter (1968) have wise discussions of the more general problem.

What is required of the administrator of a scarce ameliorative commodity to use this design? Most essential is a sharp cutoff point on a decision-criterion dimension, on which several other qualitatively similar analytic cutoffs can be made both above and below the award cut. Let me explain this better by explaining why National Merit scholarships were unable to use the design for their actual fellowship decision (although it has been used for their Certificate of Merit). In their operation, diverse committees make small numbers of award decisions by considering a group of candidates and then picking from them the N best to which to award the N fellowships allocated them. This provides one cutting point on an unspecified pooled decision base, but fails to provide analogous potential cutting points above and below. What could be done is for each committee to collectively rank its group of 20 or so candidates. The top N would then receive the award. Pooling cases across committees, cases could be classified according to number of ranks above and below the cutting point, these other ranks being analogous to the award-nonaward cutting point as far as regression onto posttreatment measures was concerned. Such group ranking would be costly of committee time. An equally good procedure, if committees agreed, would be to have each member, after full discussion and freedom to revise, give each candidate a grade, A+, A, A−, B+, B, etc., and to award the fellowships to the N candidates averaging best on these ratings, with no revisions allowed after the averaging process. These ranking or rating units, even if not comparable from committee to committee in range of talent, in number of persons ranked, or in cutting point, could be pooled without bias as far as a regression discontinuity is concerned, for that range of units above and below the cutting point in which all committees were represented.

It is the dimensionality and sharpness of the decision criterion that is at issue, not its components or validity. The ratings could be based upon nepotism, whimsey, and superstition and still serve. As has been stated, if the decision criterion is utterly invalid we approach the pure randomness of a true experiment. Thus the weakness of subjective committee decisions is not their subjectivity, but the fact that they provide only the one cutting point on their net subjective dimension. Even in the form of average ratings the recommended procedures probably represent some slight increase in committee work load. But this could be justified to the decision committees by the fact that through refusals, etc., it cannot be known at the time of the committee meeting the exact number to whom the fellowship can be offered. Other costs at the planning time are likewise minimal.

The primary additional burden is in keeping as good records on the nonawardees as on the awardees. Thus at a low cost, an experimental administrator can lay the groundwork for later scientific follow-ups, the budgets for which need not yet be in sight.

Almost all of our ameliorative programs designed for the disadvantaged could be studied via this design, and so too some major governmental actions affecting the lives of citizens in ways we do not think of as experimental. For example, for a considerable period, quantitative test scores have been used to call up for military service or reject as unfit at the lower ability range. If these cutting points, test scores, names, and social security numbers have been recorded for a number of steps both above and below the cutting point, we could make elegant studies of the effect of military service on later withholding taxes, mortality, number of dependents, etc.

This illustration points to one of the threats to external validity of this design, or of the tie-breaking experiment. The effect of the treatment has only been studied for that narrow range of talent near the cutting point, and generalization of the effects of military service, for example, from this low ability level to the careers of the most able would be hazardous in the extreme. But in the draft laws and the requirements of the military services there may be other sharp cutting points on a quantitative criterion that could also be used. For example, those over 6 feet 6 inches are excluded from service. Imagine a five-year-later follow-up of draftees grouped by inch in the 6 feet 1 inch to 6 feet 5 inches range, and a group of their counterparts who would have been drafted except for their heights, 6 feet 6 inches to 6 feet 10 inches. (The fact that the other grounds of deferment might not have been examined by the draft board would be a problem here, but probably not insurmountable.) That we should not expect height in this range to have any relation to later-life variables is not at all a weakness of this design, and if we have indeed a subpopulation for which there is a sharp numerical cutting point, an internally valid measure of effects would result. Deferment under the present system is an unquantified committee decision. But just as the sense of justice of United States soldiers was quantified through paired comparisons of cases into an acceptable Demobilization Points system at the end of World War II (Guttman, 1946; Stouffer, 1949), so a quantified composite index of deferment priority could be achieved and applied as uniform justice across the nation, providing another numerical cutting point.

In addition to the National Data Bank type of indicators, there will be occasions in which new data collections as by interview or questionnaire are needed. For these there is the special problem of uneven cooperation that would be classified as instrumentation error. In our traditional mode of thinking, completeness of description is valued more highly than comparability. Thus if, in a fellow-ship study, a follow-up mailed out from the fellowship office would bring a higher return from past winners, this might seem desirable even if the nonawardees' rate of response was much lower. From the point of view of quasi-experimentation, however, it would be better to use an independent survey agency and a disguised purpose, achiev-ing equally low response rates from both awardees and nonawardees, and avoiding a regression discontinuity in cooperation rate that might be misinterpreted as a discontinuity in more important effects.

Randomized Control Group Experiments

Experiments with randomization tend to be limited to the laboratory and agricultural experiment station. But this certainly need not be so. The randomization unit may be persons, families, precincts, or larger administrative units. For statistical purposes the randomization units should be numerous, and hence ideally small. But for reasons of ex-ternal validity, including reactive arrangements, the randomization units should be selected on the basis of the units of administrative access. Where policies are administered through individual client contacts, randomization at the person level may be often inconspicu-ously achieved, with the clients unaware that different ones of them are getting different treatments. But for most social reforms, larger administrative units will be involved, such as classrooms, schools, cities, counties, or states. We need to develop the political postures and ideologies that make randomization at these levels possible.

"Pilot project" is a useful term already in our political vocabu-lary. It designates a trial program that, if it works, will be spread to other areas. By modifying actual practice in this regard, without going outside of the popular understanding of the term, a valuable experimental ideology could be developed. How are areas selected for pilot projects? If the public worries about this, it probably as-sumes a lobbying process in which the greater needs of some areas are only one consideration, political power and expediency being others. Without violating the public tolerance or intent, one could probably devise a system in which the usual lobbying decided upon the areas eligible for a formal public lottery that would make final choices between matched pairs. Such decision procedures as the drawing of lots have had a justly esteemed position since time im-memorial (e.g., Aubert, 1959). At the present time, record keeping for pilot projects tends to be limited to the experimental group only. In the experimental ideology, comparable data would be collected on designated controls. (There are of course exceptions, as in the heroic Public Health Service fluoridation experiments, in which the teeth of

Oak Park children were examined year after year as controls for the Evanston experimentals [Blayney & Hill, 1967].)

Another general political stance making possible experimental social amelioration is that of *staged innovation*. Even though by intent a new reform is to be put into effect in all units, the logistics of the situation usually dictate that simultaneous introduction is not possible. What results is a haphazard sequence of convenience. Under the program of staged innovation, the introduction of the program would be deliberately spread out, and those units selected to be first and last would be randomly assigned (perhaps randomization from matched pairs), so that during the transition period the first recipients could be analyzed as experimental units, the last recipients as controls. A third ideology making possible true experiments has already been discussed: randomization as the democratic means of allocating scarce resources.

This article will not give true experimentation equal space with quasi-experimentation only because excellent discussions of, and statistical consultation on, true experimentation are readily available. True experiments should almost always be preferred to quasi-experiments where both are available. Only occasionally are the threats to external validity so much greater for the true experiment that one would prefer a quasi-experiment. The uneven allocation of space here should not be read as indicating otherwise.

More Advice for Trapped Administrators

But the competition is not really between the fairly interpretable quasi-experiments here reviewed and "true" experiments. Both stand together as rare excellencies in contrast with a morass of obfuscation and self-deception. Both to emphasize this contrast, and again as guidelines for the benefit of those trapped administrators whose political predicament will not allow the risk of failure, some of these alternatives should be mentioned.

Grateful testimonials. Human courtesy and gratitude being what it is, the most dependable means of assuring a favorable evaluation is to use voluntary testimonials from those who have had the treatment. If the spontaneously produced testimonials are in short supply, these should be solicited from the recipients with whom the program is still in contact. The rosy glow resulting is analogous to the professor's impression of his teaching success when it is based solely upon the comments of those students who come up and talk with him after class. In many programs, as in psychotherapy, the recipient, as well as the agency, has devoted much time and effort to the program and it is dissonance reducing for himself, as well as common courtesy to his therapist, to report improvement. These grateful testimonials can come in the language of letters and conversation, or be framed as answers to multiple-item "tests" in which a recurrent theme of "I am sick," "I am well," "I am happy," "I am sad" recurs. Probably the testimonials will be more favorable as: (a) the more the evaluative meaning of the response measure is clear to the recipient—it is completely clear in most personality, adjustment, morale, and attitude tests; (b) the more directly the recipient is identified by name with his answer; (c) the more the recipient gives the answer directly to the therapist or agent of reform; (d) the more the agent will continue to be influential in the recipient's life in the future; (e) the more the answers deal with feelings and evaluations rather than with verifiable facts; and (f) the more the recipients participating in the evaluation are a small and self-selected or agent-selected subset of all recipients. Properly designed, the grateful testimonial method can involve pretests as well as posttests, and randomized control groups as well as experimentals, for there are usually no placebo treatments, and the recipients know when they have had the boon.

Confounding selection and treatment. Another dependable tactic bound to give favorable outcomes is to confound selection and treatment, so that in the published comparison those receiving the treatment are also the more able and well placed. The often-cited evidence of the dollar value of a college education is of this nature—all careful studies show that most of the effect, and of the superior effect of superior colleges, is explainable in terms of superior talents and family connections, rather than in terms of what is learned or even the prestige of the degree. Matching techniques and statistical partialings generally undermatch and do not fully control for the selection differences—they introduce regression artifacts confusable as treatment effects.

There are two types of situations that must be distinguished. First, there are those treatments that are given to the most promising, treatments like a college education which are regularly given to those who need it least. For these, the later concomitants of the grounds of selection operate in the same direction as the treatment: those most likely to achieve anyway get into the college most likely to produce later achievement. For these settings, the trapped administrator should use the pooled mean of all those treated, comparing it with the mean of all untreated, although in this setting almost any comparison an administrator might hit upon would be biased in his favor.

At the other end of the talent continuum are those remedial treatments given to those who need it most. Here the later concomitants of the grounds of selection are poorer success. In the Job Training Corps example, casual comparisons of the later unemployment rate of those who received the training with those who did not are in general biased against showing an advantage to the training. Here the trapped administrator must be careful to seek out those few special comparisons biasing selection in his favor. For training programs such as Operation Head Start and tutoring programs, a useful solution is to compare the later success of those who completed the training program with those who were invited but never showed plus those who came a few times and dropped out. By regarding only those who complete the program as "trained" and using the others as controls, one is selecting for conscientiousness, stable and supporting family backgrounds, enjoyment of the training activity, ability, determination to get ahead in the world—all factors promising well for future achievement even if the remedial program is valueless. To apply this tactic effectively in the Job Training Corps, one might have to eliminate from the so-called control group all those who quit the training program because they had found a job—but this would seem a reasonable practice and would not blemish the reception of a glowing progress report.

These are but two more samples of well-tried modes of analysis for the trapped administrator who cannot afford an honest evaluation of the social reform he directs. They remind us again that we must help create a political climate that demands more rigorous and less self-deceptive reality testing. We must provide political stances that permit true experiments, or good quasi-experiments. Of the several suggestions toward this end that are contained in this article, the most important is probably the initial theme: Administrators and parties must advocate the importance of the problem rather than the importance of the answer. They must advocate experimental sequences of reforms, rather than one certain cure-all, advocating Reform A with Alternative B available to try next should an honest evaluation of A prove it worthless or harmful.

Multiple Replication in Enactment

Too many social scientists expect single experiments to settle issues once and for all. This may be a mistaken generalization from the history of great crucial experiments in physics and chemistry. In actuality the significant experiments in the physical sciences are replicated thousands of times, not only in deliberate replication efforts, but also as inevitable incidentals in successive experimentation and in utilizations of those many measurement devices (such as the galvanometer) that in their own operation embody the principles of classic experiments. Because we social scientists have less ability to achieve "experimental isolation," because we have good reason to expect our treatment effects to interact significantly with a wide variety of social factors many of which we have not yet mapped, we have much greater needs for replication experiments than do the physical sciences.

The implications are clear. We should not only do hard-headed reality testing in the initial pilot testing and choosing of which reform to make general law; but once it has been decided that the reform is to be adopted as standard practice in all administrative units, we should experimentally evaluate it in each of its implementations (Campbell, 1967).

Conclusions

Trapped administrators have so committed themselves in advance to the efficacy of the reform that they cannot afford honest evaluation. For them, favorably biased analyses are recommended, including capitalizing on regression, grateful testimonials, and confounding selection and treatment. *Experimental administrators* have justified the reform on the basis of the importance of the problem, not the certainty of their answer, and are committed to going on to other potential solutions if the one first tried fails. They are therefore not threatened by a hard-headed analysis of the reform. For such, proper administrative decisions can lay the base for useful experimental or quasi-experimental analyses. Through the ideology of allocating scarce resources by lottery, through the use of staged innovation, and through the pilot project, true experiments with randomly assigned control groups can be achieved. If the reform must be introduced across the board, the interrupted time-series design is available. If there are similar units under independent administration, a control series design adds strength. If a scarce boon must be given to the most needy or to the most deserving, quantifying this need or merit makes possible the regression discontinuity analysis.

References

AUBERT, V. Chance in social affairs. *Inquiry,* 1959, 2, 1–24.
BAUER, R. M. *Social indicators.* Cambridge, Mass.: M.I.T. Press, 1966.

Blayney, J. R., & Hill, I. N. Fluorine and dental caries. *The Journal of the American Dental Association* (Special Issue), 1967, 74, 233–302.

Box, G. E. P., & Tiao, G. C. A change in level of a nonstationary time series. *Biometrika,* 1965, 52, 181–192.

Campbell, D. T. Factors relevant to the validity of experiments in social settings. *Psychological Bulletin,* 1957, 54, 297–312.

Campbell, D. T. From description to experimentation: Interpreting trends as quasi-experiments. In C. W. Harris (Ed.), *Problems in measuring change.* Madison: University of Wisconsin Press, 1963.

Campbell, D. T. Administrative experimentation, institutional records, and nonreactive measures. In J. C. Stanley (Ed.), *Improving experimental design and statistical analysis.* Chicago: Rand McNally, 1967.

Campbell, D. T. Quasi-experimental design. In D. L. Sills (Ed.), *International Encyclopedia of the Social Sciences.* New York: Macmillan and Free Press, 1968, Vol. 5, 259–263.

Campbell, D. T., & Fiske, D. W. Convergent and discriminant validation by the multitrait-multimethod matrix. *Psychological Bulletin,* 1959, 56, 81–105.

Campbell, D. T., & Ross, H. L. The Connecticut crackdown on speeding: Time-series data in quasi-experimental analysis. *Law and Society Review,* 1968, 3(1), 33–53.

Campbell, D. T., & Stanley, J. C. Experimental and quasi-experimental designs for research on teaching. In N. L. Gage (Ed.), *Handbook of research on teaching.* Chicago: Rand McNally, 1963. (Reprinted as *Experimental and quasi-experimental design for research.* Chicago: Rand McNally, 1966.)

Chapin, F. S. *Experimental design in sociological research.* New York: Harper, 1947.

Etzioni, A. "Shortcuts" to social change? *The Public Interest,* 1968, 12, 40–51.

Etzioni, A., & Lehman, E. W. Some dangers in "valid" social measurement. *Annals of the American Academy of Political and Social Science,* 1967, 373, 1–15.

Galtung, J. *Theory and methods of social research.* Oslo: Universitetsforloget; London: Allen & Unwin; New York: Columbia University Press, 1967.

Glass, G. V. Analysis of data on the Connecticut speeding crackdown as a time-series quasi-experiment. *Law and Society Review,* 1968, 3(1), 55–76.

Glass, G. V., Tiao, G. C., & Maguire, T. O. Analysis of data on the 1900 revision of the German divorce laws as a quasi-experiment. *Law and Society Review,* 1969.

Greenwood, E. *Experimental sociology: A study in method.* New York: King's Crown Press, 1945.

Gross, B. M. *The state of the nation: Social system accounting.* London: Tavistock Publications, 1966. (Also in R. M. Bauer, *Social indicators.* Cambridge, Mass.: M.I.T. Press, 1966.)

Gross, B. M. (Ed.) Social goals and indicators. *Annals of the American Academy of Political and Social Science,* 1967, 371, Part 1, May, Pp. i–iii and 1–177; Part 2, September, Pp. i–iii and 1–218.

Guttman, L. An approach for quantifying paired comparisons and rank order. *Annals of Mathematical Statistics,* 1946, 17, 144–163.

Hyman, H. H., & Wright, C. R. Evaluating social action programs. In P. F. Lazarsfeld, W. H. Sewell, & H. L. Wilensky (Eds.), *The uses of sociology.* New York: Basic Books, 1967.

Kamisap, Y. The tactics of police-persecution oriented critics of the courts. *Cornell Law Quarterly,* 1964, 49, 458–471.

Kaysen, C. Data banks and dossiers. *The Public Interest,* 1967, 7, 52–60.

Manniche, E., & Hayes, D. P. Respondent anonymity and data matching. *Public Opinion Quarterly,* 1957, 21(3), 384–388.

Polanyi, M. A society of explorers. In, *The tacit dimension.* (Ch. 3) New York: Doubleday, 1966.

Polanyi, M. The growth of science in society. *Minerva,* 1967, 5, 533–545.

Popper, K. R. *Conjectures and refutations.* London: Routledge and Kegan Paul; New York: Basic Books, 1963.

Rheinstein, M. Divorce and the law in Germany: A review. *American Journal of Sociology,* 1959, 65, 489–498.

Rose, A. M. Needed research on the mediation of labor disputes. *Personnel Psychology,* 1952, 5, 187–200.

Ross, H. L., & Campbell, D. T. The Connecticut speed crackdown: A study of the effects of legal change. In H. L. Ross (Ed.), *Perspectives on the social order: Readings in sociology.* New York: McGraw-Hill, 1968.

Sawyer, J., & Schechter, H. Computers, privacy, and the National Data Center: The responsibility of social scientists. *American Psychologist,* 1968, 23, 810–818.

Schanck, R. L., & Goodman, C. Reactions to propaganda on both sides of a controversial issue. *Public Opinion Quarterly,* 1939, 3, 107–112.

SCHWARTZ, R. D. Field experimentation in sociolegal research. *Journal of Legal Education,* 1961, 13, 401–410.

SCHWARTZ, R. D., & ORLEANS, S. On legal sanctions. *University of Chicago Law Review,* 1967, 34, 274–300.

SCHWARTZ, R. D., & SKOLNICK, J. H. Televised communication and income tax compliance. In L. Arons & M. May (Eds.), *Television and human behavior.* New York: Appleton-Century-Crofts, 1963.

SELVIN, H. A critique of tests of significance in survey research. *American Sociological Review,* 1957, 22, 519–527.

SIMON, J. L. The price elasticity of liquor in the U.S. and a simple method of determination. *Econometrica,* 1966, 34, 193–205.

SOLOMON, R. W. An extension of control group design. *Psychological Bulletin,* 1949, 46, 137–150.

STIEBER, J. W. *Ten years of the Minnesota Labor Relations Act.* Minneapolis: Industrial Relations Center, University of Minnesota, 1949.

STOUFFER, S. A. The point system for redeployment and discharge. In S. A. Stouffer et al., *The American soldier. Vol. 2, Combat and its aftermath.* Princeton: Princeton University Press, 1949.

SUCHMAN, E. A. *Evaluative research: Principles and practice in public service and social action programs.* New York: Russell Sage, 1967.

SWEEN, J., & CAMPBELL, D. T. A study of the effect of proximally auto-correlated error on tests of significance for the interrupted time-series quasi-experimental design. Available from author, 1965. (Multilith)

THISTLETHWAITE, D. L., & CAMPBELL, D. T. Regression-discontinuity analysis: An alternative to the ex post facto experiment. *Journal of Educational Psychology,* 1960, 51, 309–317.

WALKER, H. M., & LEV, J. *Statistical inference.* New York: Holt, 1953.

WEBB, E. J., CAMPBELL, D. T., SCHWARTZ, R. D., & SECHREST, L. B. *Unobtrusive measures: Nonreactive research in the social sciences.* Chicago: Rand McNally, 1966.

WOLF, E., LÜKE, G., & HAX, H. *Scheidung und Scheidungsrecht: Grundfrägen der Ehescheidung in Deutschland.* Tübigen: J. C. B. Mohr, 1959.

PETER H. ROSSI

Boobytraps and Pitfalls
in the Evaluation of
Social Action Programs

I: Introduction

If one were to measure success by the popularity of evaluation research, then empirical social research has certainly arrived. Perhaps, the best example of this popularity lies in the legislation authorizing the present War on Poverty in which the agencies involved are specifically directed to set aside funds for evaluation research. Other ameliorative programs may not give as much formal recognition to such activity, but nevertheless seek social researchers to add to their staffs for this purpose or attempt to get social research centers to provide evaluations of their programs.

There are other measures of success besides popularity. If one were to measure success by the proportion of evaluation researches which are conducted with powerful enough designs to render unequivocal evaluation statements, then empirical social research does not appear to be a smashing success. For a variety of reasons—some substantive, others related to the present state of development of research methodology, and still others concerned with the "politics" of evaluation—there are very few evaluation researches which have the elegance of design and clarity of execution which would achieve widespread admiration among social researchers.

Peter H. Rossi, "Boobytraps and Pitfalls in the Evaluation of Social Action Programs," *Proceedings of the Social Statistics Section* (Washington, D.C.: American Statistical Association, 1966), pp. 127–132. Reprinted by permission.

The purpose of this paper is to explore some of the main reasons why evaluation research is hard to do well and to suggest some ways in which these difficulties can be overcome. Providing much of the materials on which this paper has been based have been the experiences with such research of the National Opinion Research Center over the past few years. However, I venture that the experiences of other research centers and of individual researchers has not been very different: At least my informal, but undoubtedly highly biased, survey would indicate strong similarities between our experiences and theirs.

In principle, the evaluation of action programs appears to be most appropriately undertaken through the use of experimental designs. All the elements which would strongly recommend such research designs are usually present: The program involved is something which is added to the ongoing social scene by purposive social action as opposed to events which are not under the control of some individual or agency. Because an action program is under someone's control, the construction of experimental and control groups is, in principle, possible. Furthermore, the program is usually not designed to cover an entire population, but only some portion of it so that some of a target population would not be covered, making it possible to think in terms of control groups. Thus, in principle, it is not difficult to design an extremely elegant program of experiments to evaluate the effectiveness of the usual action program. Controlled experiments, however, are not frequently used in evaluation research. For example, there is not a single evaluation research being carried out on the major programs of the War on Poverty which follows closely the model of the controlled experiment.

II: Action Programs and the Contemporary Scene

There can be little doubt that the present historical period is one in which there is considerable groping for new and presumably more effective treatments for a variety of presumed ills. We have rediscovered the poor, suddenly become intensely aware that Negroes are an incredibly disadvantaged group, become worried over the plight of the aged, and concerned about a presumed wasteage of brain-power. We also have enough national income to allocate some part of our resources to new programs designed to correct some of the obvious faults in our society.

However, there is an ironic twist to developing a heavy conscience in this historical period. This is because we cannot ordinarily expect that the new treatments we can devise will produce massive results. It appears as if we are in much the same position in the treatment of diseases. The introduction of modern medicine and modern sanitation procedures into a country which has had neither can very dramatically reduce morbidity and mortality, as experiences in some of the emerging nations indicate. But, in the United States of today, each new gain in morbidity and mortality can be expected to be smaller and more difficult to achieve. Providing potable water is much easier to achieve, and more dramatic in its impact on morbidity and mortality, than any attempt we can make to lower the incidence of lung cancer, especially if we try it through lowering levels of smoking in individuals.

Similarly with respect to our social ills. Dramatic effects on illiteracy can be achieved by providing schools and teachers to all children: Achieving a universally high enough level of literacy and knowledge, so that everyone capable of learning can find a good spot in our modern labor force, is a lot more difficult. Hence, the more we have done in the past to lower unemployment rates, to provide social services, etc., the more difficult it is to add to the benefits derived from past programs by the addition of new ones. Partly, this is because we have achieved so much with the past programs and partly this is because the massive efforts of the past have not dealt with individual motivation as much as with benefits to aggregates of individuals.

In part, the concern of contemporary practitioners in the applied fields with evaluation arises out of their increased methodological sophistication. But, in even larger measure, it arises out of the expectation—held at some level or other—that massive effects are not to be expected from new programs and the new treatments are going to be increasingly expensive in terms of time and money. The problem of evaluation in this historical period is that the new treatments can be expected to yield marginal improvements over present treatments and that cost-to-benefit ratios can be expected to rise dramatically. Hence, there is considerable interest in research but. considerable apprehension over what it will show concerning the effects of programs.

To illustrate, let us consider the case of Project Headstart: We have apparently wrung most of the benefits we can out of the traditional school system. Although everyone would agree that universal schooling for children up to approximately age sixteen has been a huge success, as opposed to a system of no schooling or of schooling mainly for those to pay for it themselves, there still remains considerable room for improvement, especially in the education of the poor and otherwise disadvantaged. A supplementary pre-school program bringing such children more into parity with those better off because of family background sounds like an excellent program. But, it is hardly likely to produce as much benefit as the introduction of universal elementary schooling did, especially since it is designed to do the job that a full-time institution, the family, neglected to do for one reason or another.

Effective new treatments which produce more than equivocal results are expensive. For example, each trainee at a Job Corps camp costs somewhere between five and ten thousand dollars a year (depending on which estimates you hear), as compared to considerably less than one thousand dollars per year in the usual public high school. Yet a year in a Job Corps Training Center is not going to be five to ten times more effective than a year in a public high school.

Paradoxically, the costs of evaluation are also expensive for these new programs. If effects can be expected to be small, greater precision is needed in research to demonstrate such effects unequivocally. This is another reason why I stressed the controlled experiment as the ideal evaluation research design: Its ability to detect effects is quite powerful compared to alternative methods.

Although as social scientists we can expect the new social programs to show marginal effects, the practitioner does not ordinarily share our pessimism—at least, not when he faces the Congressional Appropriating Committee. Hence, the claims made in public for the programs are ordinarily pitched much higher, in terms of expectation of benefits, than we could realistically expect with the worst of research and much better than we could expect with the best of research. Thus it turns out that one of the major obstacles to evaluation research is the interests in the maintenance of a program held by its administrators. Their ambivalence is born of a two horned dilemma: On the one hand, research is needed to demonstrate that the program has an effect; on the other hand, research might find that effects are negligible or non-existent.

III: Commitment to Evaluation

The will to believe that their programs are effective is understandably strong among the practitioners who administer them. After all, they are committing their energies, careers and ideologies to programs of action and it is difficult, under such circumstances, to take a tentative position concerning outcomes. Hence, most evaluation researches which are undertaken at the behest of the administrators of the programs involved are expected to come out with results indicating that the program is effective. As long as the results are positive (or at least not negative) relationships between practitioners and researchers are cordial and sometimes even effusively friendly. But, what happens when it comes out the other way?

A few years ago, the National Opinion Research Center undertook research with the best of sponsorships on the effect of fellowships and scholarships on graduate study in the arts and sciences fields. It was the sincere conviction, on the part of the learned societies which sponsored the research, that such fellowships and scholarships were an immense aid to graduate students in the pursuit of their studies and that heavily supported fields were thereby able to attract better students than fields which were not well supported. The results of the study were quite equivocal: First, it did not appear that financial support had much to do with selection of a field for graduate study. Secondly, it did not appear that graduate students of high quality were being held back from the completion of their graduate programs by the lack of fellowships or scholarships: Those who were committed found some way to get their Ph.D's, often relying on their spouses to make a capital investment in their graduate training. The equivocal nature of the results was quite disappointing to the sponsors whose first reaction was to question the adequacy of the study's methodology, leading to the coining of a National Opinion Research Center aphorism that the first defense of an outraged sponsor was methodological criticism. The findings affected policy not one whit: The sponsoring groups are still adamantly claiming more and more in the way of financial support for graduate students from the federal government on the grounds that such support materially affects the numbers of talented students who will go to graduate study beyond the B.A., and, furthermore, materially affects the distribution of talent among various fields of study.

Relations between the sponsoring learned societies and our researchers have been cool (if not distant) ever since. The learned societies believe their problem has been badly researched, and the researchers believe that their results have been badly ignored.

Sometimes both the researcher and the practitioner suffer from the will to believe leading to evaluation research containing the most lame sets of qualified results imaginable. Perhaps the best example can be gleaned from the long history of research on the effects of class size on learning. The earliest researches on this topic go back to the beginnings of empirical research in educational psychology and sociology in the early twenties. Since that time there is scarcely a year in which there have not been several dissertations and theses on this topic, not to mention larger researches done by more mature scholars. The researches have used a variety of designs ranging from the controlled experiment to correlational studies, the latest in the series being the results on this score obtained by James Coleman in his nationwide study of schools conducted for the Office of Education under the Civil Rights Act of 1964. The results of these studies are extremely easy to summarize: By and large, class size has no effect on the learning of students, with the possible exception of classes in the language arts. But, the net results of more than two hundred researches on educational ideology and policy has been virtually nil.

Every proposal for the betterment of education calls for reductions in the size of classes, despite the fact that there is no evidence that class size affects anything except possibly the job satisfaction of teachers. Even the researchers in presenting their results tend to present them apologetically, indicating the ways in which defects in their research designs may have produced negative findings as artifacts.

In fact, I do not know of any action program that has been put out of business by evaluation research, unless evaluation itself was used as the hatchet to begin with. Why is this the case? Why do negative results have so little impact? The main reason lies in the fact that the practitioners, first of all (and sometimes the researchers), never seriously entertained in advance the possibility that results would come out negative or insignificant. Without commitment to the bet, one or both of the gamblers usually welch.

The ways by which welching is accomplished are myriad. It is easy to attack the methodology of any study: Methodological unsophisticates suddenly become experts in sampling, questionnaire construction, experimental design, and statistical analysis, or borrow experts for the occasion. Further replication is called for. But, most often it is discovered that the goals of the program in terms of which it was evaluated are not the "real" goals after all. Thus, the important goals of school systems are not higher scores on multiple choice achievement tests, but better attitudes toward learning, a matter which the researcher neglected to evaluate. Or, the goals of a community organization in an urban renewal area were not really to affect the planning process but to produce a commitment to the neighborhood on the part of its residents while the planning took place.

Perhaps the best example of how "real" goals are discovered after goals that were evaluated were found to be poorly attained can be found in the work of a very prominent school administration group. This group, fully committed to the educational modernities of the forties and fifties, found to its surprise that whether or not a school system adopted its programs had little to do with the learning that students achieved. Hence, they dropped achievement tests as a criterion of the goodness of a school or school system and substituted instead a measure of how flexible the administration was in adopting new ideas in curriculum, producing an evaluation instrument which, in effect, states that a school system is good to the extent that it adopts policies that were currently being advocated by the group in question.

IV: Assuring Positive Results

Given unlimited resources, it is possible to make some sort of dent in almost any problem. Even the most sodden wretch on skid row can be brought to a semblance of respectability for some period of time (provided that he is not too physically deteriorated) by intense, and expensive, handling. But, to make an impact on the denizens of all the skid rows in all of our great cities requires methods that are not intensive and are not expensive case by case. There is not sufficient manpower or resources to lead each single skid row inhabitant back to respectability, if only for a short period.

Yet, many action programs, particularly of the "demonstration" variety, resemble the intensive treatment model. They are bound to produce results if only because they maximize the operation of the Hawthorne and Rosenthal effects, but cannot be put into large scale operation because either manpower or resources are not available. Hence, programs which work well on the initial run on a small scale with dedicated personnel can be expected to show more positive results than the production runs of such programs with personnel not as committed to the program in question.

The distinction I want to make in this connection is that between "impact" and "coverage." The *impact* of a technique may be said to be its ability to produce changes in each situation to which it is applied, while the *coverage* of a technique is its ability to be applied to a large number of cases. Thus, face-to-face persuasion is a technique which has high impact as a means of getting people to come in for physical examinations, but its coverage is relatively slight. In contrast, bus and subway posters may have low impact in the sense of producing a desired effect each time someone is exposed, but large coverage in the sense that many people can be exposed to bus and subway posters very easily.

An extremely effective technique for the amelioration of a social problem is one which has both high impact and high coverage. Perhaps the best example of such techniques can be found in medicine whose immunizing vaccines are inexpensive, easy to administer and very effective in reducing the incidence of certain diseases. It does not seem likely that we will find vaccines, or measures resembling them in impact and coverage, for the ills to which action programs in the social field are directed. It is more likely that we will have action programs which have either high impact or high coverage, but not both. The point I want to emphasize here is that it is a mistake to discard out of hand programs which have low impact but the potentiality of high coverage. Hence, programs which show small positive results on evaluation and which can be generalized to reach large numbers of people can, in the long run, have an extremely significant cumulative effect.

Examples of such programs in the social action field do not easily come to mind. But perhaps an illustration from the field of public health can be cited appropriately: Over the past few decades public health information specialists have been plagued by the fact that their most effective techniques have low coverage and their best mass techniques have little impact. Evaluation research after evaluation research has indicated that it is possible to raise the level of an individual's health knowledge and utilization of health facilities if you can get him to come to a course of lectures on the topic. In contrast, public health information campaigns utilizing the mass media have been shown to have minute effects. Yet, the information of the American population concerning health matters has appreciably increased over the past two decades. It is apparently the case that while no one campaign was particularly effective, their cumulative effects were considerable.

V : The Control Group Problem

The key feature of the controlled experiment lies in the control exercised by the experimenter over the processes by which subjects are allocated to experimental and control groups. In a well-designed experiment, such allocations are made in an unbiased fashion. But, there are many ways in which a well thought out plan can go awry.

Perhaps the major obstacle to the use of controlled experiments in evaluation research is a political one. The political problem is simply that practitioners are extremely reluctant to allow the experimenters to exercise proper controls over the allocation of clients to experimental and control groups. For example, the proper evaluation of a manpower retraining program requires that potential trainees be separated into experimental and control groups with a contrast being made between the two groups at a later time. This obviously means that some potential clients, who are otherwise qualified, are barred arbitrarily from training—an act which public agencies are extremely reluctant to authorize.

In part, the political problem arises because researchers have not thought through sufficiently the problem of what constitutes a control or nonexperimental experience. The logic of experimental design does not require that the experimental group not undergo *some* sort of treatment, it merely requires that the experimental group not be given the treatment which is being evaluated. In short, we have not been ingenious enough in inventing placebo treatments which are realistic enough to give the public official the feeling that he is not slighting some individuals at random. For example, a placebo treatment for a job retraining program may be conceived of as some treatment designed to help men get jobs but which does not involve retraining, and over which the training program should demonstrate some advantage. Perhaps testing and intensive counseling might be an acceptable placebo for a control group in an experimental evaluation of job training. Or, a placebo treatment for the evaluation of a community mental health center might be referrals to general practitioners for the kinds of treatment they either administer themselves or provide referrals to.

Even in the best circumstances and with the best of sponsors, the carrying out of controlled experiments can run into a number of boobytraps. There is, for example, the case of an evaluation research all set to go and well designed but whose program did not generate enough volunteers to fill up either the experimental or the control groups. Under these circumstances, the administrator opted to fill up the experimental groups abandoning all attempts at segregating the volunteers into experimental and control groups.

Or, there is the example of a well designed research on the effectiveness of certain means of reaching low income families with birth control information whose design was contaminated by the City Health Department setting up birth control clinics in areas which had been designated as controls!

Or, there is the risk that is run in long range experimental designs that the world may provide experiences to control, which would duplicate in some essential fashion, the experimental treatment. Thus, Wilner *et al.,* in the evaluation of the effects of public housing, unfortunately undertook their research in a period when the quality of the general housing stock in Baltimore was being improved at so fast a rate that the contrast in housing conditions between experimental and control groups had greatly diminished by the end of the observational period.

In sum, it is not easy either to obtain sufficient consent to undertake properly controlled experiments or to carry them out when such consent is obtained.

VI: A Strategy for Evaluation Research

There are a number of lessons to be drawn from the various sections of this paper which hopefully could go some distance toward devising a strategy for the conduct of evaluation research. While it is true that in a Panglossian best of all possible worlds, the best of all possible research designs can be employed, in a compromised real world, full of evil as it is, it is necessary to make do with what is possible within the limits of time and resources. The problem that faces us then is how can we set up the conditions for doing as best a job we can and produce research which is as relevant as possible to the judgment of the effectiveness of social policy programs.

Although the idea of evaluation research has gained wide acceptance, we are a long way from a full commitment to the outcomes of
evaluation research. It is part of the researcher's responsibility to
bring to the practitioner's attention that in most cases the effects of
action programs are slight and that there is more than an off-chance
possibility that evaluation will produce non-positive results. The
policy implications of such findings have to be worked out in advance;
otherwise the conduct of evaluation research may turn out to be a
fatuous exercise.

Secondly, we have a long way to go in devising ways of applying
controlled experiments to problems of evaluation. Political obstacles
to the use of controls often make it hard to get acceptance of such
designs, and the difficulty of maintaining controls in a non-sterile
world make full-fledged experimental designs relatively rare in use.

Earlier in this paper, I suggested that we take a lesson from medical research and search for the social analogues of placebos to be
administered to our control groups. There are other directions in
which experimental designs should go: For example, considering the
high likelihood that treatments have small effects, we need very
powerful designs to demonstrate positive results. But because power
costs money, it is worthwhile considering research designs which
evaluate several types of experimental treatments simultaneously so
that the outcomes will be more useful to the setting of program policy.
To illustrate: it is considerably more worthwhile to have the results
of an experimental evaluation which provides results on several types
of Job Corps camps than on job corps camps in general. Looking at
the differential effectiveness of several job corps camps provides more
detailed and better information for the improvement of job corps
programs than would a gross evaluation of the program all told.

This paper has stressed the model of the controlled experiment
as the desired one for evaluation research. But, it is abundantly clear
that for a variety of reasons, controlled experiments are rarely employed as evaluational devices and that they are difficult to employ.
Most frequent are some sort of quasi-experiments in which the control
groups are constructed by methods which allow some biases to operate
and correlational designs in which persons subjected to some sort of
treatment are contrasted with persons who have not been treated, controlling statistically for relevant characteristics.

The important question which faces the evaluation researchers is
how bad are such "soft" evaluational techniques, particularly correlational designs? Under what circumstances can they be employed with
some confidence in their outcomes?

First of all, it seems to me that when it is massive effects that are
expected and desired, "soft" techniques are almost as good as subtle
and precise ones. To illustrate, if what is desired as the outcome of a

particular treatment is complete remission of all symptoms in each and every individual subject to treatment, then it is hardly necessary to have a control group. Thus if a birth control technique is to be judged effective *if and only if* it completely eliminates the chance of conception in an experimental group, then the research design is vastly simplified. The question is not whether those who use the method have less children than those who do not, but whether they have any children at all, a question which can be easily decided by administering the technique to a group and counting births (or conceptions) thereafter.

The obverse of the above also holds. If a treatment which is to be tested shows no effects using a soft method of evaluation, then it is highly unlikely that a very precise method of evaluation is going to show more than very slight effects. The existence of complex and large interaction effects which suppress large differences between a group subject to a treatment and statistical control groups seems highly unlikely. Thus if children participating in a Head Start program show no gain in learning ability compared to those who did not participate in the program, holding initial level of learning constant, then it is not likely that a controlled experiment in which children are randomly assigned to experimental and controlled groups is going to show dramatic effects from Head Start programs.

Of course, if a correlational design does show some program effects, then it is never clear whether selection biases or the program itself produce the effects shown.

This means that it is worthwhile to consider soft methods as the first stage in evaluation research, discarding treatments which show no effects and retaining those with opposite characteristics to be tested with more powerful designs of the controlled experimental kind.

Although ex post facto designs of a correlational variety have obvious holes in them through which may creep the most insidious of biases, such designs are extremely useful in the investigation of effects which are postulated to be the results of long acting treatments. Despite the fact that it is possible that cigarettes cause cancer, the evidence from ex post facto studies of the correlation between cigarette smoking and lung cancer can hardly be ignored, even though the evidence is not pure from the viewpoint of a purist. Similarly, NORC's study of the effects of Catholic education on adults, despite all our efforts to hold constant relevant factors, can still be easily produced by self selection biases that were too subtle for our blunt instruments to detect. We have nevertheless gained a great deal of knowledge concerning the order of effects that can be expected, were a controlled experiment extending over a generation conducted. The net differences between parochial school Catholics and public school Catholics are so slight that we now know that this institution is not very effective as a device for maintaining religiosity and that furthermore the effects we found are quite likely to have been generated by selection biases.

From these considerations a strategy for evaluation research is beginning to emerge. It seems to me to be useful to consider evaluation research in two stages—a Reconnaissance Phase in which the soft correlational designs are used to screen out those programs it is worthwhile to investigate further; and an Experimental Phase in which powerful controlled experimental designs are used to evaluate the differential effectiveness of a variety of programs which showed up as having sizable effects in the first phase.

ROBERT S. WEISS
MARTIN REIN

The Evaluation of Broad-Aim Programs: Difficulties in Experimental Design and an Alternative

. . . Not all of the difficulties [in evaluation research] stem from the commitment to experimental evaluation. Some have to do with discord between the research group's institutional responsibilities and the values of their professional colleagues. Some stem from overoptimistic judgment regarding the potential impact of a large-scale social effort. But some of the difficulties do have their roots in the commitment to experimental evaluation, and we should examine these more closely. We begin with those which have to do with the method itself and then turn to those which have to do with the relationship between research group and administrative group which the method imposes.

1. It is difficult to select satisfactory criteria. A narrow-aim program might wish to increase an individual's facility in a language, or to prepare him for a job in the existent labor market, or to upgrade the quality of housing in an area. In these programs the criteria of success are evident in the statement of aims; or, to say this another way, the aims are very nearly operational. Broad-aim programs, in contrast, seem designed to frustrate a research person who feels he must know specifically what the program hopes to change in order that he may

Robert S. Weiss and Martin Rein, "The Evaluation of Broad-Aim Programs: Difficulties in Experimental Design and an Alternative," revision of paper given at the American Academy of Arts and Sciences Conference on Evaluation of Social Action Programs, May 2–3, 1969, pp. 20–38. Reprinted by permission. The Conference was organized under a grant from The Ford Foundation.

gather base-line data. In a narrow-aim program it is not necessary to subject the program administrator to intensive examination to force him to operationalize his goals, but in broad-aim programs there is temptation to do exactly this, since there seems to be no other way of getting operationalizations of such aims as a more responsive institutional system, a richer cultural atmosphere, or increased opportunity for the poor. Freeman and Sherwood (1965), for example, suggest that the evaluation research person "participate or even take a major responsibility for the development of the action framework."

The difficulty underlying the development of criteria in terms of which a broad-aim program may be evaluated is not that the aims of the program are unformulated, although there may be many different interpretations of their meaning which themselves will change over time, but rather that they may be specified in many different ways, any of which would be considered desirable by the program administrators. The administrators of a broad-aim program are apt not to know in advance exactly how the system change they hope to achieve will manifest itself. Although they might be prevailed on to list in advance the kinds of changes they hope will result from their program, they will nevertheless be opportunistic in their program management and will direct program energies to those system changes which appear to be within their reach, whether or not these were included among their initial aims. The attempt to evaluate the success of broad-aim programs in terms of the change in narrowly defined criteria is not only difficult; it also misrepresents the actual aims of these programs.

The question might be asked whether it is not possible to develop operational measures of system change. The appraisals of knowledgeable observers might, for example, be a possible measure. In response it might be said that while such measures are theoretically possible, and the intuitive judgments of blue ribbon panels have been used to make appraisals of local programs on a number of occasions, there are a good many practical problems impeding the use of such judgments in a tight design. To our knowledge, trustworthy measures of system change have not yet been developed, although it would seem to us that in any experimental test of broad-aim programs measures of this sort should be sought.

There is a natural response to the criterion problem in the evaluation of broad-aim action programs which appears to us to be faulty. . . . It begins with the recognition that system change may evidence itself in any of dozens of ways, and it therefore commits itself to consider each of these ways a possible criterion. Information regarding these multiple criteria are collected by means of a survey instrument, which may be administered to a sample before the introduction of the program and again after the completion of the program. The analysis of the resulting data takes the form of fishing for possible differences between "time one" and "time two" from amidst the host of possibilities. (Cf. Selvin and Stuart, 1966.) Of course, the larger the number of criteria included in the survey instrument, the more likely that some indication of system change will be found, but the more likely, too, that unaffected criteria will obscure the picture. The investigator may be unsure whether the occasional significant difference is due to a causal process stemming from the introduction of the program, or alternatively is a false positive, a difference which by chance happens to be sizeable, and which one would expect to find in a large enough population of differences. This problem of identifying which significant association to believe is intrinsic to fishing and can only be solved by good theory or other data. The comparison sample introduces no control here, although if it should happen that a number of differences favor the comparison sample (as not infrequently occurs in this style of research), it may make the investigator pause for thought.

The examination of these multiple criteria is apt to be misleading in the evaluation situation, quite apart from the likelihood of false positives. The variables which show change are likely to be identified as the more responsive aspects of the system, although in another situation the system might well have taken a different path of change and other variables might signal the change. In other words, the variables which show change are apt to be given undue attention, as though they were the successfully achieved goals of the program, whereas their status properly should be that of unanticipated indicators of system change.

Predetermined criteria have still another drawback in the evaluation of broad-aim social programs. Especially if these programs represent large-scale inputs of energy and resources, they are likely to have unanticipated consequences whose importance may rival, if not outweigh, the intended ends of the program. A poverty program may fail to change the economic condition of the poor, yet alter the political climate. An evaluation study which gives no attention to unanticipated consequences can hardly produce a full assessment of the impact of a program.

2. *The situation is essentially uncontrolled.* Setting up comparison situations is an attempt to insure that changes in the experimental condition not be mistakenly credited to the experimental intervention when in fact some other, alien, factor is responsible. The idea is that every other factor except the experimental intervention will also be present in the comparison situation and so changes in the experimental situation which do not occur in the comparison situation can confidently be taken as effects of the intervention. But this misapplica-

tion of scientific method fails to recognize the numerous ways in which any two communities are likely to differ, from the personalities of their mayors through the employment policies of their industries.

It might be objected that even in the best of laboratory experiments the situation is not totally controlled, but that if the treatments are randomly distributed to situations, then any subsequent significant difference which might theoretically have resulted from the treatment may be credited to the treatment. There are many problems in the application of this idea to broad-aim programs. First, the numbers of cases are very often insufficient to provide statistically acceptable groups for the experimental and comparison conditions. Second, the distribution of treatments to cases may confidently be assumed never to be random: almost always there is a rationale for the distribution; often the more promising candidates get the program. Third, those communities which are not chosen for a program are not unaffected by it; the diffusion effect long recognized in field studies also occurs in connection with social action programs.

In summary, from the standpoint of experimental design, comparison cases are apt to be too few, non-random, and themselves affected by the program. The second objection would tend to produce false positives, the third to produce false negatives, but the first makes it nearly impossible to put store in any result whatsoever.

3. The treatments are not standardized. The form assumed by broad-aim programs generally will differ from community to community, in response to differences in the needs and tolerances of the communities. For example, in the Model Cities planning program, different cities adopted different approaches to eliciting neighborhood participation, in part because of differences in the degree of organization of residents of their neighborhoods. Because different communities are likely to experience different forms of the program, it is misleading to take just one community, or a small number of communities, and say "the program" is there being evaluated. At best what might be evaluated would be a small number of specifications of the program.

It may happen that some ways of realizing the program turn out not to be possible, because of the nature of communities, and perhaps especially because of the nature of their political structure. In this event an important research contribution would be the description of the forms the intervention seems required to take, and of the forces which shape it. Experimental evaluation neglects such description entirely, instead assuming that what took place was what was supposed to have taken place.

4. The experimental design is limited in the information it can produce. The possible results of an experiment can be listed in advance. The independent variables under examination, singly or in combination, will or will not produce hypothesized effects. The laboratory experimenter ordinarily hopes to find at least some positive results, because these will corroborate an existent theory and direct attention to lines for its further development. Negative results are not very helpful: they signal that the theory or its operationalization is faulty, but they do not draw attention to the site of the flaw. The experimenter is apt to follow the trail of his positive results, discarding other experiments as marking out only blind alleys. A publication is apt to report only experiments which have positive results.

The situation in relation to large-scale social programs is quite different. The social program may be the only trial an idea will be given, and undoubtedly will be the only one the evaluator will study. From the perspective of the rational development of social programs, the experience cannot be shrugged off if it doesn't work. It is necessary for the research person to learn as much as he can from it, irrespective of its results. Indeed, one might assume that the capacity of communities to resist change, even when the intervention program is an ambitious one, is so great that negative results are more likely than positive ones. If this is so, the task of research cannot be merely to document that the program failed to work, but rather to identify the processes by which the program was defeated. In this way the experience of the program may become a basis for the design of programs more likely to be effective.

In any event the need in the study of broad-aim programs is for a conscientious attempt to find the forces which shaped the specification of the program, the nature of the opposition it encountered, the reasons for such failure as occurred, the program's unanticipated consequences. Then, in addition, the research might identify the anticipated changes which occurred and the ones which did not. The issue in evaluation of a broad-aim program is not "Does it work?" but rather "When such a program is introduced, what then happens?"   ·

All the above are essentially technical issues, having to do with the appropriateness of experimental design for the evaluation of broad-aim programs. The difficulties of the experimental design are serious enough on these grounds alone. But there are, in addition, administrative problems which may result from a commitment to experimental design and which also should be noted.

1. There may be conflict over program development. In the experience which we report here, the research group did not attempt to direct the development of the action program except for the suggestion that different sections of the community get different components of the action program. But in other cases the evaluation group has felt it essential that they monitor the action program to ensure that it holds still while it is being evaluated, instead of constantly metamorphosing from one form to another. But any effective administrator who is committed to the success of a program will insist on modifying the program as he learns more about his staff, his situation, and the difficulties the program faces. In response to this, the research group may raise objections for a time, but is likely eventually simply to withdraw from recognition of the extent to which the program is being modified. But this further widens the breach between administration and research.

2. *The research group may find itself dependent on uncommitted record keepers.* If the action program is multifarious and individual members of the target population can involve themselves with the program in many different ways, then the research group may want to separate out those individuals who have a great deal of involvement with particular program efforts from individuals who have less involvement or whose involvement is with other program efforts. But to do this the research will ordinarily be dependent on participation records kept by uncommitted program personnel, records that are almost certain to be unreliable and, even if reliable, difficult to coordinate with other research information. For the research group to attempt to maintain participation records themselves would be nearly impossible; but it may well prove almost as difficult for the research group to prevail on operating personnel to keep good records. (In addition, reliance on operating personnel introduces an opportunity for their attitudes to affect results.)

3. *Operationalizations may become leading goals.* If the research group, in order to establish criteria for the evaluation of a broad-aim program, has reached some agreement with program administrators that particular operationalizations of the program aims indeed represent what the administrators hope to achieve, then these operationalizations may take on an importance they would not otherwise have had. For example, if administrators of a community action program agree that one way their program could be evaluated is in terms of the numbers of unemployed or partially employed individuals who would be helped to find full-time employment, then employment will take on special importance for the research group and may well take on added importance in the minds of the administrators just because they know that this is an area in which they will be scored. The process of operationalization may present administrators with an extraneous consideration of some weight in their development of policy and may result in a focussing of the program beyond its original intent.

4. *The research staff may know less than the action group about what is going on, rather than more.* A commitment to an experimental model is apt to result in the paradoxical development of the research

staff being relatively ignorant regarding what is happening to the action program in the field. Administrators, far from being able to call on the research group for consultation, are apt to discover that the research group is totally absorbed in the management of large quantities of data, and has neither knowledge of the day-to-day operation of the action program nor desire to learn more. Not only are program administrators apt to discover that the research group can offer little by way of insight; they are apt also to discover that the research, though it competes in the present for money, of which it requires a great deal, will provide no illumination until some time after the project's close. It would be a hardy administration indeed which would not begin to define the research group as a burden.

A Role for Experimental Design in the Evaluation of Broad-Aim Programs

We do not mean to argue that there is no role whatsoever for experimental design in the evaluation of broad-aim programs. When one of the aims of the program, or a single objection to the program, assumes an importance great enough to justify the collection of data which will lead to a relatively unquestionable conclusion, and when the program has the form, or can be given the form, of repeated standardized treatments within a relatively controlled situation, then experimental design is fully justified.

The recent experiment on the consequences of negative taxation in New Jersey offers an illuminating example (Watts). Here we have an instance which meets all criteria. Although negative taxation, like other broad-aim programs, has the intent of betterment of the condition of the poor without special commitment to any particular way in which this betterment might be shown, still one specific issue, that of the impact of negative taxation on incentive to work, has assumed special importance. There is, then, a definite criterion variable of special importance, though in this case the criterion, impact on incentive, would be an undesired outcome. Negative taxation as a treatment or independent variable is perfectly standardizable; in addition, it can be repeated in enough cases so that an adequate sample of experiences can be built. It would be improper to use the results of this experiment as a basis for assessing the overall worth of the negative income tax, since only one criterion—and an undesired end at that—would be examined.

The contribution of experimental design here is that it provides a convincing test of the possible connection between the program and an undesired consequence about which critics are concerned. Where convincing statements regarding relationships are needed, and where the nature of the program permits, experimental design is clearly the methodology to be recommended.

An Alternative Methodology

We want here to sketch an outline of an approach we believe in general to be superior to experimental design as a methodology for evaluating broad-aim programs. The approach might be characterized as (a) process-oriented qualitative research, as (b) historical research, or as (c) case study or comparative research. The research approach is the same, but the first characterization emphasizes the type of data which are collected, (although there is no necessary exclusion of quantitative data), the second emphasizes the method's concern with the development of events through time, while the third emphasizes the utilization of a single case or small set of cases as a basis for generalization to a larger class. The aim of the approach is to develop a coherent and appropriately-near-to-complete description of the relevant community systems prior to the intervention of a program, of the nature of the intervention, and of the new system which then develops in which the intervention is a dynamic constituent. In what follows we shall discuss what seem to us the leading issues in this approach.

CONCEPTUAL FOUNDATION : (A) CONCEPTUAL FRAMEWORKS

A research person who intends to tell the story of an intervention attempt, or to base generalization on such a story, must have some sense of the form which would be taken by an adequate description of what happened. In experimental work this conceptual framework, as we are calling it, is organized around the idea of determination, especially causal determination. (Bunge, 1959.) There are a number of frameworks which might prove useful for historical description, including those of system theory, of an unfolding of drama-like events on which a plot-structure can be imposed, and of an interaction of political forces. In the context of program evaluation the ideas of system change seem to us central. It should be noted that these conceptual frameworks are no more in the forefront of attention for someone concerned with historical study than would be the notion of causality for an experimenter. Rather the conceptual frameworks function to guide attention to the sorts of events which should be recorded in data-gathering, to the questions which must be answered in the analysis, and to the kinds of connections which should be demonstrated in the report.

Other frameworks, in addition to those we note, may be called on, but the three noted above seem to us the most important. Far from being competitive with one another, the frameworks are more nearly complementary. The systems framework is useful in suggesting what events or phenomena should be included within the scope of one's inquiry, in suggesting the roles which might be played within the situation by various actors, and in providing general ideas regarding the functioning of interrelated actors whose manifestation may be looked for in the situation studied. The dramaturgic approach may be most useful for describing small-scale events, and for relating individual actions to their outcomes. The political framework may be most useful in describing events which unfold over longer periods of time, and involve greater numbers of individuals.

SYSTEMS

The general ideas of systems theory are well known and need not be repeated here. (See especially Miller, 1965, a and b. An excellent short bibliography appears with the first article. See also Schulberg and Baker, 1968.) Their usefulness in evaluation research extends from the initial conceptualization of the problem, which may be phrased as that of describing change in concrete intermeshed systems, to the organization of observations and conclusions in a final report, to which systems theory may supply coherence.

The systems outlook offers the research person a guide to resolution of the clash between his desire to learn about everything and the limitations of his time and energy, in its concept of "system boundaries." This instructs the research person to focus his attention on the smallest set of groups and individuals in interaction with one another which will yet account for most of the "dynamic" of the change experience; i.e., for most of what happens, and most of what determines what happens. (The systems idea of boundary is a region across which there is comparatively little interchange.)

Systems should be identified in relation to issues, and different issues might well require different system definitions. The system which would be studied in connection with an evaluation of a Model Cities planning program would be different from the system which would be studied in connection with a police department Community Relations program. Even in study of the same program, different systems may become relevant at different points.

The boundaries of systems tend to be relatively easy to identify in studies of organizations, but relatively hard to identify in studies of communities. Indeed, their relative openness is one of the important characteristics of most communities. Yet even in studies of communities key actors and institutions should be apparent. The systems perspective alerts the investigator to the need to identify the inter-relations of these actors and groupings—which may be agonistic—and then to identify the impact on these interrelations of the program, the events in which aspects of the program are met and reacted to by actors, the new actors the program introduces, and the ways in which individuals and institutions move in and out of the network of inter-relationships of which the program is a new constituent.

The systems perspective also alerts the investigator to the likeli-hood that important forces which have few interrelations with ele-ments of the system will appear on the scene. All social systems are in this sense open. These new forces can often be dealt with as "alien variables," sources of impact on the system whose prior history and subsequent fate need not be understood further. For instance, in a Model Cities planning program, the deadline for submission of the plan was changed by the office to whom the plan was to go. This had great impact on the planners and their interrelations, but it was not necessary to investigate it further; it was not necessary, for example, to ask why the deadline had been changed. But before an unexpected event is categorized as an alien variable, whose impetus stems from events in a foreign system, the investigator should consider whether there may not have been a connection between events having to do with the program and the intrusion. For example, when a radically oriented community action program, after a series of confrontations with officials of the local government, discovered that the procedure for application for new funds had been changed to its disadvantage, an investigator might with justification have decided that the program was imbedded in a larger system than he had previously attended to, a system which was activated by the controversy the program created.

THE DRAMATURGIC APPROACH

Here the basic framework is the construction of a story line involving actors within settings, often engaging in coalitions and conflicts, the course of whose interactions forms plots and subplots which move to some resolution. This framework is similar to that of "methodological individualism" which seeks to explain events by reference to the actions of individuals within situations. (Watkins, 1953.)

The dramaturgic framework seems particularly useful in the description of meetings, conferences, and other time-limited situations in which individuals interact to produce some resolution of an issue. Then observation may be structured by (a) identification of the issues which bring the individuals to the situation; (b) identification of the actors and their commitments in relation to the issues; (c) description of the action which takes place, the unfolding of the plot; and (d) statement of the resolution, the way it all turns out. (This scheme is due to Marshall Kaplan. For another, see Burke, 1945 and 1962.)

POLITICAL PROCESS

Political process is a more complex conceptual framework than the dramaturgic. It is probably more useful when the task is to deal with a connected series of events than it is when the task is to organize observation of a single event. The actors in this perspective are thought of as representing interest groups, and their actions are interpreted as expressing a strategy. Of course the investigator should check by interview or examination of documents that the interests and aims he attributes to the actors in fact exist. Groups may then be seen as bargaining with each other, producing and avoiding conflict as each strives to realize its aims, forming alliances and staking new claims and foregoing old ones. It may be useful to assume that each group has a store of resources it may deploy—staff, time, energy, money, reputation, connections, power. One of the issues in program evaluation is how groups mobilize their resources in response to the program intervention, in what way they commit themselves to affecting events, and with what success.

Again it may be said that the various outlooks described here— the systemic, the dramaturgic and the political—are not theories, any more than the notion of causation is a theory. Rather they refer to frameworks for thought which can organize and discipline observation and reporting. Other conceptual frameworks are available, though we think in this connection less likely to be useful. Two which might be noted are the *functional,* which examines phenomena in terms of their contribution to the maintenance or goals of some inclusive totality, and the idea of *patterning,* which looks for the expression of a common theme in a variety of phenomena. These outlooks may be developed independently of the systems outlook or assimilated to it. In the evaluation of an intervention attempt there would seem to be basis for a presumption that the systems outlook, as the more capable of dealing with change, should have primacy. . . .

Data Analysis

The analysis of data may aim at three different levels of generalization. First, materials may be organized to provide descriptions of what happened in the concrete cases. These case reports would describe the actual actors and events, and though there would of necessity be summarizing, there would also be a good deal of reporting in concrete detail. The analysis problem would be to organize materials into a story which can be grasped, while finding the right mix of detail and condensation. Reports might also be written on a next level of abstraction, with an emphasis on the types of systems, structures, or processes observed. Here the investigator would describe in more abstract terms the various types of situations, the program introduced in these situations, and then summarize what happened to the program in the different situations. Concrete detail would serve as illustration, and as evidence, but the focus of attention would be on the theoretical models. Finally a report might be written on a quite abstract level, presenting a general model for understanding the consequences of introduction of a program for change of the sort studied into various types of communities. On this last level there might be few references to concrete materials, although of course the investigator would check the adequacy of his model against the experience gathered in the study, as well as in part developing the model from that experience.

Any qualitative study seems to produce great quantities of data, but the more usual flood of data is here multiplied by the number of instances studied, and (if budget permits) by the utilization of field teams as data collectors. The individuals responsible for report writing will have to be almost compulsively systematic and organized in their treatment of the data if they are to avoid being overwhelmed by information. Large-scale quantitative studies can rely on coding to reduce data. Here there are no data reduction devices, only a variety of techniques for organizing the data. Different investigators develop their own analysis styles, but all concern themselves with the filing of materials, the development of preliminary statements, and the development of devices for deciding when to call a halt in data collection. (Cf. Glaser and Strauss, 1967.) . . .

The Role of Values

Evaluation is the appraisal of the extent to which a program realizes certain goals. When evaluation is performed by experimental design, the goals in terms of which the performance of the program is evaluated are those imbedded in the program at its inception. The value framework used for appraisal is for the most part that of the program's administrators, and though there is some small opportunity to do so, there is no incentive, in the experimental approach, to use alternative sets of values to develop criteria.

Qualitative study presents quite another situation. Now it is possible to describe the extent to which the program realized its initial objectives, but it is also possible to appraise the extent to which the program realized other goals as well. The investigator can ask whether members of the target population have suffered losses—perhaps by attack on a coherent way of life—as well as gains. He need not restrict his attention to the target population, but can describe what seem to have been the consequences of the program for individuals in other sectors of the community. The investigator can consider the program not only from the perspective of clients, but also from the perspective of other agencies with which it may have been competitive, or of local government, whose managers it may have by-passed. If he wishes, the investigator may evaluate the program from a radical perspective and consider the extent to which the program has patched up a destructive system rather than initiating fundamental changes.

Qualitative appraisal permits values to re-enter evaluation openly, instead of only implicitly as when the experimenter limits his attention to whether the program works. In addition, it permits the development of a set of appraisals, each from a different perspective. These are by no means the least weighty recommendations for this approach to evaluation. . . .

References

BANFIELD, EDWARD, 1964, Political Influence. New York: Free Press.

BUNGE, MARIO, 1959, Causality. Cambridge: Harvard University Press.

BURKE, KENNETH, 1945, Grammar of Motives. Englewood Cliffs, N.J.: Prentice-Hall.

CAMPBELL, DONALD, and JULIAN STANLEY, 1963, Experimental and Quasi-Experimental Design for Research. Chicago: Rand-McNally.

FREEMAN, HOWARD, and CLARENCE C. SHERWOOD, 1965, "Research in large-scale intervention programs." Journal of Social Issues, 21 : 11–28.

MARRIS, PETER, and MARTIN REIN, 1967, Dilemmas of Social Reform. New York: Atherton.

MERTON, ROBERT K., and DANIEL LERNER, 1951, "Social scientists and research policy." In Daniel Lerner and Harold D. Lasswell (eds.), The Policy Sciences, 282–307. Stanford: Stanford University Press.

MILLER, JAMES G., 1965a, "Living systems: basic concepts." Behavioral Science, 10: 193–237.

———, 1965b, "Living systems: structure and process." Behavioral Science, 10: 337–379.

Rossi, Peter, 1966, "Booby traps and pitfalls in the evaluation of social action programs." Paper presented to the annual meeting of the American Statistical Association.

Schulberg, Herbert C., and Frank Baker, 1968, "Program evaluation models and the implementation of research findings." American Journal of Public Health, 58: 1248–1255.

Selvin, Hanan C., and Alan Stuart, 1966, "Data dredging procedures in survey analysis." American Statistician, 20: 20–23.

Stufflebeam, Daniel L., 1968, "Evaluation as enlightenment for decision-making." Paper presented to working conference on assessment theory sponsored by Commission on Assessment of Education Outcomes. Evaluation Center, Ohio State University.

Suchman, Edward, 1968, "Action for what? A methodological critique of evaluation studies." Paper presented to the annual meeting of the American Sociological Association.

Thernstrom, Stephan, 1969, Poverty, Planning, and Politics in the New Boston: The Origins of ABCD. New York: Basic Books.

Vidich, Arthur J., and Joseph Bensman, 1958, Small Town in Mass Society. Princeton, N.J.: Princeton University Press.

Watkins, J. W. N., 1953, "Ideal types and historical explanation." In Herbert Feigl and May Brodbeck (eds.), Readings in the Philosophy of Science. New York: Appleton-Century-Crofts.

Watts, Harold, (no date), "Graduated work incentives: progress toward an experiment in negative taxation." Mimeographed. No place indication.

EGON G. GUBA

The Failure of
Educational Evaluation

The American educational establishment is currently making a massive effort at self-improvement. Unprecedented resources, stemming mainly from the federal government under the provisions of ESEA but coming also from foundations, state departments of education, local school systems, private industries and other agencies, are being expended on a variety of promising but as yet unproved programs. To assure the effective and efficient uses of these resources, and, even more importantly, to determine the real utility of the innovative approaches, it is necessary to gather hard data about their performance. Evaluation is the process best suited for this purpose.

The traditional methods of evaluation have failed educators in their attempts to assess the impact of innovations in operating systems. Indeed, for decades the evidence produced by the application of conventional evaluation procedures has contradicted the experiential evidence of the practitioner. Innovations have persisted in education not because of the supporting evidence of evaluation but despite it. A recent dramatic example is afforded by the Higher Horizons program in New York City. Test data failed to affirm what supervisors, teachers and clients insisted was true—that the program was making a difference so great that it simply could not be abandoned.

On a broader scale, the recent Coleman report circulated by the

Guba, Egon G., "The Failure of Educational Evaluation," *Educational Technology,* vol. 9, no. 5 (1969), pp. 29–38. Reprinted by permission.

Office of Education has shocked educators by noting that "one implication stands out above all: that schools bring little influence to bear on a child's achievement that is independent of his background and general social context."[1] More specifically, Coleman states that there is a ". . . relatively small amount of school-to-school variation that is not accounted for by differences in family background, indicating the small independent effect of variations in school facilities, curriculum and staff on achievement."[2]

This conclusion is incredible on its face. It means, if true, that it makes little difference whether a teacher is good or bad, whether good or poor materials are available, or whether the school is a barn or a geodesic dome; students will learn about the same. Now, anyone who has spent any time at all in a school knows that is just not so. Why, then, do our evaluative techniques fail to detect the effects?

When the evidence produced by any scientific concept or technique continually fails to affirm experimental observation and theory arising from that observation, the technique may itself appropriately be called into question. It shall be the burden of my remarks that evaluation as we know it has failed, and that the world of evaluation does indeed require reshaping.

Some Clinical Signs of Failure

Can this contention of failure really be supported? Let us look at some of the clinical signs that evaluation today is somewhat less than effective:

1. Avoidance. A certain sign of evaluation's failure is that everyone avoids it unless it becomes painfully necessary. This tendency toward avoidance can be noted at all levels. Local school districts rarely incorporate evaluation into any effort which they themselves fully control and finance. This is particularly clear when one consults proposed project budgets; if evaluation costs are included at all, they are contemplated only in very general terms, i.e., perhaps the salary of an evaluation "expert," or the cost of buying commercially available instruments.

The same avoidance is evident within state departments and even within the U.S. Office of Education, which, despite a great deal of talk about the desirability of evaluation for the schools, never budgets or staffs sufficiently well to provide for evaluation of its own programs.

2. Anxiety. The psychiatrist is very familiar indeed with the phenomenon of "free-floating" anxiety, which characterizes many neurotic patients. A similar affliction characterizes the practitioner and the professional evaluator when they approach an evaluation. This anxiety seems to stem from the ambiguities of the evaluation process. Since so many elements of that process are badly understood, the particular evaluation that may be applied may yield random, meaningless data. And who is there among us that would not feel anxious if judgments were to be made about our programs, our decisions, or our effectiveness by what may be a random process? Our protests that no truly professional practitioner need feel anxious when confronted by the need to evaluate are empty and worthy of contempt.

3. Immobilization. Despite the opportunity that has existed for four or more decades, schools have not responded to evaluation in any meaningful way; indeed, the mere existence of an office or functionary within the schools charged with systematic evaluation is still rare. Further, despite the federal requirements for evaluation built into legislation, particularly Titles I and III of ESEA, evaluative data are still relatively non-existent, as are programs that could be pointed to as "models" of what might be done in evaluation. This lethargy, this lack of responsiveness, this immobilization, can only be taken as symptomatic of a deeper illness.

4. Vague guidelines. The lack of meaningful and operational guidelines for evaluation is notable. Consider, for example, the statement made in the ESEA Title III manual published by the U.S. Office of Education:

> A. Where applicable, describe the methods, techniques and procedures which will be used to determine the degree to which the objectives of the proposed program are achieved.
> B. Describe the instruments to be used to conduct the evaluation.
> C. Provide a separate estimate of costs for evaluation purposes. This amount should be included in the proposal budget summary.[3]

While these three statements are expanded with some 2½ pages of text, the expansion does little to inform the reader about anything other than technical requirements. The guidelines are subject to very wide interpretation, and offer little operational assistance to the proposal developer. The inability of the very agencies that require evaluation to provide adequate guidelines for its implementation must be regarded as one of the more serious difficulties besetting evaluation.

5. Misadvice. Evaluation consultants, many of whom are drawn from the ranks of methodological specialists in educational research, fail to give the kind of advice which the practitioner finds useful. Indeed, the practitioner may be led down the primrose path instead. A recent analysis of a small sampling of Title III proposals gives the flavor of this difficulty.[4] Twenty-one proposals were examined, but only one was found that could be considered to have an adequate design from a traditional methodological point of view. Most had no design at all; while those that did offered designs known to suffer from serious deficiencies. Yet the majority of these 21 proposals purported that the services of an evaluation specialist had been employed, and that he was primarily responsible both for the planning and the implementation of the evaluation program. Usually the consultant and his institutional affiliation were named so that there was no doubt about his technical competence. It is certainly a serious symptom of disorder when the experts in the field of evaluation seem to be unable to design evaluations that meet even their own criteria of technical soundness.

6. No significant differences. Another very significant indication that evaluation is in trouble is the fact that it is so often incapable of uncovering any significant information. Over and over comparative studies of alternatives in education have ended in a finding of "no significant difference." Several conventional responses are made to this situation. It is often observed that the educationists are incapable of devising any approaches that are better than those things that they are already using. But, if this is so, we ought perhaps to applaud their remarkable consistency, since they do not devise alternatives that are any *worse* either!

Another oft heard response is to say that the lack of efficacy of comparative studies is well established by this consistent failure to find differences; educationists are then warned *not* to engage in such studies because to do so is to behave stupidly. This equally glib response, of course, ignores the fact that this comparative question is exactly the one that *must* be asked if improvement is to occur. What could be more relevant, as one gropes to change for the better, than to ask about alternatives, and to seek to determine which of several available alternatives, including present practice, is most efficacious?

This brief listing of the most obvious clinical signs of evaluation's failure is compelling. Any professional area that is so much avoided; that produces so many anxieties; that immobilizes the very people who want to avail themselves of it; that is incapable of operational definition, even by its most trained advocates, who in fact render bad advice to the practitioners who consult them; which is not effective in answering reasonable and important questions, and which has made little apparent effort to isolate and ameliorate its most serious problems—must indeed give us pause.

The Basic Lacks

How can one account for this state of affairs? Why cannot the educational community respond to the urgent need for useful evaluative information? Why cannot evaluation programs be designed and implemented that will quickly eradicate this shortage of data? The situation cannot be explained simply on the grounds of ignorance, carelessness, or unconcern. *It exists because of certain crucial lacks:*

1. Lack of adequate definition of evaluation. Evaluation, like any analytic term, can be defined in many essentially arbitrary ways. Each of the ways which have gained common acceptance have certain utilities and certain disadvantages.

An early definition of evaluation tended to equate that term with *measurement,* as it had developed in the Twenties and Thirties. We must remember that, historically, the evaluation movement followed upon the heels of, and was made technically feasible by, the measurement movement. The technique of equating a new movement with an older established movement in order to gain credibility is common, as for example, in calling "social science" a science in order to gain some of the status reserved in this society for a scientific venture. Moreover, the instrumentation developed by measurement experts provided the conceptual basis for evaluation. Finally, and perhaps of most importance, the use of measurement devices resulted in scores and other indices that were capable of mathematical and statistical manipulation, which in turn rendered possible the handling of masses of data and the easy comparison of individual or classroom scores with group norms. Thus, the idea of *interpreting* evaluative data in relation to an objective criterion could be introduced; but the criterion (norms) was devoid of value judgments and was, sociologically and culturally, antiseptic.

What disadvantages accrue from such a definition? First, evaluation was given an *instrumental* focus; the science of evaluation was viewed as the science of instrument development and interpretation. Second, the approach tended to obscure the fundamental fact that value judgments are necessarily involved (a problem to which we shall return below). Third, evaluation tended to be limited to those variables for which the science of measurement had successfully evolved instruments; other variables came to be known as "intangibles," a characterization which was equivalent to saying that they couldn't be measured; hence had no utility, and ultimately, no importance. Thus, the limits placed upon evaluation because of a lack of instrumental sophistication came to be viewed as the *real* limits to which evaluation had to be constrained. In short, this definition results in an evaluation which is too narrow in focus and two mechanistic in its approach.

Another definition of evaluation which has had great currency is that of *determining the congruence between performance and objectives,* especially behavioral objectives. This congruence definition, which grew out of the work of Tyler and others at The Ohio State University, particularly in connection with the Eight Year Study, had an enormous impact on education, as well it might. In the first place, the definition appeared in connection with an organized rationale about the entire instructional process, and provided a means whereby the teacher, administrator, supervisor and curriculum maker could make sensible judgments about what they were doing. Evaluation no longer focused solely on the student, but could provide insights about the curriculum and other educational procedures as well. The utility of evaluation was thus broadened, and, for the first time, a practical means was devised to provide *feedback* (a term unheard of at the time). Finally, evaluation came to have utility not only for judging a *product* (student achievement, for example) but also a *process* (the means of instruction, for example), a distinction whose import is only now being fully realized.

What disadvantages accrue as a result of this definition? First, with the heavy emphasis that this approach placed on *objectives,* the major task of the evaluator came to be seen as developing a set of objectives that were sufficiently operational so that the required congruence assessment could occur. The objectives themselves, in general form, were obtained by an almost mystic process that remained relatively unspecified; Tyler spoke eloquently about "screening objectives through a philosophy and a psychology," but these were vague terms. The real problem was to take the general "screened" objectives, and by a process of successively finer definition and expansion reduce them to their most operational form.

A second disadvantage of this approach was the fact that the objectives were to be stated in *behavioral* terms. A "true" evaluation could take place only by reduction to student behaviors. Thus, we are confronted with such absurdities as trying to evaluate the effectiveness of a new staff recruitment procedure, for example, by showing that this somehow related to increased achievement on the part of students.

A third and perhaps major disadvantage of this approach is that the emphasis on student behavior as the criterion caused evaluation to become a *post facto* or terminal technique. Data became available only at the end of a long instructional period. It is perhaps ironic that a definition that hinted so clearly at feedback and its utilization in improvement should have this effect. The full possibilities were thus not only *not* realized, but the form of the definition froze evaluation as a terminal event rendering product judgments. If process data were available, they could only be utilized the next time round; it was too late to use them for refinement in the ongoing program, i.e., in the program from which the evaluative data were extracted.

Thus, the definition of evaluation in congruence terms relating outcomes to objectives, while broadening the utility of evaluation considerably and providing the possibility for feedback and process data, did tend to label evaluation as a terminal process that yielded information only *after the fact*.

Neither of the two previously discussed definitions of evaluation placed much emphasis on the judgmental process. Certainly in the case of the measurement definition, and to some extent in the case of the congruence definition, the matter of *placing value* on the data was, if considered at all, taken pretty much for granted. But there was a school of thought, entertained mainly by persons who would not have labeled themselves as evaluators, that defined evaluation in yet a third way: that evaluation *is* professional judgment. Perhaps the most obvious example of this definition is in the visitation procedure used by the various accrediting associations, such as the North Central Association. While evaluative criteria do exist, these are applied mainly by school personnel whose school is being evaluated, not by the visitation teams. The chief value in their application is often understood to be the *process* of application rather than the results obtained thereby; the school personnel through this exercise gain new insights into themselves, their problems and their shortcomings. The *actual* evaluations are made not by the school personnel, however, but by the visitation teams, who come in, "soak up" the data by virtue of their expertise and experience, and render a judgment. The judgment is the evaluation.

A similar approach can be seen in the traditional school survey, and in the use of panels by the Office of Education, foundations and other funding agencies to evaluate proposals. Again, the evaluation *is* whatever judgment they render.

Advantages of this approach are fairly obvious. First, the evaluation is quickly managed. Second, the evaluators are typically experts with a great deal of experience which they can bring into play without being artificially constrained by "instruments." Third, the interplay of a variety of factors in a situation is taken into account more or less automatically, and the evaluator is thus freed of the problem of relating and aggregating data after he has collected them. Finally, there is no appreciable lag between data collection and judgment; we do not need to wait for long time periods while data are being processed.

Despite these apparent advantages, however, there are very few people who would willingly rely on this approach unless nothing else can be done. First, one has the feeling that it is not so much a matter of convenience but of ignorance that forces such an approach; if we knew more, we could be more precise and objective. Secondly, we have fears for the reliability and the objectivity of such judgments, and how can one demonstrate whether they are or are not reliable and objective? It is this inability *to apply* the ordinary prudent tests of scientific inquiry that makes us leery, even when we are willing to concede the expertness of the evaluators involved. Third, the process hides both the data considered and the criteria or standards used to assess them, because the process is implicit. Thus, even if the judgments are valid, reliable and objective, we have little confidence that we can tell *why* they are so, or to generalize to other situations. To sum up, the inherent *uncertainty* and *ambiguity* of evaluations based on this definition leave one dissatisfied.

It is apparent from this review of common definitions of evaluation that while each definition offers the evaluator certain advantages, each is also accompanied by certain disadvantages. No definition is available that does not have several serious disadvantages as concomitants.

2. Lack of adequate evaluation theory. There have been, for all practical purposes, no advances in the theory of evaluation since Ralph Tyler completed his formulations during the decade of the Forties. Since that time the professionals in the field have felt content simply to borrow from the methodology of other fields, notably educational research. Indeed, the methodology of educational evaluation has come to be equated with the methodology of research, with disastrous consequences. Let us examine some of these:

a. Laboratory antisepsis. The purpose of research is to provide new knowledge. Its methodology is designed to produce knowledge which is universally valid. The purpose of a laboratory is to provide such a context-free environment, within which universally true knowledge can be developed. The establishment of close controls makes it possible to rule out all influences except those which are the object of inquiry.

Evaluations are not designed to establish universal laws, however, but to make possible judgments about some phenomenon. In this situation, one not only does not want to establish highly controlled conditions in which possible sources of confounding are filtered out, but in fact one wishes to set up conditions of *invited interference* from all factors that might ever influence a learning (or whatever) transaction.

Thus, educational evaluation does not need the antiseptic world of the laboratory but the septic world of the classroom and the school in order to provide useful data. The use of laboratory research designs and techniques poses conditions that are simply inappropriate for the purposes for which one does an evaluation.

b. The effects of intervention. The interest of a researcher, particularly in the laboratory, is usually focused on the interplay of certain so-called independent and dependent variables. The researcher must engage in some form of manipulation or *intervention* to arrange for the conditions necessary to study this interaction. The investigator becomes an integral part of the data, since they would not have occurred without his presence.

By intervening in a situation, an investigator can achieve the controls necessary to allow him to focus upon segments and processes of particular concern to him. But he does this at a possible loss of information, because he is dealing with a contrived situation. It is also possible, however, to collect data which are natural and uncontrived, but which are also uncontrolled, difficult to analyze, and, of course, which allow all factors to exert whatever influence they might. It is about such *actual situations* that the evaluator wants information, not the contrived situations which, regardless of their utility for other purposes (e.g., establishing universally true principles) are not appropriate for the evaluator's purpose.

c. Terminal availability. The typical research design is concerned with the assessment of the effects of some "treatment" or combination of treatments. A major intent of design is to arrange matters so that the influence of factors not included in the treatment(s) are either *controlled* or *randomized* while the effect of the treatment is being detected. At the end of some period of time sufficient for the treatment to produce its presumed effect, measures are taken from which a judgment can be drawn.

This general format produces data only *at the termination* of the experiment. If the treatment is judged, let us say, to have been inappropriate or insufficient, nothing can be done to improve the situation for the test subjects from whom the insufficiency was judged. But suppose that the intent had been, as it often is in the case of education, to improve the treatment while it was being applied, so that the maximum benefit might be derived not only for the future but also for the group on which the experiment was conducted. When we try a new method of reading for disadvantaged children, we are just as interested in the children we try it on as we are in other children who may use it in the future. The evaluator cannot be content with terminal availability. The traditional methodology will not help him.

d. Single evaluations only. Evaluators operating on the basis of classic research methodology must insist, for the sake of control, that no more than one evaluation be conducted simultaneously, lest one confound the other. It is impossible, using such an approach, to distinguish the effects of two new treatments being evaluated simultaneously, at least not without very expensive refinements. But, again, moral principles prevent the educator from keeping the possible benefits of a new treatment from a group of children just because they are already being exposed to another treatment designed to remedy some other problem.

   e. *The inapplicability of assumptions.* Classical research methodology and the statistical analyses which are appropriate thereto are based upon a series of assumptions which do not meet evaluation requirements too well.

   There are, first of all, the assumptions underlying the statistical techniques. Normality of distribution, for example, is necessary to make even certain descriptive statistics meaningful, such as that the interval included between the mean plus and minus one standard deviation shall include 68 per cent of the cases. Other assumptions are built into the interpretive tables in which the "significance" of analytic statistics is determined; thus, the derivation of the F distribution depends upon certain random sampling assumptions. Finally, still other assumptions are necessary to support the logical derivation of the interpretive techniques; thus, in the case of analysis of variance, the additivity assumption, which asserts that treatments have equal effects on all persons to whom they are applied, is vital. None of these assumptions is likely to hold in typical evaluation situations. To cite one example, it is clear that good teaching tends to interact with pupils so that the able learn more than the less able. The additivity, therefore, is very tenuous.

   It is well known that statistical techniques are "robust" with respect to those assumptions; that is, the statistics tend to provide valid information even though the assumptions may be rather sharply violated. Nevertheless, it is one thing simply to deviate from certain assumptions and quite another to attempt to apply techniques in situations where their assumptions are patently not met. Even the most robust of techniques might be adversely affected if enough of its assumptions were systematically violated.

   f. *The impossibility of continuous refinement.* Perhaps the most damaging assertion that may be made about the application of conventional experimental design to evaluation situations is that such application conflicts with the principle that evaluation should facilitate the continuous improvement of a program. Experimental design *prevents* rather than promotes changes in the treatments because, as has been noted, treatments cannot be altered if the data about differences between treatments are to be unequivocal. Thus, the treatment must accommodate the evaluation design rather than vice versa.

   It is probably unrealistic to expect directors of innovative projects to accept these conditions. Obviously, they cannot constrain a treatment to its original, undoubtedly imperfect, form just to ensure internally valid end-of-year data. Rather, project directors must use whatever evidence they can obtain continuously to refine and sometimes radically to change both the design and its implementation. Concepts of evaluation are needed which would result in evaluations which would stimulate rather than stifle dynamic development of programs. Clearly, equating evaluation methodology with research methodology is absolutely destructive of this aim.

3. *Lack of knowledge about decision processes.* Programs to improve education depend heavily upon a variety of decisions, and a variety of information is needed to make and support those decisions. Since the purpose of evaluation is to provide this information, the evaluator must have adequate knowledge about the relevant decision processes and associated information requirements before he can design an adequate evaluation. At present, no adequate knowledge of decision processes and associated information requirements relative to educational programs exists. Nor is there any ongoing program to provide this knowledge.

A first question that must be considered is what model of the decision-making process is most productive for evaluators to have in mind. Most treatises on the subject of decision-making view the process as essentially *rational:* the decision-maker starts with some awareness of a problem which he must resolve; he then assembles alternative ways of responding to that problem; he chooses from among the alternative responses that one which, on balance, appears to have the highest success probability, and then he implements the choice.

But it seems highly unlikely that real-world decisions are in fact made in these ways. The mere creation of awareness of the need for a decision is a formidable task; many decision-makers seem to prefer not to be made aware unless absolutely necessary. Generally speaking, the range of possible responses available to the decision-maker is not very large; if even one alternative exists, the decision-maker is usually delighted. The choice among alternatives is not usually made on the basis of explicit and well-understood criteria; many decision-makers pride themselves on "shooting from the hip," and would not have it any other way.

Attempts have been made to define other models of the decision-making process; a notable example is the model of "disjointed incrementalism" proposed by Braybrooke and Lindblom.[5] It is likely that such other models may have more utility for the evaluator than the conventional rational model. But, meantime, it is clear that evaluators have not had a clear and useful conception in mind, a fact which has hindered them considerably in determining what evaluation methodologies are most productive and what kinds of information delivered under what circumstances would be most valuable.

A second problem relating to decision-making is the lack, to date, of adequate taxonomies of educational decisions. If evaluation is to serve decisions, it would be most useful indeed to be able to categorize or classify educational decisions by type so that, for example, evaluation designs appropriate to each type might be conceptualized. But what is the range and scope of educational decision-making? What substantive concerns are reflected in these decisions?

A third problem is the lack of methodologies for linking evaluation to the decision-maker whom it is ultimately to serve. One such linkage problem has already been alluded to—that of creating awareness in the decision-maker of the need for a decision. Another is that of helping the decision-maker to identify the criteria which he is using or might use—a difficult matter which implies a professional relationship of the highest order between evaluator and client. A third aspect has to do with reporting evaluative information to the decision-maker in ways which he finds credible and helpful. The evaluator is often thought of as a high-level technician familiar with the methodologies of research and data analysis, but it is clear that in dealing with the decision-maker he plays a series of professional roles more similar to those of the counselor or attorney than to the educational researcher. Methodologies for this role simply are lacking.

4. Lack of criteria. Most evaluators agree that the mere collection of data does not constitute evaluation—there is always at least a hint of making judgments about the data in terms of some implicit or explicit value structure. Thus, it would be unusual to speak just about whether or not objectives are achieved, but rather how *well* they are achieved. The need to introduce values gives rise to a number of problems. First there is the matter of where the values come from. It was pointed out that scholars who defined evaluation as the congruence between performance and objectives paid little attention to the origin of the objectives except that they were to be "screened" through a psychology and a philosophy. This doctrine leaves untouched the question of *what* philosophy and *what* psychology should be used as screens. When this question is made explicit, it is quickly apparent that no adequate methodology exists for the determination of values, even though, as we have already implied, such a determination may constitute the most professional task which the evaluator performs. It may, indeed, be his chief claim to a professional rather than a technical role.

Another question that arises in this domain is how to achieve consensus about the values that are to be invoked in evaluations. It may be fairly easy to achieve consensus at a micro level, as for example, when a group of English teachers attempts to define what the objectives shall be for the freshman composition course. But how can one achieve consensus on the purposes of ESEA Title I? How is one to interpret evaluative data to meet the value standards that might be invoked? In a pluralistic society in which multiple values necessarily exist side-by-side, which values will be served? Indeed, how can one even determine what are the value patterns? And when such multiple values are applied, will it not almost inevitably be the case that the *same data* when interpreted in terms of *different value standards* will give rise to antithetical evaluations?

Finally, there is a variant of the value problem which concerns the values of the evaluators themselves, and which accounts for at least some of the apparent estrangement between the evaluator and the practitioner.

The practitioner must necessarily take a variety of considerations into account when he makes any decision. At times he may find economic considerations most compelling, or political ones. But the evaluator is much more inclined to adhere, almost exclusively at times, to so-called scientific values. He prefers to make *his* decisions on "hard" data, by which, of course, he means scientifically derived data. Since he prides himself on being "rational," he cannot understand why everyone else is not rational, too. He feels disinclined to apply his scientific methods to a determination, say, of what the political climate is, because to do so would prostitute himself and pervert the ideals of the scientific community. This estrangement is severe and cannot be dismissed lightly.

5. Lack of approaches differentiated by levels. The problem of levels, as the term will be used here, stems from the fact that the evaluator's traditional point of focus has been microscopic, e.g., the individual student, the classroom, or the school building, rather than macroscopic, e.g., the school district, the state system, or the national network. This microscopic focus serves the evaluator badly when he is confronted with evaluation problems at superordinate levels, as is often the case today.

One consequence of this misplaced focus is that the *techniques* the evaluator uses are inappropriate. An example we have already noted is that, at the macroscopic level, it makes little sense to focus on behavioral objectives. Another difficulty is that the instruments have been developed for use with individuals, while the evaluator may now be concerned with system data. Finally, the evaluator is usually concerned with all of the subjects at the micro level, e.g., all of the students taking a certain science course in a certain school, while at the macro level he must lean heavily on sampling procedures with which he is not too familiar or which remain to be developed to an acceptable technical degree; as for example, using item sampling procedures rather than having all of the students answer all of the test items.

Another consequence is *faulty aggregation,* which takes two forms. First, there is the matter of summarizing operational data obtained at micro levels. Clearly the amount and kind of information required by the local project simply jams the wheels at the macro level. The second form of the aggregation problem is, in a sense, the inverse of the first; while these reports of operational data may more than meet the requirements of the micro agency, they do *not* contain information which is of vital concern to the macro agency. Thus, the local agency will not collect data relevant to the question of, say, how the Title III program is doing *as a whole,* while overloading the macro agency with information about how the specific project is doing. Overall, this aggregation problem seems often to be a matter of too much of the wrong thing.

A third consequence is that of *conflicting purposes.* Different data or information may be required at different levels, as well as different criteria to assess them. The purposes of agencies at different levels vary markedly. While there may be little question that the purpose of the teacher is to teach, or that the success of her teaching may be most appropriately assessed by reference to some criterion relating to student achievement, it is equally true that this purpose and this criterion are not relevant to, say, the evaluation of a statewide supervision or program or a national curriculum improvement effort.

Thus, the introduction of various levels of evaluation introduces problems that are by no means able to be resolved through the application of techniques, methods, criteria and perspectives developed at the micro level, where we are accustomed to working. This fact must be recognized, and steps must be taken to develop the new approaches that are clearly required. Evaluators must learn to "think big," and thinking big involves more than a quantitative increase in perspective.

6. *Lack of mechanisms for organizing, processing and reporting evaluative information.* Even if the above lacks did not exist, there still would remain an important logistical problem related to organizing, processing and reporting evaluative information. There is no central, coordinated, comprehensive system of educational data processing, storage and retrieval in existence. A few prototypes may be noted, one at the University of Iowa, but these prototypes do not begin to encompass the masses of information which will need to be processed. Meantime, one must count on the archaic and usually different systems employed by the various school systems and state departments of education.

7. *Lack of trained personnel.* Evaluation personnel have always been in short supply in this country, but the new improvement programs have magnified this shortage into catastrophic proportions. There is a purely quantitative aspect to this problem; literally tens of thousands of personnel are needed, but only a few hundred are being trained each year. Current efforts to increase the numbers being trained are confined mainly to term institutes and workshops.

But there is also a qualitative problem. The report of the "Roles for Researchers" project[6] currently being concluded at Indiana University shows that the kinds of persons needed are not likely to be developed by existing training programs that have either the flavor of educational psychology or of the traditional tests and measurements. There is, moreover, no agreement about the nature of the emergent evaluator role. So, for example, the director of a particular research and development center has said, "We are having trouble finding people who come to us with sufficient sophistication so that they can help with technical problems. We need an evaluator interested in measuring change, who is statistically competent and has all the characteristics of a stereotype methodologist in evaluation but who has a willingness to look at new kinds of problems." The model of the evaluator being developed by the Pittsburgh Public Schools has a definite linkage to the entire change process mechanism in use in that system, so that the evaluator is in fact a kind of change agent. In other instances the evaluator role is defined in terms of competence in a discipline first, and technical skills second. There is, thus, no consensus, and there are certainly few places where persons are being prepared systematically in these new orientations.

We are faced both with the lack of persons who can function in evaluator roles and with the lack of concepts and materials that are necessary to train recruits into the profession.

Where Next?

I have with malice aforethought painted a rather dismal picture of the state of the evaluative art. Surely the seven lacks that I have described (which are only the most major among literally dozens that might be identified) pose a formidable challenge to the professional community. Even the best evaluators can function only with extant theory, concepts, designs, tools, mechanisms and training. The practitioner can hardly be blamed if, when placing his faith on those extant procedures and consultant help, he produces evaluative results of little use to anyone. Nor can we fault him too much if he becomes disenchanted with the substitutes we offer—because they are not operational.

The primary task in evaluation today is the provision of sensible alternatives to the evaluator. The evaluation of educational innovations awaits the modernization of the theory and practice of the evaluative art. We need, then, a technology of evaluation.

Is there any hope that this modernization will occur soon? I believe that there is a great deal of reason to be hopeful. We can allude briefly to a few of these reasons:

On the matter of definition, a number of fruitful efforts have already been made. Cronbach,[7] Stufflebeam,[8,9] Scriven,[10] Stake,[11] Pfeiffer,[12] Suchman,[13] Quade,[14] and others have assayed new formulations that are somewhat convergent. The national Phi Delta Kappa panel convened for the purpose of writing a monograph on evaluation have pulled these definitions together into a highly useful version that links evaluation and decision-making.

On the subject of decision-making theory, the work of Braybrooke and Lindblom already referred to, together with that of Simon,[15] Hock[16] and Ott[17] have added useful dimensions to our thinking.

In relation to values and criteria, Quade,[18] Kaplan,[19] Bloom,[20] Krathwohl,[21] and Clark and Guba have made significant contributions.

In relation to data processing (particularly in the form of data banks) and the levels problem, much can be gleaned from the experience of Project Talent, the Measurement Research Center at the University of Iowa, National Assessment and Project EPIC. Computer capabilities unknown a few years ago also adds a dimension.

In the area of methodology we can look to developments such as quasi-experimental design, convergence technique, Delphi technique, item sampling, Bayesian statistics, PERT, operations research techniques, systems analysis and the like or some new insights.

Thus, the picture is by no means all drawn in shades of black or gray. The profession does show many signs of awareness to the problems that I have described. What is important now is that these first efforts be vigorously pursued and made *operational* as quickly as possible.

References

1. Coleman, James S., et al., Equality of Educational Opportunity. National Center for Educational Statistics, U.S. Government Printing Office, Washington, D.C., 1966, p. 325.

2. Coleman, *Ibid.*

3. *A Manual for Project Applicants and Grantees* (Title III Elementary and Secondary Education Act). Washington, D.C., Office of Education, Department of Health, Education, and Welfare, May, 1967, p. 48.

4. Guba, Egon G. "Report on the Evaluation Provision of Twenty-One Title III Proposals," Report to the National Panel on Title III Evaluation, Richard I. Miller, Director, October 15, 1967.

5. Braybrooke, David and Lindblom, Charles E. *A Strategy of Decisions,* New York: The Free Press, 1963.

6. Clark, David L. and Hopkins, John E. "Roles for Researchers," CRP Project No. X-022, Indiana University, in progress.

7. Cronbach, Lee J. "Course Improvement Through Evaluation," *Teachers College Record,* Columbia University, New York, 1963.

8. Stufflebeam, Daniel L. "A Depth Study of the Evaluation Requirement," *Theory into Practice,* V(3), The Ohio State University, June, 1966.

9. Stufflebeam, Daniel L. "The Use and Abuse of Evaluation in Title III," *Theory into Practice,* VI(3), The Ohio State University, June, 1967.

10. Scriven, Michael S. "The Methodology of Evaluation," *AERA Monograph Series on Curriculum Evaluation, Book I,* Chicago: Rand McNally and Company, 1967.

11. Stake, Robert E. "The Countenance of Educational Evaluation," *Teachers College Record,* Columbia University, New York, April, 1967.

12. Pfeiffer, John. *New Look at Education,* New York: Odyssey Press, 1968.

13. Suchman, Edward A. *Evaluative Research,* New York: Russell Sage Foundation, 1967.

14. Quade, Edward S. (Ed.). *Analysis for Military Decisions,* Chicago: Rand McNally and Company, 1967.

15. Simon, Herbert A. "Administrative Decision-Making," *Public Administration Review,* March, 1965.

16. Hock, Michael D. "Considerations of Decision Theory in the Reconstruction of Logic in Urban Planning," produced and distributed by the Evaluation Center, The Ohio State University, 1968.

17. Ott, Jack M. "A Decision Process and Classification System for Use in Planning Educational Change," produced and distributed by the Evaluation Center, The Ohio State University, 1967.

18. Quade, *Op. Cit.*

19. Kaplan, Abraham. *The Conduct of Inquiry,* San Francisco: Chandler Publishing Company, 1964.

20. Bloom, Benjamin S. (Ed.). *Taxonomy of Educational Objectives, Handbook I: Cognitive Domain,* New York: David McKay Company, Inc., 1956.

21. Krathwohl, David R., Bloom, Benjamin S. and Masia, Bertram B. *Taxonomy of Educational Objectives, Handbook II: Affective Domain,* New York: David McKay Company, Inc., 1964.

JOHN MANN

The Outcome of Evaluative Research

The normal channels of professional publication have made readers
with specialized interests largely unaware of the true extent of evaluative research, since such studies are published in the type of journal
associated with the method being tested. Studies of educational procedures are published in journals of educational research; research
in group psychotherapy is published in group psychotherapy journals; and human-relations training studies are published in social
psychology periodicals.

Articles published in these periodicals summarizing evaluative
studies almost invariably are developed along specialized lines. However adequate and interesting these reviews may be, they fail to
provide any comparative sense of the impact of evaluative research.
They do not indicate whether such research, taken as a whole, is likely
to determine either the general effectiveness of our attempts to change
human behavior, or the relative effectiveness of different approaches
used in the same field, or the same approaches used for different
purposes. These are basic and important questions for any science
of behavior change, and it is reasonable to suppose that the evaluation of current behavior-change methods could supply some relevant
answers.

This chapter will investigate the nature of the conclusions these
studies can reasonably be expected to provide on the basis of a review

268 OUTCOME OF EVALUATIVE RESEARCH

of the information already supplied. It is difficult to estimate the total number of such studies for several reasons. First, they appear in so many sources that it is hard to extract material from all of them. Second, much of the best such research is done as doctoral dissertations that are not readily obtainable. Finally, much evaluative research is never published because the sponsors or researchers do not want the results made known or because of its inherently poor quality. However, it is safe to say that a careful search of all literatures would accumulate three to five thousand evaluative studies of behavior-change processes.

It is neither practical nor necessary to analyze all of this research. A sample should be sufficient to gain some sense of the general tendency. Further, it is reasonable to assume that the accessibility of research has some relation to its quality and importance.

Several years ago, the author undertook a review of evaluative research conducted in a number of content areas. Since the nature and outcome of this study are directly relevant to the issues under discussion, it will be described briefly.[1]

The first step was the selection of a limited number of content areas for comparison. Two criteria were employed. First, the areas chosen had to contain a reasonable accumulation of evaluative research studies, ranging from 30 to 50, so that some general conclusion about their findings might be possible. Second, the change that the practitioners were trying to produce had to be broad, deep, and of general social significance; in this way, the evaluations would be of attempts to produce important change. With the aid of these criteria, four content areas were selected for intensive investigation: psychotherapy, counseling, human-relations training, and education. In the field of education, only studies of methods that attempted to produce basic personality changes were reviewed; this eliminated the large literature dealing with the effectiveness of educational processes as determinants of intellectual performance.

Even within these areas, it was necessary to be selective, because of the large number and variable quality of the evaluative studies that were available for review. In order to reduce the task to manageable proportions only studies of a relatively high methodological caliber were selected.

A superficial review of the literatures in psychotherapy, counseling, human-relations training, and education indicated that over six hundred studies seemed to meet these criteria. After a more careful examination, approximately two thirds proved deficient in respect to one or another of the selection criteria. It was, therefore, possible to reduce the number of evaluative studies under active consideration to 181. Because of the criteria used to select them, they contained, as a group, findings that had a greater degree of social significance and a lesser degree of experimental error than other research in their area. This sample therefore represented the most likely source for obtaining interesting and important information about the success of evaluative research in contributing to an understanding of the process of inducing behavior change and the methods by which this change can most efficiently be accomplished.

The Analysis of Evaluative-Research Studies

The central problem to be overcome in any analysis of studies obtained from diverse origins is the design and application of a common system of classification that can be applied to all of them. These categories, once they are imposed, form the frame of reference of any comparisons made among studies and thus indirectly influence the findings by limiting the kind of information that can be analyzed.

In the present instance the task of deriving a classification system was simplified by the fact that all studies utilized the same general type of research design, though they varied in complexity. They could, therefore, each be viewed as a sample of evaluative research and described in terms of the general characteristics that all such research must contain.

In order to describe any evaluative investigation, it is necessary to state the nature of the experimental design used, the number of subjects and practitioners included, the nature of the sample, the setting in which the method was tested, the nature of the method itself, the change criteria employed, the findings obtained, and the types of methodological error that may have been present. In the present instance, therefore, it was only necessary to analyze each of these aspects of evaluative research in detail in order to arrive at a coding system that could be used to describe any given study in a relatively complete manner. . . .

The first step in the preparation of the data for analysis was to code on IBM cards each of the 181 studies that constituted the experimental sample. The information on these cards was then analyzed in order to answer two central questions: first, what are the general characteristics of evaluative research when distinctions of content area are ignored; second, what are the differences in character and outcome of studies that were conducted in different areas. In general, the data analysis was intended to determine whether evaluative studies have as a group accumulated a reliable, valid, and socially significant body of knowledge that can be generalized across content areas or help to distinguish among them.

The General Character of Evaluative Research

The simplest way to attain a general picture of evaluative research when content areas are ignored is to examine the summary statistics of all categories, since these statistics, by definition, describe the general character of the studies under review.

TABLE 2

ASPECTS OF EXPERIMENTAL DESIGN

Pre post	80%
Post only	12
Pre post with follow up	7
Post only with follow up	1
One method tested with one type of control group	74
Multiple methods and one control	13
One method and multiple controls	9
Multiple methods and multiple controls	4
Subjects matched on less than 4 variables	11
Subjects matched on 4 or more variables	22
Subjects randomly assigned to experimental conditions	20
Subjects randomly assigned with equivalence of matching demonstrated	23
Partial randomization	7
Matching after the fact	3
Biased matching (groups not really from the same population)	2
Matched on unspecified variables	2
Subjects acted as their own controls	3
Basis of assignment to groups unspecified	7
No use of a factorial design	93
Use of a factorial design	6
Induced factorial design by the use of analysis of covariance	1
No use of replication	93
Use of replication	7

Table 2 shows the statistics for different aspects of experimental design. An inspection of this table suggests that evaluative research is generally formulated in the simplest possible terms, involving a pre-post test, performed both before and after the course of the experiment of one method and one control group. Factorial design and replication are used in less than 10 per cent of the studies. The method of assignment to experimental conditions is partially or totally unsatisfactory in approximately 25 per cent of the cases. In general, the design of evaluative research appears to be crude, and the method of assignment of subject to conditions only partially satisfactory.

TABLE 3

NATURE OF THE SAMPLES

Number of Subjects

Less than 10 subjects	2%
10 to 20 subjects	8
21 to 30 subjects	16
31 to 40 subjects	11
41 to 60 subjects	13
61 to 100 subjects	18
101 to 150 subjects	9
151 to 200 subjects	3
201 or more subjects	14
Number of subjects unspecified	6

Nature of Subjects

Children	8%
Adolescents	19
Young adults	30
Adults	40
Old persons	2
Nonhumans (e.g., rats)	1
Normal	49
Emotionally maladjusted (e.g., mental hospital patients)	30
Antisocial difficulties (e.g., delinquents)	11
Underachievers and retarded	9
Physically handicapped	1

Number of Change Agents

Number unspecified	53%
1	14
2	11
3	3
4	1
5	0
6	1
7	2
8 or more	9
Number not relevant	6

Table 3 describes the samples of subjects and practitioners that are used in these studies. The number of subjects varies, on the average, between forty and sixty. Their nature is partially determined by the content areas chosen for review. In the majority of studies, the number of practitioners used is not specified. Presumably, in these studies one or two practitioners are used, since a greater number would be likely to receive special mention in the description. In any case, those evaluations that do specify the number of practitioners use an average of one or two.

TABLE 4

NATURE AND SETTING OF THE METHODS EVALUATED

Nature of the Methods

Individual psychotherapy	10%
Individual counseling	11
Group psychotherapy	23
Group counseling	10
Group and individual therapy tested in the same study	9
Components and analogues of therapy	6
Human-relations training	10
Educational procedures	21

Setting of the Methods

School	61%
Prison or associated conditions such as parole	9
Out-patient or mental hygiene clinic	4
Hospital	21
Factory	1
Office	1
Home	1
Armed services	1
Private practice	1

Table 4 describes the nature of the methods tested and the settings in which they were applied. The content areas reviewed determined these components for the most part. It is interesting to note that, among the studies selected in the sample, there were twice as many of group, as of individual, therapy, in spite of the fact that group therapy has become widely used only recently.

Table 5 summarizes the frequency with which various types of measuring instruments were employed as change criteria. Many such criteria were employed in these studies, but no single type of instrument was used in more than 30 per cent of the studies.

Table 5 shows, in addition to the frequency with which a measure was used, the relationship between the change criteria utilized and the findings obtained. The most striking general conclusion suggested by this table is that change was obtained on the various instruments in about 45 per cent of the instances in which they were used as change criteria. However, since the number and nature of the

TABLE 5

INSTRUMENTS USED TO MEASURE CHANGE

Instruments	Instrument Used		Instrument Not Used
	Change Found	No Change Found	
Standard personality tests	10%	16%	74%
Self-ratings	8	10	82
Ratings by others	12	18	70
Projective tests	15	8	77
Intelligence tests	3	5	92
Interviews	2	3	95
Follow-up questionnaires	4	3	93
Attitude questionnaires	8	17	75
Interaction measures and behavioral observation	5	5	90
Measures of social sensitivity, insight, and empathy	1	4	95
School records	5	7	88
Tests of knowledge	8	11	81
Aptitude tests	1	4	95
Sociometric tests	4	5	91
Tests of psychomotor efficiency	1	0	99
Reality decisions (e.g., whether to go to college)	1	0	99
Situational tests	1	2	97
Nonverbal and performance tests	1	0	99
Behavioral records (e.g., discipline marks)	4	6	90
Degree of conformity to group norms	0	1	99
Measures related to learning (e.g., fixation, recall)	3	1	96

instruments varied from study to study, it was necessary to determine whether 45 per cent of the studies also showed evidence of change. This question was investigated by making an independent rating of the amount of change demonstrated and determining whether the amount of change determined in this way agreed with that shown in Table 5. The results of this analysis indicated that the rating of change agreed within two percentage points with the average change shown by the measuring instruments. This substantiated the conclusion that the amount of change found by each of the measuring instruments replicates the general pattern of change obtained by the global change rating and indirectly supported the reliability of the rating itself.

However, several exceptions to this pattern occurred. When projective tests were used as change criteria, change was found in 65 per cent of the cases. This is surprising in view of the generally low reliability of projective tests and the fact that they are supposed to measure aspects of personality that are presumably difficult to alter. In contrast to projective tests, ratings by others and attitude questionnaires showed changes less often than other instruments. This is also surprising, since change is often thought to occur first in surface attitudes and outward behavior. While these findings are intriguing, an over-all *chi-square* comparison of the amount of change found with various instruments failed to indicate any significant differences. The exceptions are, therefore, most reasonably interpreted as chance variation. Chi square is a statistical technique for testing whether different categories of cases occur in a predicted frequency pattern.

The conclusion to be drawn is that all instruments demonstrate the existence of change with approximately the same frequency or, conversely, that change is demonstrated in evaluative research in approximately 45 per cent of the cases regardless of the instruments used.

TABLE 6

NUMBER OF TYPES OF INSTRUMENT USED PER STUDY

Types of Instrument Used	Studies
1	64
2	57
3	32
4	20
5	5
6	2
7	–
8	–
9	–
10 or more	10

Table 6 deals with the same data from a different viewpoint by showing the number of different types of instruments used in different studies. This table indicates that fewer than 40 per cent of the studies used more than two types of change criteria. In view of the variety of instruments available, the uncertainty of the types of change to be expected, and the effort involved in even the simplest evaluative research, it is regrettable that a broader spectrum of change criteria was not employed within the confines of the individual study.

Table 7 summarizes the frequency with which various types of methodological error occurred in the studies reviewed. The impor-

TABLE 7

ERRORS IN METHODOLOGY

No control for interaction between method and measuring instrument	96%
No control for subject's degree of belief in the method	89
Impossibility of distinguishing between the effect of the therapy and the effect of the therapist	59
No control for the effect of the therapist's general level of ability	59
No control for the effect of the therapist's personality	59
No control for the previous experience of the therapist	59
No control for degree of interest of the therapist	59
No control for the effect of providing experimental subjects with attention	52
No control for differential ability of therapist with different methods	41
No objective confirmation of the method tested	31
Failure to use either matching or randomization	21
Lack of experimental control with consequent impossibility of repeating the experiment	17
Statistical ambiguities (e.g., regression effects)	17
Possible measurement bias	15
Incorrect control group	15
Failure to use appropriate change criteria	5
Failure to provide an appropriate test of the method considered	1

tance of this information is hard to overestimate, since the existence of error in the experimental procedure casts a reasonable doubt on the findings. The greater the amount of error, the greater the difficulty in interpreting the experiment. Table 7 indicates that the categorized errors occurred in the studies in from 1 to as much as 96 per cent of the cases.

The most frequent error was a failure to provide a control for the effect of interaction between test and method. Even in cases where such a control was attempted, it was not entirely satisfactory, so that this error existed in virtually all the studies reviewed.

The findings reported in Table 7 are extremely damaging to the cause of evaluative research. With two or three exceptions, the errors are of a major character. In other areas of research in the behavioral sciences, any of them would probably render a study unfit for publication. They are not errors within subtle experimental refinements. Rather, they reflect the abuse of basic scientific procedures. It is, therefore, surprising that a sample of the better examples of evaluative research should prove so contaminated with experimental error.

These findings raise grave doubts as to whether any conclusions can be drawn from such research.

An analysis of these statistics led to several basic conclusions. First, most evaluative research uses the simplest possible experimental design, substituting simplicity for efficiency. Second, the findings of evaluative research are unrelated to the ways in which change is measured. Third, the technical proficiency of this research is at a low level. To some extent, the third conclusion undermines the second, since experimental error renders experimental findings ambiguous. While change may be demonstrated an average of 45 per cent of the time, it cannot be said that it actually occurs this often. Probably the actual percentage of change is much less, since experimental error usually leads to an overestimate of the extent of change.

Evaluative Research in Separate Content Areas

The second basic question to be investigated was the differences that existed among studies that were conducted in different content areas. Presumably, comparisons among the character and outcome of evaluative research conducted in different content areas might aid in the broader formulation of evaluative research itself and help to demonstrate areas of similarity and difference. It was, therefore, with considerable interest and expectation that the comparative analysis of these studies was undertaken.

In order to determine whether studies executed in different content areas varied with respect to the analysis categories, the data were reanalyzed. Studies in the various areas were treated as separate groups. . . . An inspection of the table* suggests that fewer of the group therapy and more of the educational studies than expected had forty-one or more subjects.

However, when research in different areas was compared, no significant differences were found in any of the categories describing the experimental design that was applied, the change criteria used, or the obtained findings. These startling negative conclusions suggest that evaluative research conducted in different areas is identical in both character and outcome.

A further tabulation was made in order to determine whether certain methods, regardless of the content area in which they were applied, showed differential change patterns. For this purpose, four methods were compared: the nondirective approach, role playing, psychoanalytic therapy, and eclectic therapy. Sufficient studies of each of these approaches were available to make the comparison

* Tables 8–13 have been omitted.

meaningful. The results clearly indicated that all methods produced change about 45 per cent of the time, which indicated that there was no differential superiority among them and that in amount of change produced they did not differ from all other methods tested in the other studies.

In view of the fact that these content areas are usually treated as conceptually separate, utilize separate training procedures for the preparation of practitioners, serve different populations, and are derived from varying historical and social conditions, the lack of any demonstrable difference in the ability to induce change among them is remarkable. . . .

At this point in the analysis, it was clear that the findings of evaluative research could not provide any insight into relationships among the studies performed in different content areas, since all relevant findings were negative. It was still possible, however, that the lack of positive findings was due to the already demonstrated experimental error in the research rather than to the nature of evaluative research itself. In order to check this hopeful possibility the relationship between degree of experimental error and outcome of the study was determined.

TABLE 14

THE RELATION BETWEEN DEMONSTRATED CHANGE AND METHODOLOGICAL DEFICIENCY

	Change Demonstrated		No Change Demonstrated	
Poor methodology	4	(2.7)	2	(3.3)
Below average methodology	17	(17.6)	22	(21.3)
Average methodology	19	(22.2)	30	(26.8)
Above average methodology	32	(30.8)	36	(37.2)
Good methodology	9	(7.7)	8	(9.3)

Table 14 indicates that no relationship between the two exists. Positive findings of change are not associated with poorly designed research any more or less than they are associated with studies employing a relatively sophisticated design with elaborate experimental controls. In short, good and bad research obtained the same general finding: change occurs in approximately 45 per cent of the cases reviewed.

Several additional data analyses were undertaken in order to clarify the issues involved in arriving at a final assessment of the significance of evaluative research. These analyses appeared initially promising but proved to be either negative or puzzling in their outcome and do not affect the conclusions that have been drawn.

Summary of the General and Comparative Analysis of Evaluative Research

Two conclusions are suggested by the analysis: the quality of evaluative research is remarkably poor, and there is little difference in the results of evaluative studies conducted in different content areas. Specifically, there is no indication that the findings of evaluative research are influenced by the method tested, the content area in which the test is conducted, the change criteria used, or the methodological quality of the study of which the evaluation is made. The only clear positive finding is that change is demonstrated in approximately 45 per cent of the studies.

In considering the remarkably poor quality of evaluative research, it is necessary to remember the variety of technical and social difficulties that arise in the design and execution of these studies. However, regardless of the quality of the research itself, there remains the fact that it does not seem to produce any positive conclusions, except that change is consistently demonstrated in a certain fixed proportion of the studies. This is the heart of the problem. Evaluative research is intended to distinguish among methods of changing behavior, determining the most successful procedures, and to clarify the process of behavior change itself. To do this the demonstrated change must be related to other significant variables, such as the content area investigated, instruments used, and methods tested. None of these relationships can be clearly established. One is driven, therefore, to the inescapable conclusion that evaluative research shows no prospect of reaching these goals.

Such a damaging conclusion requires an explanation. The most reasonable explanation the author can offer, on the basis of his direct examination of the evidence, is that evaluative research is not undermined so much by the problem of its execution as by the methods it attempts to evaluate. The ingredients of evaluative studies are inappropriate to scientific methodology, which, like any good recipe, requires the use of specific pure elements that are combined in known proportions and in a fixed time schedule. Virtually all methods evaluated by the studies reviewed were of such complexity as to defy description in terms of a limited number of carefully specified variables. Such descriptive labels as psychoanalysis, nondirective therapy, or group-centered experience cover a multitude of operations whose precise nature and order of presentation are unknown. If the methods that are tested cannot be precisely described, then the results can never be cumulative, since no one can state what was tested.

The general conclusion of this comparative review is, therefore, that evaluative research represents a scientific blind alley. It has failed to validate itself in practice and the sooner its failure is accepted and recognized, the easier will be a transition to another approach to the same problem.

Studying the Components of Behavior-Change Procedures

In order to be able to study the problem of changing human behavior in a systematic and cumulative manner, it is only necessary to change the focus from the complex method as it is applied in practical situations to the components of the method, which can be examined with any desired degree of experimental precision in a laboratory setting. The number of such components is limited, and the huge variety of behavior-change techniques currently utilized represent, for the most part, variations on a few central themes.

A relatively superficial examination of the social and psychological research literature suggests that among such components of change procedures can be included the following:

1. The direction, amount, and quality of participation of both the subject and the practitioner
2. The nature of feedback mechanisms
3. The nature and extent of opportunity for the practice of the behavior patterns
4. Variations in power relationships
5. The operant conditioning of new behaviors
6. The elimination of undesired behaviors through negative conditioning
7. Elimination of undesirable reactions through deconditioning
8. The degree of faith which the subject has in the method
9. The involvement of the practitioner in the application of the method
10. The creation of stress
11. The opportunity for confession and catharsis
12. The concentration of the subject's attention on his own behavior

This list could be extended, but it sufficiently illustrates the point that it is possible to name a variety of components of the complex change processes. In addition, all of these components have been studied experimentally, so that it has already been demonstrated that they lend themselves to precise definition and measurement in keeping with customary standards in the behavioral sciences. What is more important, however, is that these components are, in fact, vital elements in most change processes. Virtually each method, for example, uses some specialized form of feedback—whether positive, negative, objective, or subjective. Further, each technique employs certain implicit or explicit laws of participation. In some, all interaction is directed toward the practitioner; in others, it is ignored and group members talk with each other. Further, the type of participation is usually specified; in psychotherapy, for example, particular stress is laid on emotionally toned materials rather than on extensive use of rational formulation.

Additional examples are easily provided. Some methods of therapy emphasize the creation of stress, opportunity for catharsis, and the continuous focus of the subject's attention on his own reaction. In other behavior-change techniques stress is minimized, and attention on the individual and opportunity for confession are both avoided. Even the same method may use different degrees of a given component at separate stages. For example, stress may be initially avoided, but emphasized at a later period.

The more known methods are reinterpreted in terms of specific components, the more one is struck by the fact that in studying the variations in given components, something is learned about the efficiency of a wide range of change processes, even though one does not test any one of them. Furthermore, testing of components is natural to the scientific method. The experimenter can control all relevant aspects of the social situation. Conflicts of interest with the practitioner need not occur, since the research involves testing components in the laboratory rather than evaluation of programs and treatment methods. This procedure also bypasses the practitioner's resistance to being evaluated, since he is not directly involved in the testing process. More generally, studies of separate components avoid all of the previously described social problems associated with evaluative research.

The major obstacle to the development of a program of research designed to test behavior-change components is that, despite the existence of a vast amount of research into such topics as attitude change, group dynamics, social influences on learning, and intergroup relations, this material has not been systematically and thoroughly examined to determine which components of change processes have been scientifically validated. It is crucial that such a critical examination of the experimental literatures involved should precede any actual research program so that central emphasis can be placed on the variables most likely to be of importance in producing behavior and attitude change.

So often in the behavioral sciences new areas are opened up in an opportunistic and superficial manner because of the development of a new and simple research technique; or they are developed one-sidedly due to a popular but limited theory that happens to be current at the time. Almost inevitably in such instances, with the accumulation of some research data a critical reaction sets in. Persons working in the area realize that much of the previous work has been misapplied, has ignored important variables and, in general, has been extremely inefficient in terms of a lasting return in secure scientific knowledge.

In the analysis of behavior change, much of this developmental inefficiency can be avoided, because a large body of relevant research studies already exists. A review of this literature can accomplish several purposes. It can help to establish precisely which components of behavior-change processes have been experimentally validated. And it can determine what is known about the effect of the simultaneous application of different components, each of which may have been independently validated. In such cases, it may be possible to judge whether components are additive or interactive in their effect. Moreover, it can establish which components have proved either difficult to measure or relatively weak as determinants of change. When this information has been accumulated and organized, it should be possible to develop a set of priorities that could dictate, on the basis of known experimental findings, which relationships among components ought to be tested, and in what order.

The power of experimental designs combining the simultaneous variation of a number of different components on a series of different levels has been greatly increased by recent developments in multiple statistical comparisons, which enable researchers using complex factorial designs to test not only for the effect of each component included in the design, but also for the relative effects of each unique combination of components. In addition, whether combined effects are additive or interactive can be determined.

An example of such a factorial study of behavior-change components might involve three variations in power relations (democratic, laissez-faire, and autocratic), four variations in feedback (subjective, objective, positive, and negative), and three variations in stress (strong, moderate, and weak). Such a factorial study would require the testing of thirty-six independent conditions if all possible combinations of power relations, feedback mechanisms, and stress were examined.

The significance of studying the behavior changes produced by various combinations can best be seen by examining several of them. For example, consider the case of an authoritarian power structure with objective feedback and high stress. Such a condition would appear to resemble certain types of staff meetings that occur in highly differentiated institutional structures. The complementary experimental condition would consist of a laissez-faire structure, subjective feedback, and low stress. This condition resembles a normal, friendly social gathering. Another of the thirty-six possible conditions would consist of a democratic structure with positive feedback and moderate stress, resembling certain types of volunteer action groups. Thus, many of the combined components tested in such a study would resemble behavior-change processes currently in use and cast some indirect light on their validity.

However, the greatest significance of this approach to the study of behavior change is not that the experimental conditions resemble practical methods currently in use, but in the degree and character of the information it provides for a given amount of effort.

The effect of each level of each component in the example would be tested not only for its absolute effectiveness, but also for its relative effectiveness in comparison to each level of every component. The absolute and differential effect of each of the thirty-six component combinations would be determined. This is particularly important, since it is of greater significance to determine how the elements of known potency combine than to know that they are individually potent. Components of behavior change are rarely, if ever, applied singly, except for experimental purposes. A complex experimental condition is the analogue of the practical treatment as applied by the practitioner. It would be determined whether certain combinations of conditions are more effective in producing specified behavior changes than knowledge about their individual effectiveness would lead one to predict.

In this manner, a complex factorial approach to the study of behavior-change components could efficiently accumulate much information directly relevant to the understanding and evaluation of a number of change-inducing procedures, while not directly testing any one of them. This, in turn, would help to provide the basis of a science of behavior change that was both systematic and comprehensive.

SIDNEY H. ARONSON
CLARENCE C. SHERWOOD

Researcher Versus Practitioner:
Problems in Social Action Research

It has become commonplace for Americans to say that a new revolution is taking place in the United States. Its main force is directed
toward improving the life chances of that still large army of the poor
consisting of Negroes, Puerto Ricans, Mexican-Americans, and some
other ethnic groups, including not a few Anglo-Saxons. As is the
case with so much of social change, the revolutionary impetus comes
not only from the bottom of the class order but also from the top. It
may be that sit-ins and other mass demonstrations produced much
of the change, but the revolution has supporters in the universities, in
federal and local government, and in that curious symbol of the business community, the Ford Foundation.

The War on Poverty is only the latest stage of the revolution.
Before this, there was the attack on delinquency by President Ken-
nedy's Committee on Juvenile Delinquency and Youth Crime and the
"grey areas" project of the Ford Foundation, the purpose of which
was to improve inner-city schools and the delivery of social and
health services to the needy. One of the more revolutionary aspects
of the earlier efforts was the insistence on the part of the President's
committee that the programs (called demonstrations) receiving its
financial support be thoroughly researched and evaluated. This article
will review the efforts of the research branch of one organization to

Sidney H. Aronson and Clarence C. Sherwood, "Researcher Versus Practitioner: Problems in Social Action Research," *Social Work,* vol. 12, no. 4
(1967), 89–96. Reprinted by permission.

evaluate a group of demonstration programs. The organization, which for purposes of this paper will be called Opportunities for Youth (OFY), was funded primarily by the Office of Juvenile Delinquency and Youth Crime and the Ford Foundation and carried on its programs in a major American city.

Projects of the President's Committee on Juvenile Delinquency and Youth Crime and the Ford Foundation have been designed as accompaniments to the massive programs of urban renewal being carried out in America's major cities. The various action-research organizations formed were to provide the human dimension for urban renewal by planning and conducting a broadly defined program of community development.

OFY, a private, nonprofit agency, was not meant to be permanent. It was intended to act as a catalyst in the development of a broad assault on the city's social problems and especially, at least in its early history, on juvenile delinquency. Its role was to stimulate other groups to co-operate in the establishment of new programs. The demonstration programs themselves were to be carried out by public and private agencies. This division of responsibility was based on the view that the programs—for obvious reasons—should be administered by agencies with more of a future.

How important research and evaluation were to the demonstration programs could be seen in Public Law 87–274, enacted by Congress to make research funds available; the purpose of this law was "to provide financial support to programs which might demonstrate effectiveness in the prevention and control of juvenile delinquency." The case for evaluation would seem to be self-evident, but the President's committee and the Ford Foundation were among the few to place an emphasis on its inclusion. A fortune was about to be spent on a variety of programs on delinquency and poverty; without evaluation no one would know which monies were well spent and which were wasted and the problems of delinquency and poverty might remain unaffected.

Agency Model

The general model adopted by OFY was that of an action-research demonstration, the purpose of which was to discover effective and efficient ways of allocating resources in attacking social problems. It assumed that efforts to reduce or prevent these should be based on evidence as to what has been done, what has worked, and how and with whom it has worked.

Ideally, an action-research demonstration has the following general features: (1) an objective or set of objectives—the criteria by which the success or failure of the demonstration will ultimately be judged, (2) a rationale—the line of reasoning by which it hopes to achieve its objectives (building upon selected variables believed to be crucial in dealing with the particular social problem, the rationale explains why changes in these variables will alleviate the problem), (3) strategies or avenues for intervention—programs suggested by the rationale and an impact model that connects the program procedures and the kinds of changes the program is designed to produce, and (4) evaluation—the procedures to determine whether the program achieved its objectives.

The over-all rationale for the programs was built around the concept of social role, on grounds that programs that provide the individual with the skills required to meet the expectations imposed on him and that improve the role performance of significant others will result in improved behavior in a number of social situations—that is, go beyond the specific role being dealt with directly—and be manifested in less law-violating behavior.

Two main kinds of programs were designed. One was aimed at the delinquency-prone population—children aged 9–16—and was based in the public schools and in summer camps. Included were programs in developmental reading, guidance, school adjustment counseling, prekindergarten training, and remedial academic work in school and in camp. The assumption underlying these programs was that the knowledge, skills, and values imparted by schools and camps were necessary for better role performance and that improved academic work will be followed by improved behavior on the streets.

The other kind of program involved the establishment of a new social service institution—the multiservice center—located in the heart of the poverty and delinquency belt, which offered under one roof a variety of co-ordinated services in employment, health, law, family services, and the like. Main focus of the multiservice center was on strengthening the role performance of adults who interacted frequently with the delinquency-prone youths, on grounds that a more stable family produced better behavior. One of the major assumptions was that many of these adults needed assistance in coping with their problems but were alienated from the network of health and welfare agencies because of the physical and social distance between themselves and the agencies and the bureaucratization of social work. By design, the multiservice center specializes in the hard-to-reach and reaches them through its neighborhood location, street workers, instant service, and development of primary relationships between the client and worker.

Three multiservice centers were established in the community. This paper will deal primarily with the relationship between the research unit and the people responsible for designing and implementing the multiservice center program and especially with the sources of discord that developed among the relevant actors in the demonstration programs.

Difficulty with Program Designers

The main source of difficulty between the researchers and their colleagues, the designers of programs, was the latter's preoccupation with the components of programs without reference to their objectives or to the connections between those components and the kinds of changes the program was intended to produce—what has been referred to as the impact model. Although it seems only logical to specify the changes that will be sought before devising strategies to produce those changes, the designer of programs typically begins with the details of the program without first defining the kinds of changes that are the intervention targets.

Nowhere was this tendency more evident than in the development of multiservice center demonstrations. To the designer, the pieces of such an enterprise fell together quite naturally—employment, family casework, health, legal, and other traditional services. But the specific goals of a multiservice center emerge much less naturally and, if at all, only with great prodding. The designer's first attempt at stating an objective is that it is the center's aim to help people. The researcher then asks what is meant by help. To regard a given client as helped, in what specific ways must he be different at some future date? Until these variables are specified, there is no way to begin to assess whether the client has been "helped." Any program designer or practitioner ought to want to know what effects the program is trying to produce, but the research responsibility of a demonstration program cannot be fulfilled unless these outcomes are defined in terms that can be operationalized and measured. It was not always possible to get the designers to define the goals; researchers frequently had to suggest what the goals were and attempt to get the designers to go along.

The designer is also so intent on producing a program that he is likely to think little about the program's impact model. Limitations in space do not allow for a complete discussion of the importance of the impact model; without it there is no way, for example, to determine what connections there are between the program and the intermediate variables that presumably are producing the changes desired in the outcome variables. As was the case with the specification of goals, it remained for the researchers themselves to infer the impact model from the components of the program or constantly to prod the designers to state the theoretical links.

Problems Around Control Groups

This is not to say that interaction between the researchers and the program designers was characterized by continual conflict. It was not. Indeed, a major contribution toward implementing the action-research demonstration was the deep commitment of the program designers to the evaluation of their programs. For example, whenever feasible the researchers wanted to set up a comparison or control group that would not be exposed to the program. Little difficulty was experienced in getting the designers to set up the programs in such a way that there was not room enough for all those eligible to participate. However, although the problem of the control group was not one that involved the researchers and the program designers, it brought the OFY staff into conflict with practitioners of the agencies that actually ran the programs OFY designed and evaluated.

The practitioners—social workers, lawyers, teachers, probation officers, guidance and adjustment counselors, and camp directors—frequently did not understand the necessity for the comparison group. Deliberately denying some sufferers of a particular condition access to a program designed to alleviate that condition seems like a heartless denial of service. "When are you going to stop experimenting with people and let us start helping them?" was a typical reaction. Despite these objections the necessity of a control group came to be accepted in principle by the practitioners. All the programs instituted in the schools and camps utilized at least a version of the classical experimental design.

Other problems were also involved in the construction of experimental and comparison groups: (1) Practitioners did not always keep to the requirements for maintaining equivalent groups. (2) In the case of the neighborhood multiservice centers, random assignment into experimental and comparison groups was not feasible. It would have been virtually impossible to enumerate a sample of potential multiservice center clients and then arrange for a random group to go to the center and another to be kept out.

Obtaining Clients' Records

Evaluation of the effectiveness of any of the programs required that the research unit know by name and other identifying information the people who were given service, since these people would have to be followed over the period of the intervention (and ideally beyond) and some method developed to measure how much they had changed, if at all. This meant more than knowing names. Since outcomes may be associated with different problems and differential exposure it was important to know why the person had come to the center, what types of practitioners had been seen, how many different visits had been made, and so on.

The practitioner, however, looks at records from a different perspective. Because of his concern solely with the client's problems, he may feel that his ability to provide service would not be impaired if all he recorded was the client's name. Furthermore, he does not always see the justification for the categories of information that appear on the records. The category "religious affiliation," for example, caused much difficulty. Although religion has ·long been regarded as an explanatory variable in sociological theory, practitioners frequently ignored that category on grounds that to ask about religion would violate the client's right of privacy. That sociologists have had little difficulty in obtaining such information from survey respondents or that the practitioners as social workers probe areas that really do violence to the privacy of the client made no difference. Attempts to convince practitioners that they needed this and other types of information to help them do a better job met with varying success.

Uneasiness about records also results from the fact that the practitioner often fears that records will be used as a projective device to tell about him, that they will be used as a measure of his ability as a diagnostician or of his judgment in devising treatment methods. There is some validity to this, for despite the fact that the researchers were not trying to evaluate the competence of the practitioners it was impossible not to form judgments from such records.

Success in obtaining the names of clients and other identifying information varied from one program to another and even within the same program from one director to another. In one major program—the legal services program—there was complete failure to obtain client records from practitioners.

In this program provision was made for legal aid to indigents who needed help in civil cases (such as divorce, desertion, eviction, repossession of property) and in criminal cases as well (including misdemeanors and felonies). Furthermore, for criminal cases a bail project was designed to investigate the background of defendants so that some could be recommended for release by the judge on their own recognizance. In addition to broadening the range of legal services for the indigent, a major innovation of the program was its co-ordination with social services. The program assumed, for example, that a person who has faced eviction year after year needs more than a lawyer. Thus it was planned that in such cases the lawyer —who was housed in the multiservice center—would make a referral to a home development worker for aid in budgeting and marketing, to an employment worker to see if steady employment could be arranged, or perhaps to a training program to upgrade skills. Conversely, a person who sought a family service worker about a husband who had deserted would be referred to a lawyer so that support payments could be arranged. Since some legal aid lawyers were given storefront offices outside a multiservice center, it would have been possible for the research unit to compare a legal aid program integrated within a broad social service program with a more traditional type of program.

Unanticipated in the planning stage was the fact that the legal agencies that subcontracted to operate the programs would be unwilling to turn over copies of their clients' records on grounds that to do so would violate the confidential lawyer-client relationship. The lawyer, their argument went, could not be subpoenaed to testify about information revealed to him by the client. To make such information available to a researcher who could be subpoenaed jeopardized the privileged communication enjoyed by the lawyer. The argument that the researcher can be required to testify in court cannot be denied. But more may have been involved since the lawyer-directors of the programs refused to furnish even the names of their clients on grounds that the mere fact that a person sought or spoke to a lawyer was confidential.

At this writing, the names of people served by the lawyers in the program are not being made available, nor are they likely to be, but every client who appears at the multiservice center—including those seeking the services of a lawyer—must register, so it is known which have been referred to lawyers. However, the director of the local legal aid society hopes to re-route clients seeking a lawyer directly to the lawyer's office without registering at the receptionist's desk. So far he has not succeeded, but there is talk of removing the lawyers from the multiservice centers and establishing all of them in storefront offices. The names of defendants who are connected with the criminal components of the legal services program are not being made available.

A multiservice center director who did not want to turn over copies of his records also felt that to do so violated the confidential relationship between the social service worker and the client. Although he recognized that the relationship did not have legal sanctions he felt that professional ethics were involved. It was fruitless to argue that the research unit was not interested in the names of people per se, that their interest was in people as social types, but that without clients' names their progress (or lack of it) could not be measured over the years or data from other institutions and agencies connected.

The research unit was, in fact, also concerned with the problem of confidentiality. An elaborate security system was constructed, involving storing information in locked steel cabinets, later translating it into data processing language, and ultimately destroying the original forms.

Responsibility for Designing Interventions

A major source of difficulty between the researcher and program designer, on the one hand, and the practitioner, on the other, centers around the responsibility for designing interventions. It has been noted that OFY designed programs that were then farmed out. The practitioners were expected to be consulted as the designs took shape and it was assumed that no agency would accept a program if it did not agree with its approach. However, for various reasons these expectations were not always fulfilled. (1) Some programs did not exist until OFY established them. The staffs of these programs were not yet assembled and could hardly be expected to participate in designing the programs. They could be expected to be suspicious about a program that was imposed on them externally. (2) Such consultation that did go on often resulted in such challenges to what was designed that to take them seriously would have jeopardized the experimental nature of the program. (3) Some subcontractors, who signed contracts agreeing to operate the program as designed, proceeded to change many—if not most—of the program components once they began operating. The practitioner's commitment to the program, then, was sometimes less than enthusiastic.

Much of the tension between researchers and practitioners resulted from failure to convince the practitioners that what was being evaluated was the impact of a program and not their ability or competence. The researchers were unable to invoke the "pharmacology model," that is, to convince the practitioners that a particular intervention could be viewed by them the same way as a doctor viewed an experimental drug, that *it* was being tested and not they, and that if the program did not work, the failure was that of the designers rather than of the implementers.

The pharmacology model is especially appropriate in understanding another major problem in social action experiments, that is, holding the practitioners to the program design. The developer of a new drug does not have to worry about the possibility that the doctor who tries it for him will change the *contents* of that drug. Yet almost every social action program written by the program department was changed by the practitioners almost as soon as the program began.

There is a genuine problem here. The practitioner has responsibility for the day-to-day operation of an ongoing program and is apt to define success in administrative terms. Success to the designers of the programs means that the outcomes for which they were hoping were achieved and it is the researcher's job to measure the extent to which this is so. For example, a summer camp program designed by OFY had as its outcome variable better school work (in subsequent academic years). Success to the camp staff, on the other hand, meant that all the boys expected arrived and all were returned home, that no one drowned, there were not too many fights, everyone seemed to have fun, and the boys respected the counselors. This definition of success was manifested in a brief speech made by a camp director at a meeting of camp staff at the end of the summer. He announced to his colleagues that he suspected that the researchers would soon declare his program a failure but that he *knew* that it had triumphed, and that he could see its achievements "in the smiling faces of the campers." The researcher does not doubt that the boys smiled frequently at the camp, but this is not how the outcome variables were operationalized.

Role of "Anchor Workers"

A new and intriguing concept in the program design of the multiservice center was that of the role of the "anchor workers." One of the assumptions of the program was that poor people with problems are reluctant to take advantage of the network of available social services because of the impersonality of the bureaucratic organizations that dispense aid. A client may never see the same person at these agencies twice but instead is shunted about from worker to worker and agency to agency. As noted previously, the bureaucratization of the social welfare agencies is felt to produce alienation in the people who need the services the most.

The role of the anchor worker was designed to facilitate rapport between the client and the social worker. The person in need of help would not be pushed around; the first worker assigned to him was designated the anchor worker and would stay with him and develop a primary relationship. He would provide as much direct service as he could, but in the event that he could not provide a particular service—and this was to be expected in a multiservice center—he would, of course, make a referral. Even then the worker would keep in touch and provide needed support; he would go along with the client even if it meant traveling to an agency outside the building.

Two of the three multiservice centers abandoned the idea of the anchor worker from the outset on grounds that it did not or would not work or was not necessary. What this meant was that it was difficult to administer, not that it would not produce the planned-for impact. To the researcher, something that does not work is something that has a faulty connection between the input and the intended outcome.

Failure To Adhere to Program Design

Insistence that the practitioners adhere to the program design frequently resulted in the charge referred to before that the researchers were more interested in research than in people. It availed little to present the case for social action experiments to the practitioners or the fact that it was the program designers who had a stake in a specific intervention, not the researchers. In desperation the researchers sometimes said that the program could also be evaluated as the practitioners wanted to run it, to which the practitioners would respond: "Then let us run it our way and you research that." At that stage of the intervention, however, this was no longer a feasible or a justifiable position. The practitioners had, after all, signed a contract agreeing to do the program as it had been designed. Furthermore, this position completely overlooks the interdependence between program and research. Collaboration is possible only if the design is researchable, if its goals are stated and can be operationalized, if it is possible for impact to be assessed.

Every program design has its research design in a demonstration, one that depends on the program design, one that must be ready *prior* to the beginning of every program, because readings on variables as they are distributed among the experimental and comparison populations must be taken before exposure to the intervention. The research design operationalizes the goals of the intervention in terms of indicators that become the outcome variables, it determines the instruments that measure those variables, and so on. Once the program has begun it is too late for the practitioners to ask that what has happened be evaluated even if it included precise goals and an impact model. Furthermore, it is not logical to measure the outcome variables as specified in the original proposal in evaluating the drastically revised version since there may be no theoretical connection between the new program components and the outcome variables.

The number of examples of program components being discarded is manifold. The net result is that there are pressures to keep the programs from standing still and the researcher is frequently not sure just what it is he is trying to evaluate unless he develops some mechanism for policing the intervention.

Accomplishments and Weaknesses

This paper should not be concluded without listing some of the accomplishments of the project or without conceding some of the weaknesses of this research effort. It must be said that at the beginning little was known about evaluation research and few people were around who had training or experience in this special field. That a research assistant had specialized in one of the social sciences in college did not mean that he came to his job skilled. Indeed, former academicians on the staff who had taught the methodology of the social sciences were amazed at the complexities of evaluation research. Among other things, the academician learned the difference between randomly assigning a group of college students to experimental and control groups and assigning a group of truculent delinquents to such groups. But in the frequently clumsy implementation of the research designs many members of the research department have upgraded their skills and together with their colleagues from sister organizations now form a nucleus of persons who are better able to do evaluation research.

The researchers learned that skill in their craft requires more than technical knowledge. In fact, the ability to be diplomatic is perhaps as important as any. We learned that success requires close cooperation among the researchers, the program designers, and the practitioners.

Although our hopes and plans were far from being fully realized, as the struggles described earlier indicate, we feel that the best measure of our accomplishments can be seen in the fact that several social action programs have been evaluated utilizing classical experimental principles. At least a step has been made toward providing a more rational basis for planning future social action programs.

JACK ELINSON

Effectiveness of Social Action Programs in Health and Welfare

It has been a sort of hobby of mine to collect studies of social action programs on health and welfare. I select the studies on the basis of certain rough criteria. Mainly, I feel that the study should be prospective. Secondly, that the study should involve some planned intervention designed to achieve desired ends—that is, to do good in some way. Next, that some sort of control group in an approximation of the classical experimental design be used. Lastly, the material should have been reported in the scientific literature, in a book or in an article, monograph or other format. In other words, the material should be generally available to a scientific audience.

Now, when you look around for evaluative studies meeting these criteria, I do not think you will find too many. The ones listed in Table 1 may not be all that have been completed and meet the criteria

TABLE 1

Published Studies

1. J. Cumming and E. Cumming: *Closed Ranks* (Harvard University Press, 1957).
2. K. R. Hammond and F. Kern: *Teaching Comprehensive Medical Care* (Harvard University Press, 1959).

Jack Elinson, "Effectiveness of Social Action Programs in Health and Welfare," *Assessing the Effectiveness of Child Health Services*, Report of the Fifty-sixth Ross Conference on Pediatric Research, Abraham B. Bergman, ed., Columbus: Ross Laboratories, 1967, pp. 77–81. Reprinted by permission.

3. H. J. Meyer and E. F. Borgatta: *An Experiment in Mental Patient Rehabilitation* (Russell Sage, 1959).
4. D. M. Wilner, et al.: *Housing Environment and Family Life* (Johns Hopkins University Press, 1962).
5. H. R. Kelman: "An Experiment in the Rehabilitation of Nursing Home Patients," *Public Health Reports* (April 1962).
6. G. Silver: *Family Medical Care* (Harvard University Press, 1963).
7. G. W. Fairweather: *Social Psychology in Treating Mental Illness* (New York, Wiley, 1964).
8. A. Sheldon: "An Evaluation of Psychiatric After-Care," *British Journal of Psychiatry* (1964).
9. H. J. Meyer, E. F. Borgatta, and W. C. Jones: *Girls at Vocational High* (Russell Sage, 1965).
10. D. Wallace: "The Chemung County Research Demonstration with Dependent Multi-Problem Families" (State Charities Aid Association, New York, 1965).

I have outlined, but in the past ten years they are the ones that have come to my attention. They have come to my attention at about the rate of one per year.

Abstracts of these studies have been prepared by my research assistant, Cyrille Gell, two of which I present as examples.

Abstract of TEACHING COMPREHENSIVE MEDICAL CARE, by K. R. Hammond and F. Kern (Harvard University Press, 1959)

Objectives. In 1953 the University of Colorado School of Medicine initiated a General Medical Clinic Program to teach fourth-year students the techniques and philosophy of comprehensive medical care. Comprehensive medical care is defined as: responsibility for patient's total health; recognition of importance of social and psychological factors; awareness of preventive techniques.

Description of Program. During the 3-year study period (1954–56), half of each senior class of 80 students was assigned to the GMC Program for 24 weeks. Operating principles of GMC: (1) Give student maximum possible responsibility for his patients. (2) Increase continuity of contact with patient. (3) Incorporate preventive techniques in clinical teaching. (4) Stress importance of family interpersonal relations (Family and Home Care Program). (5) Stress importance of social and psychological problems in medicine.

Study Design. Each year senior students were divided into thirds according to class standing, and an equal number from each third was randomly assigned to experimental and control groups. The experimental group entered the GMC Program, while controls went through the usual clinical clerkship in medicine.

Criterion Variables. Nine dependent variables were examined: knowledge, skills and attitudes in medicine, psychology and sociology. Pre- and post-test multiple-choice questions on filmed doctor-patient interviews requiring application of knowledge and skill in all 3 areas were administered. Students also took Medical Attitudes Test on social aspects of medicine.

Outcomes. The GMC Program did not greatly affect the acquisition of either medical knowledge or psychological and social components of medicine or skill in applying such knowledge. The experimental student was *not* more inclined to deal with psychological problems or even to develop more fully his relations with patients. His attitude toward comprehensive care remained the same, while that of the control students became increasingly negative.

Abstract of FAMILY MEDICAL CARE, by George Silver (Harvard University Press, 1963)

Objectives. The Family Health Maintenance Demonstration aimed at combining prevention and treatment of both physical and emotional disorder, emphasizing health promotional activities. Family health was seen in terms of appropriate functioning in work, play, sex, family life—particularly mother's role vis-a-vis children's needs. Supplementing role of family physician (internist), services of social worker and public health nurse were provided to improve family relationships and health practices, respectively.

Description of Demonstration Program. The demonstration was carried out over 8 years in the context of a comprehensive prepaid medical group affiliated with HIP and Montefiore Hospital. The treatment teams of internist, social worker and public health nurse performed research observations and evaluations; gave preventive and therapeutic services; consulted with medical specialists, psychiatrist, psychologist, health educator and social scientist. In addition to regular comprehensive medical care from HIP Montefiore Medical Group, study families received family guidance and emotional support from health team for up to four years. An active health promotional program included literature, meetings, films and small group conferences.

Study Design. Criteria for inclusion in demonstration: families belonging to Montefiore Medical Group, resident in its zone of coverage; both parents alive and father not more than 45 years old; at least one child. Approximately 150 study families were paired randomly with equal number of controls meeting same criteria but not offered special team services. Eighty-five percent of families selected for study (124) agreed to participate. Study and control groups found very similar initially on demographic data, but no baseline examinations made on controls. Demonstration teams collected initial, interval and final data on study families and also examined controls at completion. Research instruments designed to measure improvement or deterioration in health and interpersonal relationships.

Criterion Variables. Twelve areas of family functioning examined. Physician rated family medical history and each member's physical condition. Nurse scored nutrition, sleep and rest, educational achievement of children, recreational adjustment and housing. Social worker evaluated personal adjustment; family relationships of spouses, children and father, children and mother; occupational adjustment of father. Each area rated excellent, good, fair or poor on scale from 4 to 1.

Outcomes. Members of study families improved in physical condition (from 2.7 to 3.1), but not superior to controls at end (3.0). At final evaluation, 88.5 percent of study subjects rated good or excellent, vs. 75.6 percent of controls. Improvement in 4 or 5 areas evaluated by nurses was greatest in housing. Of 5 areas evaluated by social worker (emotional health), average rating *declined* in 4. No greater improvement among study families than among controls in educational achievement of children. Controls did better in 9 out of 12 evaluation areas. Improvement not related to over-all high utilization of medical services or to prevalence of symptoms and difficulties.

I think you will agree with me that as evaluative studies go, the quality of the evidence developed in these studies is reasonably scientific and statistically standard.

I think it is also correct to say for all ten studies that in most instances the programs that were developed to effect desired changes were designed by acknowledged experts in the respective fields, with the full expectation that real and important changes would take place in the target population.

It is very difficult to characterize the results of all ten of these evaluative studies in a few sentences.

However, I think it is not an unduly harsh judgment to make when I say that *none of the ten programs of social intervention achieved striking positive results.* There are glimmerings of a positive and meaningful effect to be observed here and there. Possibly the effects, where there are any, are slight, and in a few instances there are some negative effects. In short, there is scarcely a basis here for generating or supporting enthusiasm, I would say, for any of the experimental programs which were evaluated in this way.

In fact, I have come to the following tentative tongue-in-cheek conclusions:

When one wishes to show that a program has been successful, the evaluation should include the following:

1. A control group should not be used.
2. If a control group is used, it should be selected purposively, rather than by random methods, and matched on "relevant variables."
3. If a prospective design cannot be used, the matching for the control groups should be done retrospectively.
4. Effort variables should be used as criteria of success rather than effect variables.
5. The evaluation should be done preferably by those in charge of the program.
6. The results should not be published in the scientific literature, but should be issued as a report to one's self or the program director.

Exceptions:

1. Training programs—almost invariably effective.
2. Evaluations in small parts of programs can be shown to have at least short-term effects; e.g., comic books in health education.
3. Specific drugs—some of these have been found to be effective.

Things yet to be evaluated:

1. Narcotic addiction treatment programs.
2. Major systems of psychotherapy.

Evaluations, however, are not only based on controlled studies of this kind; evaluation also means placing value on something done every day of the week on whatever evidence people have, or on no evidence. This will continue to be the case.

Of course, some questions have been raised by this racking up of evaluative studies in the field of social action and health and welfare. I would put before you just a few of these questions.

Are the measures that are used too insensitive? If they are, who will devise the more sensitive measures?

Are the sights set too high? This is a little different than measuring sensitivity but, on the other hand, should one look for more modest kinds of achievements? Maybe less ambitious goals would show more positive results when the intervention is applied more seriously.

Are the health and welfare professions really incapable of conceiving and implementing effective programs on a broad scale?

I think these questions need some attention.

DAVID A. WARD

GENE G. KASSEBAUM

On Biting the Hand That Feeds: Some Implications of Sociological Evaluations of Correctional Effectiveness

Daniel Glaser has written an article in which he refers to correctional research as "an elusive paradise."[1] Gene Kassebaum and I have been skittering around this paradise for the past five years and the principal theme of this paper is a concern that paradise may be lost.

While we do want to describe briefly the design and principal findings of our investigation, our real intent is to raise some points for discussion regarding not the whole process involved in assessing correctional effectiveness, but mainly the things that happen after the study is reported. This is relevant because we seem to be in a stage in the development of the field of corrections where the programs in which we placed our hopes, our best theories, and sometimes our professional reputations are being subjected to the test of empirical assessment and in the main, are found to be wanting.

In the field of corrections, as in education, public housing, medicine and public health, sociology has enjoyed a decade of well financed, large-scale evaluation research, often with the cordial, whole-hearted cooperation of the agencies being evaluated. By evaluation research we mean the use of public agencies as the source of data about the reactions of people to the programs of these agencies. The distinctive feature of such research—as opposed, let us say, to merely using an agency as a convenient pool of MMPI's, life histories, etc.—is that evaluation research produces data which directly refer

David A. Ward and Gene G. Kassebaum, "On Biting the Hand That Feeds." Paper presented at the 61st annual meeting of the American Sociological Association, Miami Beach, Florida, August 1966.

professionals or the possibility that programs may be designed for reasons other than modifying the behavior of inmates, some comment is necessary about the use of the phrase "correctional effectiveness."[3] It is clear that some people will assess correctional effectiveness in terms of improved inmate behavior (that is the absence of negative reports), others in terms of a strengthened ego or greater emotional stability, others in terms of improved performance on a civilian job or in keeping employed, others in terms of relating more effectively to a caseworker, a correctional officer, a therapist, a parole agent, or a wife. Still others argue that committing fewer or less serious crimes or staying out longer on parole constitutes criteria of program success. There is nothing unusual about multiple criteria, but these are sometimes put forward in sequence as preceding assertions fail to be confirmed by the evaluation of the program. There is even the possibility of formulating program goals so that with some programs, you can't lose. In the case of a community (nalline) testing program, for narcotics users, it is not clear how an evaluation study could avoid justifying the program. If the recidivism rate is lower for the treatment group than the control group, one could say that the fear of detection by nalline deterred men from using drugs, or at least markedly reduced drug use. On the other hand, if the treatment group has higher recidivism rates, the figures can be said to show that nalline is an effective detection device resulting in the reconfinement of drug addicts. In either case, the program would have been found to be worth using.

Measurement of outcome by the use of sliding criteria reflects in part the effort to justify programs on grounds other than a demonstrated impact on inmate behavior or reduction of recidivism. It is our contention, however, that departments of corrections are agencies whose publicly stated principal concern is with the surveillance and control of inmate and parolee behavior. The real "pay off" of treatment programs cannot be measured in terms of making happier or better adjusted inmates, or parolees who commit fewer or less serious crimes, but in maintaining order in the prison community and in reducing recidivism.

The complexity of this situation can be seen in our own experience of conducting an evaluation study in California. From the beginning, the Department of Corrections was supportive, open in its dealings, cooperative at all levels. The department agreed to every major condition required in the design (not always a convenience to the institution) ; it did not go back on its original commitment to us throughout the five years. The study was initiated largely because of the interest of the Department of Corrections in having an assessment made of a group counseling program that was becoming a key part of the department's treatment effort. In 1961 some 12,000 inmates and several thousand staff members were involved in this program as well as many departmental dollars.

While the authors were interested in the effects of group counseling as a treatment technique, we were particularly interested in the use as group leaders of staff members who were, from the point of view of clinical disciplines, professionally untrained. That is, the great majority of group leaders were rank and file custodial officers, school teachers, shop instructors, and clerical personnel who had in common only several hours of instruction about group counseling techniques. The program consisted of these people meeting with groups of ten or twelve inmates on a once-a-week basis.

We began with the assumption that a likely effect of the group counseling approach would be increased communication between staff and inmates. Also, this communication would be subject to fewer conventional restrictions in that it was supposed to encourage confrontations and disclosures between keeper and captive which are taboo according to the tenets of the inmate code. The virtue of solidarity would presumably be called into question by inviting inmate criticism of other inmates in the counseling session. In these terms, what was anticipated was not depth psychology but lessened endorsement of values which sanction further antisocial behavior.

We thus were led to suppose that if adherence to the inmate code were weakened, there would be greater possibility of acceptance of conventional values and of alternatives to post-release crime. Thus we hypothesized that:

1. Participation in group treatment would result in lessened endorsement of inmate code, and
2. Parolees who have received group treatment would have lower recidivism rates than those who do not. The differences would be higher for inmates who score lower on endorsement of the inmate code.

The next consideration in the development of the study design was prompted when it was brought to our attention that negative outcome findings of the existing program could be interpreted as not measuring the impact of a program "run as it should be run." Because this seemed sensible and because it was brought to our attention by two N.I.M.H. site visitors, we added a variation to the regular group counseling program in terms of a substantial increase in the training of the group leaders. This training was conducted by an outside consultant, Dr. William Schutz, a psychologist then at Berkeley who had extensive experience in conducting groups and training group leaders. Thirty-one of the 160 group counselors who participated in the study received this supplementary training which began with an intensive three-day training period and was followed by half-day sessions every other week for four months.

A final aspect of the design was added when we decided to include an assessment of the department's version of the therapeutic community called community living. This program involved four meetings a week of all inmates who lived in a fifty-man cell block with three custodial and treatment personnel responsible for them and a fifth meeting of three smaller groups.

With this final variation, we then had four treatment programs to assess: regular group counseling, the specially trained group leaders in what we called research group counseling, community living, and a control group which participated in all other aspects of the prison's treatment programs but organized group counseling. The problems of imposing this design on one prison or several prisons were dramatically reduced when we learned of the completion of construction of a new medium security prison. This 2,400-man prison was designed on the theory that smaller units make for better control and treatment and was comprised of separated quadrangles of 600 men each, linked to a central service area.

Each of the quadrangles was intended to be run, insofar as possible, as a semi-autonomous institution under the immediate supervision of a program administrator. However, there would be a superintendent and central staff who would make for uniform policy and be concerned with overall supervision of the quandrangles and the central services.

The quadrangles are the basic sleeping, eating, recreational and social units of the prison. The quadrangles may be entered only through controlled gates from the central plaza. Contamination of study samples occurs to the extent that inmates have contact with men from other quads in connection with centralized activities. However, Men's Colony industries provide work for only a few hundred men. Far more time is spent in recreational activities in their own quads. The quadrangular construction of Men's Colony was ideal for our research design and eliminated the problems of comparing different prisons containing differing populations and of the extensive contact between study samples that would occur in prisons of traditional architectural design. Another great advantage was that we reached agreement with the department on the selection of the site before inmates were admitted to the prison. Thus we were able to achieve comparability of study samples through a specified random assignment procedure which was applied from the opening date of the institution.

The final design consisted of one quadrangle containing 300 men eligible for regular group counseling and 300 men in the second building who were required to participate in research group counseling; a second quadrangle where 450 men were eligible for regular group counseling and 150 men were required to participate in the community living program; and a third quad containing 600 men who lived in the same physical setting and under the same overall administration as the other men and who were eligible for all aspects of the treatment program except that no counseling or community living groups were organized.[4]

We do not have time here to describe the conduct of the study, except to say that the inmates were tested and retested, interviewed and observed, their files were examined, the group counselors were queried, tested and observed in action, and parole agent reports, arrest records, and parolee interviews were gathered. Of special importance were questionnaire data which measured inmate loyalty and solidarity over time, the reports of prison rules violations and the reports of arrest and parole board actions against parolees.

Minimal criteria for inclusion in the follow-up sample were at least six months' participation in one of the treatment varieties and at least six months of parole supervision after release. Approximately one thousand men were included in our follow-up sample under these terms. Our follow-up is a better measure of treatment outcome than has been obtained in most other studies because we were able to take advantage of California's indeterminate sentencing laws and parole policy. Approximately 95 percent of the men released from Men's Colony left with at least twelve months of parole supervision ahead of them. This is a key factor in evaluating treatment outcome because: (1) there are no distinctions made between good risks who get parole and poor risks who are released at expiration of sentence, (2) the indeterminate sentence makes for longer periods of parole supervision, and (3) parole supervision means the keeping of records on the experiences of releasees. Finally, it should be added that the research division of the California Department of Corrections has a well ordered system for reporting status on parole at six, twelve and twenty-four month intervals after release from prison. Because we were fortunate to have these conditions operant, we were able to have a follow-up period of at least 24 months for 70 percent of our sample. At that point after release we can tell you that 26 percent of the sample had no reported problems, that 20 percent were reported for minor problems such as an arrest or short term jail confinement, that 11 percent were reported for major problems such as frequent arrests, longer jail terms, and that 43 percent of the sample were returned to prison. Contrary to the expectations of the treatment theory, there were no significant differences in outcome between the various treatment groups or between the treatment groups and the control group. Furthermore, contrary to sociological expectations, participation in group counseling and community· living did not lessen endorsement of the inmate code, and did not result in a demonstrable decrease in frequency of prison discipline problems for inmates in counseling as opposed to controls.

Complete reporting of the multivariate analysis of various combinations of variables related to in-prison and post-release experience is far beyond the scope of this paper. In the few minutes remaining we wish to return to the tactical issues raised earlier.

It will be noted that we attempted to cope in this design with some of the defenses to adverse findings sometimes raised by treatment professionals. For one thing, we made every effort to obtain a fair test of good correctional treatment. We studied a system which is directed and run by some of the best men in corrections. The inmates studied were neither the more intractable offenders confined in maximum security prisons nor were they the good treatment potential inmates found in first term, minimum security facilities. The study subjects are representative of the majority of inmates in a correctional system. Furthermore they are confined in the most up-to-date prison in the department in terms of physical plant and staffing.

In the second place, we have extended the follow-up period to a reasonable length. Our data indicate that follow-up periods of six and even 12 months are inadequate as measures of post-release adjustment. Even at 12 months, only 35 percent of our study sample had reports of either major arrests or return to prison; that figure at 24 months was 54 percent. The number of parolees with no reported problems dropped from 41 percent to 26 percent. The extended follow-up, which was undertaken in the main to anticipate criticism, turned out to be of signal importance in understanding the post-release experiences of the men.

Finally, we can argue that the program was evaluated through the use of a research design that included randomly assigned and comparable samples, a control group, minimal contamination of treatment groups and controls, a large enough study population, a long enough follow-up period, and outcome data collected and provided by the department itself.

With this array of evidence and these arguments, what are the implications of the negative results of the study for a department which has now made group counseling and community living programs a part of the program of every prison in the department, has made inmate participation in the programs compulsory in some institutions, and has just made participation in post-release group counseling mandatory for every parolee in the state?

It seems to us that if the department wishes to continue this widespread use of counseling, perhaps some new arguments such as: participation in group counseling gives custodial officers a real part in the treatment program and improves their morale; group sessions add a little variety to inmate life and take up time, will have to be advanced. In other words, defensive arguments, can be raised against our findings if other outcome criteria are suggested. Some of the arguments about the impact of this program on grounds other than reduction of prison disciplinary problems and recidivism seem entirely legitimate to us and are, by intention, beyond the scope of our study. On the other hand, the department may wish to alter the development of the group treatment program as the chief of the department's research division has suggested, perhaps in anticipation of a study such as ours . . .

> the impact of group counseling on the correctional apparatus cannot be appraised until some models can be set up for tests. The task now is not to prove that group counseling works. Eager advocates of research must be patient with an era of experimentation in group counseling. Nothing will be settled in any massive study which could conceivably be executed now. Dozens of small issues must be resolved before group counselors can be adequately trained. In the meantime, the gains which the correctional apparatus makes from the mere existence of this practice within its gates should sufficiently reward its tolerance.[5]

While the lack of evidence on the efficacy of group counseling certainly has not discouraged the expansion of this program, nevertheless there are going to be problems for the supporters of this program if they argue that inmates behave better and parolees return less often for having participated in it.

But our real concern here is with the implications of this study for the administrators of the department of corrections. How are they to justify the amount of time and effort of these staff members and the substantial funds that are devoted to these programs? Particularly when it is recalled that these people have to answer the questions of legislators and state budget analysts who are less receptive to arguments that "staff morale is better," that "one man was saved" or that inmates or parolees are happier or better able to relate to others when they return to the community.

In informal conversations at academic and correctional society meetings, and at institutions around the country, one occasionally gains the impression that some correctional administrators are alarmed at the political implications of negative findings. It should be stressed that we actually do not have clear evidence that a critical study or academic book or article has necessarily led to or influenced legislative cuts in funds, to say nothing of a public hue and cry. But, the tightening up of administrative procedures towards outside scrutiny, and an inclination toward increased reliance on departmental staffs doing the evaluation, with more discreet circulation of detailed results should they prove disappointing, would appear to be possible consequences of the way correctional administrators define the situation.

As we look about us in 1966 it seems a reasonable surmise that there will be mixed reactions to the current crop of correctional evaluations which report no impact of treatment. On the one hand, such findings may give impetus to a wider variety of new treatment programs being tried out on small scale. However, it is also likely that prudent departmental administrators will possibly question the wisdom of encouraging program evaluations conducted by outside experts and given extensive publication in speeches, papers, articles and books. They may feel that the same ends can be achieved in a different and less damaging way. If one's own staff members, particularly one's own research division, conducts these studies, then control over the reporting of the findings is feasible. It is the authors' impression that so-called "confidential department reports" with "restricted circulation" will increasingly be concerned not only with any investigation of "sensitive" areas such as inmate homosexuality and the bases of staff decision making, but also with program evaluation. There is already precedent for not releasing reports of prison incidents and recidivism figures by institutions "because the press and the public don't understand what is involved." There is no reason to think that this argument cannot be extended to reports of programs that do not reduce recidivism. We would remind you that the departments of corrections which have been most innovative in regard to correctional treatment and most supportive of research by outsiders (and who consequently get most of the bad reviews), are also the departments which have research divisions clearly capable of conducting program evaluations. Obviously the control of the areas to be examined is also likely to be the result of decisions by departmental administrators. The problem, however, is not only that research will be limited but that restriction will be placed on circulation of findings. This development would at most certainly result in redundant studies not to mention the maintenance of ineffective programs in departments of corrections which do not do evaluation. Remote as it may seem, we should not overlook the possibility that corrections may turn to criteria other than recidivism reduction. Perhaps in keeping with the realities of the situation, it will be asserted that the rationale for imprisonment is that prison confinement and parole supervision are systems of control and surveillance of persons troublesome to the community. That day is not upon us, but it does not seem to us at all impossible.

We are at any rate concerned with the general problem posed by the fact that, although corrections has turned to evaluation research to support its general organizational aims, the treatment evaluation study results are not much to take to the legislature. Hence we are led to speculate that future studies may be less geared to overall program evaluation, the results may be confined to departmental circulation, or outcome criteria may change. These inclinations might be averted however, if someone—if even one of you— could report a study of a correctional treatment program that really did make a difference.

Footnotes

1. Daniel Glaser, "Correctional Research: An Elusive Paradise," *The Journal of Research in Crime and Delinquency,* Vol. 2. No. 1, January, 1965.

2. Jerome Rabow, "Research and Rehabilitation: The Conflict of Scientific and Treatment Roles in Corrections," *The Journal of Research in Crime and Delinquency,* Vol. 1, No. 1, January, 1964.

3. We feel the inevitability of the validating use of statistics has been established. See Paul Meehl, *Clinical Versus Statistical Prediction.*

4. A modification of the original design occurred when the department required the use of one quadrangle for special categories of inmates. The population of this quad was comprised of psychotics in partial remission, particularly troublesome homosexuals, aged inmates with arson histories, young toughs who were management problems in other prisons, and transients. This conglomerate group was so unusual that we excluded it from the study, a decision we later regretted.

5. John Conrad, *Crime and its Correction: A Survey of International Practices,* University of California Press, Berkeley, California, 1965, pp. 246–7.

ROBERT LONGOOD

ARNOLD SIMMEL

Organizational Resistance
to Innovation Suggested by Research

Public health workers are fond of the phrase: "The huge gap between knowledge and its application." There is good reason for this.
Public health organizations have indeed been slow to put to work the
results of research. Sometimes there are sound technical reasons for
this delay. Not everything that is possible is economically or politically feasible. But the purpose of this paper is to discuss the tendencies to resist innovation which are rooted in the nature of organizations and society. Our examples are chosen from the field of public
health, and we conclude with some comments on a matter that is of
particular concern to social scientists—the resistance they themselves
have met in public health organizations.

There are three vectors of organizational resistance to innovation: the individual personalities that make up the organization, the
organization itself, and the culture in which the organization is em-
bedded. Let us consider a few cases which may be usefully studied
from these three perspectives.

An organization draws its personnel from the society in which it

Robert Longood and Arnold Simmel, "Organizational Resistance to Innovation Suggested by Research." Paper presented at the 57th annual meeting of the
American Sociological Association, August 1962, in Washington, D.C.

NOTE: This paper was the outcome of some differences of opinion, much
discussion, some mutual influence of the co-authors, and, for good measure, a
little bit of research. It is not a scientific treatise; it is rather an exhortation. As
an exhortation it is as valid today (1970) as it was in 1962. So we have let it
stand, except for minor editorial changes, and the exclusion of details of our
survey of the opinions of public health administrators about social scientists.

has its existence. It is therefore inextricably bound to, and limited by the culture of that society. Ours is a society dominated by middle class values; it follows that the organizations in our society reflect middle class interests, tastes, attitudes, and morals. Even organizations whose reason for existence is to aid the underprivileged reflect middle class perspectives. Long have the social welfare leaders cried for an integrated attack on the syndrome of poor housing, poor health, poor educational and job opportunity, that freezes succeeding generations of a huge segment of our population in poverty. But their cries have been in vain. The middle class view of poverty—as expressed by legislator and bureaucrat—is grounded in the immemorial attitude of "alms for the poor." That a fundamental solution to the problem of continuing poverty is possible has not been given serious consideration by our middle class society.

How, specifically, does middle class culture infiltrate an organization, causing it to resist and ultimately reject innovations suggested by research? In the following example the researcher himself, acting as a representative of his organization and of middle class values, did not perceive what should have been an obvious conclusion of his investigation.

The research consisted of an evaluation of the tuberculosis casefinding program of a public health organization. The elimination of tuberculosis depends on finding and treating the tuberculous, so that the reservoir of virulent tubercle bacilli in the population is annihilated. This, according to prevailing theory, will stop the spread of tuberculosis and lead to the practical eradication of the disease. Because the disease thrives best in squalid living conditions, most cases of tuberculosis are found in the poverty-stricken lower class. Responsible experts in tuberculosis control work agree that case-finding strategy must take this fact into account.

Realizing this, one might naturally expect that mass screening of the population for tuberculosis would be conducted primarily among the poor—those on social welfare, unskilled marginal workers, slum dwellers.

The investigation of the tuberculosis case finding program to be discussed here was carried out by a highly skilled epidemiologist in 1958. He found that mass surveys by means of chest x-rays—the principal tuberculosis screening method—were directed at five types of target population: students at schools and colleges, patients admitted to general hospitals, the employees of state agencies, visitors at agricultural fairs, and entire communities. Over-all, the aim was rather skewed toward middle class participation; self-selection insured that x-rays of middle class individuals were obtained in far greater proportion than x-rays of lower class individuals. The lower class was clearly under-represented. And, in fact, the program un-

need for changes which would strike at established relationships and patterns of work. For example, residents might have to be lured with a division of labor more favorable to their interests, with greater participation in decision making and greater opportunities to gain experience at other hospitals which are not so specialized. We do not know of any such investigation, but we can easily see organizational interest in its neglect.

The third vector of organizational resistance to the application of research—the motives of individuals in the organization—is a many-faceted one. We shall restrict our discussion again to one very common and general motive of executive decision makers—the drive for prestige and economic betterment, for "getting ahead." In particular let us consider the effect of this motive on the entry of social scientists into public health organizations, not forgetting that social scientists, as middle class Americans, are driven by the same motive.

In any bureaucratic organization there is a constant competition for the attention and benevolence of the chief decision maker. This is a no-holds-barred fight since to win it is to gain prestige and to further one's career; to lose it is to lose prestige and frustrate one's career. Every organization has its horrible examples of executives who, for one reason or another, have lost favor with the chief decision maker. As far as the organization is concerned, they are the walking dead. In the scramble for official blessing, no less aggressive for its veneer of friendly organizational solidarity, the competitors seek to eliminate as much uncertainty as possible. The admission of unknown or unpredictable elements complicates the game and heightens the perceived risk. The social scientist, a newcomer on the scene of the health organization, could become a dangerous adversary in the game. Who knows what information he will dig up that would discredit or cast suspicion on the thinking or working habits of the more established competitors? Social scientists have made themselves particularly vulnerable by their insistence on the label "scientist." In the game of scientism, all the advantage goes to the home team, and in the case of health organizations, the physicians are the home team. Social scientists, many somewhat insecure in their methodology, are an easy mark for harassment by those playing the scientism game. This harassment may be partly motivated by the desire to keep the social scientist out of the power structure of the organization.

We do not see this trauma for the social scientist as an unmitigated evil. It is in the crucible of this interprofessional push and shove that the social scientist will learn to keep his guard up, and to adapt and establish his discipline in the organization. If he should withdraw from the struggle, both he and the health organizations would be worse off. Good social scientists can be vital components of the organizations that govern society today. Many physicians working in public health organizations recognize that social scientists, performing at their best, can provide vital links between administrative procedures and human needs.

Evidence for the willingness of public health physicians to work with social scientists can be derived from the joint publications of physicians and social scientists and from the fact that social scientists have been hired in public health agencies. A small survey of 29 physician-administrators supported the general idea that physicians are well disposed toward social science. Most of them claimed that their opinion about social scientists had become more favorable during the preceding ten years; there was remarkably high agreement that social science has made or is likely to make important contributions to public health. Without reporting further details, it is perhaps interesting to note some comments made by the respondents. "It would be a help," ruminates one physician, "if the behavioral scientists as a group were less insecure and defensive. Most of the problems encountered between behavioral scientists and physicians and others in public health administration would be eased if the social scientists showed greater ability, first, to define problems, and second, to decide which approach would be most likely to pay off. At present the habit is almost invariably . . . population sampling and interviewing, usually without first attempting to identify goals in an adequately objective fashion."

Another respondent, who seemed very favorably inclined toward social scientists, complained of their inadequacy as members of a public health organization. "Social science people," he wrote, "are not fully aware of the science and techniques of epidemiology or of the hard practical realities of local problems in public health."

Another respondent simply asked what social scientists hope to do in public health and what their unique capacities are. He also, interestingly, would like to know whether the social scientists will "replace or supplement existing professions." One respondent thinks that it is "too easy for someone to get a job as a social scientist" and wonders "if the fault isn't in the schools." And so on.

Some responsibility for resistance to social science belongs to the social scientists. Individual antagonisms will account for nothing, since they exist the world over and we have to live with them wherever we go. But there is some systematic basis for the opposition to social science in public health—and other—organizations, in the relationship between the nature of the organization and the contribution social science can make. Anyone else can blame the organization—but social scientists have no excuse if they do not analyze their own organizational setting and if on the basis of this analysis they cannot improve their relations to other professions and other occupations. If this is done right it will make their work more acceptable, both by avoiding pre-existing bases for resistance and by making their work more suitable to the needs of the institution that hired them.

Social scientists will not help their cause if they remain reluctant to emerge from the womb of their profession into the rough and tumble of organizational give and take. Some have reacted to the hostility they have found by snuggling into a jargonized way of communicating what they have to say, as if to tell their tormentors: "If you won't appreciate me, I won't bother talking to you at all. At least my colleagues in the field will appreciate what I am saying." This is their version of the segregationist chant: "Two, four, six, eight, we don't wanna integrate." The end product of this reaction can only isolate the social scientist more completely than ever, reducing his contribution to mere academic exercises. These exercises will be abided for the sake of paying lip service to the harmless vogue of social scientism in public health. In one easy step, from cerebration to ceremony.

We believe that both the public health physician and the social scientist need not less engagement, but more. For an effective partnership, they must confront each other both as professionals and as full-blown human beings, arguing differences on their merits and working towards synthesis. It is not an academic atmosphere that will help social scientists who range into field of application, but engagement with the organizational ferment.

Our quarrel is not with the sociology of knowledge. We do not claim that the social scientist's work can be in all respects independent of its social context. Quite the contrary, our quarrel is with the social scientists who do no more than tentatively flirt with the field of application in which they are working. If one strongly identifies with professional standards, maintains some contact with one's professional reference group, and exposes oneself to its criticism, one's scientific objectivity will not be undone by lively personal involvement in the organization whose practical problems are the social scientist's intellectual problems. But we go one step further. If these problems are no more than distant intellectual problems for the social scientist, he will discover that he and his findings are ignored. If he is not willing to share in the responsibility of his organization he himself becomes the principal source of resistance to the innovations which his research may suggest.

Notes

1. See Sills, David L., *The Volunteers,* esp. Ch. II and IX, where the general statement is very effectively contradicted—though by appeal to facts about organizations of a type with which we are not here concerned.

2. Sills, David L., *ibid.*

CAROL H. WEISS [*]

Utilization of Evaluation: Toward Comparative Study

The problem to which this paper is addressed is the frequent failure of decision-makers to use the conclusions of evaluation research in setting future directions for action programs. I will offer some hypotheses on conditions under which evaluation is or is not utilized, and propose that research be done to test them. In short, this is a proposal for empirical evaluation of evaluation research.

The basic rationale for evaluation is that it provides information for action. Its primary justification is that it contributes to the rationalization of decision-making. Although it can serve such other functions as knowledge-building and theory-testing, unless it gains serious hearing when program decisions are made, it fails in its major purpose.

The record to date appears to be an indifferent one. There are some well-known examples of prompt utilization of evaluation. The New York City Higher Horizons program is one. Evaluation demonstrated the effectiveness of the prototype "Demonstration Guidance Program" in one junior high school, and steps were taken to implement the program in other schools in the system. Unfortunately, in the process, budgets were cut and authority diffused, and the ensuing

Carol H. Weiss, "Utilization of Evaluation: Toward Comparative Study." Paper presented at the American Sociological Association meeting, Miami Beach, Florida, September 1, 1966. Printed in U.S. House of Representatives, Committee on Government Operations, Research and Technical Programs Subcommittee, *The Use of Social Research in Federal Domestic Programs,* vol. 3 (Washington, D.C.: Government Printing Office, 1967), 426–432.

program never again realized similar success. But this was a problem of inappropriate administration rather than of failure to accept and act on the basic findings.

On the other hand, institutions often do not change their activities in response to evaluation. They explain away the results, sometimes casting aspersions on the evaluator's understanding, the state of his art, and his professional or theoretical biases. Evaluators complain about many things, but their most common complaint is that their findings are ignored.

What accounts for the high rate of non-utilization? I will give some suggestions, which are to be taken as hypotheses for study rather than as an addition to the flood of advice and exhortation to social scientists on how to win more friends and influence more people. The first class of factors leading to non-utilization lies in the organizational systems that are expected to use the evaluation results, and the second class lies in the current state of evaluation practice.

Organizations invariably respond to factors other than the attainment of their formal goals. Even rudimentary knowledge of organizational behavior indicates the salience of the drive for organizational perpetuation, personnel's needs for status and esteem and their attachment to the practice skills in which they have invested a professional lifetime, conservatism and inertia and fear of the unknown consequences of change, sensitivity to the reactions of various publics, costs, prevailing ideological doctrines, political feasibility, and the host of other considerations that affect the maintenance of the organization. Evaluation's evidence of program outcome can not override all the other contending influences.

What evaluation can do is add its weight to the thrust for change. Few organizations are so monolithically self-satisfied that counterpressures do not exist. Most of them face some discrepancy between the ideal and the actual that generates a search for better ways of operation. (This discrepancy sometimes provided the impetus that led to embarking on evaluation in the first place.) There is at least a potential for utilization. But rather than ignore the forces that tend to subvert the implementation of evaluation results and trust in the good will and rationality of the organization, evaluators might well pay greater attention to the organization-maintenance imperatives that influence decision-making, perhaps even address the covert goals as well as the formal goals of the organization in their research. With better knowledge of the kinds of resistance to be expected, they may be able to devise more effective strategies for defining evaluation issues and for gaining their results a hearing.

A fascinating example of resistance to utilization can be borrowed from military history. In 1940–41 the RAF Bomber Command refused to accept the evidence of aerial photography on the failure of its missions. Photographs indicated that only one of every four air-craft reporting an attack on target had actually gotten within five miles of it. An officer who passed on to his chief an interpretation showing that an attack had missed its mark found it later on his desk with a note scrawled across it in red: "I do not accept this report." The author of the account of these events states, in words that will echo familiarly to social evaluators, "it was very natural that many of those whose work it affected jumped to the comforting conclusion that something must have been wrong with the camera or the photographs or the man who wrote the report."[1]

Fortunately the case had a happy ending, the style of which has implications for our discussion. Professor Lindemann, Churchill's scientific adviser, found the evidence convincing and urgent, and brought it directly to Churchill's attention. "So it was at these top-most levels that the evidence of the photographs was finally faced, and at these levels that the necessary priority was given to develop-ing the new navigational aides . . . which were to change the entire outlook for British night bombing."

Use of evaluation appears to be easiest when implementation implies only moderate alterations in procedure, staff deployment, or costs, or where few interests are threatened. For example, in the Bail Bond project of the Vera Foundation,[2] where only the bail bondsmen stood to lose, use of the evaluation was immediate and dramatic.

On the other hand, application of results can threaten the func-tion of a total organization or an occupational group—such as a de-tached-worker agency whose program for gangs is found ineffective in reducing delinquency, or psychotherapists, if treated and untreated patients show similar recovery rates. In such cases, even overwhelm-ing demonstration of failure is unlikely to convince the practitioner group or its sponsoring agency to use the findings and go out of business. Use must be made at higher (or lower) levels, by groups that set policy and determine the allocation of resources, or at least hypothetically, by the clients or potential clients themselves.

The other major limitation on use of evaluation results is the current state of evaluation practice. Much evaluation is poor, more is mediocre. Evaluation in action settings is a difficult and demanding enterprise, and calls for a high order of imagination and tenacity as well as research ability. Much has been written in anguished prose about the problems that plague the conduct of evaluation, and just about all of it is true.[3]

---

[1] Constance Babington-Smith, *Air Spy*, Ballantine, 1957.

[2] National Conference on Bail and Criminal Justice, *Interim Report, May 1964–April 1965*.

[3] The catalog includes inadequate academic preparation for research in ac-

The achievement is that good evaluations can be done at all, and yet they are. They use appropriate change criteria and relatively reliable measuring instruments; they use control groups or apply other checks to rule the possibility that observed effects are attributable to non-program factors; their statistical methods and interpretation are sound. If they are not models of exemplary or sophisticated methodology, they do meet the basic canons of research.

But technical competence by these standards does not imply the absence of methodological problems. Evaluation has special requirements. One of the most serious difficulties in evaluation is the imprecision of the program that is subjected to study. Evaluators usually accept the description of the program given by practitioners as sufficient. They rarely attempt to specify the theoretical premises on which it is based, define the principles that guide its practice, or even monitor its operation so that there is confidence that the program as officially described actually took place—and at a reasonable level of competence. It is possible that the evaluation is attributing the observed effects (or "no effects") to a phantom program, or to one of such marginal caliber that it hardly provides a fair test of the program concept.

The imprecision of program input poses even more basic difficulties. Social action programs are complex undertakings. To quote John Mann :[4]

> A positive change in behavior may be found. Assuming that the study itself was carefully designed and executed, this finding may be accurate. But to what is it to be attributed? When the method [program] is carefully examined, it is quickly seen to be an amalgam of components of unknown or partially controlled proportions.

We will return to some of these problems later. Let me turn now to the theme of the paper—a proposal for systematic study of conditions associated with utilization of evaluation results.

---

tion agencies; the low status of evaluation in academic circles; program ambiguity and fluidity; practitioner suspicion and resistance; organizational limitations on boundaries for study, access to data, and design requirements; inadequate time for follow-up; inadequacies of money and staffing; controls on publication; etc. Cf. Sidney H. Aronson and Clarence C. Sherwood, "Social Action Research: Some Problems in Researcher, Program Designer, and Practitioner Relationships," May 4, 1966, mimeo; Hyman Rodman and Ralph L. Kolodny, "Organizational Strains in the Research–Practitioner Relationship," in Alvin Gouldner and S. M. Miller (eds.), *Applied Sociology,* Free Press, 1965; Carol H. Weiss, "Planning an Action Project Evaluation," in Department of HEW, *Learning in Action* (1966) ; John Mann, *Changing Human Behavior,* Scribner's, 1965, Appendix A.

[4] Mann, *op. cit.,* p. 12.

The Study of Utilization

There may be value in taking the kinds of impressions discussed here and subjecting them to empirical study. If we can discover patterns and regularities, if we can get better leads to where, by whom, and under what conditions evaluation results are most likely to be applied, it may become possible to wedge a wider opening.

We can differentiate three major types of use. First is use within the ongoing program, to improve its operation as it goes along. Although this is the type of use that program administrators often expect, it calls for a special kind of short-term, limited-effect, quick-feedback study, and is not always compatible with the evaluation design and schedule that researchers develop. The second use is also at the original site of the program, but occurs at the completion of a total cycle of programming, to decide whether to terminate, modify, or restructure the program, or to continue it and possibly carry it over to other units of the organization. The third use is in outside settings—by agencies operating similar programs, by standard-setting or granting bodies, or by policy-making units at federal, state, or local levels. Such groups make decisions of wider scope, which can affect the initiation or discard of programs throughout a federal, state, or voluntary system. An intermediary "use" can also be recognized—the transmission of evaluation results by linking agents who, persuaded by the evidence, become advocates for its application. State and federal consultants and faculty members of professional schools are examples of such linking intermediaries, whose commitment and influence provide the potential for future utilization. In these days of maximum feasible representation, target group members may be able to play a similar role.

For a study of conditions associated with utilization, one variable must be the direction of results—positive or negative. The implementation of negative results poses issues different in kind as well as degree from the use of positive results.

To eliminate confusion arising from non-use of incompetent, unduly small-scale or fragmentary evaluation (where lack of use can be viewed as a responsible position), it is proposed to limit the study to results of relevant and technically sound evaluations, preferably confirmed by replication or the accumulation of independent evidence.

Types of conditions to be studied include those both outside and inside the evaluator's purview. A study, or more properly a series of inquiries, might look into such diverse questions as these:

Are new and relatively innovative agencies more responsive to implementing evaluation results than long-established agencies? Is the rigidity of agency doctrine important? What combinations of evaluation results and political or elite pressures are effective? What kinds of threat, and to which levels of staff, generate most resistance? Is utilization affected by the support of top-level administrators for the study—or the evaluator's position or influence in the organizational hierarchy—or the conduct of the evaluation by a university or other outside research organization—or publication of results in books or professional journals? Effects of such factors, and others mentioned earlier in considering organizational behavior, can be studied singly, additively, and in interaction.

I am particularly interested in investigating ways in which evaluation itself is carried out that enhance its utilization. At present, evaluation usually examines conditions before and after the program and comes up with global findings on the extent of change. But rarely can it answer questions about which elements of the program amalgam worked or did not work, and how and why. Yet it is just such information that is vital for institutionalizing a program into routine practice and transferring it to other locations. Without it we are saddled with a load of irrelevant specificities and likely to miss the essential ingredients.

Therefore, utilization might be increased if the evaluation included such elements as these:

1. the explication of the theoretical premises underlying the program, and direction of the evaluation to analysis of these premises,
2. specification of the "process model" of the program—the presumed sequence of linkages that lead from program input to outcome, and the tracking of the processes through which results are supposed to be obtained,
3. analysis of the effectiveness of components of the program, or alternative approaches, rather than all-or-nothing, go or no-go assessment of the total program.

Evaluation can—and some evaluations have—selected a limited number of program theories or notions and concentrated study on these. They run the gamut from narrow to very broad-range issues. An example of relatively restricted scope can be taken from the evaluation of a program for using young indigenous aides in a community action program. Rather than look at the effectiveness of their total performance, which is a slippery undertaking at best when standards are ambiguous and functions change to fit people, it is possible to look at one premise. This might be the notion that as on-the-job workers, previously unemployed adolescents learn skills more readily than they do as pupils in a work training program. This type of evaluation begins to provide a test for a concept that can be generalized to other places and structures, rather than merely a description of the outcomes of one specific project.

The "process model" diagrams the expected channels of change. For example, a group counseling project is operated for problem girls in an effort to reduce delinquent behavior. By what causal chain is the counseling expected to reach this goal—by changing the girls' self-image? by providing information on other opportunities for self-expression and self-esteem? by motivating them to greater interest in school and vocational achievement? by providing role models for alternative behavior? After the initial stage, what ensuing consequences are expected? The process model makes clear what intermediate effects the evaluation has to look for, and directs attention to the essentials. Tracking the progress of the program input along its putative path allows a test of the theoretical linkages and enables the evaluation to say useful things about the stage where things go awry and adjustment is needed.

Analysis of components of the program and of alternative approaches can provide information on the effectiveness of specific strategies. The issue for decision is rarely the choice between this program and no program, but the choice among alternative ways of programming.

For utilization, the immediate advantage of these related ways of pursuing evaluation is that they tend to avoid the dead-end of finding the whole program ineffective (or even effective) without any indication of *why* or what alternative courses of action are likely to be better. Moreover, evaluation findings are more apt to be comparable and additive, and contribute to the building of knowledge.

Some other evaluation procedures also appear to hold promise for utilization and are worth study:

1. Early identification of potential users of evaluation results and selection of the issues of concern to them as the major focus of study.   .

Theoretically it is possible for a single study to provide information that can be used by an array of audiences—practitioners, administrators, higher policy makers, professional schools, clients—each of whom has different motivation and capacity to apply the results. In practice, study requirements often diverge. For maximum pay-off, it may be effective to decide in advance where the major potential for utilization lies, and to gear the study to the relevant users.

2. Involvement of administrators and program practitioners, from both inside and outside the project, in the evaluation process.

Not only does their participation help in the definition of evaluation goals and the maintenance of study procedures, but it may help change the image of evaluation from "critical spying" to collaborative effort to understand and improve. Outside consultants may even become spreaders of the word to other focal sites.

3. Prompt completion of evaluation and early release of results.

Evaluation reported a year or two, or more, after completion of the program, is often too late to affect decisions, whose schedule is determined by the budgeter's—not the evaluator's—calendar. Long-term follow-up may well be essential, but considerations of use may dictate at least preliminary reporting of the direction of results in early phases.

4. Effective methods for presentation of findings and dissemination of information.

There are at least four sub-items here. One is the clarity and attractiveness of the presentation of evaluation data to non-research audiences. Another is the spelling out of the implications that the study offers for action. This might extend to analysis of the probable consequences of the implied changes for the organization. Third, there may be inventive mechanisms to reach remote audiences impervious to bulky reports and journal articles. And finally, aggressive advocacy by the evaluators for the positions derived from evaluation may gain them a hearing in councils of action. This involves the evaluators' abandoning the stance of detached professional appraisal and engaging in the rough and tumble of decision-making both within the organization and in the wider spheres of policy formation.

A first study on utilization of evaluation could select and refine one or two of the notions from this speculative assortment—perhaps the position of the evaluator inside or outside the project staff, an issue with a hardy (mainly oral) tradition, or the inclusion in the evaluation of analysis of alternative program strategies—and investigate their association with subsequent use of results.

If factors such as those discussed here do in fact increase utilization, there are clear implications for future evaluation practice. If none of these factors has much discernible impact, efforts to apply social science to the solution of social problems must seek new directions. Some critics, for example, have suggested that evaluation be replaced by laboratory experimentation with specific and carefully delimited program components. Although this approach has some appeal, it avoids the effects of the natural setting and the constraints and counterpressures in the larger social system that can nullify program efforts.

What concerns me is the current disenchantment with the utility of evaluation in some influential government agencies and foundations. It is possible that the sins of the program are being visited on the evaluation. Premature disenchantment can clamp limits on creative experimentation in evaluation. Better knowledge of what kinds of evaluation have an impact on decision-making, and under what conditions, should help to encourage more effective development of evaluation practice.

CAROL H. WEISS

The Politicization
of Evaluation Research

Researchers who undertake the evaluation of social action programs
are engaged in an enterprise fraught with hazards. They are beset by
conceptual and methodological problems, problems of relationship,
status, and function, practical problems, and problems of career and
reward. To add to the perils of the evaluation career, evaluation is
now becoming increasingly political.

Increasing Visibility and Scope
of Evaluation Research

Evaluation reports are becoming front-page news. Policy decisions
sometimes hinge on whether evaluation shows good results from
an action program or not. The Westinghouse Learning Corporation–
Ohio University evaluation of Head Start made waves at the White
House. The Coleman Report has received explicit attention from the
President and the Congress, and if its meaning and its implications
are still a matter of debate, the study clearly has had an influence on
the formation of educational policy. Where once evaluators bemoaned
the neglect of their results by policy makers, they are more and more
being given an active role in decision making.

Most evaluation studies, of course, are still filed and forgotten.

Carol H. Weiss, "The Politicization of Evaluation Research," *Journal of
Social Issues,* vol. 26, no. 4 (1970), pp. 57–68. Reprinted by permission.

But the case of the exceptional headliner today is likely to be common tomorrow. Increasingly, legislation and administrative regulations require evaluation of social programs, large sums of public monies are being expended, and results are publicized and considered in decision-making councils.

Evaluation has always had explicitly political overtones. It is designed to yield conclusions about the worth of programs and, in so doing, is intended to affect the allocation of resources. The rationale of evaluation research is that it provides evidence on which to base decisions about maintaining, institutionalizing, and expanding successful programs and modifying or abandoning unsuccessful ones. This function as handmaiden to policy is probably the characteristic of evaluation research that has attracted competent researchers, despite all the discontents and disabilities of its practice.

Not so long ago, innovative social action programming and its accompanying evaluation were small-scale enterprises. The greatest effect that evaluation could have would be to encourage further street work with gang youth (by the sponsoring agency and maybe one or two agencies like it) or discouraging individual counseling sessions for clinic patients. The effects tended to be localized, since programs and their evaluations were bounded. Even where similar programs were operated nation-wide, program staffs were so aware of the unique circumstances of their own school or hospital or organization that they saw little carryover of the results on someone else's program to their own operations.

The big change is that both programming and evaluation are now national in scope. Programs may actually be no more standardized in form, content, and structure than they ever were, but they are funded from a common pot and bear a common name: "community action program," "Head Start," "model cities," "legal services," "neighborhood service centers," "Title I of the Elementary and Secondary Education Act," "maternal and child health program," and so forth.

The evaluation, too, is large-scale, not limited as in the past to the "pilot" or "demonstration" program. Evaluation is mandated in much recent legislation in the areas of poverty, manpower, and education—and funds provided. Thus the evaluation of the Work Incentive Program (WIN), sponsored by the Departments of HEW and Labor, is looking at fifty projects in all parts of the country. The NORC study of the impact of community action agencies on local institutions has been expanded from fifty to a hundred communities. The evaluation of multi-service centers sponsored by the Office of Economic Opportunity now includes study of fifty multipurpose programs, twenty limited-purpose programs, and twenty grass roots organizations. Such extensive coverage is common practice in many recent evaluation endeavors. A recent Urban Institute review of federal evaluation practice (Wholey *et al.,* 1969) explicitly recommends jettisoning the single-project evaluation in favor of multi-project evaluation.

With studies of this scope and concomitant expense, it is not unexpected that some fanfare attends their completion. The evaluator, unaccustomed to the political spotlight, finds old difficulties exacerbated and new problems burgeoning.

Criticisms of methodology. Once evaluation studies are seen as likely to have important political consequences, they become fair game for people whose views are contradicted (or at least unsupported) by the data. A first line of attack is the study's methodology. Critics of every persuasion seem able to locate experts who find flaws in the sampling, design, choice of statistics, measurement procedures, time span, and analytic techniques—even though their real criticisms derive less from methodology than from ideology. Whatever the motivation, a study whose conclusions enter the political arena must be prepared for searching scrutiny of its methods and techniques.

The experimental model remains the ideal in evaluation methodology, with random assignment of subjects to an experimental group which is exposed to the program stimulus or to a control group which is not. An added advantage of experimental design in political terms is that it is scientifically respectable. But the difficulties of applying the experimental model in field studies are legion; in large-scale social programs they are often overwhelming. Control groups with random assignment are rare amenities.

Nor is it clear that the experiment is always the best and most relevant model. Critics (Weiss & Rein, 1969; Guba & Stufflebeam, 1968) have pointed out its customary limitations. Traditional experimental design deals with a stable standardized treatment; it collects before and after measures over a "full cycle" of the program, and uses specified goal criteria. Its results, then, disclose the extent to which a consistent program has reached its stated goals, but rarely *why* the observed results occur, what processes intervene between input and outcome, or what the implications are for improving the effectiveness of the program. For programs whose goals and emphases shift in midcourse, the experiment cannot distinguish the effects of the old from the new, nor will it provide much feedback to programs that need quick help in planning and implementing changes. Most of these limitations are not intrinsic to the experiment—e.g., if interim measures of success are available, short-cycle quick-feedback results are possible—but they are accurate assessments of most experimental evaluation practice.

Quasi-experimental designs (Campbell & Stanley, 1966) free

the evaluation from some of the experiment's restrictive conditions, particularly in randomization, and are more compatible with the program environment in which the evaluator works. As a means of ruling out plausible rival explanations (other than the effect of the program) for the outcomes observed, they can be highly effective and useful; additional controls can be added on one at a time to protect against sources of invalidity that the designs leave free. But again the usual—although by no means inevitable—thrust of the study is the degree of change toward the desired goals. Little attention is generally paid to how the program develops, to variations among units, outside events that affect programming and participation, adequacy of program operation, unanticipated consequences, etc.

Interesting developments are taking place in methodology to study the series of events that ensue from the development of a theoretical program strategy through its implementation and short-run and long-term effects. Systems approaches and process-oriented qualitative analyses, for example, are being applied to large-scale programs. But none of these departures, not even the quasi-experiment, has attained the legitimacy of experimental design. When methodology is subject to attack, evaluators are wary of the untried tack. Many apparently prefer to stick unimaginatively to the book, rather than risk the penalties of pioneering.

Relationships with funding bodies. The new-style evaluation money, although larger in amount than ever before, comes ringed around with restrictions. Not only do the government "RFPs" (requests for proposal, the specifications of the research to be done and its scheduling) specify many of the details of objectives, indicators, timing, analysis, and reporting which used to be thought of as the evaluator's bailiwick, but government agencies are requiring increasingly close surveillance during the course of the study. Some are requiring biweekly conferences or monthly reports. The reason is, clearly, the sad experience that many agencies have had with evaluation. Academic evaluators have been known to bend the purposes of the study to suit their own disciplinary interests. (One story, possibly apocryphal, is that one three-year evaluation of public services, because of the investigators' interest, was turned into a study of the speech patterns of local residents.) Their adherence to schedules and deadlines has been characterized by "academic freedom." Commercial investigators, on the other hand, while generally sticking more closely to the intent of the contract, have cut some uncuttable corners, and the credibility of the research has suffered.

Whatever valid reasons gave rise to agencies' current supervisory practices, they inevitably raise questions about the autonomy of the evaluation. Government agencies may seek only to enforce standards of relevance and research quality, but they almost inevitably become suspect of political pressure, pressure to vindicate the program and justify its budget. The agency retains, after all, the authority to cut off the study in the middle if "progress" is poor. The evaluator can be forgiven for uneasiness about the direction of his research.

Relationships with program personnel. Program staff have rarely liked evaluators poking their noses into the operation of programs or measuring outcomes. Whatever soothing explanations are offered about "testing program concepts" or "accountability to taxpayers," the evaluator is a snoop. To the program operator, who knows that his program is doing well, evaluation is at best unnecessary and at worst, if it shows few positive effects, a calumny and a threat to the future of the program, his job, and needed help to clients.

Today, with the visibility of evaluation becoming greater, program staff are increasingly aware of the implications of releasing data. They see the inferences that will be drawn even from service figures (if temporary beds for overflow patients are not included in the hospital's figures on "number of beds," budgetary allotments will be lower), and they are wary of feeding data into the evaluator's "insensitive indicators" of program success. Thus, access to data may be restricted. Occasionally what program staff deem "more relevant" data may be supplied. Even where this is not so, the general atmosphere of uncordiality can dim the evaluator's spirits and his study.

Drawing recommendations. In the increasingly political context of evaluation, the act of drawing implications from study data becomes chancier than ever. Many evaluations are "black box" studies: the evaluator takes "before" measurements on factors relevant to program goals, the subjects are then exposed to the program (an unexamined entity like a black box), and then he records "after" measurements. He concludes that the program has succeeded in achieving its goal(s) to the observed extent.

To go from such data to recommendations requires what Paul Lazarsfeld calls a leap; in many cases, the data do not provide even a jumping-off point. If a job training program doesn't improve the rate of employment, what do you know about future directions? The data aren't informative about the kinds of modifications that should be made. There is a discontinuity between the study and recommendations of a course of action. With large-scale decisions hanging in the balance, evaluators exercise their non-data-based speculatory talents at their own risk.

Null results. Probably the most serious political problem of all is that evaluation results, with dismaying frequency, turn out to be negative. Over the past several years, careful and competent studies have shown few positive effects from such varied programs as psychotherapy, probation services, casework, school desegregation, public housing, and compensatory education. Elinson (1967), reviewing the results of ten of the most competent and best known published evaluations, found that none of them demonstrated much success. To judge from evaluations, most action programs do not make much change in the behavior of individuals and groups. The evaluator thus is in the position of turning thumbs down on someone's program. The problem is particularly troublesome because old established programs are rarely evaluated. It is the new and innovative program that is subjected to evaluation. The evaluator and his negative findings are gutting the venturesome program and giving aid and comfort to the barbarians.

We say, of course, that null evaluation results need not lead to the abandonment of programs but to their improvement. The Nixon administration, after the poor showing of Head Start in the national evaluation, did after all increase its budget and call for more experimentation in its content. Nevertheless, the proclivity to the negative remains a fact of evaluation life, and there are those who are uneasy about the effects of this saturnine cast. They fear that not only will it lead to premature abandonment of new programs; it may be more likely to lead to the abandonment of evaluation. As an illustration, Ward and Kassebaum (1966), in a paper reporting the null results of group counseling in a correctional institution, report that the state agency's response to the study was to expand the program and close down access to researchers. The next section of this paper discusses alternatives to traditional evaluation procedures with a view to accentuating the positive.

ALTERNATIVES

A number of courses are open. One hopeful direction is to place less stress on evaluations of over-all impact, studies that come out with all-or-nothing, go/no-go conclusions. More resources should be allocated to evaluations that compare the effectiveness of variant conditions within programs (differing emphases and components of program, attributes of sponsoring agency structure and operation, characteristics of participants) and begin to explain which elements and sub-elements are associated with more or less success. Such an approach produces data of interest across a wide range of programs and has high utility in pointing direction for further program development.

The Follow Through program has developed an elegant evaluation design to do this kind of study, with several different program strategies being studied in 60 or 70 sites.[1] Some early reports were not hopeful about the possibilities of carrying out the study as designed.

> However, political considerations apparently resulted in complete local choice of strategy, with the result that the planned variations are not present in the design, and the finest evaluation techniques, even if applied to each local program, will not yield very useful information as to which strategies tend to work best in which demographic situations. . . . Finally, the lack of use of comparable pretest and posttest measures over the various Follow Through strategies essentially assures an ultimate lack of comparability [Light, 1968, pp. 765–66].

More recent reports indicate that all is not lost yet (Stanford Research Institute, 1969). Although communities do select the Follow Through program model that they implement, it is still possible for researchers to compare the results of each model in different sites. (The main problems that the study is having involve the communities' difficulties in implementing the program with sufficient intensity to make a difference in the classroom and their inability or unwillingness to maintain the program strategy as prescribed in the model.)

Comparative study, even without conscious and orderly variation, can have great power. If the evaluator is clever, he can capitalize on variations that occur naturally. Many government programs, as noted above, are not so much unitary programs as a congeries of diverse efforts addressed to the same problem. Within the programs there are different emphases and different content and procedures. The evaluator may be able to identify the different theories that underlie the differing emphases, categorize them—and the program activities—along a number of significant dimensions, and then relate the types of program to program outcomes. Through meticulous specification of program inputs, of participants, and of environmental conditions, evaluation can increasingly locate and identify the factors that make for relative program effectiveness.

Another circumstance that evaluators (and people who fund evaluations) would do well to avoid is premature evaluation. Evaluators have been lecturing their program counterparts for a generation

---

[1] That there is a continuing effort to develop and implement sophisticated evaluation designs despite all the buffeting that evaluators take, is a tribute to the people that man the field. One suspects that a good part of the optimism and ambition results from turnover; as one year's crew of hopeful evaluators burns out during re-entry into the atmosphere of program reality, a new generation comes in.

on the need to involve them even before the program begins operation. Don't just bring us in on the ground floor, they have said, bring
us in to help dig the foundation. That is all to the good, and people in
various locations have evidently learned the lesson. But sometimes
this has led to evaluation's assessment of results during the start-up
period, before the program has learned how to organize itself and
put its concepts into practice. When evaluation goes on while the
program is still groping for direction, misinterpretations can occur.
Lack of success may be attributed to a particular program and
program model that never had the chance to see the light of day.

Etzioni (1960) has suggested another order of approach, a
"system model" rather than a "goal model." Although his original
paper was directed at the study of organizations, it is almost equally
applicable to evaluation. The system model recognizes that organizations engage in activities other than achievement of their goals. A
study, therefore, should not focus exclusively on goal attainment but
should look also at measures of the effectiveness of other organizational functions, such as recruiting resources, maintaining the structure, achieving integration into the environment.

A study that adopted the system model for analyzing a delivery
organization (Georgopolous & Tannenbaum, 1957) used three
measures to judge effectiveness: organizational productivity (the
goal), flexibility in terms of adaptation to change, and relative absence of intraorganizational strain or tension. The latter two characteristics can be conceived as means to the goal and investments in the
organization's capability to achieve its goal over the long run.

In evaluation research, the system model might include indicators of such other aspects of program effectiveness as the ability
to get grants, recruit qualified staff, gain political support in the
community, etc. This would have advantages in assessing the latent
functions of programs, as well as in identifying the real and important
second-order effects (e.g., providing an organization that speaks for
the poor). But over the long run, whatever its other contributions,
a program may well be expected to demonstrate some positive results
on client outcome measures as well.

IMPLICATIONS OF EVALUATION: A RADICAL CRITIQUE

In a basic sense, the bent toward the negative that is characteristic
of social action evaluations is not something to be masked or shunted
aside. To the extent that null results are real and not an artifact of
primitive methodology, they betoken serious weaknesses in social
programming. The spate of negative results across a whole gamut of
programs betokens a series of important shortcomings.

Basic social science. One component is the shortcomings in basic social science. The behavioral sciences do not give many answers to questions on the causes and processes of social ills. Nor do they have much to say about the processes of social change and the conditions necessary to bring desired changes about. Therefore, evaluation may well be revealing the error in the theories and assumptions on which programs are based.

Suchman has stated the issue beautifully :

> If a program is unsuccessful, it may be because the program failed to "operationalize" the theory, or because the theory itself was deficient. One may be highly successful in putting a program into operation but, if the theory is incorrect . . . the desired changes may not be forthcoming: i.e., "the operation was a success, but the patient died." Furthermore, in very few cases do action or service programs directly attack the ultimate objective. Rather they attempt to change the intermediate process which is "causally" related to the ultimate objective. Thus, there are two possible sources of failure (1) the inability of the program to influence the "causal" variable, or (2) the invalidity of the theory linking the "causal" variable to the desired objective [Suchman, 1969, p. 16].

Obviously much remains to be known in order to plan social change efforts wisely. Programs based on intuitive wisdom and extrapolations from past experience are not good enough. Important theoretical and research contributions are due.

Program development. Even with basic knowledge at less than adequate levels, we do not put into practice all we know. Instead of profound re-thinking of program services, there is quick adoption of some fashionable prescription which, whatever its other virtues, is likely to attract funding. Instead of innovative approaches to programming, there is tinkering with the mixture as before to give it a shiny new surface but leave the essential ingredients unchanged.

Very few programs are born without roots in the existing order of things. There are ties and obligations to old agency philosophies and ways of work and to the assumptions and methods of traditional professions. The people engaged in program development activities are not likely to come from, or particularly value, the social science frontier. Nor, on their side, are social scientists doing much applied research on the development of programs. Little is done to apply existing theory and knowledge to program development, to study means for securing acceptance of new programs, or to analyze alternative methods for their implementation within bureaucratic structures. On no side does there seem to be encouragement for radical departures from the past.

Management. The administration and management of new programs, particularly the large-scale programs of recent years, have been woefully deficient. In part this has been because of the effort to bring members of new groups (blacks and other minorities) into management when previous experience had been denied them. But much of the problem has no such justification. In fact, a good share of the fault lies in Washington with its shifting rules, perpetual crises and demands, incredibly complicated procedures for funding and refunding, and political pressures.

Program structure. Certainly a major reason for null evaluation results on social action programs lies in the structure of programs. Fragmentary projects are created to deal with broad-spectrum problems. We know about multiple causality. We realize that a single-stimulus program is hardly likely to make a dent in deep-rooted ills. But the political realities are such that we take what programs can get through Congress (or other sources) when we can get them. Each then becomes elaborated in its own structure. Even when successive programs are legislated that are broader in scope and resources, as in the case of programs to deal with poverty, the early structures survive. Each continues doing its own thing with sparse recognition of their interrelatedness. The fragmentation of program structures and authority leads to disjointed (and ineffective) services. Competing and conflicting bureaucracies, jockeying for power and prestige, are not apt to make big inroads in the problem.

Today's programs are the result of a series of uncoordinated decisions, disjointed, poorly matched, often working at cross-purposes. They are run by different levels and organs of government—city, county, independent school system, state, special district. They are funded by, and responsive to, different federal agencies with differing purposes and ideologies. Rarely are they responsive directly to the local governmental unit or to the people whom they serve.

The influx of federal programs and federal funds in the social service field has been an attempt to meet needs that local government has largely ignored for generations. But the organizational structures that accompany federal programs and money have complicated an already intolerable fragmentation of services and authority. What is seriously required is basic reform in local governmental institutions, so that services are provided and coordinated at a level meaningful to individuals. No federal patching or categorical funding has been able to coax, bribe, or order this kind of control. The political scientists' prescription—metropolitanization of area services and decentralization of local services to a level responsive to the people—sounds even more important today than it did a generation ago, if no more politically feasible. Local control of government services, which theoretically can bring about coordination on the neighborhood level, has a host of hurdles to surmount before it even gets to tackle the job.

Time for risk-taking. It is time that we recognized the failure of our moderate, piecemeal, cheap solutions to basic social problems. They have been tried, and evaluation research has found them wanting. Bold experiments are called for. It is a fraud to perpetuate variations on outmoded solutions to problems that are rooted in our system of social stratification. If more and more services to the poor do not enable people to move out of poverty, perhaps we have to look to ways of redistributing income so that the poor are no longer poor. Similarly, we may have to question such hardy assumptions as compulsory education to age sixteen, imprisonment of lawbreakers, the private practice of medicine.

Evaluation research may even be able to help chart the new and risky courses if Congress will appropriate funds for small-scale, truly experimental, pilot programs. The programs would be designed for research, not service, and would be under research control to ensure minimal interference with experimental conditions. Although years of melancholy experience with "demonstration" programs should caution against great optimism, it may be possible to develop program-and-evaluation pilots that are neither co-opted, politically pressured, nor ignored.

Summary

In the deepest sense, there is nothing null about recent evaluation research. The newly-visible large-scale evaluations are progressively disclosing the bankruptcy of piecemeal approaches to social programming. Unless society's limited domestic resources are invested more wisely, significant changes are not likely to occur. This is as important a conclusion as evaluation can provide.

References

Campbell, D. T., & Stanley, J. C. *Experimental and quasi-experimental designs for research.* Chicago: Rand McNally, 1966.

Elinson, J. Effectiveness of social action programs in health and welfare. In *Assessing the effectiveness of child health services,* report of the Fifty-sixth Ross Conference on Pediatric Research. Columbus: Ross Laboratories, 1967.

ETZIONI, A. Two approaches to organizational analysis: A critique and a suggestion. *Administrative Science Quarterly,* 1960, 5, 257–78.

GEORGOPOLOUS, B. S., & TANNENBAUM, A. S. A study of organizational effectiveness. *American Sociological Review,* 1957, 22, 534–70.

GUBA, E. G., & STUFFLEBEAM, D. L. Evaluation: The process of stimulating, aiding, and abetting insightful action. Working paper, Evaluation Center, Ohio State University, November, 1968.

LIGHT, R. J. Report analysis: National Advisory Commission on Civil Disorders. *Harvard Educational Review,* 1968, 38, 756–67.

STANFORD RESEARCH INSTITUTE. Highlights of the longitudinal evaluation of the national follow through program, 1968–9. Working paper, Stanford University, 1969.

SUCHMAN, E. A. Evaluating educational programs. *The Urban Review,* 1969, 3(4), 15–17.

WARD, D. A., & KASSEBAUM, G. G. Biting the hand that feeds. Paper presented at the meeting of the American Sociological Association, 1966.

WEISS, R. S., & REIN, M. The evaluation of broad-aim programs: A cautionary case and a moral. *Annals of the American Academy of Political and Social Sciences,* 1969, 385, 133–42.

WHOLEY, J. S., DUFFY, H. G., FUKUMOTO, J. S., SCANLON, J. W., BERLIN, M. A., COPELAND, W. C., & ZELINSKY, J. G. *Federal evaluation policy: An overview.* Washington, D.C.: The Urban Institute, 1969.

3 / BIBLIOGRAPHY

Conceptual &
Methodological Issues

ALKIN, MARVIN C. "Evaluation Theory Development." *Evaluation Comment,* vol. 2, no. 1 (1969), 2–7.

AMERICAN INSTITUTES FOR RESEARCH. *Evaluative Research Strategies and Methods.* Pittsburgh: American Institutes for Research, 1970.

ANDREW, GWEN. "Some Observations on Management Problems in Applied Social Research." *The American Sociologist,* vol. 2, no. 2 (1967), 84–89, 92.

ARONSON, SIDNEY H., and CLARENCE C. SHERWOOD. "Research Versus Practitioner: Problems in Social Action Research." *Social Work,* vol. 12, no. 4 (1967), 89–96.

BAKER, ROBERT L. "Curriculum Evaluation." *Review of Educational Research,* vol. 39, no. 3 (1969), 339–358.

BARTON, ALLEN H. *Studying the Effects of a College Education.* New Haven: The Edward H. Hazen Foundation, 1959.

BATEMAN, WORTH. "Assessing Program Effectiveness: A Rating System for Identifying Relative Program Success." *Welfare in Review,* vol. 6, no. 1 (1968), 1–10.

BELSHAW, CYRIL S. "Evaluation of Technical Assistance as a Contribution to Development." *International Development Review,* vol. 8 (June 1966), 2–23.

BENEDICT, BARBARA A., PAULA H. CALDER, DANIEL M. CALLAHAN, HARVEY HORNSTEIN, and MATTHEW B. MILES. "The Clinical-Experimental Approach to Assessing Organizational Change

Efforts." *Journal of Applied Behavioral Science,* vol. 3, no. 3 (1967), 347–380.

BENNIS, WARREN. "Theory and Method in Applying Behavioral Science to Planned Organizational Change." *Journal of Applied Behavioral Science,* vol. 1, no. 4 (1965), 337–360.

BERLAK, HAROLD. "Values, Goals, Public Policy and Educational Evaluation." *Review of Educational Research,* vol. 40, no. 2 (1970), 261–278.

BIGMAN, STANLEY K. "Evaluating the Effectiveness of Religious Programs." *Review of Religious Research,* vol. 2, no. 3 (1961), 97–121.

BLENKNER, MARGARET. "Obstacles to Evaluative Research in Casework." Parts 1 and 2. *Social Casework,* vol. 31, nos. 2–3 (1950), 54–60, 97–105.

BLUM, HENDRIK L., and ALVIN R. LEONARD. "Evaluation Research and Demonstration." In *Public Administration: A Public Health Viewpoint.* New York: The Macmillan Company, 1963, pp. 286–322.

BORGATTA, EDGAR F. "Research Problems in Evaluation of Health Service Demonstrations." *Millbank Memorial Fund Quarterly,* vol. 44, no. 4, part 2 (1966), 182–199.

———. "Research: Pure and Applied." *Group Psychotherapy,* vol. 8, no. 3 (1955), 263–277.

BORUS, MICHAEL E., and WILLIAM R. TASH. *Measuring the Impact of Manpower Programs: A Primer.* Policy Papers in Human Resources and Industrial Relations, No. 17. Ann Arbor: Institute of Labor and Industrial Relations, 1970.

BRIM, ORVILLE G., JR. "Evaluating the Effects of Parent Education." *Journal of Marriage and Family Living,* vol. 19 (February 1957), 54–60.

BROOKS, MICHAEL P. "The Community Action Program as a Setting for Applied Research." *Journal of Social Issues,* vol. 21, no. 1 (1965), 29–40.

BRUNNER, EDMUND DES. "Evaluation Research in Adult Education." *International Review of Community Development,* nos. 17–18 (1967), 97–102.

BYNDER, HERBERT. "Sociology in a Hospital: A Case Study in Frustration." In Arthur B. Shostak (ed.) *Sociology in Action.* Homewood, Illinois: Dorsey Press, 1966, pp. 61–70.

CALDWELL, MICHAEL S. "An Approach to the Assessment of Educational Planning." *Educational Technology,* vol. 8, no. 19 (1968), 5–12.

CAMPBELL, DONALD T. "Administrative Experimentation, Institutional Records, and Nonreactive Measures." In J. C. Stanley (ed.) *Improving Experimental Design and Statistical Analysis.* Chicago: Rand McNally & Co., 1967, pp. 257–291.

————. "Reforms as Experiments." *American Psychologist,* vol. 24, no. 4 (1969), 409–429.

————. "Considering the Case against Experimental Evaluations of Social Innovations." *Administrative Science Quarterly,* vol. 15, no. 1 (1970), 110–113.

CARO, FRANCIS G. "Approaches to Evaluative Research: A Review." *Human Organization,* vol. 28, no. 2 (1969), 87–99.

———— (ed.) *Readings on Evaluative Research.* New York: Russell Sage Foundation, 1971.

CHERNEY, PAUL R. (ed.) *Making Evaluation Research Useful.* Columbia, Maryland: American City Corporation, 1971.

CHERNS, A. "The Use of the Social Sciences." *Human Relations,* vol. 21, no. 4 (1968), 313–325.

COHEN, DAVID K. "Politics and Research: Evaluation of Social Action Programs in Education." *Review of Educational Research,* vol. 40, no. 2 (1970), 213–238.

COLVIN, C. R. "Reading Program that Failed, or Did It? Hawthorne Effect." *Journal of Reading,* vol. 12, no. 2 (1968), 142–146.

COMMUNITY COUNCIL OF GREATER NEW YORK, RESEARCH DEPARTMENT. *Issues in Community Action Research.* Report of the Spring Research Forum on Evaluation Efforts in Three New York City Community Action Programs. New York: The Council, 1967.

CRONBACH, LEE. "Evaluation for Course Improvement." *Teachers College Record,* vol. 64, no. 8 (1963), 672–683. Also reprinted in Norman Gronlund (ed.) *Readings in Measurement and Evaluation.* New York: The Macmillan Company, 1968, pp. 37–52.

DAILY, EDWIN F., and MILDRED A. MOREHEAD. "A Method of Evaluating and Improving the Quality of Medical Care." *American Journal of Public Health,* vol. 46, no. 7 (1956), 848–854.

DAVIS, JAMES A. "Great Books and Small Groups: An Informal History of a National Survey." In Phillip E. Hammond (ed.) *Sociologists at Work: Essays on the Craft of Social Research.* New York: Basic Books, Inc., Publishers, 1964, pp. 212–234.

DENISTON, O. L., I. M. ROSENSTOCK, and V. A. GETTING. "Evaluation of Program Effectiveness." *Public Health Reports,* vol. 83, no. 4 (1968), 323–335.

————, I. M. ROSENSTOCK, W. WELCH, and V. A. GETTING. "Evaluation of Program Efficiency." *Public Health Reports,* vol. 83, no. 7 (1968), 603–610.

————, and IRWIN M. ROSENSTOCK. "Evaluating Health Programs." *Public Health Reports,* vol. 85, no. 9 (1970), 835–840.

DONABEDIAN, AVEDIS. "Evaluating the Quality of Medical Care." *Millbank Memorial Fund Quarterly,* vol. 44, no. 3, part 2 (1966), 166–203.

DEXTER, LEWIS A. "Impressions about Utility and Wastefulness in Applied Social Science Studies." *American Behavioral Scientist,* vol. 9, no. 6 (1966), 9–10.

DORFMAN, ROBERT. "Introduction." In *Measuring Benefits of Government Investments.* Washington, D.C.: The Brookings Institution, 1965, pp. 4–22.

DOWNS, ANTHONY. "Some Thoughts on Giving People Economic Advice." *American Behavioral Scientist,* vol. 9, no. 1 (1965), 30–32.

DRESSEL, PAUL L. (ed.) *Evaluation in Higher Education.* Boston: Houghton Mifflin Company, 1961.

DREW, ELIZABETH B. "HEW Grapples with PPBS." *The Public Interest,* no. 8 (Summer 1967), 9–29.

DUBOIS, PHILIP H., and E. DOUGLAS MAYER (eds.) *Research Strategies for Evaluating Training.* AERA Monograph Series on Curriculum Evaluation, no. 4. Chicago: Rand McNally & Co., 1971.

DYER, H. S. "Pennsylvania Plan: Evaluating the Quality of Educational Programs." *Science Education,* vol. 50, no. 3 (1966), 242–248.

EATON, JOSEPH W. "Symbolic and Substantive Evaluation Research." *Administrative Science Quarterly,* vol. 6, no. 4 (1962), 421–442.

EDUCATIONAL TESTING SERVICE. *On Evaluating Title I Programs.* Princeton: ETS, 1966.

EIDELL, TERRY L., and JOANNE M. KITCHEL. *Knowledge Production and Utilization in Educational Administration.* Eugene: Center for the Advanced Study of Educational Administration, University of Oregon, 1968.

ELINSON, JACK. "Effectiveness of Social Action Programs in Health and Welfare." In *Assessing the Effectiveness of Child Health*

Services (report of the Fifty-sixth Ross Conference on Pediatric Research). Columbus, Ohio: Ross Laboratories, 1967, pp. 77–88.

Etzioni, Amitai. "Two Approaches to Organizational Analysis: A Critique and a Suggestion." *Administrative Science Quarterly,* vol. 5, no. 2 (1960), 257–278.

————, and Edward W. Lehman. "Some Dangers in 'Valid' Social Measurement." *The Annals of the American Academy of Political and Social Science,* vol. 373 (September 1967), 1–15.

"Evaluating Educational Programs: A Symposium." *Urban Review,* vol. 3, no. 4 (1969), 4–22.

Evans, John W. "Evaluating Social Action Programs." *Social Science Quarterly,* vol. 50, no. 3 (1969), 568–581.

Fairweather, George. *Methods for Experimental Social Innovation.* New York: John Wiley & Sons, Inc., 1967, pp. 24–36.

Fellin, Phillip, Tony Tripodi, and Henry J. Meyer (eds.) *Exemplars of Social Research.* Itasca, Illinois: F. E. Peacock Publications, 1969.

Ferman, Louis A. "Some Perspectives on Evaluating Social Welfare Programs." *Annals of the American Academy of Political and Social Science,* vol. 385 (September 1969), 143–156.

First National Conference on Evaluation in Public Health. Continued Education Series No. 89. Ann Arbor: University of Michigan, School of Public Health, 1960.

Flanagan, John C. "Evaluating Educational Outcomes." *Science Education,* vol. 50, no. 3 (1966), 248–251.

————. "Project Talent: The First National Census of Aptitudes and Abilities." In Norman Gronlund (ed.) *Readings in Measurement and Evaluation.* New York: The Macmillan Company, 1968, pp. 413–421.

Fleck, Andrew C., Jr. "Evaluation as a Logical Process." *Canadian Journal of Public Health,* vol. 52, no. 5 (1961), 185–191.

————. "Evaluation Research Programs in Public Health Practice." *Annals of the New York Academy of Sciences,* vol. 107, no. 2 (1963), 717–724.

Fox, David J. "Issues in Evaluating Programs for Disadvantaged Children." *Urban Review,* vol. 2 (December 1967), 7, 9, 11.

Freeman, Howard E., and Clarence C. Sherwood. "Research in Large-Scale Intervention Programs." *Journal of Social Issues,* vol. 21, no. 1 (1965), 11–28.

Getting, Vlado. "Part II—Evaluation." *American Journal of Public Health,* vol. 47, no. 4 (1957), 409–413.

GLASER, EDWARD M., and HUBERT S. COFFEY. *Utilization of Applicable Research and Demonstration Results*. Los Angeles: Human Interaction Research Institute, n.d.

GLASS, GENE V. *The Growth of Evaluation Methodology*. AERA Monograph Series on Curriculum Evaluation, no. 7. Chicago: Rand McNally & Co., in press.

GLENNAN, THOMAS K., JR. *Evaluating Federal Manpower Programs: Notes and Observations*. Santa Monica: The RAND Corporation, 1969.

GLOCK, CHARLES Y., et al. *Case Studies in Bringing Behavioral Science Into Use: Studies in the Utilization of Behavioral Science*. Vol. 1. Stanford: Institute for Communication Research, 1961.

GOLLIN, ALBERT E. "The Evaluation of Overseas Programs: Applied Research and Its Organizational Context." In Robert Campbell, Bert King, and John Nagay (eds.) *Education and Training for International Living: Concepts*. Arlington, Virginia: Beatty Publishers, 1970.

GORHAM, WILLIAM. "Notes of a Practitioner." *The Public Interest*, no. 8 (Summer 1967), 4–8.

GREENBERG, BERNARD G., and BERWYN F. MATTISON. "The Whys and Wherefores of Program Evaluation." *Canadian Journal of Public Health*, vol. 46, no. 7 (1955), 293–299.

GRIESSMAN, B. EUGENE. "An Approach to Evaluating Comprehensive Social Projects." *Educational Technology*, vol. 9, no. 2 (1969), 16–19.

GROBMAN, HULDA. *Evaluation Activities of Curriculum Projects: A Starting Point*. AERA Monograph Series on Curriculum Evaluation, no. 2. Chicago: Rand McNally & Co., 1968.

GRUENBERG, ERNEST M. (ed.) "Evaluating the Effectiveness of Mental Health Services." *Millbank Memorial Fund Quarterly*, vol. 44, no. 1, part 2 (1966), whole issue.

GUBA, EGON G. "Development, Diffusion and Evaluation." In Terry L. Eidell and Joanne M. Kitchel (eds.) *Knowledge Production and Utilization in Educational Administration*. Eugene: Center for the Advanced Study of Educational Administration, University of Oregon, 1968, pp. 37–63.

————. "The Failure of Educational Evaluation." *Educational Technology*, vol. 9, no. 5 (1969), 29–38.

————, and JOHN HORVAT. "Evaluation During Development." *Bulletin of the School of Education, Indiana University*, vol. 46, no. 2 (1970), 21–45.

————, and Daniel L. Stufflebeam. "Evaluation: The Process of Stimulating, Aiding, and Abetting Insightful Action." Address at Second National Symposium for Professors of Educational Research, sponsored by Phi Delta Kappa, November 21, 1968. Columbus: Evaluation Center, College of Education, The Ohio State University.

Hagen, Elizabeth P., and Robert L. Thorndike. "Evaluation." *Encyclopedia of Educational Research.* 3rd ed. New York: The Macmillan Company, 1960, pp. 482–486.

Hall, Richard H. "The Applied Sociologist and Organizational Sociology." In Arthur B. Shostak (ed.) *Sociology in Action.* Homewood, Illinois: Dorsey Press, 1966, pp. 33–38.

Hardin, Einar, and Michael E. Borus. "An Economic Evaluation of the Re-Training Program in Michigan: Methodological Problems of Research." *Proceedings of the Social Statistics Section.* Washington, D.C.: American Statistical Association, 1966, pp. 133–137.

Hastings, J. Thomas. "Curriculum Evaluation: The Why of the Outcomes." *Journal of Educational Measurement,* vol. 3, no. 3 (1966), 27–32. Also reprinted in Norman Gronlund (ed.) *Readings in Measurement and Evaluation.* New York: The Macmillan Company, 1968, pp. 53–60.

Havelock, Ronald G. *Planning for Innovation through Dissemination and Utilization of Knowledge.* Ann Arbor: Institute for Social Research, University of Michigan, 1969.

Hayes, Samuel. *Measuring the Results of Development Projects.* Paris: UNESCO, 1959.

Hemphill, John K. "The Relationships between Research and Evaluation Studies." In Ralph W. Tyler (ed.) *Educational Evaluation: New Roles, New Means.* 68th yearbook of the National Society for the Study of Education. Chicago: The Society, 1969, pp. 189–220.

Herman, Melvin. "Problems of Evaluation." *The American Child,* vol. 47 (March 1965), 5–10.

————, and Michael Munk. *Decision Making in Poverty Programs: Case Studies from Youth-Work Agencies.* New York: Columbia University Press, 1968, pp. 139–181.

Herzog, Elizabeth. *Some Guide Lines for Evaluative Research.* Washington, D.C.: Government Printing Office, 1959.

Hesseling, P. "Principles of Evaluation." *Social Compass,* vol. 11, no. 1 (1964), 5–22.

Hill, Marjorie J., and Howard T. Blane. "Evaluation of Psychotherapy with Alcoholics." *Quarterly Journal of Studies on Alcohol,* vol. 28, no. 1 (1967), 76–104.

HOLLIDAY, L. P. *Appraising Selected Manpower Training Programs in the Los Angeles Area.* Santa Monica: The RAND Corporation, 1969.

HOUGH, ROBBIN R., "Casualty Rates and the War on Poverty." *American Economic Review,* vol. 58, no. 2 (1968), 528–532.

HOVLAND, CARL I. "Reconciling Conflicting Results Derived from Experimental and Survey Studies of Attitude Change." *American Psychologist,* vol. 14, no. 1 (1959), 8–17.

————, ARTHUR A. LUMSDAINE, and FRED D. SHEFFIELD. *Experiments in Mass Communication.* Princeton: Princeton University Press, 1949.

HUTCHISON, GEORGE B. "Evaluation of Preventive Services." *Journal of Chronic Diseases,* vol. 11, no. 5 (1960), 497–508.

HYMAN, HERBERT H., and CHARLES R. WRIGHT. "Evaluating Social Action Programs." In Paul F. Lazarsfeld, Willam H. Sewell, and Harold L. Wilensky (eds.) *The Uses of Sociology.* New York: Basic Books, Inc., Publishers, pp. 741–782.

JAMES, GEORGE. "Research by Local Health Departments: Problems, Methods, Results." *American Journal of Public Health,* vol. 48, no. 3 (1958), 353–361.

————. "Planning and Evaluation of Health Programs." In *Administration of Community Health Services.* Chicago: International City Managers Association, 1961, pp. 114–134.

JENKS, CHARLES L. "Evaluation for a Small District." *Educational Product Report,* vol. 2, no. 5 (1967), 8–17.

JONES, JAMES A. "Research." In *Breakthrough for Disadvantaged Youth.* Washington, D.C.: U.S. Department of Labor, Manpower Administration, 1969, pp. 235–250.

JUSTMAN, JOSEPH. "Problems of Researchers in Large School Systems." *Educational Forum,* vol. 32, no. 4 (1968), 429–437.

KANDEL, DENISE B., and RICHARD H. WILLIAMS. *Psychiatric Rehabilitation: Some Problems of Research.* New York: Atherton Press, Inc., 1964.

KELMAN, HOWARD R., and JACK ELINSON. "Strategy and Tactics of Evaluating a Large Scale Medical Care Program." *Proceedings of the Social Statistics Section.* Washington, D.C.: American Statistical Association, 1968, pp. 169–191.

KLINEBERG, OTTO. "The Problem of Evaluation Research." *International Social Science Bulletin,* vol. 7, no. 3 (1955), 347–351.

KOGAN, LEONARD S., and ANN W. SHYNE. "Tender-Minded and Tough-Minded Approaches in Evaluative Research." *Welfare in Review,* vol. 4, no. 2 (1966), 12–17.

KRAUSE, ELLIOTT A. "After the Rehabilitation Center." *Social Problems,* vol. 14, no. 2 (1966), 197–206.

LASORTE, MICHAEL A. "The Caseworker as Research Interviewer." *American Sociologist,* vol. 3, no. 3 (1968), 222–225.

LEMKAU, PAUL V., and BENJAMIN PASAMANICK. "Problems in Evaluation of Mental Health Programs." *American Journal of Orthopsychiatry,* vol. 27, no. 1 (1957), 55–58.

LEMPERT, RICHARD. "Strategies of Research Design in the Legal Impact Study." *Law and Society Review,* vol. 1, no. 1 (1966), 111–132.

LERMAN, PAUL. "Evaluative Studies of Institutions for Delinquents: Implications for Research and Social Policy." *Social Work,* vol. 12, no. 4 (1968), 55–64.

LEVINE, ABRAHAM S. "Evaluating Program Effectiveness and Efficiency: Rationale and Description of Research in Progress." *Welfare in Review,* vol. 5, no. 2 (1967), 1–11.

LEVINE, ROBERT A. "Evaluating the War on Poverty." In James L. Sundquist (ed.) *On Fighting Poverty: Perspectives from Experience.* New York: Basic Books, Inc., Publishers, 1969, pp. 188–216.

LEVINSON, PERRY. "Evaluation of Social Welfare Programs: Two Research Models." *Welfare in Review,* vol. 4, no. 10 (1966), 5–12.

LEVITAN, SAR A. "Facts, Fancies and Freeloaders in Evaluating Anti-Poverty Programs." *Poverty and Human Resources Abstracts,* vol. 4, no. 6 (1969), 13–16.

LIKERT, RENSIS, and RONALD LIPPITT. "The Utilization of Social Science." In Leon Festinger and Daniel Katz (eds.) *Research Methods in the Behavioral Sciences.* New York: Holt, Rinehart & Winston, Inc., 1953, pp. 581–646.

LINDVALL, C. M., and RICHARD C. COX. *Evaluation as a Tool in Curriculum Development: The IPI Evaluation Program.* AERA Monograph Series on Curriculum Evaluation, no. 5. Chicago: Rand McNally & Co., 1971.

LIPPITT, RONALD. "The Use of Social Research To Improve Social Practice." *American Journal of Orthopsychiatry,* vol. 35, no. 3 (1965), 663–669.

————, JEANNE WATSON, and BRUCE WESTLEY. *The Dynamics of Planned Change.* New York: Harcourt, Brace and Company, 1958, pp. 263–272.

LUCHTERHAND, ELMER. "Research and the Dilemmas in Developing Social Programs." In Paul F. Lazarsfeld, William H. Sewell, and Harold Wilensky (eds.) *The Uses of Sociology.* New York: Basic Books, Inc., Publishers, 1967, chapter 18.

MANGUM, GARTH L. "Evaluating Manpower Programs." *Monthly Labor Review,* vol. 91, no. 2 (1968), 21–22.

MANN, JOHN. "The Outcome of Evaluative Research." In Mann, *Changing Human Behavior.* New York: Charles Scribner's Sons, 1965, pp. 191–241.

MARRIS, PETER, and MARTIN REIN. "Research." In Marris and Rein, *Dilemmas of Social Reform: Poverty and Community Action in the United States.* New York: Atherton Press, Inc., 1969, pp. 191–207.

MAULDIN, W. PARKER, and JOHN A. ROSS. "Family Planning Experiments: A Review of Design." *Proceedings of the Social Statistics Section.* Washington, D.C.: American Statistical Association, 1966, pp. 278–282.

McDILL, EDWARD L., MARY S. McDILL, and J. TIMOTHY SPREHE. *Strategies for Success in Compensatory Education: An Appraisal of Evaluation Research.* Baltimore: The Johns Hopkins Press, 1969.

McINTYRE, ROBERT B., and CALVIN C. NELSON. "Empirical Evaluation of Instructional Materials." *Educational Technology,* vol. 9, no. 2 (1969), 24–27.

MERTON, ROBERT K. "Role of the Intellectual in Public Bureaucracy." In Merton, *Social Theory and Social Structure.* Glencoe, Illinois: The Free Press, 1964, pp. 207–224.

MEYER, ALAN S., and STANLEY K. BIGMAN. "Contextual Considerations in Evaluating Narcotic Addiction Control Programs." *Proceedings of the Social Statistics Section.* Washington, D.C.: American Statistical Association, 1968, pp. 175–180.

MILLER, S. M. "The Study of Man: Evaluating Action Programs." *Trans-action,* vol. 2 (March/April 1965), 38–39.

MOREHEAD, MILDRED A. "The Medical Audit as an Operational Tool." *American Journal of Public Health,* vol. 57, no. 9 (1967), 1643–1656.

MOSS, L. "The Evaluation of Fundamental Education." *International Social Science Bulletin,* vol. 7, no. 3 (1955), 398–417.

NAGPAUL, HANS. "The Development of Social Research in an Ad Hoc Community Welfare Organization." *Journal of Human Relations,* vol. 14, no. 4 (1966), 620–633.

OTT, JACK M. "Classification System for Decision Situations: An Aid to Educational Planning and Evaluation." *Educational Technology,* vol. 9, no. 2 (1969), 20–23.

OWENS, THOMAS R. "Suggested Tasks and Roles of Evaluation Specialists in Education." *Educational Technology,* vol. 8, no. 22 (1968), 4–10.

PERRY, S. E., and LYMAN WYNNE. "Role Conflict, Role Definition, and Social Change in a Clinical Research Organization." *Social Forces,* vol. 38, no. 1 (1959), 62–65.

POPHAM, W. JAMES, *et al. Instructional Objectives.* AERA Monograph Series on Curriculum Evaluation, no. 3. Chicago: Rand McNally & Co., 1969.

PROVUS, MALCOLM. "Evaluation of Ongoing Programs in the Public School System." In Ralph W. Tyler (ed.) *Educational Evaluation: New Roles, New Means.* 68th yearbook of the National Society for the Study of Education. Chicago: The Society, 1969, pp. 242–283.

RODMAN, HYMAN, and RALPH L. KOLODNY. "Organizational Strains in the Researcher–Practitioner Relationship." In Alvin Gouldner. and S. M. Miller (eds.) *Applied Sociology: Opportunities and Problems.* New York: The Free Press, 1965, pp. 93–113.

ROSENBLATT, AARON. "The Practitioner's Use and Evaluation of Research." *Social Work,* vol. 11, no. 2 (1966), 248–251.

ROSENSHINE, BARAK. "Evaluation of Classroom Instruction," *Review of Educational Research,* vol. 40, no. 2 (1970), 279–300.

ROSSI, PETER H. "Boobytraps and Pitfalls in the Evaluation of Social Action Programs." *Proceedings of the Social Statistics Section.* Washington, D.C.: American Statistical Association, 1966, pp. 127–132.

————. "Evaluating Social Action Programs." *Trans-action,* vol. 4, no. 7 (1967), 51–53.

————. "Practice, Method, and Theory in Evaluating Social-Action Programs." In James L. Sundquist (ed.) *On Fighting Poverty: Perspectives from Experience.* New York: Basic Books, Inc., Publishers, 1969, pp. 217–234.

SADOFSKY, STANLEY. "Utilization of Evaluation Results: Feedback into the Action Program." In June L. Shmelzer (ed.) *Learning in Action.* Washington, D.C.: Government Printing Office, 1966, pp. 22–36.

SCANLON, R. G. "Innovation Dissemination." *Pennsylvania School Journal,* vol. 116 (March 1968), 375–376.

SCHULBERG, HERBERT C., and FRANK BAKER. "Program Evaluation Models and the Implementation of Research Findings." *American Journal of Public Health,* vol. 58, no. 7 (1968), 1248–1255.

————, ALAN SHELDON, and FRANK BAKER. *Program Evaluation in the Health Fields.* New York: Behavioral Publications, Inc., 1970.

SCHWARTZ, RICHARD D. "Field Experimentation in Sociolegal Research." *Journal of Legal Education,* vol. 13, no. 3 (1961), 401–410.

SCRIVEN, MICHAEL. "The Methodology of Evaluation." In Ralph W. Tyler, Robert M. Gagné, and Michael Scriven (eds.) *Perspectives of Curriculum Evaluation.* AERA Monograph Series on Curriculum Evaluation, no. 1. Chicago: Rand McNally & Co., 1967, pp. 39–83.

————. "An Introduction to Meta-Evaluation." *Educational Product Report,* vol. 2, no. 5 (1969), 36–38.

SHELDON, ELEANOR B., and HOWARD E. FREEMAN. "Notes on Social Indicators: Promises and Potential." *Policy Sciences,* vol. 1 (1970), 97–111.

SHERWOOD, CLARENCE C. "Issues in Measuring Results of Action Programs." *Welfare in Review,* vol. 5, no. 7 (1967), 13–18.

SLOCUM, W. L. "Sociological Research for Action Agencies: Some Guides and Hazards." *Rural Sociology,* vol. 21, no. 2 (1956), 191–199.

SMITH, BRUCE L. R. *The RAND Corporation.* Cambridge: Harvard University Press, 1966.

SMITH, JOEL, FRANCIS M. SIM, and ROBERT C. BEALER. "Client Structure and the Research Process." In Richard N. Adams and Jack J. Preiss (eds.) *Human Organization Research.* Homewood, Illinois: Dorsey Press, 1960, chapter 4.

SOMERS, GERALD G. "Research Methodology in the Evaluation of Retraining Programmes." Madison: University of Wisconsin, Industrial Relations Research Institute, reprint series, no. 61. Reprinted from *Labour and Automation,* Bulletin No. 1, Geneva, 1965.

STAKE, ROBERT E. "The Countenance of Educational Evaluation." *Teachers College Record,* vol. 68, no. 7 (1967), 523–540.

————. "Generalizability of Program Evaluation: The Need for Limits." *Educational Product Report,* vol. 2, no. 5 (1969), 38–40.

————. "Objectives, Priorities, and Other Judgment Data." *Review of Educational Research,* vol. 40, no. 2 (1970), 181–212.

————. "Testing in the Evaluation of Curriculum Development." *Review of Educational Research,* vol. 38, no. 1 (1968), 77–84.

STEIN, HERMAN D. "The Study of Organizational Effectiveness." In David Fanshel (ed.) *Research in Social Welfare Administration.* New York: National Association of Social Workers, 1962, pp. 22–32.

———, GEORGE M. HOUGHAM, and SERAPIO R. ZALBA. "Assessing Social Agency Effectiveness: A Goal Model." *Welfare in Review,* vol. 6, no. 2 (1968), 13–18.

STEMBER, CHARLES H. "Evaluating Effects of an Integrated Classroom." *The Urban Review,* vol. 2, no. 7 (1968), 3–4, 30, 31.

STEWARD, M. A. "The Role and Function of Educational Research —I." *Educational Research,* vol. 9, no. 1, 1966, 3–6.

STOUFFER, SAMUEL A. "Some Observations on Study Design." *American Journal of Sociology,* vol. 55, no. 4 (1950), 355–361.

STUFFLEBEAM, DANIEL L. "Evaluation as Enlightenment for Decision-making." Address delivered at the Working Conference on Assessment Theory, sponsored by the Commission on Assessment of Education Outcomes, The Association for Supervision and Curriculum Development, Sarasota, Florida, January 19, 1968. Columbus: The Evaluation Center, College of Education, The Ohio State University, 1968.

———. "Toward a Science of Educational Evaluation." *Educational Technology,* vol. 8, no. 14 (1968), 5–12.

———. "The Use and Abuse of Evaluation in Title III." *Theory into Practice,* vol. 6, no. 3 (1967), 126–133.

STURZ, HERBERT. "Experiments in the Criminal Justice System." *Legal Aid Briefcase* (February 1967), 1–5.

SUCHMAN, EDWARD A. "Action for What? A Critique of Evaluative Research." In Richard O'Toole (ed.) *The Organization, Management and Tactics of Social Research.* Cambridge: Schenkman Publishing Company, 1970.

———. *Evaluative Research: Principles and Practice in Public Service and Action Programs.* New York: Russell Sage Foundation, 1967.

———. "A Model for Research and Evaluation on Rehabilitation." In Marvin Sussman (ed.) *Sociology and Rehabilitation.* Washington, D.C.: American Sociological Association, 1966, pp. 52–70.

TAKISHITA, JOHN Y. "Measuring the Effectiveness of a Family Planning Program: Taiwan's Experience." *Proceedings of the Social Statistics Section.* Washington, D.C.: American Statistical Association, 1966, pp. 268–271.

TAYLOR, PHILIP H. "The Role and Function of Educational Research." *Educational Research,* vol. 9, no. 1 (1966), 11–15.

THERKILDSEN, PAUL, and PHILIP RENO. "Cost-Benefit Evaluation of the Bernalillo County Work Experience Project." *Welfare in Review,* vol. 6, no. 2 (1968), 1–12.

TURVEY, RALPH, and A. R. PREST. "Cost-Benefit Analysis: A Survey." *Economic Journal,* vol. 75, no. 300 (1965), 683–735.

TYLER, RALPH W. "Assessing the Progress of Education." *Science Education,* vol. 50, no. 3 (1966), 239–242.

——— (ed.) *Educational Evaluation: New Roles, New Means.* 68th yearbook of the National Society for the Study of Education. Chicago: The Society, 1969.

———, ROBERT M. GAGNÉ, and MICHAEL SCRIVEN. *Perspectives of Curriculum Evaluation.* AERA Monograph Series on Curriculum Evaluation, no. 1. Chicago: Rand McNally & Co., 1967.

U.S. DEPARTMENT OF HEALTH, EDUCATION AND WELFARE, NATIONAL ADVISORY MENTAL HEALTH COUNCIL. *Evaluation in Mental Health.* Washington, D.C.: Public Health Service, Publication no. 413, 1955.

U.S. DEPARTMENT OF HEALTH, EDUCATION AND WELFARE, OFFICE OF EDUCATION. *Preparing Evaluation Reports: A Guide for Authors.* Washington, D.C.: Government Printing Office, 1970.

U.S. HOUSE OF REPRESENTATIVES, COMMITTEE ON GOVERNMENT OPERATIONS, RESEARCH AND TECHNICAL PROGRAMS SUBCOMMITTEE. *The Use of Social Research in Federal Domestic Programs.* 90th Congress, 1st session. Washington, D.C.: Government Printing Office, 1967, vol. 3.

WALL, W. D. "The Future of Educational Research." *Educational Research,* vol. 10, no. 3 (1968), 163–169.

WARD, DAVID A., and GENE G. KASSEBAUM. "Evaluations of Correctional Treatment: Some Implications of Negative Findings." In S. A. Yefsky (ed.) *Law Enforcement Science and Technology.* Proceedings of the First National Symposium on Law Enforcement Science and Technology, IIT Research Institute. Washington, D.C.: Thompson Book Co., 1967, pp. 201–209.

WARDROP, JAMES L. "Generalizability of Program Evaluation: The Danger of Limits." *Educational Product Report,* vol. 2, no. 5 (1969), 41–42.

WEINBERGER, MARTIN. "Evaluating Educational Programs: Observations by a Market Researcher," *Urban Review,* vol. 3, no. 4 (1969), 23–26.

WEISS, CAROL H. "Evaluation of In-Service Training." In *Targets for In-Service Training.* Washington, D.C.: Joint Commission on Correctional Manpower and Training, October 1967, pp. 47–54.

———. "Planning an Action Project Evaluation." In June Shmelzer (ed.) *Learning in Action.* Washington, D.C.: Government Printing Office, 1966, pp. 6–21.

———. "The Politicization of Evaluation Research." *Journal of Social Issues,* vol. 26, no. 4 (1970), pp. 57–68.

———. "Prevention of Juvenile Delinquency: Research and Evaluation." In *Papers on Research in Crime and Delinquency.* Washington, D.C.: U.S. Department of Health, Education, and Welfare, Office of Juvenile Delinquency and Youth .Development, 1966, pp. 1–21.

———. "Utilization of Evaluation: Toward Comparative Study." In *The Use of Social Research in Federal Domestic Programs.* U.S. House of Representatives, Committee on Government Operations, Research and Technical Programs Subcommittee, 90th Congress, 1st session, April 1967. Washington, D.C.: Government Printing Office, vol. 3, 1967, pp. 426–432.

Weiss, Robert S., and Martin Rein. "The Evaluation of Broad-Aim Programs: A Cautionary Case and a Moral." *The Annals of the American Academy of Political and Social Science,* vol. 385 (September 1969), 118–132. A revised version also appears in *Administrative Science Quarterly,* vol. 15, no. 1 (1970), 97–109.

Welch, Wayne W. "Curriculum Evaluation." *Review of Educational Research,* vol. 39, no. 4 (1969), 429–443.

Welty, Gordon A. "Experimental Designs and Applied Research." *California Journal of Educational Research,* vol. 20, no. 1 (1969), 40–44.

Westbury, Ian. "Curriculum Evaluation." *Review of Educational Research,* vol. 40, no. 2 (1970), 239–260.

Wholey, Joseph S., *et al. Federal Evaluation Policy.* Washington, D.C.: The Urban Institute, 1970.

Wilder, David E. "Problems of Evaluation Research." In Edmund deS. Brunner, David E. Wilder, Corinne Kirchner, and John S. Newberry (eds.) *An Overview of Adult Education.* Chicago: Adult Education Association, 1959, pp. 243–273.

Wilkins, Leslie T. "Evaluation of Training Programs." In *Social Deviance.* London: Tavistock Publications, 1964, pp. 288–293.

———. *Evaluation of Penal Measures.* New York: Random House, Inc., 1969.

Williams, Walter. "Developing an Agency Evaluation Strategy for Social Action Programs." *Journal of Human Resources,* vol. 4, no. 4 (1969), 451–465.

————, and JOHN EVANS. "The Politics of Evaluation: The Case of Head Start." *The Annals of the American Academy of Political and Social Science,* vol. 385 (September 1969), 118–132.

WITTROCK, M. C. "The Evaluation of Instruction: Cause and Effect Relations in Naturalistic Data." *Evaluation Comment* (journal of the Center for the Study of Evaluation, UCLA), vol. 1, no. 4 (1969), 1–7.

————, and DAVID WILEY (eds.) *The Evaluation of Instruction: Issues and Problems.* New York: Holt, Rinehart & Winston, Inc., 1970.

WRIGHT, CHARLES R., and HERBERT H. HYMAN. "The Evaluators." In Phillip E. Hammond (ed.) *Sociologists at Work: Essays on the Craft of Social Research.* New York: Basic Books, Inc., Publishers, 1964, pp. 121–141.

WORTHEN, BLAINE R., "Toward a Taxonomy of Evaluation Designs." *Educational Technology,* vol. 8, no. 15 (1968), 3–9.

Illustrations of
Evaluation Studies

ALDRICH, NELSON (ed.) "The Controversy Over the More Effective Schools: A Special Supplement." *Urban Review,* vol. 2, no. 6 (1968), 15–34.

BENEDICT, BARBARA A., PAULA H. CALDER, DAVID M. CALLAHAN, HARVEY HORNSTEIN and MATTHEW B. MILES. "The Clinical-Experimental Approach to Assessing Organizational Change Efforts." *Journal of Applied Behavioral Science,* vol. 3, no. 3 (1967), 347–380.

BERLEMAN, WILLIAM C., and THOMAS W. STEINBURN. "The Execution and Evaluation of a Delinquency Prevention Program." *Social Problems,* vol. 14, no. 4 (1967), 413–423.

BOGART, LEO, et al. *Social Research and the Desegregation of the U.S. Army.* Chicago: Markham Publishing Co., 1969.

BOOCOCK, SARANE S., and JAMES S. COLEMAN. "Games with Simulated Environments in Learning." *Sociology of Education,* vol. 39, no. 3 (1966), 215–236.

CAIN, GLEN, and GERALD SOMERS. "Retraining the Disadvantaged Worker." In Cathleen Quirk and Carol Sheehan (eds.) *Research in Vocational and Technical Education.* Madison: Center for Studies in Vocational and Technical Education, University of Wisconsin, 1967, pp. 27–44.

———, and ERNST W. STROMSDORFER. "An Economic Evaluation of Government Retraining Programs in West Virginia." In Gerald G. Somers (ed.) *Retraining the Unemployed.* Madison: The University of Wisconsin Press, 1968, pp. 299–335.

CAMPBELL, DONALD T., and H. LAURENCE ROSS. "The Connecticut Crackdown on Speeding: Time-Series Data in Quasi-Experimental Analysis." *Law and Society Review,* vol. 3, no. 1 (1968), 33–53.

CAPLAN, NATHAN. "Treatment Intervention and Reciprocal Interaction Effects." *Journal of Social Issues,* vol. 24, no. 1 (1968), 63–88.

CHAMBERLIN, C. D., ENID CHAMBERLIN, N. E. DROUGHT, and W. E. SCOTT. *Adventure in American Education.* Vol. 4: *Did They Succeed in College?* New York: Harper & Row, Publishers, 1942.

CLARK, BURTON R. *The Open Door College: A Case Study.* New York: McGraw-Hill Book Company, 1960.

COLEMAN, JAMES S., ERNEST G. CAMPBELL, and others. *Equality of Educational Opportunity.* Washington, D.C.: Government Printing Office, 1966.

CUMMING, JOHN, and ELAINE CUMMING. *Closed Ranks: Study of Mental Health Education.* Cambridge: Harvard University Press, 1957.

DAVIS, JAMES A. *Great Books and Small Groups.* Glencoe, Illinois: The Free Press, 1961.

DENTLER, ROBERT. *The Young Volunteers: An Evaluation of Three Programs of the American Friends Service Committee.* Chicago: National Opinion Research Center, 1959.

DRESSEL, PAUL L. *Evaluation in General Education.* Dubuque, Iowa: William C. Brown Company, 1954.

FAIRWEATHER, G. W. *Social Psychology in Treating Mental Illness.* New York: John Wiley & Sons, Inc., 1964.

GOLLIN, ALBERT E. *Education for National Development: Effects of U.S. Technical Training Programs.* New York: Praeger Publishers, Inc., 1969.

GRANGER, R. L., *et al. The Impact of Head Start: An Evaluation of the Effects of Head Start on Children's Cognitive and Affective Development.* Vol. 1: *Report to the Office of Economic Opportunity by Westinghouse Learning Corporation and Ohio University.* June 1969.

GREELEY, ANDREW M., and PETER H. ROSSI. *The Education of Catholic Americans.* Chicago: Aldine Publishing Company, 1966.

HAMMOND, K. R., and F. KERN. *Teaching Comprehensive Medical Care.* Cambridge: Harvard University Press, 1959.

HYMAN, HERBERT H., CHARLES R. WRIGHT, and TERENCE K. HOP-

KINS. *Applications of Methods of Evaluation: Four Studies of the Encampment for Citizenship.* Los Angeles: University of California Press, 1962.

JACOB, PHILIP E. *Changing Values in College.* New York: Harper & Bros., 1957. (See Allen H. Barton, *Studying the Effects of a College Education,* in Section I.)

KATZ, IRWIN. "Review of Evidence on Effects of Desegregation on the Intellectual Performance of Negroes." *American Psychologist,* vol. 19, no. 6 (1964), 381–399.

KELLNER, ROBERT. "The Evidence in Favour of Psychotherapy." *British Journal of Medical Psychology,* vol. 40, no. 4 (1967), 341–358.

KELMAN, H. R. "An Experiment in the Rehabilitation of Nursing Home Patients." *Public Health Reports,* no. 77 (April 1962), 356–366.

KENDALL, PATRICIA. "Evaluating an Experimental Program in Medical Education." In Matthew B. Miles (ed.) *Innovations in Education.* New York: Teachers College, Bureau of Publications, 1964, pp. 343–360.

LANDERS, JACOB. *Higher Horizons: Progress Report.* New York: Board of Education of the City of New York, 1963.

LIPTON, DOUGLAS, ROBERT MARTINSON, and JUDITH WILKS. *Treatment Evaluation Survey* (tentative title). State of New York (forthcoming).

MAIN, EARL D. "A Nationwide Evaluation of M.D.T.A. Institutional Job Training." *Journal of Human Resources,* vol. 3, no. 2 (1968), 159–170.

McCORD, WILLIAM, and JOAN McCORD. *Origins of Crime: A New Evaluation of the Cambridge–Somerville Youth Study.* New York: Columbia University Press, 1959.

McDILL, EDWARD L., MARY S. McDILL, and J. TIMOTHY SPREHE. *Strategies for Success in Compensatory Education: An Appraisal of Evaluation Research.* Baltimore: The Johns Hopkins Press, 1969.

MEYER, H. J., and E. F. BORGATTA. *An Experiment in Mental Patient Rehabilitation.* New York: Russell Sage Foundation, 1959.

———, E. F. BORGATTA, and W. C. JONES. *Girls at Vocational High.* New York: Russell Sage Foundation, 1965.

MILES, MATTHEW. "Changes During and Following Laboratory Training: A Clinical-Experimental Study." *Journal of Applied Behavioral Science,* vol. 1, no. 3 (1965), 215–242.

MILLER, WALTER B. "The Impact of a 'Total-Community' Delinquency Control Project." *Social Problems,* vol. 10, no. 2 (1962), 168–190.

NEWCOMB, THEODORE M. *Personality and Social Change.* New York: Dryden Press, 1957.

PATTISON, E. MANSELL, RONALD COE, and ROBERT J. RHODES. "Evaluation of Alcoholism Treatment: A Comparison of Three Facilities." *Archives of General Psychiatry,* vol. 20, no. 4 (1969), 478–488.

POPHAM, W. J., and J. M. SADNAVITCH. "Filmed Science Courses in the Public School: An Experimental Approach." *Science Education,* vol. 45, no. 4 (1961), 327–335.

POWERS, EDWIN, and HELEN WITMER. *An Experiment in the Prevention of Juvenile Delinquency: The Cambridge–Somerville Youth Study.* New York: Columbia University Press, 1951.

PRICE, BRONSON. *School Health Services: A Selective Review of Evaluative Studies.* Washington, D.C.: U.S. Department of Health, Education and Welfare, Social Security Administration, Children's Bureau, 1957.

RIECKEN, HENRY. *The Volunteer Work Camp: A Psychological Evaluation.* Cambridge: Addison-Wesley Publishing Co., Inc., 1952.

ROSENTHAL, ROBERT, and LENORE JACOBSON. *Pygmalion in the Classroom.* New York: Holt, Rinehart & Winston, Inc., 1968.

ROSS, H. LAURENCE, DONALD T. CAMPBELL, and GENE V. GLASS. "Determining the Social Effects of a Legal Reform: The British 'Breathalyser' Crackdown of 1967." *American Behavioral Scientist,* vol. 13, no. 4 (1970), 493–509.

SHELDON, A. "An Evaluation of Psychiatric After-Care." *British Journal of Psychiatry,* vol. 110 (1964), 662–667.

SILVER, G. *Family Medical Care.* Cambridge: Harvard University Press, 1963.

SMITH, E. R., and R. W. TYLER. *Appraising and Recording Student Progress.* New York: Harper & Row, Publishers, 1942.

STROMSDORFER, ERNST W. "Determinants of Economic Success in Retraining the Unemployed: The West Virginia Experience." *The Journal of Human Resources,* vol. 3, no. 2 (1968), 139–152.

THOMSON, CAPTANE P., and NORMAN W. BELL. "Evaluation of a Rural Community Mental Health Program." *Archives of General Psychiatry,* vol. 20, no. 4 (1969), 448–456.

U.S. DEPARTMENT OF AGRICULTURE, AGRICULTURAL MARKETING SERVICE, FOOD DISTRIBUTION DIVISION. *The Food Stamp Pro-*

gram: An Initial Evaluation of the Pilot Project. Washington, D.C.: U.S.D.A., 1962.

U.S. DEPARTMENT OF HEALTH, EDUCATION AND WELFARE, NATIONAL ADVISORY MENTAL HEALTH COUNCIL. *Evaluation in Mental Health.* Washington, D.C.: Public Health Service, publication no. 413, 1955.

————. *A Bibliographic Index of Evaluation in Mental Health.* Prepared by James K. Dent. Washington, D.C.: Public Health Service, publication no. 1545, 1962.

VANECKO, JAMES J. "Community Mobilization and Institutional Change." *Social Science Quarterly,* vol. 50, no. 3 (1969), 609–630.

WALLACE, D. *The Chemung County Research Demonstration with Dependent Multi-Problem Families.* New York: State Charities Aid Association, 1965.

WALLEN, NORMAN E., and ROBERT M. W. TRAVERS. "Analysis and Investigation of Teaching Methods." In N. L. Gage (ed.) *Handbook of Research on Teaching.* Chicago: Rand McNally & Co., 1963, chapter 10.

WEEKS, H. ASHLEY. *Youthful Offenders at Highfields.* Ann Arbor: University of Michigan Press, 1958.

WEISBROD, BURTON A. "Preventing High School Dropouts." In Robert Dorfman (ed.) *Measuring Benefits of Government Investments.* Washington, D.C.: The Brookings Institution, 1965.

WILNER, DANIEL M., R. P. WALKLEY, T. C. PINKERTON, and M. TAYBACK. *Housing Environment and Family Life.* Baltimore: The Johns Hopkins Press, 1962.

WRIGHTSTONE, J. WAYNE, SAMUEL D. McCLELLAND, JUDITH I. KRUGMAN, HERBERT HOFFMAN, NORMAN TIEMAN, and LINDA YOUNG. *Assessment of the Demonstration Guidance Project.* New York: Board of Education of the City of New York, Division of Research and Evaluation, n.d.

Design, Measurement, Sampling, & Analysis

ADAMS, GEORGIA S. *Measurement and Evaluation in Education, Psychology, and Guidance.* New York: Holt, Rinehart & Winston, Inc., 1964.

BARTON, ALLEN H. "Measuring the Values of Individuals." *Religious Education*, Supplement (July–August 1962), pp. 62–97.

———. *Organization Measurement.* Princeton: College Entrance Examination Board, 1961.

BLALOCK, HUBERT M., JR. *Causal Inferences in Nonexperimental Research.* Chapel Hill: University of North Carolina Press, 1961.

BLOOM, BENJAMIN S., *et al. Taxonomy of Educational Objectives. Handbook I: Cognitive Domain.* New York: David McKay Co., Inc., 1956.

BONJEAN, CHARLES M., RICHARD J. HILL, and S. DALE McLEMORE. *Sociological Measurement: An Inventory of Scales and Indices.* San Francisco: Chandler Publishing Co., 1967.

BUROS, OSCAR (ed.) *Sixth Mental Measurements Yearbook.* Highland Park, New Jersey: Gryphon Press, 1965.

CAMPBELL, DONALD T., and ALBERT ERLEBACHER. "How Regression Artifacts in Quasi-Experimental Evaluations Can Mistakenly Make Compensatory Education Look Harmful." In J. Hellmuth (ed.) *Compensatory Education: A National Debate.* Vol. 3 of *The Disadvantaged Child.* New York: Brunner/Mazel, Inc., 1970.

————, and DONALD W. FISKE. "Convergent and Discriminant Validation by the Multitrait-Multimethod Matrix." *Psychological Bulletin,* vol. 56, no. 2 (1959), 81–105.

————, and JULIAN STANLEY. "Experimental and Quasi-Experimental Designs for Research on Teaching." In N. L. Gage (ed.) *Handbook of Research on Teaching.* Chicago: Rand McNally & Co., 1963. Reprinted as *Experimental and Quasi-Experimental Design for Research.* Chicago: Rand McNally & Co., 1966.

COCHRAN, WILLIAM G. *Sampling Techniques.* New York: John Wiley & Sons, Inc., 1953.

COX, DAVID R. *Planning of Experiments.* New York: John Wiley & Sons, Inc., 1958.

DUNCAN, OTIS DUDLEY. "Path Analysis: Sociological Examples." *American Journal of Sociology,* vol. 72, no. 1 (1966), 1–16.

GRONLUND, NORMAN (ed.) *Readings in Measurement and Evaluation.* New York: The Macmillan Company, 1968.

GROUP FOR THE ADVANCEMENT OF PSYCHIATRY. *Psychiatric Research and the Assessment of Change.* New York: The Group, 1966, vol. 6, Report no. 63.

HANSEN, MORRIS H., WILLIAM N. HURWITZ, and WILLIAM G. MADOW. *Sample Survey Methods and Theory.* Vol. 1: *Method and Applications.* New York: John Wiley & Sons, Inc., 1953.

HARRIS, CHESTER W. (ed.) *Problems in Measuring Change.* Madison: University of Wisconsin Press, 1963.

HOCHSTIM, JOSEPH R. "A Critical Comparison of Three Strategies of Collecting Data from Households." *Journal of the American Statistical Association,* vol. 62, no. 319 (1967), 976–989.

HYMAN, HERBERT. *Survey Design and Analysis: Principles, Cases, and Procedures.* Glencoe, Illinois: The Free Press, 1955.

KAHN, ROBERT L., and CHARLES F. CANNELL. *The Dynamics of Interviewing.* New York: John Wiley & Sons, Inc., 1957.

KENDALL, PATRICIA L. "A Review of Indicators Used in 'The American Soldier.'" In Paul F. Lazarsfeld and Morris Rosenberg (eds.) *The Language of Social Research.* Glencoe, Illinois: The Free Press, 1955, pp. 37–39.

KISH, LESLIE. "Selection of the Sample." In Leon Festinger and Daniel Katz (eds.) *Research Methods in the Behavioral Sciences.* New York: Dryden Press, 1953, pp. 175–239.

————. *Survey Sampling.* New York: John Wiley & Sons, Inc., 1965.

KRATHWOHL, DAVID R., BENJAMIN S. BLOOM, and BERTRAM B. MASIA. *Taxonomy of Educational Objectives. Handbook II: Affective Domain.* New York: David McKay Co., Inc., 1964.

MICHAEL, WILLIAM G., and NEWTON S. METFESSEL. "A Paradigm for Developing Valid Measurable Objectives in the Evaluation of Educational Programs in Colleges and Universities." *Educational and Psychological Measurement,* vol. 27, no. 2 (1967), 373–383.

MILLER, DELBERT C. *Handbook of Research Design and Social Measurement.* New York: David McKay Co., Inc., 1964.

MONROE, J., and A. L. FINKNER. *Handbook of Area Sampling.* New York: Chilton Company, Book Division, 1959.

OPPENHEIM, A. N. *Questionnaire Design and Attitude Measurement.* New York: Basic Books, Inc., Publishers, 1966.

PLUTCHIK, R., S. R. PLATMAN, and R. R. FIEVE. "Three Alternatives to the Double-blind." *Archives of General Psychiatry,* vol. 20 (1969), 428–432.

ROBINSON, J. P., R. ATHANASIOU, and KENDRA B. HEAD. *Measures of Occupational Attitudes and Occupational Characteristics.* Ann Arbor: Survey Research Center, University of Michigan, 1967.

————, JERROLD G. RUSK, and KENDRA B. HEAD. *Measures of Political Attitudes.* Ann Arbor: Survey Research Center, University of Michigan, 1968.

————, and PHILLIP R. SHAVER. *Measures of Social Psychological Attitudes.* Ann Arbor: Survey Research Center, University of Michigan, 1969.

ROSENBERG, MORRIS. *The Logic of Survey Analysis.* New York: Basic Books, Inc., Publishers, 1968.

RUSSETT, BRUCE M., *et al. World Handbook of Political and Social Indicators.* New Haven: Yale University Press, 1964.

SHAW, MARVIN E., and JACK M. WRIGHT. *Scales for the Measurement of Attitudes.* New York: McGraw-Hill Book Company, 1967.

SJOBERG, GIDEON, and ROGER NETT. *A Methodology for Social Research.* New York: Harper & Row, Publishers, 1968.

SJOGREN, DOUGLAS D. "Measurement Techniques in Evaluation." *Review of Educational Research,* vol. 40, no. 2 (1970), 301–320.

SLONIM, MORRIS JAMES. *Sampling.* New York: Simon & Schuster, Inc., 1966.

STEPHAN, FREDERICK F., and PHILIP J. McCARTHY. *Sampling Opinions: An Analysis of Survey Procedure.* New York: John Wiley & Sons, Inc., 1958.

SUDMAN, SEYMOUR. *Reducing the Cost of Surveys.* Chicago: Aldine Publishing Company, 1967.

THORNDIKE, ROBERT L., and ELIZABETH HAGEN. *Measurement and Evaluation in Psychology and Education.* 2nd ed. New York: John Wiley & Sons, Inc., 1961.

UNDERHILL, RALPH. *Methods in the Evaluation of Programs for Poor Youth.* Chicago: National Opinion Research Center, June 1968.

U. S. BUREAU OF THE BUDGET, EXECUTIVE OFFICE OF THE PRESIDENT. *Household Survey Manual, 1969.* Available from Clearinghouse for Federal Scientific and Technical Information, Springfield, Virginia 22151, document no. PB-18-7444.

WEBB, EUGENE J., DONALD T. CAMPBELL, R. D. SCHWARTZ, and L. B. SECHREST. *Unobtrusive Measures: Nonreactive Research in the Social Sciences.* Chicago: Rand McNally & Co., 1966.

WEISS, CAROL H. "Interviewing Low-Income Respondents." *Welfare in Review,* vol. 4, no. 8 (1966), 1–9.

WINER, B. J. *Statistical Principles in Experimental Design.* New York: McGraw-Hill Book Company, 1962.